TEACHING LANGUAGES IN COLLEGE

CURRICULUM
AND
CONTENT

Wilga M. Rivers

National Textbook Company
NTC a division of *NTC Publishing Group* • Lincolnwood, Illinois USA

Published by National Textbook Company, a division of NTC Publishing Group.
© 1992 by NTC Publishing Group, 4255 West Touhy Avenue,
Lincolnwood (Chicago), Illinois 60646-1975 U.S.A.
Manufactured in the United States of America.

1 2 3 4 5 6 7 8 9 ML 9 8 7 6 5 4 3 2 1

Contents

Preface

THE TITLE OF THIS BOOK HAS FIVE KEY TERMS, ALL SIGNIFICANT:
Teaching—Languages—College—Curriculum—Content. The book limits its
discussion to the many aspects of the *language program* (which subsumes, as an
integral part, the study of the culture associated with it), specifically as it takes
shape at the undergraduate *college level,* with particular emphasis on the *design
of the program* as it relates to student interests and needs at the present time,
and as that program fits into the department and college *curriculum.* All
important in building and implementing a curriculum are the kinds of *content*
that will enable the students in the program to grow in their use of the language:
in their understanding of all that is involved in using a language, and in the
types of capabilities they will need as they continue to use this language within
the parameters of another culture. Curriculum design and content are not in
themselves sufficient without *teaching* that is adapted to the needs of the
students—teaching in the sense of facilitating individual learning, with all its
idiosyncrasies, internal tensions, and seemingly erratic external manifestations. This teaching is *teaching language* (with its associated culture), which is
quite different from teaching history or sociology or fine arts. We know much
more about how languages are learned than we did twenty years ago, and this
new knowledge should affect the way we present languages, formally and

informally, and prepare learning materials. Although the emphasis of the book
is on curriculum and content, chapter 19, *Ten Principles of Interactive Language
Learning and Teaching,* provides the basis for the approach to the language
class that underlies the many teaching suggestions incorporated into the
various chapters.

While considering programs, we must not forget those who are administratively and pedagogically responsible for them, the kind of preparation we
may look for in appointees, and the nature of the responsibilities they may be
expected to assume (chapter 15). Before taking up the newly established
professorship of modern languages at Bowdoin College in 1829, Henry
Wadsworth Longfellow spent three years in France, Spain, Italy, and Germany,
assiduously studying the languages and literatures of those countries, and his
later appointment in 1834 as Smith Professor of Modern Languages at
Harvard University came with the stipulation that he spend another year to
eighteen months abroad to perfect his knowledge of German.[1] During his
tenure at Harvard, Longfellow was almost a department on his own, teaching
French and German language (at one stage 115 students of the former and 30
students of the latter) and supervising Spanish and Italian; he also gave lectures
on literary texts being studied by the students in all four languages in
succession, as well as public lectures on such leading literary figures as Goethe
and Dante.[2] We are all much more specialized these days, as far as languages
go, than was Longfellow, but most of us still have strong interests in both
language and literature (discussed in chapter 12) or language and linguistics
(chapter 13). Broad interests make for interesting and challenging teachers.

Finding few textbooks available, Longfellow, while at Bowdoin, wrote
grammar textbooks, exercise manuals, and books of readings for French,
Spanish, and Italian.[3] At Harvard, he also supervised and critiqued classroom
instruction regularly. He was expected to "observe the manner, in which each
instructer [sic], performs his duty, make such remarks and give such directions
as circumstances may require,"[4] "being present at least once a month at the
recitation of every student in each language"[5]—a procedure that to some of his
instructors "assumed an appearance of *espionnage.*"[6] Even in those days, it
seems, professors of modern languages were overworked and expected to be
all things to all people.

Despite his herculean labors, Longfellow had to endure a committee
report, accepted by the Harvard Faculty in the spring of 1840, which remarked
on the "deleterious effects of a too unrestricted study of modern languages,"
which, "on account of the simplicity of their grammatical structure, and the
enticing character of many of their productions,[7] is apt to give a distaste for
severer and more disciplining studies."[8] Apparently students were enjoying

their language study too much for hidebound conservatives. Just such objections to modern language study are still heard today, a good hundred fifty years later. (A rationale for language study in the liberal arts curriculum is given in chapter 1.) Cornell University seems to hold the distinction for the establishment of the first modern language *department* a little over a hundred years ago. In the years since, unfortunate and unnecessary tensions have often simmered, and even boiled over, between language and literature interests within departments, and even between language and linguistics—three interests that should be convergent.

Language is a natural acquisition for each of us—one that enables and empowers us to interact, to work, to express our deepest thoughts and wishes. Language is the essence of all forms of literature. Literature is one of the richest and most powerful expressions of language and culture, and one that fulfills our deepest emotional, intellectual, and esthetic needs. The more we know about how languages work and their relationship to the culture, and the deeper our knowledge of the language we are studying, the better is our work in linguistics and in literature. We respect and value all three central concerns of our department: language and culture, literature, and linguistics. Surely it is time, however, to consider that modern language studies have come of age after such a long period and give serious consideration to language as an autonomous study, with a logic and *droit d'existence* of its own—a status already accorded to literature and linguistics. The plea in this book for strong language and culture programs with autonomous aims can only strengthen literature and linguistics programs, providing these with students with the necessary knowledge and capabilities to draw the most from what they have to offer. A strong and effective language program will arouse genuine interest in linguistic problems associated with that language and deepen and strengthen the students' appreciation of its literature. It will also provide for a great number of other interests and educational experiences for language students who are not necessarily attracted to linguistics and literature as their major areas of study. Many such collateral interests are discussed in the various chapters.

This book is a call for serious rethinking of the language program, developing and establishing it as a powerful force within the curriculum of the college. The language program can serve many needs, some yet to be identified, providing students with a deep, enriched knowledge, not only of the language itself but also of the culture it permeates, thus preparing them for harmonious interaction, in whatever capacity, with persons of other cultures. Languages have come of age as mature partners with literature and various forms of linguistic study in our departments. With this new maturity, they cease to be in tutelage or vassalage and become peers in the educational enterprise of the college.

Along with Bok of Harvard, we recognize that "the debates [on higher education] of the 1980's have been superficial. We must step back and ask what our society needs from colleges and universities,"[9] and, we may add, from language and culture programs within those institutions. The discussions of language programs in this book ask this question, as they outline new directions for study. We begin with the essential but preliminary basic or requirement courses (chapter 1) and discuss forms of language requirement and placement (chapter 3), what is meant by proficiency, and how we may ascertain that it has been achieved (chapter 10). Multitudinous suggestions are provided for possible intermediate and advanced courses, with details of content and indications for implementation. A carefully crafted long sequence of advanced courses is advocated as the core of a strong departmental program that serves the needs of all students in the college (chapter 2). We examine the teaching of language through literature (chapter 4) and the improvement of students' ability to read and interpret with comprehension (chapter 5); the development of courses for a diversity of career purposes (chapter 6); the long-deferred but eventually inevitable marriage of language and international studies (chapter 14); and the penetration of other cultures through authentic personal and vicarious contact (chapter 11), much of this facilitated by new and old, if underused, technologies (chapter 7). We do not limit our discussion to the commonly taught languages—the ubiquitous French, Spanish, and German—but consider also the needs of such languages as Japanese, Korean, Russian, Latin, and Greek (chapters 8 and 9).

Within the departments, much soul-searching is in order and in evidence with regard to the structure of an end-of-the-century major and minor (or concentration) in language and literature departments (chapter 2). Diversification in this area is elaborated, as well as the contributions linguistics can make to strengthening all aspects of the work of the department (chapter 13).

Discussion is not limited in this book to the undergraduate programs of large research universities. The self-examination that should be undertaken by the small four-year colleges, where the survival of well-developed language programs is in many cases threatened, is analyzed and elaborated, as well as the particular features of the situation faced by adult and continuing education schools (chapters 16 and 17).

If programs are to be strong and forward-moving, governance and organizational factors cannot be ignored. Who should direct the language and culture program? After what preparation and in anticipation of what rewards? How do we prepare future instructors in the language program so that the momentum of new thinking on content and classroom practice may be maintained in imaginative but observedly effective ways? What kinds of production should be recognized for promotion and tenure? What do coordination and supervision imply in practice (chapter 15)? Finally, the exciting new developments in language resource centers indicate another growing edge of our work. How have they been organized thus far in various institutions to serve the cause of languages and assist LTCS's (Language Teaching and Culture Specialists) in their work? What are the professed aims of existing centers and how are these being achieved (chapter 18)?

There is so much concerning language and culture programs that needs to be aired and openly discussed in our departments and across faculties. Here are some places to begin.

This book is not designed to be read necessarily in strict succession, although we hope some readers will become so engrossed that they will wish to do so! Many will want to leap first into a chapter that seems to deal with an immediate problem or proposal in their department. Before doing so, however, most would probably profit from a careful reading of the first two chapters on the undergraduate program, so that the other chapters may be seen within the perspective of a carefully conceived language program; otherwise, one may end up with a well-developed tail wagging the dog. We hope the book will be useful for departmental curriculum discussions as well as personal perusal; that it will strengthen the hand of department heads (and even deans!) who feel that their faculty need to take their language program more seriously, updating and enriching it; and, alternatively, that it will provide ammunition for language program directors and coordinators who would like to experiment and innovate, but need to win the support of department heads and colleagues. Finally we must look to the future, which lies in the hands of the future language and literature department members whom we are presently preparing in our departments—the hardworking teaching assistants, who will most probably teach and develop courses as they have encountered them when in graduate school. This book should prove useful for teaching assistant training, where this is established, or for distribution among all the teaching staff in a department as a prelude to full discussion of the needs in a particular context. In whichever situation this book is used, we look forward to a meeting of the minds with you. May your programs prosper and give you and your students much satisfaction.

Finally, all of us who have contributed to this book owe much to our mentors, colleagues, and students, whom we thank most warmly for all that they have contributed to our thinking. Like you, we are a part of all that we have met.[10]

Wilga M. Rivers
Watertown, Mass.

NOTES

1. *The Poetical Works of Longfellow,* With a New Introduction by George Monteiro, Cambridge Edition (Boston: Houghton Mifflin, 1975), p. xx.

2. Carl L. Johnson, *Professor Longfellow of Harvard,* Studies in Literature and Philology, No. 5 (Eugene, OR: Univ. of Oregon Press, 1944), p. 1.

3. Titles of these textbooks are given in Johnson (1944), p. 1, n. 4.

4. *Ibid.,* p. 24.

5. *Ibid.,* p. 26.

6. *Ibid.,* p. 28.

7. I take this to mean literary productions, that is, the texts read in the language class, which, apparently, the students found too enjoyable.

8. *Ibid.,* p. 40.

9. D. Bok, President of Harvard University, in an address to the 14th Annual Meeting of the National Association of Independent Colleges and Universities, 1990, reported in the *Harvard University Gazette,* vol. 35, no. 21 (February 2, 1990), p. 1.

10. With acknowledgments to Tennyson's *Ulysses.*

Author Biographies

MARVA A. BARNETT is currently Associate Professor of French and Director of the Teaching Resource Center at the University of Virginia. An experienced TA trainer, she has pursued research on foreign-language reading and writing processes and learners' strategies. Her publications include *More Than Meets the Eye* and *Lire avec plaisir,* as well as articles in *The Modern Language Journal, Foreign Language Annals,* and *The French Review.*

TRUETT CATES has taught at Williams College, Johannes Gutenberg University in Mainz, and, since 1979, at Austin College. He has worked in the fields of foreign-language reading, comprehension-based instruction, and authentic materials preparation. Since 1989 he spends afternoons and weekends as varsity soccer coach.

ILONA CHESSID has taught language and literature at Harvard University, where she was also Demonstration Teacher for new instructors, and at Haverford College in the summer Total Immersion French Workshop. At Harvard she collaborated in the production of several teacher training videos on interactive language instruction, teaching language through literature, and teaching ethics through masterpieces of French literature. She is now teaching at Hunter College.

RAYMOND F. COMEAU, Assistant Dean of Harvard University Extension School and Director of Foreign Language Instruction for Continuing Education, has published, lectured, and given workshops on a variety of topics dealing with the teaching of foreign languages. He is co-author of the *Ensemble* series, an intermediate French program consisting of three coordinated texts, now in its fourth edition, and *Échanges,* a first-year program. A Lecturer in French at the Extension School, he was named the first recipient of its Carmen S. Bonanno Prize for Excellence in Foreign Language Teaching in 1990.

VERÓNICA CORTÍNEZ is an Assistant Professor at the University of California, Los Angeles. She studied at the Universidad de Chile and the University of Illinois at Urbana–Champaign and received her Ph.D. from Harvard. For a long time, the teaching of literature has been her primary interest.

BARBARA FREED is Professor and Chair of Modern Languages at Carnegie Mellon University. Her interests include research on classroom-based language learning, input in second-language acquisition, and the linguistic impact of study-abroad experiences. She has published in the areas of proficiency-oriented teaching, language loss, and the training of foreign-language teaching assistants. She has also edited the major collections *Contextes, The Loss of Language Skills,* and *Foreign Language Acquisition Research and the Classroom.*

JUDITH G. FROMMER, Coordinator of Language Instruction in the Romance Languages at Harvard University, has been teaching "Le Français économique et commercial" since 1982. She is co-editor of *Transformations in French Business: Political, Economic, and Cultural Changes from 1981 to 1987.* She is the developer of the MacLang Authoring System for creation of computer-assisted language-learning materials in ten languages and has also written textbooks and articles on language teaching.

ROBERT FRYE is Associate Professor and Chair of the Department of French at Regis College. He was founding Director of Wellesley College's Maison Française. In addition to studying in Rouen, France, as an undergraduate, he served as administrative assistant to the Illinois Year Abroad Program in Paris. Frye writes on Proust and Robert Merle as well as matters of pedagogical interest.

GILBERTE FURSTENBERG was born and educated in France, where she received the Agrégation. She is a Senior Lecturer of French at the Massachusetts Institute of Technology. For the last five years she has been involved in the Athena Foreign Language Learning Project. She is the author and Director of Pedagogical Design for the interactive videodisc project *Direction Paris,* which explores the uses of videodisc technology, in both the fictional and the documentary mode, for language learning and teaching.

THOMAS J. GARZA, Assistant Professor of Slavic Languages at the University of Texas at Austin, has been both participant in and administrator of numerous study-abroad programs in the Soviet Union. He has also taught Russian and EFL at Harvard University and the University of Maryland, supervised Serbo-Croatian instruction at the Foreign Service Institute, and conducted teacher-training workshops in the Soviet Union and Eastern Europe. His publications include articles and teaching guides on integrating authentic materials, especially video, into foreign language and culture curricula.

BRIGITTE GOUTAL has taught French language and literature at Harvard University and in the Middlebury College Summer School. She has been Director of the summer Total Immersion French Workshop at Haverford College, which she designed herself and for which she has trained teachers. She has collaborated in a video and made presentations on the interaction of language and literature. She is completing her doctoral studies in French literature.

CHRISTINE HÉROT has taught French language and linguistics at the University of Oregon, at Harvard University (to undergraduates and adult extension students), and in a magnet middle school in Miami, where students obtain both French and American credits. She is presently engaged in doctoral research on conceptual development in children.

ELEANOR HARZ JORDEN is currently University Professor/Distinguished Fellow at the National Foreign Language Center, The Johns Hopkins University, and the Mary Donlon Alger Professor of Linguistics, Emerita, Cornell University. A former President of the Association for Asian Studies and of the Association of Teachers of Japanese, she founded the Cornell Japanese FALCON Program and served as its Director from 1972 to 1987. Her Japanese language textbooks, *Beginning Japanese* (Parts 1 and 2), *Reading Japanese,* and *Japanese: The Spoken Language* (Parts 1, 2, and 3), are among the most widely used in college programs around the world.

RICHARD A. LAFLEUR, Professor and Head of Classics at the University of Georgia, has authored more than sixty publications on Latin literature, language, and pedagogy; a past president of the American Classical League and editor of *The Classical Outlook* since 1979, he has been recipient of grants totaling more than $300,000 for a variety of school–college collaboratives and of numerous awards, including the Georgia Governor's Award in the Humanities, the *Ovatio* of the Classical Association of the Middle West and South, and the American Philological Association's national award for Excellence in the Teaching of Classics.

RICHARD D. LAMBERT is founder and Director of the National Foreign Language Center at The Johns Hopkins University in Washington, D.C., Professor Emeritus of Sociology and South Asian Studies at the University of Pennsylvania, and editor of *The Annals* of the American Academy of Political and Social Science. He is the author of *Points of Leverage: An Agenda for a National Foundation for International Studies; Beyond Growth: The Next Stage in Language and Area Studies;* and *International Studies and the Undergraduate* (the result of an extensive two-year study of undergraduate international éducation in the United States conducted for the American Council on Education); and co-editor, with S. J. Moore, of *Foreign Language in the Workplace.*

MARGUERITE A. MAHLER is Associate Professor of French and Linguistics at Framingham State College. She has coordinated and developed courses at Harvard University and the University of Michigan and is currently Coordinator for French at Middlebury College Summer School. She taught linguistics at Harvard and teaches applied linguistics for International Education Programs Overseas (in Costa Rica, Mexico, Brazil, and Italy). She is preparing an advanced grammar textbook for French, which incorporates her model of tense and aspect, and has published several articles in theoretical and applied linguistics.

BERNICE MELVIN is currently Dean of Humanities at Austin College. She has taught at the University of Texas at Austin, Haverford College, and, since 1980, at Austin College. She has published articles on memory and foreign-language learning and on the use of authentic materials in the foreign-language classroom.

DOUGLAS MORGENSTERN, Senior Lecturer in Spanish at MIT, is a designer with the Athena Language Learning Project and an adviser to the WGBH/McGraw-Hill Spanish telecourse series project. He has created text and audio materials for Harcourt Brace Jovanovich; Holt, Rinehart and Winston; and Heinle and Heinle Publishers and has authored articles and made numerous presentations on interactive video, simulation, and language learning.

MARLIES MUELLER, Director of Teacher Training for French in the Department of Romance Languages and Literatures at Harvard University since

1975, has developed curricula for language courses at the elementary and intermediate level and language and literature courses at the advanced level, researched foreign-language teaching in American high schools for the American Academy of Arts and Sciences, and consulted for the American Council on Education evaluating tests used by the United States Armed Forces. Her publications include a textbook for elementary French; articles on language and literature teaching; demonstration videos for interactive language teaching, cultural literacy, and the teaching of poetry; and a work of socio-historical criticism of literature.

JUNE K. PHILLIPS is Executive Director of the Tennessee Foreign Language Institute. She edited four volumes in the ACTFL Foreign Language Education Series, chaired the Northeast Conference on the Teaching of Foreign Languages in 1984, and currently serves on the ACTFL Executive Council. She has written numerous articles, monographs, and textbooks and has conducted workshops and seminars throughout the United States and abroad. Professional affiliations include ACTFL, MLA, AATF, and TFTLA.

WILGA M. RIVERS, Professor Emerita of Romance Languages and Literatures at Harvard University, has taught at the University of Illinois, Northern Illinois University, Monash University (Australia), Columbia University, and Harvard, where she was Coordinator of Language Instruction in the Romance Languages. She has published numerous books on the theory and practice of language teaching, drawing insights from psychology and linguistics, with specific books on the teaching of French, German, Spanish, Hebrew, and English as a second or foreign language. She has lectured and taught courses and seminars in thirty-three countries and throughout the United States and Canada. Her books and articles have been translated into nine languages.

REBECCA M. VALETTE, Professor of Romance Languages and Literatures at Boston College, has published extensively in the fields of foreign-language methodology and measurement. Her book *Modern Language Testing* has been translated into German and French. She and her husband Jean-Paul Valette are authors of widely used teaching materials, which include *French for Mastery, Spanish for Mastery,* and *Contacts.*

1
The Undergraduate Program I: Courses for All Comers

Wilga M. Rivers
Harvard University

CHANGING ATTITUDES FOR A NEW CENTURY

"The telephone, fax, personal computer, minicam, and satellite are all strands in a tightening global communications network that affects the political, economic, social, and cultural life of virtually everybody on the planet, in a geometrically increasing way," says Marvin Kalb.[1] The "global village" (McLuhan and Fiore 1967: 67) is becoming a reality. Across the world people are talking to each other in languages that are not their own. Europe is drawing together and insisting that the new Europeans be able to communicate; they are putting their convictions into practice by sending their young people to study in each other's universities, through the ERASMUS project, and by providing money for the improvement of language teaching through LINGUA (Kieffer 1990). Eastern Europeans are moving swiftly to ensure that their young people are in a good position to interact with the new Europeans. Japan, Korea, and Taiwan send to prospective business partners everywhere representatives who speak their languages, while these same prospective partners are beginning to realize the value to them of knowing Japanese, Korean, and Chinese. University leaders in the United States call for the internationalization of their campuses, for bringing in more foreign students, and for sending more and more of their own students to study in other countries. Bok of Harvard, as keynote speaker for the National Association of Independent Colleges and Universities, sets out steps to be taken by colleges to help the nation deal with its most serious problems, putting in first place that "colleges and universities should stress foreign languages and international studies to prepare students for 'a more global, competitive, interdependent world.'"[2]

In all these pronouncements there is a sense of urgency. We are no longer in the leisurely Belle Époque, when one learned a language to make the Grand Tour, concentrating on a knowledge of its literature as a social grace or intellectual imprimatur. The times they are a-changing. Students sense the need to be able to mix freely and easily in social and professional settings with people of other cultures, many of whom have been learning languages since their elementary school days. This is a time of opportunity for our language departments, akin to the opportunities of the Sputnik era. Will our departments seize this moment of the cresting tide, or will they ignore it, immersed in their old ways and the pursuit of more and more specialized interests?

For departments to profit from this changing atmosphere, professors of languages and literatures will need to give much more thought to the needs and aspirations of the wider student body, rather than devoting so much of their time and energy to the few majors with potential for graduate studies in their specialized fields or subfields. Many professors have already been developing innovative core courses in literature and foreign cultures in the last few years. Can they also meet the needs of all comers in the language area, providing courses of diverse contents at the level of proficiency or language control that interested students bring with them, with incentives to continue to any level that meets the students' needs?

This approach may require for some a considerable reversal of attitudes toward language programs and some planning. We are now in a period when students recognize the need to study languages, but they expect to emerge from their studies with a useful competence. They wish to be able to communicate at a level above polite exchanges and utilitarian convenience; to read stimulating and interesting material and even write appropriate messages acceptably. They enjoy reading and discussing literary texts, although for many their interests do not lie with literary theory and criticism; they prefer direct contact with the author's own words. Above all, they wish to understand how to interact with persons of other cultures, so that they can establish cordial relations at a deeper level than: "Hi! How're things?" and they appreciate experience with the other culture, either in person or vicariously through authentic materials.

What Can Departments Do
to Welcome This Voluntary, Nontraditional Clientele?

Many departments consider language courses to be equivalent to "service courses," "requirement courses," "basic courses," "elementary courses," and "intermediate courses." Why this truncated view? we may ask. The terms *elementary* and *intermediate* presume the existence of something beyond and convey to students a sense of incompleteness, even futility, rather than any promise of a usable proficiency for their efforts. We must begin to see these courses as educational courses of value to students at any level, and their course titles should indicate this. Only then will we devote time and energy to thinking in new ways about course content that will make the language learning experience worthwhile, however brief it may be. We need content that students will be anxious to use and that will encourage them to look for more advanced courses to develop their proficiency still further. We must demonstrate that we consider all courses important and deserving of respect, as are all students who come to our department.[3]

Learning a language is a long process. Language is internalized through constant use, not in short intensive bursts followed by long periods of passivity. Students who wish to reach a high level of proficiency must have continual opportunities to exercise their language use in interesting and profitable ways, and this requires *a long sequence of courses.* Offering a seven- or eight-year sequence within a department is not excessive. No student will participate in all courses; some will begin the language at college level and, because of particular aptitudes and high motivation, leap through the sequence to the top level; others will come in midway and profit from the variety of approaches and contents as long as they are able; some will enroll in the top-level courses as entering students because of thorough preparation at elementary and secondary schools or because they have studied and traveled abroad; while others, with an interest in languages, will begin a third or fourth language and leave when they have a good foundation on which to build at a later stage.[4] If the opportunities are there, students will seize them avidly. The early courses should be motivational so that students learn to enjoy and use their new language and look forward to further interesting experiences within the department. (Word-of-mouth recommendation is also not to be underestimated.) The constantly evolving nature of the entire program, with new courses being proposed and replacing those that have ceased to attract students, also keeps the teaching staff alert and alive, allowing them to use as subject matter what they know and love best or to develop new interests through experimentation. (See chapter 2 for suggestions on developing the advanced level.)

THE APPRENTICESHIP LEVEL

Diversification at the "Basic" or "Requirement" Level

It has been the habit of many departments to provide a very bland diet in early courses, with banal content, on the assumption that these students are captive and will endure anything until they get their freedom. This is a very short-sighted policy. It ignores a number of important realities. It ignores the fact that a boring language experience for great masses of students across the nation develops and perpetuates anti-language attitudes in the adult community, who ultimately decide on funds for educational programs; these attitudes infect future generations of college students, through parental and societal influence, with a resistant reaction to taking language study seriously. Exciting programs at this level can and have won over many seemingly uncaring students to a love of language, just as "required" science courses have interested many in biology or astronomy without making of them professional biologists or astronomers. Many of them, we know, come back to study languages in evening or extension classes (see chapter 17). Most importantly, such an unreflective approach ignores the fact that students in these so-called "basic" courses are by no means homogeneous as a group. They are not all, by any means, coerced "requirement" students.

The diversity of population in first-year courses was clearly demonstrated in research conducted at the University of Illinois at Urbana–Champaign (a large state institution with a very diverse intake) at a time (1972) when students were protesting loudly against having to study languages obligatorily. Results showed that 20 percent of elementary and intermediate students, across 11 languages, were taking language as an elective; a further 27 percent were requirement students who would have chosen to study a language even if there had been no requirement; and yet another 27 percent were studying the language only because there was a requirement but were enjoying their language study nevertheless; so that finally only 26 percent of the students were just going through the motions because the courses were imposed on them (Rivers 1976: 172–3). The Illinois questionnaire, reprinted in Rivers 1976, also elicited a clear picture of student interests and desires at that time and served as a basis for program planning.

At Harvard in 1980 (with a highly selected and self-selected student body) 56 percent of first-year students across 4 Romance languages were studying the language because it was a requirement, so 44 percent were not in the class because of a requirement at all. At this level, 72 percent said they would have studied the language even if there had been no requirement; 86 percent were enjoying their language study; and 44 percent intended to continue to a further level (another 20 percent would have liked to continue but had scheduling impediments). At the intermediate level, 51 percent were requirement students, so 49 percent were elective; 63 percent said they would have studied the language even if there had been no requirement; 77 percent said they were enjoying their language study; 49 percent intended to continue studying the language at the advanced level (where a diversity of language courses was available to them), while a further 14 percent would have liked to continue but had scheduling impediments.[5]

An investigation of student attitudes in the 90s, with the growing societal uneasiness about national competitiveness, would probably reveal figures, in a variety of institutions, that were somewhere between the Illinois and Harvard figures. Departments can easily obtain this kind of information through questionnaires. Such investigations of the nature and interests of the student body are an essential first step in devising programs to meet the needs of a diversity of students, providing absorbing and enticing activities for requirement and nonrequirement students alike.

Rationale for Language Study

At some time all departments face questioning from other areas of the university about the reasonableness of requiring students to study languages as part of their education as young adults. One justification relates to the very purpose of undergraduate education. In the early college curriculum, we aim at providing students with some familiarity with different areas of knowledge and various ways of thinking about and working with old and new information, in order to open to them new perspectives and new experiences. Learning other people's languages and accessing their cultural experiences and preoccupations through their language cannot be ignored as a unique window on the world of thought and action. The value of personal experience with a language and a culture other than one's own and the doors this opens to discovery and enlightenment in the worlds of people, books, and modern communications are not unsubstantial. What has become so familiar as to be unremarkable in our own language and culture is now seen in a vivid new light.

Rivers (1981) sets out seven categories of objectives teachers may pursue in developing language courses:

1. To develop the students' intellectual powers through the study of another language

2. To increase the students' personal culture through the study of the great literature and philosophy to which the new language is the key

3. To increase the students' understanding of how language functions and to bring them to a greater awareness of the functioning of their own language

4. To teach students to read another language with comprehension so that they may keep abreast of modern writing, research, and information

5. To give students the experience of expressing themselves within another framework, linguistically, kinesically, and culturally

6. To bring students to a greater understanding of people across national barriers, by giving them a sympathetic insight into the ways of life and ways of thinking of the people who speak the language they are learning

7. To provide students with the skills that will enable them to communicate orally—and to some degree in writing—in personal and career contexts with speakers of another language and with people of other nationalities who have also learned this language

Each of these objectives has at some time or in some place predominated in the stated aims of language teachers (Rivers 1981: 8).

In fact, in this list we can almost read a history of the progress of language teaching over the last hundred years or so. The most popular objectives at the present time are the last three, although the fourth predominates in many parts of the world, and the linguists among us would like to see the third come more to the fore (see chapter 13). Emphases continually change in synchrony with national trends and societal pressures. An objective that is foremost in one decade may, rightly or wrongly, be rejected outright in the next. Which of these objectives (or others that may be proposed) is most appropriate in a particular institution will depend on the kinds of students in the program (their ages, backgrounds, career orientations, general interests) and the overall educational objectives of the college.[6]

Each of the categories listed constitutes a worthy educational objective. The problem is whether, in the average "basic" or "requirement" course, we are perceived by our students, or other members of the university, as achieving such objectives to any substantial or recognizable degree. The common complaint that "just learning irregular verbs and a lot of useless vocabulary" is not an educational experience that should be required of students is quite justified and should give us pause. We may talk in idealistic terms when we feel our bailiwick (read: budget) is threatened; the point is: Do we act with these noble ends in mind in our actual semester-by-semester practice?

Course Design

In any program large enough to permit it, courses should be devised, even at the elementary level, that accommodate choice of approach and content. In designing these courses, we keep in mind not only objectives but also the diversity among our students of aptitude for various aspects of language and of learning styles (oral-aural preference versus visual; learning through use versus abstract analysis—for two instances). We have the possibility of developing courses that emphasize the aural-oral from the beginning—some courses begin with a strong listening component before speaking is expected, as in Terrell's Natural Approach (1977, 1982), while others encourage attempts at communication, both listening and speaking, from the earliest stages (Rivers 1987: 6–8). (In the Harvard French program, first-year students meet with the instructor once a week, individually or in pairs, to try their hand at communication from the first weeks.) Alternatively, we can plunge students directly into reading, particulary with cognate languages (Rivers et al. 1988-9: 171–77). We may give language knowledge a privileged position, especially for students of linguistics, or we may adopt a functional–notional approach (Rivers 1981: 232–35), where functions of language are practiced in contexts of use (rules are performed), before systematization is attempted. For the beginning level, many departments adopt a four-skills approach, teaching listening, speaking, reading, and writing together (sometimes overlooking the "fifth skill"—coping with the foreign culture). Chapter 4 discusses ways of using authentic literary texts as language-learning aids as early as the second semester to provide students with interesting and worthwhile content. The important questions are not which objective is given priority and which approach is adopted, but whether a judicious decision has been taken after reflection on the nature of the student body, the needs of the types of students in the college, and the specific problems the particular language being taught poses for these students (see chapter 8). This reflection may well result in changing the current offerings so that more choice of approach and content is available.

Elementary Courses

In planning the early levels of our language program, we do not seek above all articulation with later courses. We plan for the students a well-rounded and satisfying experience with the language, which is not regarded as pre-anything, but which ensures that all who pass through it will leave with the ability to use effectively and confidently whatever level of language they have acquired. We endeavor to provide a comfortable and enjoyable experience by reducing as much as possible the pressures of the one final all-determining, future-deciding examination, experimenting with alternative modes of evaluation.

Regular self-testing (which is what all tests should be) keeps the students aware of their progress (see chapter 10 and Principle 8 in chapter 19), while the demands of using what they are learning in an active way in interesting activities acts as an incentive to keep up with the work assigned. Students will be able to leave the course with confidence in their achievement, while being well enough grounded to be able to continue, if they wish, or return to language study at a later date, as their needs dictate.

Early language learning can be active and participatory, with students discussing and role-playing within the level of language they control. Original dramatizations created in the classroom are popular, and these can be video-taped so that students can see and hear themselves and recognize the need for improvement or change. As students see themselves communicating, kinesics becomes more strikingly obvious, as do the all-important features of intonation and rhythm. Modern media allow much of what used to be presented and explained in class to be studied at an individual pace by computer or in a multimedia laboratory, where students can interact vicariously with members of the other culture, thus enriching the course and liberating the classroom for communicative activities. If a complete course is built around individual work with computers,[7] this should be supplemented with at least two interactive group sessions per week, where students are able to use what they have been learning in active person-to-person communication. For computer programs requiring decision making at certain points to advance the program and determine its direction, working in pairs or small groups encourages students to use the language orally (see chapter 7).

Authentic language and cultural experiences can be brought into class not only via magazines, radio, film, videodisc, and satellite transmissions, but also through direct modem links with classrooms in other countries. Native speakers can be contacted in the community or by telephone or encountered in restaurants and at local community events. Video interviews made by the instructor with visiting native speakers, using the actual questions and language of the first-level textbook, are valuable because they can be used over and over again. Commercials in the language provide interesting insights into aspects of the culture in simple, often repetitive, memorable language, with native speakers reacting normally in a variety of culturally typical situations. Should these forms of authentic contact seem out of reach, there is still correspondence, written or taped, with peers in the other culture. One instructor in German encouraged students to write to people in a Düsseldorf phone book, requesting information on customs, songs, and food at Christmas time, with notable success.[8] The author, when teaching French in a small country town, used the simple device of a pin and a map of France and wrote to the head of the English language department in the educational institution of the randomly selected town to establish correspondence links; the chamber of commerce or tourist information center will do as well, and these sources will often send the students a rich store of documentation as well. Correspondence often leads to telephone conversations and, later, exchanges of visits. If teachers will think ahead, plan carefully, and incorporate what is available reflectively into the semester's work, the future of the development of comprehensible and acceptable language use without traveling abroad is very bright indeed (see also chapter 11).

Extension and Enrichment

Intensive Courses   Even a small program should be able to provide, beyond the general course, at least one specialized intensive course for fast third- or fourth-language learners with a strong, clearly defined motivation. A group like this, willing to spend much more class and individual time on language study than those in the regular course, can usually acquire in one or two semesters a solid enough foundation to develop advanced linguistic control on their own initiative at a later date in the context in which they will need it. Because of their previous successful experience with a second language, they will have already acquired an understanding of how languages differ from their own and the features that require special attention. Their rate of acquisition is often spectacular.

Reading Courses   Nor must we forget the needs of students who wish only—for academic, career, or personal reasons—to read the language. Even in the first year of cognate languages, courses can be developed to meet this special need, encouraging students to plunge as directly as possible into reading for information in areas of particular concern to them (see chapters 5 and 6; and Rivers et al. 1988–9: chapter 6).

Reading courses should never be considered an easy ride to the college language requirement. If recognized as one choice for fulfilling such a requirement, they should demand a higher level of reading achievement than that expected of students who are trying to acquire four skills at once. In practice, they provide a valuable course for upper-level students in other disciplines who will need to read source material in another language—comparative literature, world literature, medieval studies, history, philosophy, area studies, and international studies (see chapter 14) come readily to mind—and they can also provide a home for graduate students who have a Ph.D. language requirement to fulfill. Groups within the class should be encouraged to choose and read together material in the professional area of interest to them.

Study Abroad   Another set of students whose needs require careful course planning is the study abroad group from other departments. Sometimes departments like architecture, music, journalism, engineering, or international studies decide to send their students abroad to further their studies. Often, optimistically, they expect their students to acquire within one semester sufficient control of the language of the target country for residence and even study purposes. The course designed for this special group should be intensive; and here the Dartmouth model is worth investigating (see chapter 11). At least three hours a day (including practice sessions and language laboratory or computer work) should be expected. The course should be designed with the actual communication (and study) intentions of this particular group of students in mind, so that on arrival in the country they will have had ample practice in the types of situations for which they will need the language. (Close consultation with the students' home department is advisable, if real needs are to be met.) An important segment of the course will be learning about the culture and how to live and work harmoniously within it (see chapter 19, Principle 9). Students will be given plenty of vicarious exposure to the culture through videos, television, radio, and print media, and they will be given opportunities to discuss freely with native speakers in their area various aspects of life and work in the country they will visit. This type of course should be taught by a person with considerable experience in the country and some specialized knowledge or interest in the students' area of concern. Even without the study abroad objective, certain groups of students with specialized interests may be gathered into one section designed to meet their special needs. The University of Cincinnati, for instance, offers Elementary German for Music Students, with special attention given to pronunciation, musical vocabulary, and readings with topics of interest to students of music. This could well be extended to students of Italian.

Alternatives to the Language Requirement   In colleges where courses in literature in translation or the study of other cultures are accepted in lieu of the language requirement for some students who have difficulty learning another language, the foreign-language departments should not react as though jilted. These courses are taught most effectively by instructors who know the language and its literature and culture well. Sometimes students in the "hard" sciences or engineering also are attracted to such courses as an option; they are seeking a complete change of pace from their regular routine. In some places, faculties of science and engineering require their students to broaden their studies with such humanistic exploration. Students of this type have a refreshingly different approach to literary and cultural interpretation, which is revitalizing for the instructor. This is an area to be explored by departments seeking to be of service to all comers.

Diversity in First-Year Students   A perennial problem for beginning language courses is the mixed group they enroll. Usually there is great variation in precollege preparation (the latter may vary within one first-year group from 0 to 5 or more years; see Rivers 1976: 221). "True beginners" are intimidated from the first lesson when other members of the class, including some bilinguals, seem to know all the answers and can rattle off sentences and ask relatively sophisticated questions about grammar. Care should be taken to see that the true beginners are carefully shepherded during the first month. Experience has shown that by the second month or so most hardworking beginners catch up with those who have already studied the language (with no great success) for two or three years in high school and have placed back in the beginning level, especially if the course is fast-paced and concentrates on what is being learned in this particular class. (Others who have previously studied the language for several years have suffered from a long break since they actually used what they learned, and these too catch up as the semester proceeds.)

Bilinguals   Of more concern are the bilinguals. Elementary courses frequently enroll students who have heard or even spoken the language at home all their lives, but have never encountered it in written form. Some of these students, without realizing it, may speak a dialect very different from the standard variety of the class textbook. Because they comprehend rapidly and have a better pronunciation than the beginners around them, their fellow students often feel intimidated, while the bilinguals, who believed they knew the language, feel denigrated to be placed in the beginning level, usually as the result of a formal, impersonal placement test. An effort must be made to provide special sections or a separate course for these bilinguals so that their distinctive needs may be met in a supportive and encouraging atmosphere where they may discuss shared problems as well as develop appreciation of their ethnic heritage and hone an important career skill. Special classes for bilinguals can discuss the differences among dialects and between these and the accepted norm. Usually two one-semester courses are necessary to accommodate all bilingual students: a lower-level course for those whose active language skills are weak and who have had little experience reading the language, and a continuing course to take these students to higher levels of native speaker competence in speech and writing while introducing them to interesting and well-written texts of their own culture. The upper-level course will also attract more fluent bilinguals who are looking to bring their control of the language, including writing, to the level of peers in their native culture. Courses of this type should be taught, where possible, by a well-prepared bilingual of similar background to the students—a person who understands their linguistic and cultural problems and how to overcome them and can appreciate the contributions of the different dialects to the richness of the language.

Two-Stage Approach

In some languages, those with distinctive structure spoken in a very different culture, not all students attracted to the classes realize how long it will take to be able to use the language in conversation and negotiation or for reading. Consequently, the first-year courses are often inflated with students with unrealistic expectations, who finish the year disappointed and frustrated with their achievement. To obviate this problem, a two-stage approach can be tried. (This approach is also useful for junior colleges and adult education classes in more commonly taught languages.)[9]

In the two-stage approach, we make a distinction in our planning between continuing and terminal courses. In many institutions, because of the progressive and cumulative nature of language learning, most language courses are designed as continuing courses: high school classes prepare students for college; elementary courses prepare students for the intermediate level; intermediate courses prepare students for advanced study; and undergraduate majors prepare students to undertake graduate-level literary studies. This meets the needs of some, but by no means all. When a course is designed as terminal, this does not mean that the students who do continue will not be prepared to do so; it does, however, provide those who will not go on with a satisfying and rounded experience with the language at that level, making sure that they can do something with the knowledge and skill they have acquired.

With this orientation, the Stage One course is considered an entity in itself, of educational and humanistic value. It provides students with a serious introduction to the culture in which the language is embedded, along with some ability to "get around" in the language orally and (where the nature of the writing system permits it) graphically as well, at least at the utilitarian, informational level. At the end of this one-semester course (or two semesters in slower-paced programs), students will have had some experience with language learning and the differences between languages and cultures, and they will be in a position to decide whether this is a study they wish to pursue. Students who do decide to continue with the language then go on to Stage Two, where the course will be peopled with students who know what they are undertaking, are enthusiastic about it, and are committed to achieving a higher level of language control. This system is worth trying with languages where there is a high dropout rate in the first year. It is an approach that considers any language learning a valid educational experience and tries to make it so.

No matter what type of course is selected as appropriate at the elementary level, the course should be proficiency-oriented; in other words, course designers and instructors alike must keep in the forefront of their thinking the question, What will these students be able to do with the material when they leave the course? Facing up to this question will affect every classroom activity or homework assignment and the selection and testing of them.

DEVELOPING A WORKING COMPETENCE—
THE INTERMEDIATE LEVEL

Diversification at the Intermediate Level

Once we are beyond the elementary level and students have some grasp of how the language works and what is involved in learning and using it, we are out in an open field. Languages can be learned through all kinds of content and through any activity that requires use of the language in interaction with others who share similar interests (and this includes the instructor). Here imagination should have free play. In designing courses to meet students' needs and interests, we do not have to offer 300 choices of content for 300 students to give a feeling of individual choice. Experience has shown that students' choices tend to center around several nuclei.

1. *The Pragmatic.* These students want access to the language for immediate use, within their own field of study or for oral survival, either in a country where the language is spoken or with native speakers at home.

2. *The Humanistic.* These students want to acquire the language, but at the same time to experience its poetry, films, art, music, or prose masterpieces. They want to be able to interact at a cultivated level, but they are not necessarily interested in literary theory as such (in which case they would have enrolled in literature courses).

3. *The Anthropological.* These students want to understand how persons of other cultures think, what things matter most to them, and how to establish harmonious relations with them.

4. *The Utilitarian.* These students want to be able to read the language for scientific, philosophical, or political reasons, and they wish to attain this objective by the shortest possible route. Alternatively, they want to be able to conduct business, work in some capacity, or do some kind of research in another country. We can also include under this heading students who say bluntly: "I have to do a requirement. Let's get on with it!"

Each of these categories can inspire a number of possibilities for course content.

Whether there is one section or twenty parallel sections, instructors should consider seriously the many possibilities for intermediate level courses that will give such diverse students a sense of satisfaction with their achievement. Where there are parallel sections instructors should have a choice as well as students. Instructors teach more competently and enthusiastically when they are teaching what they know and love. At the intermediate level, we can decide on a core of language knowledge that students in all sections will be expected to acquire, while giving students choice to enroll in sections according to the additional subject matter individual instructors wish to offer in that section. This is a proven way in large programs to arouse the interest of teaching assistants, who may feel that language teaching has been imposed on them as an inescapable chore because of their need to earn their daily bread. It also perks up fourth-semester requirement students, who may have a tendency to "sit on their hands" and seek to complete the semester with the least possible hassle. It undoubtedly attracts "free spirits"—students who are attracted to languages and want to do further study as an option. Logistically this approach means, given four or five classes a week, allotting two days for study and practice of the common core and two or three days for studying the particular materials or carrying out the specific activities designed for each individual section. Alternatively, two-week or four-week segments can be allotted to the section-specific material at intervals during the semester. (This is particularly useful where the section is producing a video or a play or studying a film or novel in detail.)

What Course Options Can We Provide?

The following are ideas for intermediate level courses (full courses or parallel sections) that have been tried out in different places. Some are more suitable for fourth-semester or advanced intermediate level. Each department, of course, will need to establish its own priorities after careful consultation with its instructors and some study of the student body. Where variety of content is introduced in different sections, there should be no attempt to impose a uniform across-the-board final examination. Some of the courses proposed will be evaluated on a final product created by the students as well as on their language proficiency; others will involve testing of specific skills rather than overall control of language.

1. Some students will opt for a *continuing four-skills* course, in which case the choice of major textbook and any supplementary materials will revolve around the content that will interest the students most: litera-

ture (short stories, poems, plays, short novel); film; history; or contemporary culture. Above all, the intermediate course should not become just another review of grammar. Grammar needs context, and students need content for intellectual stimulation. To learn how to express oneself through the language by observing grammar in action and performing rules in interesting language activities should continue to be the focus.

2. Some programs will need at this level a special section for those who have already decided that they wish to *major* or *concentrate* in the language or make it a *minor* area of study. This section will be designed as a continuing section, building up students' control of the language in speech and writing and preparing them to interpret texts and discuss them in the language. Where there is a multitrack major, there will be more diversity in what students expect to accomplish. It is appropriate for senior faculty to join in discussions of what they would like future majors and minors to be able to do.

3. An *oral survival* course is an attractive option. In this course, students learn to make passive knowledge of the language active. The course implicitly promises that, if the graduates of the course were helicoptered into a country where the language is spoken, they would be able to understand what is said to them (even on the telephone!), be understood, and make their way comfortably within the culture. A course of this type is usually based on contemporary materials that clarify cultural mores and preoccupations for the students, or it may set the students the task of developing a visit to the country: arrival, finding lodgings, selecting a travel itinerary with certain objectives, budget, and so on. It will certainly include a strong listening component. The emphasis will be on developing confidence in communicating in the language, without undue emphasis on stringent correction (Rivers 1981: 242–44).

4. A course entirely in the target language may study the *culture* of its speakers, explicitly and in depth, through authentic print materials (magazines, books, newspapers), but also through television, radio, film, or videodisc. This course will aim at regular contact with native speakers, either visited in their communities or brought into the classroom to discuss with students what they have been learning.

5. A *contrastive cultures* course may be conducted partly in the foreign language and partly in the native language of the students. Students will study the target culture as seen by its bearers and as seen through the eyes of their own compatriots, while simultaneously viewing their

native culture as perceived by speakers of the target language; they will also discuss the influence of one culture on the other. Print and visual materials will be used, brought into class or brought to the attention of the class by students as well as by the instructor.

6. A course studying the *literature* of the target language, with *discussion in that language*. (Since this is a language course, not a literature course, techniques and activities will be of the type discussed in chapter 4.)

7. A course studying the *literature* of the target language with in-depth discussions *in the native language* of the students. Further writings by some of the authors being studied may be read in translation to give students a broader view of their work. This course will interest students majoring in other literatures or in comparative literature, as well as students from other faculties who love to read literature.

8. A course in *reading for information* may use scientific, technological, philosophical, sociological, mathematical, or other texts. The emphasis will be on extracting information and writing reports, abstracts, and summaries of the contents in the students' native language. The selection of reading materials will be individualized according to the professional interests of the students (see chapter 5).

9. A course in which students learn language through *drama* is always an attraction for some and provides excellent material for active language use when all aspects of the preparation are kept in the target language (Via 1987).

10. Courses specially geared to specific *professions* can be designed to give useful career-oriented preparation. Some departments have developed Spanish courses for health professionals, law enforcement personnel, or fire fighters (especially in areas where persons in these professions frequently have to deal with large concentrations of Hispanics); this approach can be extended to other languages where the need exists. Italian for Musicians has proved useful. French, German, Spanish, and Japanese for Business are also popular, although at this level they might better be called Commercial French (German, etc.) and concentrate on preparing students for the full-fledged courses for business—which will require much more sophisticated control of language and understanding of the culture of the business world (see chapter 6).

11. A course in *film,* using the scenario of a foreign film as the major text. The film is then studied in detail, and students reenact scenes or, in groups, write, act, and film new scenes that fit in with the original characterization and plot, or variants of existing scenes.

12. *Comic books* and *cartoons* provide an area of rich insight into popular culture and cultural preoccupations and assumptions. A very interesting course can be developed around these, exploring the culturally defined situations they depict; comparing them with the local product; filling in dialog in balloons and subscripts left blank and comparing these with those of others for peer assessment of authenticity and appropriateness; and preparing new episodes (if someone in the group can sketch, this helps, of course). In Europe, certain comic books even have an academic status, with university courses devoted to their study as cultural artifacts of semiotic significance. They are a way of bringing a new excitement into a fourth-semester requirement group.

13. *Desktop publishing* of a newspaper, jointly planned and written from coast to coast via modem, has been the material of a fourth-semester French course taught by Frommer at Harvard and Barson at Stanford for several years (see chapter 6). This is *purposeful, task-oriented* language learning, and further ways of learning useful skills while practicing language could well be devised.

14. *Print media* provide material for a very topical course. Students study the press in a target-language country, becoming acquainted with available newspapers and magazines; analyzing their philosophical, political, and social orientations; discussing contrasting reports of events and social problems; and studying and interpreting political cartoons.

15. Learning language while concentrating on learning *content* is frequently advocated. This makes most sense when the content being studied is in some way connected with the target language or culture, for example history, sociology, philosophy, art appreciation, or musicology, with special focus on the target-country or target-language contributors to the discipline. In these courses all readings as well as classroom discussions and assignments are in the target language. (See also chapter 2.)

16. *Contemporary global concerns* may be probed, analyzed, and discussed through television and video segments from countries where the language is spoken, supplemented by radio and print materials and songs that reflect social involvement. Students become aware of the fact that speakers of the language are equally involved in preserving the planet, conserving their cultural heritage, working for full participation of all citizens within their societies, eliminating poverty, illiteracy, homelessness, and endemic diseases, and utilizing technological advances to improve and prolong life. Discussions can often be supplemented with carefully selected short stories, poems, or excerpts from plays or

novels. The essence of this type of course is student involvement in selecting topics and full participation in cooperative research, discussion, and proposing solutions.

No institution will offer all these options at one time, and many others could be listed. Instructors will use their imagination, according to the particular setting and clientele of their institutions. No matter what provisions are made, there should always be the option for students to "proficiency out" of the language requirement through testing that is unrelated to coursework, should students prefer to learn the language on their own or in an area where the language is spoken. Our aim with a requirement should be to expose students to language learning, not to hassle and irritate them with bureaucracy. For the volunteers, we hope to have met their needs in an exciting encounter with another language and culture, and we look forward to meeting them again at the advanced level.

NOTES

1. M. Kalb, director of the Harvard University Kennedy School of Government's John Shorenstein Barone Center on the Press, Politics, and Public Policy, cited in C. Lambert, "Global Spin," *Harvard Magazine* (Jan.–Feb. 1990): 18.

2. *Harvard University Gazette* 85 (Feb. 2, 1990): 2.

3. For a thorough statistical study of the foreign-language situation in colleges and universities, with discussion of implications, see Lambert (1990).

4. For a discussion of different student learning styles, see Breiner-Sanders (1991).

5. Results of the Harvard Questionnaire 1980 can be obtained from the author. It closely parallels results in 1976, which are to be found, along with the questions asked, in Rivers 1976, pp. 221–23. Replication of the Harvard or Illinois studies at a later period in different types of institutions would provide valuable information about changing attitudes.

6. For objectives of language teaching in fifty states of the USA and fifty countries, see Rivers 1983b, chapter 2, "Educational Goals: The Foreign-Language Teacher's Response," and Rivers 1983a, Appendix: "Results of Questionnaire on Foreign Language Learners' Goals."

7. The Ohio State University has for a number of years individualized first-year language study across several languages, using computers to assist students in their learning.

8. R. Di Donato, while teaching German at MIT.

9. For a discussion of languages in junior and community colleges, and particularly a detailed discussion of the two-stage approach, see "Conservation and Innovation: Foreign Languages in Two-Year Undergraduate Institutions," in Rivers 1983b: 183–90.

REFERENCES

Breiner-Sanders, Karen. 1991. "Higher-Level Language Abilities: The Skills Connection," pp. 54–88 in June K. Phillips, ed., *Building Bridges and Making Connections.* Report of the Northeast Conference on the Teaching of Foreign Languages. Middlebury, VT: The Northeast Conference.

Kieffer, Claude. 1990. "Development of School Programs in the European Perspective." *Language Association Bulletin* [New York Association of Foreign Language Teachers] 41,4: 8–11.

Lambert, Richard D. 1990. *Language Instruction for Undergraduates in American Higher Education.* Occasional Papers of the National Foreign Language Center, no. 7. Washington, DC: NFLC.

McLuhan, Marshall, and Q. Fiore. 1967. *The Medium Is the Massage.* New York: Bantam.

Rivers, Wilga M. 1976. *Speaking in Many Tongues: Essays in Foreign-Language Teaching.* Expanded 2d ed. Rowley, MA: Newbury House.

————. 1981. *Teaching Foreign-Language Skills.* 2d ed. Chicago: Univ. of Chicago Press.

————. 1983a. *Communicating Naturally in a Second Language: Theory and Practice in Language Teaching.* Cambridge, Eng., and New York: Cambridge Univ. Press.

————. 1983b. *Speaking in Many Tongues: Essays in Foreign-Language Teaching.* 3d ed. Cambridge, Eng., and New York: Cambridge Univ. Press.

————. 1988. *Teaching French: A Practical Guide.* Lincolnwood, IL: National Textbook Company.

————, ed. 1987. *Interactive Language Teaching.* Cambridge, Eng., and New York: Cambridge Univ. Press.

————; Milton M. Azevedo; and William H. Heflin, Jr. 1988. *Teaching Spanish: A Practical Guide.* Lincolnwood, IL: National Textbook Company.

————; Kathleen M. Dell'Orto; and Vincent J. Dell'Orto. 1988. *Teaching German: A Practical Guide.* Lincolnwood, IL: National Textbook Company.

————, and Moshe Nahir. 1989. *Teaching Hebrew: A Practical Guide.* Tel Aviv, Israel: University Publishing Projects.

Terrell, Tracy D. 1977. "A Natural Approach to Second-Language Acquisition and Learning." *Modern Language Journal* 61: 325–37.

————. 1982. "The Natural Approach to Language Teaching: An Update." *Modern Language Journal* 66: 121–32.

Via, R. 1987. "The Magic 'If' of Theater: Enhancing Language Learning through Drama," pp. 110–23 in Wilga M. Rivers, ed., *Interactive Language Teaching.* Cambridge, Eng., and New York: Cambridge Univ. Press.

2
The Undergraduate Program II: The Advanced Level— A Plethora of Possibilities

Wilga M. Rivers
Harvard University

FIVE DIRECTIONS FOR COURSE CONTENT

At the advanced level we are providing opportunities for students from all disciplines to achieve the level of language control they are seeking; courses are not devised specifically with majors and minors, or concentrators, in mind, although many of the latter will profit from the most advanced of the courses. We are advocating an open-door policy by which the department welcomes all who love languages, without any form of exclusion by content, and tries to develop their knowledge in language-related fields while they are delving more deeply into the language. If languages could be learned as quickly as some advertisements boast, there would be no need for long and arduous study, but we who have learned languages as nonnative speakers know that this is not the case. Students appreciate the opportunities provided by integration into long sequences and register in great numbers. This is the direction language departments will do well to investigate if they are to flourish in future years in an increasingly competitive academe.

For many departments, "advanced" courses mean just two: a "Review of Grammar" (for a third or fourth time in approximately the same terms) and "Con and Comp" (Conversation and Composition). In the latter one-semester course, there is presumably concurrent practice of the fluent use of everyday, informal language (with any introduction the department provides to the pragmatics of intercultural communication) and written expression (the study of formal language use, according to the norms of educated society, along with a cursory look at stylistics and cohesive discourse features). Can these two be easy bedfellows, if we are to do justice to both of them? In one semester, is it possible to develop an advanced competence in either? Furthermore, should these two essential areas be separated from the "review of grammar," which can be effective at this level only when students are "performing rules" in the context of expressing their own meanings in speech or writing (see chapter 19, Principle 5)? Language knowledge grows and language control is consolidated in *living language* courses (Rivers 1983: 161–62), where students are focusing their attention on content and meaning while internalizing the finer points of phonology, syntax, or pragmatics as they need them at any particular moment.

If the embedding of language learning in purposeful and interesting activity with the language is taken as a basic principle, then we can "review" grammar, pronunciation, or whatever while considering challenging questions and texts, or performing tasks, that catch and maintain the students' attention and involvement. Living language courses at any level can be designed to have whatever focus we feel is needed for student development (writing, speaking, listening, sound production, reading), provided that this particular aspect of language is integrated into some form of realistic use. Thus, instead of a remedial pronunciation class, we work on play reading or class dramatic performance (whether to the level of theatrical production or not), or we concentrate on the reading of poetry. Both of these activities require of students constant repetition with increasing clarity of articulation and expres-siveness. For the improvement of writing, we organize a section to produce a departmental news bulletin in the target language. Or we establish a class in creative expression, where students study short stories or poems and write their own. Is it oral expression that needs work? Then students meet around a project they must jointly develop through discussion, often in small groups, after which they go out to interview native-speaking informants to obtain information that is to be shared with the class orally or through recorded tapes or videos. Literary texts provide an excellent focus for developing ability to use the language when students become actively involved with the material (see chapter 4).

Since language learning is a continuum that goes on throughout life, it is inevitable that there will be some overlapping between the kinds of courses one may propose for the advanced level and those described for the higher intermediate level. Numbers 4, 6, 9, 10, 11, 14, and 16, described for the intermediate level (see chapter 1), can quite appropriately be taught at a higher level of linguistic complexity, and further courses along the lines of 13, where tasks are performed that involve useful skills for work or leisure, can easily be devised after some reflection.

There are five directions in which advanced language programs can develop (Rivers 1983: 171–80) in providing intellectually challenging courses that allow for linguistic consolidation and increasingly nativelike control, and these will be discussed in relation to specific course proposals. In a long program, each course is allotted a particular level for admission, which can be related to a score on the placement test used in the department. In this way, students are working together at a similar level of competence. With clear indications of entry levels, students can select courses more judiciously and avoid frustration.

1 Interdisciplinary Studies

The marriage between language and literature has historic roots, and a minor liaison has been established in some departments with linguistics (see chapter 13). These are not, however, the only possible alliances; others offer promise for future development. In this connection, a natural association would appear to be *foreign language and international studies,* which is discussed in detail in chapter 14. With due regard to the contributions of speakers and writers of particular languages to various fields of endeavor, we may wish to establish links with philosophy, psychology, anthropology, history, geography, architecture, visual arts, music, theater arts, or film, among others. In these disciplines foreign-language professors, with some notable exceptions, are not the experts at the college level, even if they have a strong interest in the subject. Such courses are best team-taught with experts from the relevant disciplines, with the language specialist attending the main lecture, conducting discussion sections on documentation and contemporary material that is not available in translation, and helping with practice sessions in the language. Students also do assignments in the foreign language. (This development of language use through study of subject matter in another discipline is referred to as *content-based instruction.*) To take part in such a program, the foreign-language instructor must be well-read and must keep up with the area. If the link is with international studies, the course should be linked with the departmental Study Abroad program (see chapter 11), for which students will be assigned well-defined research projects that take them into the community and give them background for interpreting national attitudes and aspirations.

Jurasek (1988) reports the development at Earlham College of a program of *foreign language across the curriculum,* in which professors in such areas as

philosophy, European history, or law, usually with at least a reading competence in a foreign language, discuss in English texts in the foreign language that
would normally be included in their regular courses. (With selected groups this
discussion may be in the foreign language.) These professors "do not teach
foreign languages. Rather, their goal is to heighten the students' concentration
on the course material and open new windows to content" (p. 54). During the
period 1980–86, eighty-six new courses were developed with a foreign-
language component and about 90 percent of the students in the college
participated at some level of language skill, ranging from intermediate to
advanced (p. 55).

Brown University, in another language-across-the-curriculum endeavor,
integrates the study of four foreign languages into social science courses,
linking French with international relations; Spanish with political science;
Portuguese with both history and Afro-American studies; and Russian with
Soviet studies. Students are introduced to the vocabulary and discourse of the
discipline, read primary sources in the language, and use the language for
discussion and written assignments. These courses are for intermediate and
advanced students, as well as for native speakers.[1]

The content-based approach was expanded by the University of Minnesota, which added to such courses as French and Spanish history, Latin-
American politics, or Central European geography one-credit "trailer courses"
taught in the foreign language by the professors teaching the main course,
assisted by foreign-language graduate students. St. Olaf College in Minnesota
adds to core courses taught in English an optional "applied foreign-language
component," in which a foreign-language teacher leads a discussion in the
foreign language on original texts selected by the core course professor.

Departments interested in the content-based approach will find instruc-
tive accounts of initiatives in other schools in the professional journals.[2]

2 Language and Intercommunity Understanding

Learning to accept difference and to cooperate with "different" others are
important skills in the modern world. A unit on using the telephone in another
country or buying a train ticket does not ensure this kind of understanding.
Neither does talking about facts and details of another culture. Students must
learn to cope within another culture, and for this they need personal contact
wherever possible or else vicarious contact, provided by interactive video or
radio and television materials that capture the actuality of the living culture.
They need to "see" the other culture on its own terms, its similarities and
differences, and recognize their own culturally acquired prejudices and

assumptions. They profit from experience in studying possible points of conflict between cultures. Di Pietro's Strategic Interaction, in which students work out cultural dilemmas through scenarios, is useful here (Di Pietro 1987).

2.1 Community-Based Courses

Where there is a local community of immigrants, migrants, or émigrés who speak the target language, access to this living laboratory should be worked into an advanced course. Students may work in pairs, with clearly defined assignments, collecting data and interview material (written and taped) on the community's history, folklore, customs, employment patterns, child-rearing practices, philosophy of life, leisure activities, and so on, and reporting back at intervals to the class group. Students should be encouraged to attend community celebrations, help the local community in its contacts with the majority culture, with child care (much useful practice can be gained in using the language with children), or in tutoring. Telephone links can be established with members of the community in old people's homes or with shut-ins. Bilinguals within the college community should be brought into class to explain their community to their peers. Archival material gathered may be shared with the community through a target-language newspaper or local access news show, or stored in the local library. This type of course can be a continuing enterprise, as new sets of students carry on where others have left off.

2.2 A Systematic Study of Certain Aspects of the Target Culture

This more customary approach may be developed in a number of ways.

- The course may concentrate on particular regions or levels of society, applying sociolinguistic methods of analysis. This investigation may be linked with a study of the phonological and lexical distinctiveness of the local dialect, for which regional novelists and poets often provide very useful and interesting source material. Alternatively, the study may focus on political institutions and their bearing on national and international policy; or on the economic climate and the roots of the local business culture, as a companion course for the Language for Business course.

- A very popular Spanish course at Harvard uses *telenovelas* (soap operas) from Hispanic America, taken from satellite transmissions, as course material. Students learn much about the life and language of ordinary people in various Spanish-speaking countries, while they are perfecting their language skills, using what they have learned in further episodes that they write in small groups and then film, observing and critiquing their own use of language and rerecording for improvement and authenticity.

- A similar course can be evolved using target-language *advertisements* and *commercials*. The analysis of the semiotics of advertising is very revelatory of cultural assumptions, mores, and values, since advertisers play very much on these, sometimes at an implicit level, to increase sales effectiveness. Students study differences in approach to the consumer via print and via video. As with 2.2b, students prepare, record, and critique their own commercials.

- A lively interest in the contemporary scene in target-language countries can be aroused in a course linked to regular target-language *radio broadcasts*. In this course, students write up a weekly bulletin for language classes across all levels, bringing them up to date not only on political developments, but also on many aspects of contemporary life and leisure pursuits. This activity improves their listening and writing skills, and, if they discuss the details and format of their bulletins together, their speaking ability.

3 Understanding the Process of Communication

We often maintain that learning another language helps us to understand how language functions in communication: Such things as how meanings are encoded and decoded; the pragmatics of discourse (how we achieve our purposes in social situations); how to interpret what others are trying to communicate, not only through words, but by nonverbal means; the relationship between language and social structure, and how it defines inner and outer relationships through our reactions to language varieties and our swift adaptation to levels of language use. Despite our lofty claims, however, we rarely devise courses that relate directly and unambiguously to this objective.

Some of this material will, of course, form part of undergraduate linguistics courses (see chapter 13). Advanced language courses should also provide for this area of concern. In many departments there is an advanced conversation course, which, unfortunately, is often palmed off on a newly arrived native speaker with little knowledge of the complexity of what a course like this should be accomplishing. It should not surprise us, therefore, if it ends up as a course in listening to long monologs by the inexperienced instructor, interspersed with occasional comments by the bolder or more fluent members of the group, or lengthy oral reports, read by each student in turn in a soporific monotone from a written script. Other possibilities exist.

3.1 Advanced Communication Skills

A course of this type will be linked with a careful study of the nature of interpersonal discourse in the target language—not only the politenesses that smooth the way in formal and informal relationships, but also the nature of exchanges within the culture: Who speaks first to whom using what level of language? How close do people stand? What are the social rules of eye contact and touching? What are appropriate opening and closing gambits for different kinds of communicative exchanges? How are pauses filled to retain speaker priority? How does one take the floor? How are interruptions engineered? How does one accept, refuse, deny, hedge, negotiate, or navigate in a conversation in different contexts? How does one correct oneself or change direction unobtrusively? (See also Kramsch 1981; 1987). Students have a great deal to learn about the deep emotional impact of culturally determined semantic differences expressed in the lexicon: even simple elements of daily life have vastly different connotations for persons of different cultures, as do common allusions, whether historical, folkloric, or topical.

None of these elements can be fully appreciated and assimilated out of context. A Communication Skills course needs context and should be integrated into a close study of the culture of the speakers of the language, through analysis of carefully selected print and video sources. These need not necessarily be sociological: authentic dialog in modern plays, novels, films, and television programs, or in personally recorded discussions among native speakers, are rich sources of information in an area where students will learn more from personal observation and analysis than from lecturettes and scholarly descriptions. Although the course will be evaluated mainly on demonstrations of success in communicative exchanges, some part of the grade will also be allotted to individual analyses of communicative tactics in personally collected data.

3.2 Advanced Oral and Written Expression

After successful completion of an Oral Survival course at the intermediate level (see chapter 1), some students feel the need for an advanced course (or courses), in which they can learn to express themselves more formally and accurately.[3] A course of this type is based on debates and formal discussions of contemporary societal and global problems, carefully researched and prepared by groups of students, who also write out in expository form the viewpoints they will support. Students discuss improvements to each other's scripts, which are then carefully corrected by the instructor and discussed with the individual authors before being included in the debate. During actual debates, the students take the floor and the instructor remains on the periphery, available for consultation and advice on less successful aspects of the activity. Students learn how discussions and formal presentations are developed in the language, and the stages of exposition and the formal cohesive features of written argument. Students are evaluated on the same types of activities as those in which they have been engaged during the semester.

3.3 Kinesics and Communicative Interaction

Wylie (1985) has studied the way the whole body is involved as a unit in communicative dyads. "All communication," he maintains, "is highly and regularly rhythmic" (p. 780). Students of a new language must learn to control not just their vocal organs but the degree of relaxation of the torso and the amount of space in which they move, and they must synchronize eye and body movements with those of their interlocutors. "Pronunciation and even grammar," he says, "appear to be more easily learned in the context of cultural rhythm" (p. 781). He feels that nativelike expression is not attainable when these bodily factors are out of harmony with the vocal output, as so often happens in conventional language classes. He developed a novel course (described in Crook 1985) in which students endeavor to loosen up their habitual bodily movements and approximate those of native speakers. Students make a close study of film clips of native speaker interactions and learn to reproduce these interactions word for word, movement for movement, intonational pattern for intonational pattern. In this way, they learn that nativelike production is an entity that cannot be acquired piecemeal.[4]

3.4 Cours de Perfectionnement (Perfecting Language Skills)

There is always a need at the highest level for a course for those students who have returned from study abroad; for those who have lived for some time in a country where the language is spoken, but have not necessarily studied the language while abroad; for those who have lived for some time in a country where the language is spoken, but have not necessarily studied the language while abroad; for students who have completed a long sequence in elementary school and junior and senior high school (often with Advanced Placement); and for majors, minors, concentrators, and graduate students needing extra work to improve their fluency and accuracy. Such a course may use literary texts or materials dealing with contemporary culture, or both, but always actively: listening to materials on tape, video, or film; practicing pronunciation, stress, and intonation to as near-native a level as possible; reading extensively self-selected texts as well as those discussed in class; writing creatively; discussing ideas from their listening and reading and their own ideas, frequently and in depth; making tapes and videos for which they have written the scenarios themselves and remaking them until they are proud of their efforts; making contacts with native speakers, conducting interviews, and developing friendships. The emphasis is always on culturally authentic discourse in speech or writing. An innovative instructor has a wide world of possibilities to explore and the students will propose many of their own. Sometimes more than one semester is needed to satisfy the aspirations of these groups. This is the prototype of a *living language* course.

3.5 Translation

Much neglected in recent years has been the valuable skill of translation, called by Duff (1981) "the third language." The swing of the pendulum away from translation was understandable, because of the overuse of it at one time as the quintessential language teaching device and, consequently, the artificiality of much translation practice. Although some translation has its place as a clarifying and memory-testing device at earlier stages (Rivers et al. 1988–9, chapter 9), study of translation at the advanced level as a craft and a potential career skill is quite another undertaking.

Although it might appear that a course in translation should be discussed under the rubric of "Languages for Specific Purposes and Career Preparation" (below), it has considerable relevance for the understanding of how languages work and how we communicate through different languages. As an intellectual activity, it teaches students much about the way two languages express reality (the sum total of human experience); how they reflect in different terms such basic concepts as time, space, and motion, as well as more abstract notions (philosophical, economic, or political); how one language can represent what can be mentally comprehended but expressed only by implication or circumlocution in another (see Rheingold 1988); as well as the richness of idiom and metaphor and the complications of style.

In fact, a course of this type becomes a learning experience in both the foreign and the native languages. Duff wonders "why it is that translation, no matter how competent, often reads like a 'foreign language'" (1981: vi), and discusses the fundamental problem of penetrating the original writer's thought and successfully transferring this in well-written form to one's own language. A course in translation from the target language to the native language not only develops the student's ability to penetrate to the deepest meaning of a target-language text and increases knowledge of many fields, but it also sharpens control of the written forms of one's own language. Translation from the native language to the target language forces the student to consider fundamental differences in ways of expressing reality, and demands precision of lexical and syntactic choice, with accuracy in structural formulation. Both can become absorbing activities. It hardly needs to be added that the instructor should keep well abreast of research in theory of translation.

A translation course should not impose repetitive, routine activity on students. Many new approaches can be included. For instance, as well as actual translation of texts and group discussion of these translations, students may

- Study several translations of the same text and discuss the strengths and weaknesses of these before attempting their own translations of problematic passages

- Study a B-grade translation made by a student in an earlier class (name deleted, of course) and make a critique of it before embarking on their own translations, thus becoming aware ahead of time of particularly difficult sections

- Analyze in schematic form passages in the source language expressing complex ideas, in such a way as to reveal the stages of development of the argument, and then rebuild the argument in comprehensible and acceptable form in the target language

- Work cooperatively in groups on translations, discussing problems fully with each other as they examine the text; or exchange individual translations within a group, discussing and editing each other's work and rewriting before submitting a final translation to the instructor

- As a loosening-up exercise, practice rapid translation of texts as dictated, then, after polishing up their work briefly, discuss in groups the virtues and shortcomings of the individual translations (this makes them very conscious of the dangers of miscomprehension resulting from coming too rapidly to conclusions)

- At times, practice simultaneous and consecutive oral interpretation, as an exercise in flexibility (although this activity warrants a special course, where it is to be considered as a possible career skill)

Translation courses at this level can accommodate graduate students as well as undergraduate students. Further courses at an even higher level of difficulty should be considered an integral part of the graduate program, enabling students to develop a sophisticated understanding of their new language.

4 Languages for Specific Purposes and Career Preparation

Many students who love languages will be drawn to other disciplines as their career orientation, but with the realization that further work in languages can enhance their professional potential; others will discover that their chosen careers require language competency. Departments must be open to the needs of these groups, devising courses that interest them and help them in their professional development. (Possibilities for such courses are discussed in detail in chapter 6.)

5 Languages as the Key to Humanistic Studies

Da Vinci wrote in his *Notebooks:* "He who can go to the fountain does not go to the water-jar."[5] Many people who love literature are anxious to read foreign literatures in the original tongue, thus going directly to the fountainhead. Literature is an area dear to the heart of all foreign-language departments (now frequently called departments of foreign languages and literatures), and it is the area of study for which most provision is made in traditional programs. We may wonder, then, why it is reappearing in a discussion on the advanced language program. Surely students can enroll in the already existing literature courses?

Unfortunately, many students interested in maintaining and further developing their language competency have found that their language skills deteriorate in lecture courses on literature, sometimes given in the native language, where much time is taken up with the study of literary theory and criticism, rather than the actual writings of the authors on the program. (For the teaching of literature, see chapter 12.) Discussion may be rare, and what discussion there is may well be in the native language, on the assumption that students will feel less inhibited in expressing complex and subtle ideas. Written assignments in literature courses often allow for the use of either the native language or the target language, as the student feels inclined. Consequently, skills of literary analysis may be honed, but ability to express oneself in the target language is soon perceived by the students to be of little importance in the course.

5.1 Advanced Language Courses with Literary Content

If students enjoy the aesthetic satisfaction of a good book, a good play, or a good poem, but have as their primary concern the further development of their language competency, they will look for an advanced language course with literary content—a course that elicits thoughtful discussion, debate, and involvement in the target language. The aim of such a course will not be to develop future literary critics or theorists, but to bring students into direct contact with writers and thinkers through their work, while pursuing ideas in a lively context—discussing, imagining, acting out, and creating in the language they are learning to control (see also chapter 4). For such courses, literature is conceived in the broadest terms, introducing texts representative of various target-language areas and diverse ethnic groups within those areas, and accepting as worthy of study not only accepted masterpieces but also genres such as detective and science fiction, travel chronicles, picaresque tales, folklore, and film. The success of the course is judged by the enthusiasm of the students to go on reading in the language as a pleasurable leisure pursuit.

Apart from the general course with literary content, the following variations may stimulate further innovative thinking.

5.2 Creative Writing through Literature

Comeau developed an advanced language course in which students began by reading and discussing many short poems by a diversity of poets, looking at these poems as creative acts. After this examination of the process of making a poem, students began to write their own in the target language, not imitating models, but launching out as poets, expressing their own personal insights. The poems were corrected for grammaticality by the instructor and then read aloud and enjoyed in class. The course then turned to short stories, with a similar objective—to encourage students to write their own. Comeau considers the course as accomplishing three goals: "(1) to encourage students to exhibit their literary creativity within a classroom context; (2) to encourage students to react both personally and critically to literature; and (3) to improve written and spoken language by asking students to produce creative pieces."[6]

5.3 Dramatic Expression

Dramatic activities provide an excellent vehicle for perfecting language use, with special advantages for improvement of pronunciation, stress, intonation, kinesics, and general verbal fluency. Dramatic texts are studied in detail, largely through acting them out, all preparations and decisions on interpretation being made in the target language (see Via 1987). Sometimes the course leads to the full-scale production of a play or sections of a play; at other times to the writing by the students of their own dramatic interludes, which are then videotaped, critiqued, and reenacted, until a satisfactory version is arrived at, which is then shown to other language classes or at a language club.

5.4 Literature and Film

Literary works are frequently made into films. In this course, films are studied and discussed in close relationship with the original texts, with discussion centering on the purposes of the original writer, the purposes of the film producer, and the correspondence or lack thereof between the two; students study the artistic reasons for decisions made by both.

5.5 Film as Artistic Expression

This course centers on films produced in the target language.

- It may take a historical approach, studying the evolution of film in the target-language milieu.

- It may study the ways in which films reflect the culture and aspirations of speakers of the language.

- It may concentrate on the filmmaking process, examining scriptwriting, dramatic and photographic techniques, settings, costumes, lighting, décor, and so on, culminating with the creation of several short films by groups of students who demonstrate in their own productions in the course what they have learned.

Whichever approach is taken, one product of the course will be regular reviews of target-language films being shown on campus, or in the area, for circulation among other students of the language.

5.6 Literature and Other Forms of Aesthetic Expression

Two possibilities are

- An instructor with a background in art or music relates selected literary texts to the art and music of the period in which they were written.

- A study of the music (including opera) or art of the target culture is related to poetry, song, and folklore manifestations, demonstrating the *Zeitgeist* influencing the various arts at particular periods in cultural history. "Song" should be broadened beyond concert material to include the songs enjoyed by ordinary people in their leisure hours.

A broadening of offerings at the advanced level presupposes a willingness in the department to break new ground, an interest in imaginative planning and experimentation on the part of some, and recognition in promotion and tenure decisions of the value of time-consuming work that may be unconventional.

Within the Family—
Majors and Concentrators

To maintain the emphasis on building programs to meet student interests and concerns, many departments have been redesigning their requirements for majors or concentrators. Once again, many could be attracted, since graduates with a broad humanistic education are now being welcomed for admission to many professional schools (of business, law, medicine, journalism, and international studies). Majors or concentrations centered on a language, together with a broad but critical study of the literature and intellectual thought and endeavor associated with its use and its users, provide a training in analyzing and thinking about problems and solutions that is recognized as an excellent basis for any career-oriented advanced studies.

Since the early seventies, when the Stanford German Department transformed itself into a Department of German Studies and the French Department at the University of Illinois at Urbana–Champaign began to consider seriously the implications of Expanded French Studies, numerous institutions have been experimenting with multitrack concentrations, double majors, and dual majors, while trying to maintain intellectual rigor and coherence within individual students' plans of study. Such broadening of possible paths to the undergraduate major should not, and need not, lead to a fuzzy, diluted wishwash of a program, and this is where the undergraduate advisor or head tutor plays a decisive role in shaping students' vague aspirations into well-structured, intellectually demanding, coherent plans of study. Many of these programs, especially in institutions with a relatively small group of concentrators, are intentionally individualized. For this approach to be successful, structures (so beloved of administrators and computers) must be designed flexibly, to capture the imagination of the brilliant maverick as well as the conscientious conformist, and careful early advising is crucial.

Lohnes has given us an excellent metaphor for this changed perspective on the department's work. In the past, he says, we were accustomed to "a pyramid, with large numbers of students in the beginning language courses at the base . . . with a very small number of advanced graduate students at the top" being "trained as research scholars for the pursuit of lofty goals"—a situation in which we doubtless did "justice to the few who reached the top, but . . . paid very little attention to all those that (fell) by the wayside." In its place, he proposes "a stack of cubes that can easily be rearranged or added on to. The right angles of the new system have produced a number of plateaus which can be clearly defined as to objectives and achievements," so that the various sections of the department's work "have become recognizable units within themselves, while also providing continuity for those who want to proceed all the way to the top" (1976: 78–80).

Once we consider the major or concentration as a recognizable unit within itself with adjustable segments "that can easily be rearranged or added on to," we are mentally and administratively liberated to think broadly and flexibly about possible combinations of language, literature, and culture studies and related interdisciplinary areas.

The Stanford Program

Stanford's flexible thinking finally developed a five-pronged program that allowed students to major in

- German Language and Linguistics, with links with the English and Linguistics Departments and with a segment of Language Pedagogy

- German Literature, which focuses on genres and specific developments and topics of German literature and culture

- German Thought *(Geistesgeschichte),* with offerings linked to English, French, philosophy, history, and religious studies, among others

- Culture Studies, which may combine study of German language and literature with such disciplines as art history, musicology, political science, history, economics, anthropology, or comparative literature, and presumes a period at the Stanford Center in Berlin

- Double majors with the Departments of Economics, International Relations, Political Science, History, and Engineering. For the social sciences and engineering, internships in Germany are available after a quarter at the Berlin Center[7]

The Cincinnati Program

The Department of Germanic Languages and Literatures at the University of Cincinnati has developed a German Cluster, which can complement or supplement another major. The Cluster, with a segment of basic German, includes courses that may be used to fulfill the College of Arts and Sciences language requirement and the humanities and literature requirements (for the latter, courses in German Culture and Literature in Translation are taught in English); in this way, students who had not considered German studies as an option may be attracted to the department. After the Cluster, students may continue with:

- The German Literature major, which includes language, literature, and some area studies courses

- The German Studies major (with language, area studies, and some literature), which allows the possibility of earning some credits through the National Work-Study Program in Germany, and permits about one-third of the credits available to be applied to combined studies with Art History, Judaic Studies, Philosophy, Music History, or Political Science

- The Certificate in Business Administration combined with major study in German (a four-year program), or a five-year Co-op program leading to a B.A. in German, a Certificate in General or International Business, and a Certificate of Professional Development (these are also available in English, French, and Spanish)—both the four-year and five-year programs being filled out, of course, with a carefully selected schedule of business courses. For nonmajors, Certificates in Basic Business German and in Competence in Business German and German Area Studies are available for shorter sequences of study

- A combined program with the College of Education by which the student earns a major in German and the Ohio Teaching Certificate

The Cincinnati Department of Germanic Languages and Literatures also provides opportunities for advanced level German students to take the examination for the Goethe Institute Certificate in German as a Foreign Language *(Zertifikat Deutsch als Fremdsprache)*, which is accepted by most universities in Germany as a language proficiency entrance examination. Finally, students from outside the department can earn a Certificate in German-American Studies for which they study the German-American Experience and electives from Anthropology, Architecture, Art History, Geography, German, History, Judaic Studies, Music History, and Philosophy, along with a special project of independent study.[8]

Observations

These detailed descriptions of two extensive programs in one language show what can be done. Clearly, well-developed programs like these have many aspects that would transfer to other languages. Nevertheless, one would expect different languages to think out variations appropriate for the special situations and contributions associated with that language. Spanish departments, for instance, have tended to expand in the direction of Latin American Studies, often with a minor in Portuguese, Chicano Studies, and Spanish for Business. At the University of Southern California, students from the School of Journalism have been able to do a double major with Spanish, which not only prepares them for fluent use of the language, but also gives them a broad background in

Hispanic literature and culture. The Department of French at the University of Illinois at Urbana–Champaign has a French Studies major that includes language, literature, civilization, film, and a cognate area. It also has a special joint B.A. major in the Teaching of French with the College of Education, and a joint major in Commercial French Studies with the Department of Business Administration, which combines French with professional studies in business administration, accounting, economics, and finance and leads to the *Certificat pratique du français commercial et économique* of the Chamber of Commerce of Paris (see also chapter 6). Carnegie Mellon University is in the process of developing a Modern Languages major that will be based partly on content-based language instruction and will establish links between the Modern Languages Department and History, English and Literary and Cultural Studies, Psychology, Cognitive Studies, and Computational Linguistics. The trend in the departments is clearly toward providing majors with opportunities to explore widely in areas of particular interest and value to them while developing a solid foundation in language, literature, and culture.

No matter what the particular thrust of the specialized track of the major, there should be a core course required for all students in basic principles of linguistics, particularly as applied to this language, some required courses in nineteenth and twentieth century literature, and a core course in the understanding of other cultures. Literature students are dealing with works that derive their importance and meaningfulness within the culture from the way the author has created them in the language; basic linguistic concepts will help them read these works with deeper appreciation of this craft. Linguistics students need to see language not only in abstractions, but in one of the highest forms of use, and need to learn to enjoy and appreciate the culture through its artifacts. Students of culture and intercultural relationships need to understand how language works in order to appreciate the close intertwining of language and culture and to recognize the cultural ethos that is so vividly manifested in the literature its culture-bearers produce, read, and enjoy. Students in practical fields of business, engineering, law, and so on, need the humanistic experience that closer contact with language science, literature, and culture studies can bring them and thus be prepared not only to use the language more precisely and effectively within the culture and read for pleasure and profit the best the culture has to offer, but also to interact effectively with the culture-bearers. Future teachers of the language need a well-rounded experience in the language they will be teaching. Basic courses in these disciplines tie together the various segments of a multitrack concentration that unites the department in a common endeavor, while accepting and welcoming diversity.

The Language Component in the Major

Nor should the language component of the major, minor, or concentration remain unmentioned. Students soon sense whether some element of the program is considered central or peripheral. One way of ensuring that students consider the aural-oral language component important enough to make a serious effort to keep raising their level of proficiency is to require the passing of an Oral Proficiency Interview (OPI) at the Superior or Advanced Plus level on the ACTFL/ETS scale (see Appendix A), or some similar alternative, before graduation.[9] The decision on level will depend on the language being presented. Preferably, the students should be able to choose for themselves just when they feel ready to pass this oral test, which would be offered on several occasions during the year. Some students may need to take the test more than once, assessing their level of proficiency, then working at improving their communication skills to bring them up to the standard required by the department; for this reason, students should be encouraged to take the test for the first time in their junior year.

Serious consideration should be given to requiring (or strongly recommending, depending on the institution and availability of supplementary funding to cover expenses) that all majors spend a certain period in a target-language country in a meticulously designed and supervised program of language improvement. This may be for a year, a semester, or a summer. Students should be given preparation in the home institution that will ensure their deriving the maximum benefit from their stay, which should, if possible, be with a carefully selected family or in residence with native speakers, not other foreign students. Students should be expected to carry through a well-structured research or study project that requires them to use the language with target-language speakers. This project should be sufficiently demanding to warrant credit toward the major (see also chapter 11).

Methodology

Some may wonder why ways of teaching the language have not been discussed in chapters 1 and 2. Decisions on methodology of language teaching or techniques (the *how*) can only be considered after we have identified the *who* (who our students are and what their particular needs and interests may be— for what reasons they are studying the language), and the *what* (what kind of curriculum and content will meet these needs and further stimulate their interest). Once curriculum and content are established, we can look more sensibly and perceptively at *how* we will go about helping students learn this content. Decisions on how to teach the language will respect teacher and student personality, maturity of students, nature of the subject matter, and preferred learning styles. (This is a separate issue that is taken up in chapter 19.) Approaches to the actual teaching should never be doctrinaire but flexible and innovatory, so that students and teachers together experiment with more and more effective ways of learning specific content for clearly defined purposes; in this way the dynamism of a constantly revised and adapted program is maintained.

NOTES

1. Reported in Newsletter 5 (spring 1990) of The Center for Language Studies, Brown University, Rhode Island.

2. Information on the Earlham College, University of Minnesota, and St. Olaf College initiatives has been drawn from Kramsch (1991), which contains a detailed analysis of the content-based instruction (CBI) and "language across the curriculum" approaches to developing usable language competence while illuminating culturally based aspects of the content. For Earlham College, see also Jurasek (1988).

3. J. Frommer developed a course of this type at the request of students in her Oral Survival course at Harvard.

4. Laurence Wylie, Professor Emeritus of Romance Languages and Psychology, Harvard University, taught this course, which he called "Communicating with the French," in Harvard College and Harvard Extension. A video of the class in progress may be viewed in the Modern Language Center at Harvard.

5. Quoted by Duff (1981), p. 1.

6. R. Comeau, Assistant Dean of Harvard Extension, personal communication.

7. The University of Rhode Island also integrates the study of German and an internship with an engineering company in Germany into the undergraduate engineering curriculum.

8. Professor R. Schade of the Department of Germanic Languages and Literatures at the University of Cincinnati reports that they have now "largely licked the 2nd to 3rd year attrition rate . . . Aggressive 'marketing' and good teaching combine to make for an experience sufficiently meaningful to entice students beyond the 2-year language requirement" (personal communication, Oct. 22, 1990).

9. Details of the ACTFL Proficiency Guidelines may be found in Rivers 1983 Appendix (Provisional Generic); in Rivers et al. 1988-9 (Provisional Language-specific); and in H. Byrnes and M. Canale, eds. (1987), pp. 15–24 (Generic 1986).

REFERENCES

Byrnes, Heidi, and Michael Canale, eds. 1987. *Defining and Developing Proficiency: Guidelines, Implementations, and Concepts.* The ACTFL Foreign Language Education Series, vol. 17. Lincolnwood, IL: National Textbook Company.

Crook, Jere L. 1985. "Teaching Communication with the French." *French Review* 58: 786–92.

Di Pietro, Robert J. 1987. *Strategic Interaction: Learning Languages through Scenarios.* Cambridge, Eng., and New York: Cambridge Univ. Press.

Duff, Alan. 1981. *The Third Language: Recurrent Problems of Translation into English.* Oxford, Eng.: Pergamon.

Jurasek, Richard. 1988. "Integrating Foreign Languages into the College Curriculum." *Modern Language Journal* 72: 52–58.

Kramsch, Claire J. 1981. *Discourse Analysis and Second Language Teaching.* Language in Education No. 37. Washington, DC: Center for Applied Linguistics.

————. 1987. "Interactive Discourse in Small and Large Groups," pp. 17–30 in Wilga M. Rivers, ed., *Interactive Language Teaching.* Cambridge, Eng., and New York: Cambridge Univ. Press.

————. 1991. "Foreign Languages and International Education in the United States," in C. Gnutzmann, F. Konigs, and W. Pfeiffer, eds. *Fremdsprachenunterricht im Internationalen Vergleich: Perspektive 2000.* Tubingen, Ger.: Gunter Narr.

Lohnes, Walter F. 1976. "German Studies: The Stanford Model. The Evolution of a Program," pp. 78–87 in W. F. Lohnes and V. Nellendorfs, eds., *German Studies in the United States: Assessment and Outlook.* Madison: Univ. of Wisconsin Press.

Rheingold, Howard. 1988. *They Have a Word for It: A Lighthearted Lexicon of Untranslatable Words and Phrases.* Los Angeles: J. P. Tarcher; New York: St. Martin's.

Rivers, Wilga M. 1983. *Speaking in Many Tongues: Essays in Foreign-Language Teaching.* 3d ed. Cambridge, Eng., and New York: Cambridge Univ. Press.

————, et al. 1988–89. *Teaching French/German/Spanish/Hebrew: A Practical Guide.* Lincolnwood, IL: National Textbook Company; Tel Aviv, Israel: University Publishing Projects.

Via, Richard. 1987. "The Magic 'If' of Theater: Enhancing Language Learning through Drama," pp. 110–23 in Wilga M. Rivers, ed., *Interactive Language Teaching.* Cambridge, Eng., and New York: Cambridge Univ. Press.

Wylie, Laurence. 1965. "Language Learning and Communication." *French Review* 58: 777–85.

3
The Foreign-Language Requirement

Barbara F. Freed
Carnegie Mellon University

THE ROLE OF THE FOREIGN-LANGUAGE REQUIREMENT, NOT UNLIKE MANY general education requirements within the undergraduate curriculum, has been debated over several centuries of American education. Originally viewed as the means of introducing students to classical studies, primarily through instruction in Greek and Latin, the language requirement was broadened in many institutions toward the turn of the century to include modern languages. Throughout the twentieth century, the foreign-language requirement has reflected, in a cyclical pattern, our alternating national concern and indifference to the teaching and learning of foreign languages. While there are many philosophical issues related to the decision whether language study should be required, how much should be required, and of whom, the purpose of this chapter will not be to debate such fundamental issues, nor even to defend the existence of a language requirement within a liberal education,[1] but rather to describe traditional and innovative models of foreign-language requirements and to discuss some of the practical issues related to implementing and maintaining such requirements.

RECENT STATISTICS

After several decades of decline, language enrollments are increasing. This phenomenon is due to a renewed national interest and awareness of the importance of language and cultural study and to growing efforts to internationalize the curriculum and the campus. This resurgence of interest in language study is reflected in the growing number of institutions that are implementing, reinstituting, or strengthening the foreign-language requirement. Following the peak reached in 1965–66, when close to 90 percent of the institutions that responded to a national Modern Language Association (MLA) survey reported foreign-language requirements for the B.A. degree, foreign-language requirements plummeted to a low of 47 percent in 1982 (Brod and Lapointe 1989). The most recent survey of postsecondary institutions has indicated an encouraging reverse in this trend: 58 percent of B.A.-granting institutions now report a foreign-language requirement for the B.A. degree, while almost 26 percent of the responding institutions have a foreign-language entrance requirement (Brod and Lapointe 1989). This trend is evident not only in B.A.-granting institutions, but in two-year and community colleges as well. As will be discussed below, the nature of these requirements varies considerably from institution to institution and sometimes even within the same institution.

TYPES OF REQUIREMENTS

Traditionally foreign-language requirements have been of two types: admission and degree requirements. Admission requirements stipulate that students must have completed a specific amount of language study prior to college entrance. For example, institutions might require two high school units of a foreign language; or three high school units of one foreign language or two units in each of two foreign languages. Other institutions might require a specific number of high school units as well as a satisfactory score on a standardized achievement test (Brod and Lapointe 1989).

Degree requirements, by contrast, prescribe the amount of language study that must be completed before or during the college career in order to receive the undergraduate degree, usually but not always the Bachelor of Arts degree. Degree requirements sometimes state that a student must complete a specific number of additional semester hours of a language studied in high school or a higher number of semester hours for a new foreign language. Alternatively, some institutions require a specific score on either a nationally recognized or a departmental examination (Brod and Lapointe 1989).

Traditionally, both admissions and degree requirements have been limited to colleges of arts and sciences or their equivalent. With growing frequency, however, we find other schools within a university that now require foreign-language study: for example, foreign-language degree requirements in schools of nursing, engineering, fine arts, and business. The specific number of courses or credit units that are required to satisfy the language requirement varies considerably from institution to institution, and even from school to school within an institution where more than one school requires foreign-language study. For example, at the University of Pennsylvania, the College of Arts and Sciences has one type of requirement, while the School of Nursing has a more traditional and less stringent requirement, and the School of Engineering has a humanities requirement that includes language study as one option. It is also not uncommon to find institutions that have both admission and degree requirements. In some of these institutions students who do not satisfy the admission requirement are expected to take a requisite number of language courses for which no credit is given.

DEFINING LANGUAGE REQUIREMENTS

Of the many issues related to language requirements one is the decision of how they should be defined. That is, what should students be expected to do to satisfy the language requirement? How much language study should be required? Which languages should be acceptable as part of the language requirement?

As is obvious from the preceding examples, traditional foreign-language requirements have tended to be described, if not actually defined, in terms of semesters or years of study, credit units, or test scores, on the assumption that time or test scores measure language learning and language use. Requirements based on number of semesters or credit units completed have sometimes been called "seat-time requirements," implying that they are satisfied by completing an appropriate number of courses or amount of time in foreign-language courses. These foreign-language requirements stipulate that students must complete a predetermined number of courses, usually at the elementary or intermediate level of language study, and occasionally they specify a minimum acceptable grade for the course. Sometimes, however, more advanced levels of literary study are required. Examples from the 1989 MLA Survey suggest that two to four semesters of language study are the most common current requirements. On occasion these requirements are described in school catalogs as "competence" requirements, but close inspection of the criteria for satisfying them frequently reveals that they too may, in fact, be satisfied by taking a required number of courses or by achieving the appropriate score on a traditional test (Freed 1981). For example, scores ranging between 550 to 650 on the College Entrance Examination Language Achievement Test (CEEB) or an Advanced Placement (AP) test score of 3 or 4 are frequently accepted as criteria for satisfying an undergraduate foreign-language requirement. The advantage of the test option is that it requires prior student achievement, encourages language study beyond the requirement level, and permits students to acquire their knowledge in other ways (such as residence in the country) if they prefer. It meets the needs also of students with some knowledge of the language who prefer to work on their own to regain a former level of competence or improve on a semibilingual competence.

With respect to languages that may be used to satisfy the language requirement, it is current practice to accept both modern and ancient languages. Therefore, within the same school students may satisfy the language requirement by studying French, Spanish, German, or Russian or languages such as Latin, classical Greek, or Sanskrit. While the majority of students still tend to enroll in the more commonly taught languages, enrollments in the less commonly taught languages are growing at a tremendous rate, with Japanese being the fastest-growing language in the country. In addition to living and ancient languages, there are also a small number of institutions that are willing to accept nontraditional languages as acceptable courses for the language requirement. These include courses in American Sign Language, computer languages, and artificial intelligence. While these innovations may be acceptable in some specialized programs, they tend not to provide the broad-based cultural component that most programs now wish to emphasize.

We are also beginning to witness a new type of language requirement, one that is used either as an admission or graduation requirement. This new requirement, frequently a redefinition or strengthening of an existing requirement, is described and measured in terms of students' actual performance in the language, as determined by out-of-course testing. Sometimes these requirements are called "proficiency requirements" and are satisfied by requiring students to demonstrate a specific level of "communicative language proficiency" in one or several skills.

Despite their labor-intensive nature, proficiency-based requirements overcome the inconsistencies of course grades and the inherent limitations of the multiple-choice discrete-point achievement tests that represent the basis of measurement in many traditional requirements. Proficiency requirements stress what students are able to do with the language as opposed to what they know about the language. Institutions that have adopted proficiency requirements have taken the position that a specific number of classroom hours spent in language study or specific scores on traditional achievement tests are not indicative of students' abilities to use the language in any purposeful way. It is their contention that a meaningful requirement is one that expects students to demonstrate their ability to utilize the language in a variety of contexts and for a variety of purposes that span the oral–literate continuum.

It is important to point out, however, that departmental or institutionally defined criteria for satisfying a language requirement do not necessarily reflect or reveal the teaching philosophies that underlie them. Official statements regarding the language requirement also fail to describe the number and, most significantly, the type of contact hours students have with a language, nor do they describe the general orientation of language departments. That is to say, four semesters of language study in one institution may be the equivalent of two or even six semesters of study elsewhere. The same may obviously be true for grades. While it may also be assumed that those institutions that have recently adopted proficiency-oriented requirements have also implemented communicatively oriented curricula, teaching, and testing approaches, some departments within institutions that have maintained more traditionally described requirements may also have adopted similar, more current, and interactive teaching approaches and may already test for proficiency in language use within the course structure (Rivers 1990).

Within the context of new types of language requirements, there are also innovative programs. As our understanding of second-language acquisition grows, concurrent with a desire to integrate into the undergraduate curriculum an appreciation and awareness of linguistic and cultural diversity, increasing numbers of institutions are introducing "language across the curriculum" options and requirements. These requirements may stipulate that students take a content area course taught in a foreign language (as at the Monterey Institute for International Studies, Brown University, and Rice University) or that discipline-specific courses include references and readings in a foreign language (Jurasek 1988). Other new initiatives include efforts to develop a foreign-language studies program that is multidisciplinary and extends far beyond the notion of foreign-language learning as a basic skill and a service function of a department (Hugot 1990).

CASE STUDIES

Given the range of language requirements that may be found in various types of undergraduate programs, the following case studies are offered to illustrate the diverse ways in which language requirements have been developed and defined. The first two sets of case studies describe existing language requirements at selected institutions. The third set of case studies, content-based requirements, deal more with innovative language "options" than with requirements per se. They are offered both because they reflect a growing national concern for integrating language study into the general curriculum rather than isolating language as a "skill and content-getting" tool, and because it is anticipated that options such as these, which are beginning to make a national impact, will eventually evolve into a new type of foreign-language requirement.

Requirements Based on Course Credit, Time, and Test Scores

Harvard University   The foreign-language requirement at Harvard University requires that incoming students achieve a score of 560 on the Harvard Placement Examination (HPE) or on the CEEB; failing this, they are required to study a language for one year (two semesters) at the level (elementary or intermediate) at which they placed on the HPE, or they may begin a new language. Thus students who have previously studied a language, participated in study abroad programs, or worked on their own need not enroll in classes as long as they achieve the requisite score. Students who have not had contact with the language for several years sometimes pass the HPE at the 560 level after one semester of refreshing their knowledge at the intermediate level. The test option, therefore, allows for much flexibility and student choice.[2]

Ohio State University   The foreign-language requirement at Ohio State University varies from college to college. Within the College of Arts and Sciences, four ten-week quarters are required to satisfy the requirement. Exemptions from the requirement are determined by departmentally prepared language examinations.

University of Michigan   The College of Literature, Science and Arts at the University of Michigan has recently changed the nature of its language requirement. Prior to the fall of 1988, students could satisfy the requirement if they had completed four years of high school language instruction. The new requirement stipulates two required years of language study in college for all students except those who are exempted from the requirement on the basis of oral and written departmental examinations or a documented learning disability.

Proficiency Requirements

University of Pennsylvania   In the fall of 1981, the French section of the Department of Romance Languages in the School of Arts and Sciences at the University of Pennsylvania initiated a foreign-language proficiency requirement to replace its long-standing four-semester time/credit requirement.

Within the course of the next eight years, French was joined by Spanish, Italian, German, Russian, Arabic, and Hebrew. Several other languages adopted a proficiency orientation (Hindi, Chinese, Japanese), although these languages did not formally redefine the criteria for satisfying the language requirement.

The foreign-language proficiency requirement is satisfied when a student has passed a multiskill (listening, speaking, reading, and writing) proficiency test. This test uses the ILR-ACTFL Oral Proficiency Interview (OPI) to measure oral interaction and departmentally developed tests of functional proficiency to measure listening, reading, and writing. The minimal acceptable scores are determined by individual departments and vary from language to language. In the Department of Romance Languages the range of scores is from Intermediate–Mid (on the ACTFL Guidelines; see Appendix A) in speaking, to Advanced in reading and listening. (For a more complete description of this requirement and the variations in departmental requirements on the proficiency test, see Freed 1981, 1984, and 1987a). The proficiency test is usually taken after a student has spent four semesters or the equivalent studying a foreign language. In many instances, however, students take and pass this test at the completion of three semesters of study. On occasion, students are unable to pass the proficiency test at the end of four semesters. Such students continue with language study until they are able to pass the test successfully. Exemption from the language requirement upon admission to the university is based on a relatively high CEEB score (650) or a combination of a high CEEB score (600) and an OPI score of Intermediate–Mid.

University of Minnesota   The University of Minnesota has taken another approach to a proficiency requirement. In 1986, the university approved a new requirement, which is based on proficiency test scores and replaces a prior requirement of five foreign-language courses (or three foreign-language and three English courses). The objective of this new requirement is to help students acquire an acceptable level of functionally useful skills in a foreign language. The requirement is unique in that it, in essence, combines an entrance and a graduation requirement. By "encouraging students to complete a significant amount of language study before arriving at the university" ("Second Language" 1990: 2) it ensures that many students will have completed the equivalent of three years of language study in high school. The requirement uses the ACTFL Guidelines as an organizing principle and establishes a certain level of skills for entrance (Intermediate–Low in reading and listening and Novice–High in writing and speaking) and a higher level of skills for the graduation requirement (Intermediate–High in reading and listening; Intermediate–Mid in writing and speaking ("Second Language"

1990: 22). (For a more detailed description of this requirement see Lange et al.
1986; Lange 1987.)

Content-Based Language Requirements

Monterey Institute of International Studies   While not for an undergraduate program, the language requirement for the Master's degree at the Monterey
Institute of International Studies is described because of its very innovative
design. The degree requirement can be satisfied only by completing a twelve-
unit language "component" from which there are no exemptions and which is
related to the student's professional degree. Once students achieve the equivalent of a junior-level ("fifth semester") language proficiency, they are required
to participate in a series of content-based (discipline-specific) courses that are
taught totally or in part in a foreign language. For example, Western European
Politics is taught in French, Spanish, and German; Ecological Politics in the
Soviet Union is taught in Russian; Chinese Management is taught in Mandarin;
and Politics and Government in the Near East is taught half in English and half
in Arabic.

Earlham College   In an effort to enhance the role of foreign languages in
the undergraduate curriculum, Earlham College has recently instituted a
language-across-the-curriculum program. By virtue of this program, more
than 80 percent of Earlham students—who are enrolled in eighty-six courses
in philosophy, history, anthropology, economics, and literature—are exposed
to various uses of a foreign language. Depending on the language skills of the
course instructors, the exposure may involve the use of course-relevant terminology in which a translation is insufficient, the introduction of key concepts in
the foreign language, reading selected portions or even a complete text in the
foreign language, and participating in related discussions of the materials.
(Jurasek 1988: 54–55).

Brown University   A more recent exploration of the language-across-the-
curriculum option is currently being explored at Brown University. The goal
of this program is to encourage the use of foreign languages in the social sciences by integrating the study of four languages with work in five content
areas: International Relations—French; Political Science—Spanish; History
and Afro-American Studies—Portuguese; Soviet Studies—Russian. In these
courses, carefully designed reading and writing assignments in the various
target languages are integrated into the content-area courses for the purpose of
introducing students to the vocabulary of the discipline as well as to the
academic discourse of that discipline. In addition to the discipline-specific

courses mentioned above, related language courses will be developed to concentrate on "discourse strategies used in the fields of international relations and political science" in the various target languages.[3]

Observations

It should be noted that, in addition to the programs at Earlham and Brown, similar initiatives have been undertaken at the University of Rhode Island, the Colorado School of Mines, the University of Minnesota, and St. Olaf's College. Carnegie Mellon University is in the process of developing a Modern Languages major that will be based in part on content-based language instruction.

The preceding case studies reflect a variety of traditional and innovative approaches to the role of required (or sometimes "strongly encouraged") foreign-language study. In all cases the examples presented constitute individual institutions' responses to the need for introducing American undergraduates to the study of foreign languages and foreign cultures as an accepted and integral part of the undergraduate curriculum.

IMPLEMENTATION OF LANGUAGE REQUIREMENTS

The practical implications of implementing, redefining, or strengthening a language requirement are many. The obvious first step is to define the nature of the requirement: the goals of the requirement, the type of requirement, the students to whom it applies, and the criteria for measuring satisfaction of the requirement. (For a discussion of various types of tests and the issues related to testing for both placement and proficiency, see chapter 10.)

In establishing realistic expectations and guidelines for the requirement, it is important to consider the backgrounds of the students, the size of the faculty, and the presence of graduate teaching assistants. It is equally important to consider the overall philosophy of the department with respect to the role of language studies within the general context of the department's educational mission. Involving students in discussions about their needs and expectations for language learning has also proven to be a useful part of the process of establishing a meaningful requirement.

The next step is to obtain institutional commitment to instituting and maintaining the requirement. Institutional commitment must be expressed in terms of philosophical agreement with the nature of the requirement, administrative endorsement, and financial support. Obtaining the necessary institutional commitments will guarantee support for the inevitable increases in student enrollment, probable increases in expenditures for new materials, technologies, testing materials, and workshops in professional development that may be considered necessary for both standing faculty, adjunct lecturers, and graduate teaching assistants.

Finally, both individual language departments and the appropriate university officials must acknowledge the need for and provide funds for language program coordinators or directors, whose roles and responsibilities within a language department must be clearly defined, with attention given to their status. Moreover, an appropriate reward structure for their work must be established. It has recently and repeatedly been recognized that the expertise of language program coordinators or directors is indispensable to the smooth functioning of a well-designed program (Barnes et al. 1990).

Once the necessary assurances have been acquired, it is wise to pilot-test various aspects of the new or revised requirement. This may include working with only one language or with small groups of students or faculty in several language departments, pretesting evaluation instruments, and providing the appropriate "grandfather clauses" for exempt students. This phase provides the opportunity to identify and deal with weaknesses and unforeseen limitations within the proposed requirement. Once a trial phase has been completed, it is crucial to disseminate as much information as possible about the nature of the requirement and how and when it may be satisfied. In planning for the requirement, it is necessary to review the course sequence leading to the language requirement to be certain that the courses are carefully articulated, with an appropriate recycling of material from one level to the next. Optimally, the recycling provides necessary review and reuse of material but avoids the unnecessary duplication that has proved to be so inefficient in typical standard four-semester requirement sequences. This is also an opportune time to think about bridging the gap between language requirement courses and advanced language sequences, courses that are introductions to literary studies, and content-based language courses. It is also advisable to pretest current students in an effort to establish realistic standards and valid measurement devices and then to phase the requirement in gradually. A frequently forgotten item in program building is appropriate evaluation devices. Little is currently known beyond our negative impressions that many students do not continue beyond the language requirement sequence. As part of the planning phase for instituting or improving a language requirement it is appropriate to initiate a study of student enrollment patterns beyond the language requirement as a point of comparison with a follow-up study of the same patterns after the institution of the new requirement.

In redefining a language requirement it is also useful to think in terms of building appropriate motivation and incentives into the program so that the coerced are convinced of the value and pleasures of language study. This has been accomplished in many programs by placing greater emphasis on communicative language proficiency and on helping students develop a full range of skills that they perceive as potentially useful on a continuum that spans oral and written expression. Such options include developing skills of oral interaction, reading of a literary or nonliterary nature, writing of texts other than standard "compositions," learning other subject matters through the language (history, politics, art, or music), and the development of cultural discourse and insight into other ways of thinking. Student motivation is also increased by developing interdisciplinary sequences of courses so that the values of language study are continually reinforced.

EXEMPTIONS FROM THE LANGUAGE REQUIREMENT

Inevitably there will be students who, for one reason or another, request exemptions from the language requirement. These requests fall into three general categories: previous study, bilingual or native competence, and learning disabilities. Institutions with long-term language requirements are accustomed to dealing with the first category, exemptions based on previous language study. Fewer, however, have well-developed policies for providing exemptions for bilingual students, native speakers, or students who have documented learning disabilities.

Previous Study

In discussions above we saw that many schools provide exemptions to students who achieve a specific score on an appropriate foreign-language test. These tests are usually nationally standardized or otherwise recognized tests (e.g., the MLA Cooperative Tests, the College Entrance Examination Board Language Achievement Test [CEEB], the Advanced Placement Examinations [AP], and the Oral Proficiency Interview [OPI]). Many institutions use their own departmentally developed tests in lieu of or in addition to nationally recognized tests.

Exemption policies vary from institution to institution. Students at the University of Pennsylvania, as we saw, may be exempted from the language requirement in the more commonly taught languages with a CEEB score of 650 or a CEEB score of 600 and an OPI score of Intermediate–Mid. At

Harvard University, students may be exempted from further required study with a score of 560 on the CEEB or on the Harvard Placement Examination. At the University of Minnesota, by contrast, exemptions are granted for proficiency test scores of Intermediate–High in reading and listening and Intermediate–Mid in writing and speaking. A number of other institutions that responded to the 1988 MLA survey indicated language requirement exemptions for students that score between 550 and 650 on the CEEB.

Native Competence

With the growing emphasis on student diversity, minority enrollments, and internationalizing the university, we are finding on our campuses an increasing number of students whose mother tongue is not English. Many institutions are thus faced with the dilemma of whether students should be exempted from a language requirement on the basis of their competence in English, which is their second (and sometimes third) language, or on their language skills in their first language, which is a foreign language in an American institution. Some institutions, the University of Pennsylvania for example, have developed a policy that permits bilingual students who have received their secondary school education in a language other than English and who, therefore, have both an oral and literate command of the language, to be exempted from further required language study. In the event that students have lived abroad and acquired proficiency (although not bilingual competence), they are expected to pass a specially prepared multiskill proficiency test. Such exemptions do not carry with them course credit, either for courses in English as a Second Language or for courses in the student's first language. Emphasis in fact is placed on the expectation that students demonstrate competence in English by being successfully enrolled in an undergraduate study through the medium of English. Some institutions, Harvard for instance, provide special courses or sections to enable bilingual students who have not been educated in the language to satisfy the requirement while perfecting their skills in a standard form of the language.

Learning Disabilities

Students with learning disabilities present a unique set of problems in the foreign-language classroom, as well as in other courses. Federal legislation and growing sensitivity to the needs of learning-disabled students have encouraged institutions to develop appropriate accommodations for these students. Institutions such as the University of Pennsylvania, Harvard, Dartmouth, and the

University of Wisconsin have defined specific policies and procedures for exempting students from the standard language requirement (Freed 1987b; Dinklage 1985; Heilenman 1985; Chancellor's Committee 1983).

Most often these policies require that students who have not been admitted to the institution with documented learning disabilities enroll in a regular language course in the hope that they will be able to complete it successfully. In the event that these students experience extreme difficulty in their language courses, they are then referred to a trained specialist or university administrator for an interview; and they are frequently asked to complete a battery of special tests. Students who receive an exemption from the standard language requirement are usually expected to satisfy an alternate course of study. This alternate requirement may combine courses in linguistics, language and culture, and literature in translation. (For a description of the University of Pennsylvania alternate requirement, see Freed 1987b).

Two institutions have experimented with developing special foreign-language courses for learning disabled students. Unfortunately these courses have been offered as a result of special funding and have tended not to be continued over more than a few semesters. Physical disability has not proved to be a handicap: students with hearing deficits lip-read specially administered tests and blind students work with special materials, recorded or in braille (Pica 1989; Dinklage 1985).

Beyond the Language Requirement

Despite the prevailing belief that many of the students who are obliged to satisfy an undergraduate language requirement never enroll in higher-level courses, there are few documented studies that indicate what percentage of students do go on to more advanced study. It is commonly believed that less than 50 percent go beyond the second year of study (Steele 1989: 160). Institutions should conduct their own surveys in this area, since large-scale surveys mask differences due to local contextual factors. Nonetheless, it is well known that American institutions, on the whole, do not prepare large numbers of students for advanced-level use of foreign languages (Lambert 1985).

With the growing interest in language instruction and the emphasis on preparing students to use the language in functionally useful ways, we are finding increasing motivation among students. The obligation remains, however, to create language programs that are sufficiently motivating to encourage students to continue beyond the requirement level. This is first a question of departmental attitudes toward language study. The dimensions of the problem, however, are larger than language departments themselves. Within our university community we must strive to create an environment and culture that values multilingual and multicultural competence. Only in this way will the coerced become the convinced and will our students continue their study of a language until some advanced level of proficiency is assured and can be maintained.

Notes

1. A publication by the Consortium for Language Teaching and Learning (*Language Learning and Liberal Education,* 1989, P. Patrikis, ed.) devotes several chapters to defining the role of language within a liberal education.

2. It should be noted that the one-year course at Harvard meets five days a week.

3. Wording is from Brown University Title VI Proposal, Abstract and p. 1

References

Barnes, B. K., C. Klee, and R. Wakefield. 1990. "A Funny Thing Happened on the Way to the Language Requirement." *ADFL Bulletin.* 22,1: 35–39.

Brod, Richard I., and Lapointe, Monique. 1989. "The MLA Survey of Foreign Language Entrance and Degree Requirements." *ADFL Bulletin* 20,2: 17–41.

Chancellor's Committee for Persons with Disabilities. 1983. Report on Undergraduate Foreign Language Requirement. Unpublished report, University of Wisconsin, Madison.

Dinklage, K. T. 1985. "Regarding College Students' Inability to Learn a Foreign Language." Paper presented at the University of Pennsylvania Colloquium on Learning Disabilities and Foreign Language Learning, Philadelphia.

Freed, Barbara F. 1981. "Establishing Proficiency-Based Language Requirements." *ADFL Bulletin* 13,2: 6–12.

_____. 1984. "Proficiency in Context: The Pennsylvania Experience," pp. 211–40 in S. Savignon, and M. Berns, eds., *Initiatives in Communicative Language Teaching: A Book of Readings,* vol. 1. Reading, MA: Addison-Wesley.

_____. 1987a. "Issues in Establishing and Maintaining a Language Proficiency Requirement," pp. 263–73 in A. Valdman, ed., *Proceedings of the Indiana University Invitational Symposium on the Evaluation of Foreign Language Proficiency.* Bloomington, IN: Indiana University.

_____. 1987b. "Exemptions from the Foreign Language Requirement: A Review of Recent Literature, Problems and Policy." *ADFL Bulletin* 18,2: 13–17.

Heilenman, Laura K. 1985. "Exemptions from the Foreign Language Requirement: Notes from the Field." Paper presented at the annual meeting of the MLA, Chicago.

Hugot, François. 1990. "Foreign Languages across the Curriculum." Paper presented at the Brown University FIPSE lecture, Providence, RI.

Jurasek, R. 1988. "Integrating Foreign Languages into the College Curriculum." *Modern Language Journal* 72: 52–58.

Lambert, Richard D. 1985. "Foreign Language Instruction: A National Agenda." *ADFL Bulletin* 16,3: 1–4.

Lange, Dale L. 1987. "Developing and Implementing Proficiency-Oriented Tests for a New Language Requirement at the University of Minnesota: Issues for Implementing the ACTFL-ETS-ILR Proficiency Guidelines," pp. 275–90 in A. Valdman, ed., *Proceedings of the Indiana University Invitational Symposium on the Evaluation of Foreign Language Proficiency.* Bloomington, IN: Indiana University.

————, Jermaine Arendt, and R. Wakefield. 1986. "Strengthening the Language Requirement at the University of Minnesota: An Initial Report." *Foreign Language Annals.* 19,2: 149–56.

Patrikis, P. C., ed. 1989. *Language Learning and Liberal Education.* Proceedings of the University of Chicago and Consortium for Language Teaching and Learning Conference on Language Learning and Liberal Education. New Haven, CT: CLTL.

Pica, T. 1989. "Report on Special Spanish Course for Learning Disabled Students." Unpublished report presented to the Consortium for Language Teaching and Learning, Yale University.

Rivers, Wilga M. 1990. Personal telephone communication.

"Second Language Requirements." 1990. *MLA Newsletter* 22: 2–22.

Steele, R. 1989. "Teaching Language and Culture: Old Problems, New Approaches," pp. 153–62 in J. Alatis, ed., *Language Teaching, Testing and Technology: Lessons from the Past with a View toward the Future.* Georgetown University Round Table on Languages and Linguistics. Washington, DC: Georgetown Univ. Press.

4

A Step toward Cultural Literacy: Language through Literature

Marlies Mueller
Brigitte Goutal
Christine Hérot
Harvard University

Ilona Chessid
Hunter College

THE PAST QUARTER CENTURY HAS SEEN SUBSTANTIAL PROGRESS IN language teaching. Modern, communicative approaches have revitalized our classes and brought enthusiastic students back to our courses, even in colleges and universities that had dropped the foreign-language requirement. Student-centered methodologies have stemmed from the realization that one must speak a foreign language in order to master it. The joy of meaningful communication in the target language can be experienced almost from the beginning of language studies. The results of these communicative techniques have been impressive. Our students' control of grammar and vocabulary proves to be acceptable, and in many cases their accents receive compliments from native speakers. They travel abroad, ask directions, reserve hotel rooms, shop, and accomplish myriad day-to-day tasks with surprising confidence, having been thoroughly prepared in our classrooms.

Unhappily, in many institutions, the focus of language learning has been shifted from literary works to purely informational texts of contemporary relevance. Although these have their place, students have paid a certain price for their linguistic competence. Too often, achieving "literacy" in another culture (which for earlier generations was the essence of foreign-language learning) has been exchanged for a relatively rapid command of the everyday spoken language.

In programs where literature remains a part of the language class, teaching often clings to the traditional lecture format: an accumulation of titles, dates, and authors' names, followed by translation exercises and discussions in English. From time to time, with an apologetic bow toward the language component of the course, grammatical exercises are grafted onto the minilectures. These drills and exercises have only the most tenuous connections to the texts being studied. This artificial separation between the introduction of literary works and communication-oriented methodology is quite unnecessary (see Kramsch 1985; Muyskens 1983; Kaufman 1987). In fact, there are a number of important advantages to the use of fictional, dramatic, and poetic masterpieces in the language classroom.

Interactive language teaching is highly rewarding for the student, yet emotionally demanding. Some of this pressure can be deflected by funneling language lessons through a fictional work. The same emotional risks are involved as students attempt to express their ideas in a new idiom, but the students are distracted from their anxiety about correct use of grammatical forms by the interesting nature of the material and the kinds of tasks in which they are involved. In addition, the practice of combining culturally rich literature with language study is supported by research on reading comprehension. These findings suggest that there are advantages to providing students with substantive cultural information, from the early stages of language learning, to enable them to comprehend what they read.[1] (See also chapter 5.) This same cultural information will serve students well as they practice their oral skills in culturally authentic settings.

It has become clear that the overt meanings of any written or spoken communication are merely "the tip of the iceberg of meaning; the larger part lies below the surface and is composed of the reader's own relevant background knowledge" (Hirsch 1987: 34). Every authentic text, however simple, implies information that it takes for granted and does not explain, but which students must, nevertheless, integrate into a mental structure built from prior knowledge. These structures provide the full meaning of the text for the reader and are essential to understanding and remembering discourse. Models from both artificial intelligence research and psychology show that this process can work efficiently only if there is quick access to the appropriate structures. Expert performance in a new language depends on the rapid deployment of approximations to those mental structures that are second nature to native speakers.

Consequently, an article in *Le Monde* about contemporary French politics will be incomprehensible to American students unless they have certain facts at their fingertips. Without these facts about French political, intellectual, and social history, they will transpose the French politicians to the familiar

American scene and ascribe to them American motivations. This kind of transposition can lead to grave misunderstandings. It can be combatted by a language program that takes seriously both the linguistic competence and the cultural literacy of its students.

Reading, writing, listening, and speaking in a foreign language should not, therefore, be treated as mere "skills," independent of solid cultural knowledge. By cultural knowledge we do not mean the stereotypical and picturesquely touristic kind often found in textbooks, but the fundamental cultural knowledge that expresses the values, attitudes, and self-image of a people and constitutes an indispensable referent in any discussion of literature. This, combined with the cultural awareness necessary for successful social interaction (which is also amply demonstrated in literature), will truly enable our students to put their grammatical skills to use.

How, in the limited class time available to us, do we transmit cultural literacy, cultural awareness, grammar, and vocabulary in interactive ways so as to engage the imagination of our students, while guiding them to creative use of the target language? This article will discuss various means of refining use of structure and lexicon, while simultaneously reinforcing cultural literacy and cultural awareness. The methods described are all interactive and share one other essential trait: by anchoring all linguistic activities in the literary text and exploiting its cultural and creative richness, they teach language on many levels, each of which clarifies and strengthens the others.

The text, as a pivotal point from which one constantly departs and to which one continually returns, must therefore be chosen very carefully. In selecting a work of fiction for a second-semester elementary language course, we asked ourselves the following questions:

- Is the text part of the shared experience of the foreign culture we teach, in the sense that a speaker of that language must have read it to be called educated?

- Is the author an authentic interpreter or considered one of the builders of the culture of the language we are teaching?

- Is the text linguistically feasible for second-semester students at the elementary level?

- Will the language used by the author help students learn the everyday spoken language of the twentieth century?

- Will the text engage the students' imagination?

One text that meets these criteria for students of French is *Huis Clos (No Exit)* by Jean-Paul Sartre.[2] We shall discuss how it may be taught to students who have had twenty weeks of instruction in French at the elementary level.

The indications given can be easily transposed to an appropriate modern text in some other language.

The aims of our teaching are

1. To convey substance in the form of sophisticated historico-cultural information that will further the student's literacy in the language

2. To increase the students' cultural awareness, i.e., to aid their understanding of the contemporary social and cultural ambience of the speakers of that language

3. To help students "live" with the text by stepping out of themselves and communicating the complex emotions of the characters as they understand them, and ultimately to help them enter the text creatively

4. To integrate the above aims with interactive use of the grammatical structures and vocabulary of a first-year program

The following three sections show how such a text can be used to achieve these goals. We will begin by discussing how the students' cultural and literary sensitivity can be expanded while they continue to develop their language skills, particularly grammar and vocabulary. We will then present examples for teaching cultural awareness by extending the literary text, i.e., extrapolating from its content in order to explain similar situations in the "nonliterary" world of the target culture. Finally, we will suggest ways to "open up" and analyze the text, inviting students to improve their grammatical skills through textual analysis and encouraging them to increase their understanding of the characters through in-depth examination of the literary work.

CULTURAL LITERACY

An American student, lacking the cultural background of the average French reader, will be confused by the very first words of *Huis Clos*.[3] "Un salon style Second Empire. Un bronze sur la cheminée" (A drawing room in Second Empire style. A massive bronze ornament stands on the mantelpiece).[4] Here the student meets a cultural enigma before even entering Sartre's world. Unfortunately, all but the most enterprising students will respond to this "cognitive overload" (Hirsch 1987: 68) by skipping over the important first line. Thus they will not only lack a textual element crucial to a thorough appreciation of the play, but they will also miss an opportunity to advance toward cultural literacy. The very first words of *Huis Clos* offer the opportunity to introduce information that will (1) demystify the text, (2) provide students with the cultural vocabulary to hone their interpretive skills, and (3) add to the mental structures necessary for decoding French cultural information in the future.

How then does the teacher proceed with the play? We propose the introduction of key vocabulary items and cultural concepts before they are encountered in the text, so that students can approach it with confidence. Merely providing the traditional vocabulary sheet with the inclusion of "cultural" vocabulary is not enough. We suggest a technique called "cultural priming," whereby the student discovers and decodes cultural messages with the teacher's guidance. For example, returning to the first line in *Huis Clos* and the "salon Second Empire," the teacher must begin by exploring the meaning the word "salon" holds for an educated French person.

In a literary/historical context it will evoke a number of different associations, such as the artistic salons of the nineteenth century, the salons of the eighteenth-century *philosophes,* and the seventeenth-century salon culture (when artistic, philosophical, or literary lights congregated to discuss ideas). Without summarizing three centuries of French intellectual history to explain the cultural content of one word, the instructor can nevertheless highlight the role of the salon in French literary history.

Given that literary texts, even at this level, should be taught exclusively in the target language, visual aids can be used to familiarize students with the term "salon." Slides, prints, or film clips are extremely helpful in presenting concepts from intellectual history, such as the early "salons," dominated by the elegant, cultivated ladies of the aristocracy. The contrasts and comparisons with Sartre's salon, also dominated by the female sex, will become obvious as students advance in their reading of the play.

The reproduction or slide of a seventeenth-century salon in a painting by J. F. de Troy (1670–1752) entitled *Lecture de Molière,* could inspire the following socratic teaching:

1. How many men and how many women are there in the picture? To which social class do they belong? (There are more women than men. They belong to the aristocracy.)

2. Describe the décor of this salon. (It is very rich and elegant.)

3. What are these elegant ladies and gentlemen doing—drinking tea or coffee? (No, they are reading a play by Molière, and, judging from their expressions, they are analyzing the play critically.)

4. What kind of atmosphere does the picture convey? (The atmosphere is a scholarly one; although everyone looks relaxed, they are obviously discussing the play seriously.)

5. What is the painter suggesting about the role and importance of a salon? (The salon was a place where men and women gathered to dis-

cuss and to learn about literature, art, architecture, and music. It fulfilled, in essence, the function of a kind of modern liberal arts college.)

6. What is Sartre's aim in placing his characters in a salon? (Sartre used the salon as a setting where men and women have traditionally met, communicated on an equal footing, and learned about each other as well as about themselves.)

With each answer, the teacher can seize the opportunity to enlarge and give depth to the students' understanding. When, later on in their university career, students encounter European culture in history courses, they will see another facet of something already somewhat familiar, and the chances of retention will increase. In addition, their reading of *Huis Clos* will be enhanced by a deeper understanding of its underlying historical background, and their developing language skills will become part of a broader and better informed perspective.

Once the mental structures touched upon by the word *salon* are well in place, the next step is to illuminate the significance of "style Second Empire."

1. To what does "Second Empire" refer?

2. When was the First Empire?

3. Who was the Emperor?

4. When one speaks of Napoleon, to whom does one generally refer, Napoleon I or Napoleon III?

5. Discuss the difference between the two emperors with respect to the Sartrian concepts of authenticity and imitation, reality and falsity.

Turning to the second line of the description of the salon, "Un bronze sur la cheminée," the bronze can be introduced along the same pedagogical lines:

1. What is a "bronze"? (A statuette)

2. This is later referred to as a "bronze de Barbedienne." Why is there a capital B in Barbedienne? (It is the name of a person.)

3. Who could Barbedienne be? (The name of the person sculpted or the sculptor; here, it is the latter.)

4. Copies of his statues were mass-produced. Why do you think Sartre includes one such copy in this play? (Sartre is again depicting the décor as imitative and false.)

5. Members of what social class would display such a sculpture in their salon? (The discussion of this question can be taken up again at the later mention of a "salle à manger Louis-Phillippe," a concept equally

rich in cultural allusions, and one that Sartre obviously inserted for similar reasons.)

A series of carefully structured questions of this type can help students realize that behind a simple description of a salon is hidden a world of historico-cultural allusions that create the tone and atmosphere of the play. The stage is thus set for thematic discussions of such topics as the conflicts of social classes, the personalities of the characters, their expectations of one another, and each one's desire to hide behind some kind of mask.

The importance of the "salon Second Empire" is underscored when it becomes the subject of the first discussion between two characters.

GARCIN: C'est comme ça . . . (And this is what it looks like?)

LE GARÇON: C'est comme ça . . . (Yes.)

GARCIN: Je pense qu'à la longue on doit s'habituer aux meubles. (Well, I dare say one gets used to it in time.)

LE GARÇON: Ça dépend des personnes. (Some do. Some don't.)

To understand this passage the reader must perceive the cultural clues inherent in the salon. Indeed, the interaction between Garcin and *le garçon* (the usher) can only be understood within the context of those underlying cultural assumptions. For instance, Garcin's observation: "Je pense qu'à la longue on doit s'habituer aux meubles" reveals how awkward he feels in this particular setting. This observation indicates more than personal taste; it announces Garcin's social background and introduces the character's personal conflict with the bourgeoisie.

The bronze de Barbedienne is also highlighted by Garcin's immediate recognition and reaction: "Un bronze de Barbedienne. Quel cauchemar!" (A bronze of Barbedienne, of all people! What a horror!) Garcin's violent response to the statue and desire to destroy the lamp with it ("Et si je balançais le bronze sur la lampe électrique, est-ce qu'elle s'éteindrait?—And suppose I took that contraption on the mantelpiece and dropped it on the lamp—would it go out?") reveal a significant aspect of his explosive personality. They also indicate his total disdain for bourgeois society and for everything it represents. He is, however, forced to accept the statue and the lamp; indeed, the "salon" in its entirety. In this scene the reader learns about Garcin through his reactions to the surroundings. The presentation of the character is subtle and implicit, but no French reader would misunderstand it. By presenting vocabulary as inseparable from the historico-cultural context in which it is found, we not only teach our students the linguistic symbols in which the text is written, but also encourage them to master the cultural code through which the ideas of the play are conveyed.

CULTURAL AWARENESS

We hope to lead our students toward a more satisfying encounter with literature and a more facile manipulation of grammatical constructs in a cultural context. We also wish to familiarize them with the contemporary cultural ambience in which speakers of the language live and move. Traditional methodologies that emphasized cultural literacy eliminated any consideration of what we shall call "cultural awareness." We consider this a mistake. Cultural literacy should be accompanied by competence in ordinary target-culture situations. Our students should, of course, be well read and well informed, but also prepared for practical encounters and contacts.

In many courses, "culturally relevant" situations are presented in a style reminiscent of a Berlitz manual. Topics like "in the post office," "at the hotel," or "in the restaurant" recreate a cultural ambience for which the student learns the necessary locutions. Teaching these and similar vocabularies through use is more effective than reading them or repeating them in dialogs. Yet here again, a new dimension is added to this interactive framework when such learning is grounded in a literary work. A fictional text, which pervades and unifies lessons on various cultural concepts, can anchor cultural and linguistic data, while increasing the students' exposure to literature.

It is essential to remember that the social and cultural phenomena familiar to our students are different from those of the target culture. Therefore, this method requires a continual readjustment of the students' perspective. Discussions in the language, stemming, as they often do, from experiences with native cultural phenomena, need to be purged of that peculiarly American twist often found in improvisations in the classroom. (For example, in a role-playing activity, American students may show their drivers' licenses in order to purchase wine.) This process of supposition of cultural appropriateness with subsequent correction by a culturally competent teacher sensitizes students to potential misunderstandings. In addition, the data with which the activity provides them will help avoid such errors in the future.

In applying this method, one might use a text like *Huis Clos* to drill grammatical points in the following manner:

1. Vous êtes le psychologue d'Inès, donnez-lui des conseils. (You are Inès's psychoanalyst. Give her some advice.)
   (drills use of the imperative)

2. Si vous étiez l'avocat d'Estelle, qu'est-ce que vous diriez pour la défendre? (If you were Estelle's lawyer, what would you say in her defense?)
   (drills use of the conditional)

Questions such as these stimulate discussions of contemporary cultural issues while language use is being practiced. For example, the above drills might trigger questions such as:

1. What cultural stigma or attitudes are attached to psychoanalysts in France?

2. How does the French judicial system operate?

Thus, as we have already demonstrated with cultural literacy, the introduction of contemporary cultural information goes hand in hand with the improvement of language use in a meaningful context. Cultural awareness heightens the effectiveness of the learning process by preventing misconceptions or skewed impressions. Just as a literary work can mesh with a whole range of linguistic exercises (such as structural practice, cloze passages, compositions, listening comprehension exercises), so can issues of cultural awareness.

The instructor must first identify those textual elements that would trigger a discussion of cultural issues. The next step is to construct exercises based on the text but having to do with nonfictional circumstances. A brief introduction conveying the necessary background information can be provided or assigned to students as homework. By using elements of the literary text as starting points for a discussion of cultural topics, we enlarge our students' perspectives and further their understanding of the characters and issues in the play.

The following are examples of such "jumping off" points that might be used to explore elements of cultural background.

1. General social or political concerns that are explicit or easily identified in the text. For example:

   a. Garcin's political views

   b. The class conflict between Inès and Estelle

   How would these be seen and evaluated by the French reader?

2. Cultural data connected to objects, places, or allusions in the text. In these cases, at least one character from the play should be retained in role-playing or compositions. For example:

   a. Inès at work in the post office (topic: the French postal system)

   b. Garcin at his typewriter in the pressroom (topic: journalism in France)

3. Independent cultural settings examined through the perspective of a particular character. For example:

   a. Estelle chez le coiffeur (Estelle at the hairdresser's)

   b. Garcin et sa femme au restaurant (Garcin and his wife at a restaurant)

Other activities would explore themes in the play by isolating various conflicts and interpersonal dynamics. Brief dramatic scenes or group problem-solving activities are constructed around situations with conflicts similar to those in the text being studied. Each student takes on the personality (and name) of one character. The activity turns on similar emotional and psychological issues while bringing in new vocabulary and specific cultural circumstances. The following examples use the characters from *Huis Clos:*

a. Garcin, Inès, and Estelle are roommates who have been evicted because of their constant arguing. They find a new apartment but it is only large enough for two. They must decide which of the three will be excluded. (topic: living conditions in Paris)

b. Garcin and Inès plan to lead the inmates of hell in a revolutionary uprising. Estelle objects and attempts to dissuade them. (topic: political tendencies in France)

An exercise such as the latter provides an excellent opportunity for discussing the political context of the play. The teacher might provide background information on France in 1944 or have a student (or all students) prepare a brief exposé on the resistance. These activities increase the students' exposure to important historical and political elements of the culture being studied. They also provide information necessary for a sophisticated understanding of the chosen literary work.

In another activity, a scene may be broken down and rewritten, keeping the general structure intact while changing specific elements. Students are asked to describe a scene, for instance, in four statements. With *Huis Clos,* the scene in which Estelle reveals her crime (she killed her unwanted child) could be broken down in the following way:

1. Three people are shut in a room together.

2. Two try to get the third to reveal a secret.

3. The third resists and then gives in.

4. The secret is a shocking one.

The students, with the help of the instructor, then propose several relevant settings, like those below, within which such a scene might occur. (One or more of the characters maintains his or her identity.) Students in groups work the situation out in the four stages outlined in the statements.

a. Three waiters are trapped in the wine cellar at the Tour d'Argent (or another famous restaurant).

b. Three salespeople are stuck in an elevator at the Galeries Lafayette (or some other well-known department store).

c. Three students are accused of a murder during a student demonstration. They are locked up in the same cell.

Activities and exercises like these introduce students to many French social and professional relationships. The instructor should note any cultural errors in the students' scenarios and comment on national differences. In this way, not only are the students interacting with French language and literature, they are preparing for practical encounters in various social contexts and becoming familiar with the customs of the French in their home environment.

Textual Analysis

Finally, we will want to combine cultural literacy and cultural awareness with textual analysis to exploit the linguistic richness of the play and practice language use in a literary context. One technique, which has proved very interesting to the students, encourages the "intrusion of fiction into fiction." The text becomes malleable as we enter it through fantasy (Peytard 1982: 99). The story line is stretched, but the original content is not deformed. New fictional elements serve to bring forth the substance of the play, encouraging students to remain within the logic of the text and practice the vocabulary and grammar used by the author.

For example, students play the role of reporters interviewing the characters of the play, who stand accused of a robbery.[5] The robbery and the reporters are fictitious, but the reactions of the characters must be compatible with their personalities and reveal the students' understanding of them. This type of activity, now widely recognized as useful for extracting the main ideas from a text, can also be used at an elementary level to practice grammar in a directed but stimulating way. An exercise constructed around the use of the informal past tense and the past perfect might be as follows:

The instructor or a student, taking the part of a police inspector, asks what one of the students (playing the role of a character from the play) did the night before. The student answers using the informal past and actual elements of the play. Another student, playing the role of a reporter, reports the facts to the class using the past perfect. Each response fits the text and places the grammatical usage in a familiar and relevant context. Similarly, again in order to practice the conversational past, a judge can be introduced into the play. He or she demands that each of the characters name one good action performed during his or her lifetime. Or, a doctor might inquire about the past activities of a character who has fallen seriously ill.

As the introduction of a new figure brings forth crucial aspects of the characters' personalities, the facts of the plot are stretched in order to highlight significant elements of the play. For instance, in order to practice interrogative forms, a psychiatrist can enter the scene and question a character. A judge may sentence the three protagonists to return to earth, telling them (using the future construction) what they are to do in their new lives, the sentences being related to facts of the play.

For example:

THE JUDGE TO ONE OF THE STUDENTS: "Estelle, tu seras une maîtresse d'école dévouée." (Estelle, you will be a devoted grade school teacher.)

TEACHER TO STUDENT: "Que feras-tu sur terre?" (What will you do on earth?)

ESTELLE: "Je m'occuperai des petits enfants." (I'll take care of small children.)

This answer, despite its playful aspect, fits perfectly into the context of the original story line. In *Huis Clos* Estelle was sent to hell for committing infanticide.

From the elementary level on, textual analysis, grammar, and vocabulary practice merge, as in the following situations, which help review a wide range of vocabulary items:

- The prison cook takes the order for their last earthly meal from the three characters in *Huis Clos*. (conditional for expressing requests)

- A masked ball is being organized in hell. The characters decide on their costumes. (immediate future)

The situations proposed must trigger responses that uncover actual traits of character. Thus Garcin might choose to appear at the ball as Don Juan, Estelle as a courtesan, and Inès as the revolutionary Charlotte Corday.

The fictional domain grows in complexity as we practice increasingly difficult areas of grammar. For example, to practice the subjunctive in French, interviews are arranged during which a student, posing as a character from the text, is asked what he or she would like the other characters to have, see, or do in their salon. For example:

Qu'aimeriez-vous que Garcin fasse? (What would you like Garcin to do?)

J'aimerais qu'il s'en aille. (I'd like him to go away.)

The past conditional can be elicited by asking students to imagine which objects the three characters would have saved had there been a fire in their home on earth. A further communicative element can be added by asking students which objects they think their classmates might choose in a similar situation. After the initial stage, where the focus of the activities is primarily on elements of grammatical structure, other interactional situations can be developed to lead directly to an analysis of the substantive content of the play:

- The victims of the characters in the play arrive in hell. How do the characters react? What do they say to their victims? What do they do?

- Students imagine themselves waking up in the salon with Estelle, Inès, and Garcin. They must explain their presence and communicate with the characters.

- Students are asked to eliminate one of the characters from the play and give either moral or dramaturgical reasons for their choice.

These activities, timed to last not more than ten minutes each, are highly interactive, creating a strong triangle of communication among the text, the student, and the instructor. To stimulate the students' imagination, the instructor may give the initial example and then encourage students to interact. Having entered the text immediately from a linguistic as well as a literary angle, students feel at ease with both analysis and expression. They develop an ability to use form and content naturally.

On one level, the intrusion of fiction into fiction helps students in various ways:

- They approach the text from within. Students become part of the text. They are "on the inside," like writer and characters. In this way, they can take possession of the text, make it their own, not deforming what already exists but rather extending it. Through this penetration, they come to grips with the process of creating. "They reconstruct the process of creation of the author" (Kramsch 1985: 357).

- They take control of their learning. In this method the instructor adjusts to the students' direction in the fictionalizing process.

On another level, by these means, students discover the text as a mechanism. By uncovering the grammatical and thematic structures involved in the adequate functioning of the narration, "by delving into the very fabric of the work—the language" (Mueller and Rehorick 1984: 475), they discover the essential role of grammar in conveying nuances of meaning. This sensitization to words and grammatical constructions can initiate a revalorization of grammar in the students' experience.

To introduce a work of world literature in this manner early in language learning necessarily entails the desacralization of the literary text. Though this may seem heretical to some, we believe it is in no way detrimental but, on the contrary, beneficial to both language learning and literary appreciation. Our method, in which language practice and textual analysis become thoroughly intertwined, prevents the development of one at the expense of the other. Thus literature no longer represents the ultimate point to be reached after a long period of language study but is revealed as an integral part of the culture, one of many means of expression specific to the language and available to its users. By inserting "fiction into fiction," students approach the text as the text approaches the reader—through the imagination. Literature as a realm of creativity inspires and demands more creativity. Through this process, students take possession of the text and make it part of their creative world. The creative process that reading inspires is thus maintained and extended as a vital element in language learning.

Interactive language teaching can be highly effective when steeped in and structured around a particular literary work. A synergistic method of this type, in which literature enhances language learning and language acquisition increases literary sensitivity, has proven to be very useful for encouraging students to take their first steps toward cultural awareness and literacy.

NOTES

1. Carrell and Eisterhold (1988) give details of research in reading, particularly schema theory, that emphasizes the fact that "the background knowledge that second language readers bring to the text is often culture-specific" (p. 81).

2. *No Exit* is Sartre's portrayal of hell. The three main characters are Garcin, a pacifist journalist, womanizer, and deserter; Estelle, a class-conscious socialite, guilty of infanticide; and Inès, a manipulative, lesbian postal worker. The three are consigned, for eternity, to a sparsely furnished salon in which they must incessantly confront one another. The incompatibility of their social, political, and moral attitudes makes their imprisonment together an existential hell.

3. The title itself, *Huis Clos,* requires a brief explanation. Its meaning, no exit, refers to both the immediate physical predicament of the characters and a more general, abstract interpretation of the human condition. Since, however, the discussion of the title's cultural and literary implications will become relevant only after students have become thoroughly familiar with the play, we begin our discussion with the opening lines of the play itself.

4. Translations of *Huis Clos* are taken from Jean-Paul Sartre, *Huis Clos,* trans. Stuart Gilbert (New York: Random House, 1946), with some adaptations.

5. Some of the techniques described here may be viewed on the videotape *Cultural Literacy and Interactive Language Instruction,* directed by Marlies Mueller (1990).

REFERENCES

Carrell, Patricia L., and Joan C. Eisterhold. 1988. "Schema Theory and ESL Reading Pedagogy," pp. 73–92 in P. L. Carrell, J. Devine, and D. E. Eskey, eds., *Interactive Approaches to Second Language Reading*. Cambridge, Eng., and New York: Cambridge Univ. Press.

Hirsch, E. D., Jr. 1987. *Cultural Literacy: What Every American Needs to Know*. Boston: Houghton Mifflin.

Kaufman, M. R. 1987. "An Effective Communicative Approach for the Introduction of French Literature." *French Review* 60: 825–34.

Kramsch, Claire J. 1985. "Literary Texts in the Classroom: A Discourse." *Modern Language Journal* 69: 356–66.

Mueller, Marlies, director. 1990. *Cultural Literacy and Interactive Language Instruction*. Video. Lincolnwood, IL: National Textbook Company.

————, and Sally Rehorick. 1984. "Reaching for Caligula's Moon: Teaching Modern Drama in Advanced Language Classes." *French Review* 57: 475–84.

Muyskens, Judith 1983. "Teaching Second-Language Literatures: Past, Present and Future." *Modern Language Journal* 67: 413–23.

Peytard, J. 1982. "Sémiotique du texte littéraire et didactique du F.L.E." *Études de linguistique appliquée* 45: 91–103.

5

The Reading Component Articulated across Levels

Marva A. Barnett
University of Virginia

*A*lice *had been looking over [the Mad Hatter's] shoulder with some curiosity.
"What a funny watch!" she remarked. "It tells the day of the month, and doesn't tell what
o'clock it is!"*

"Why should it?" muttered the Hatter. "Does your *watch tell you what year it is?"*

*"Of course not," Alice replied very readily: "but that's because it stays the same year
for such a long time together."*

"Which is just the case with mine," *said the Hatter.*

*Alice felt dreadfully puzzled. The Hatter's remark seemed to her to have no sort of
meaning in it, and yet it was certainly English.*

(LEWIS CARROLL, *Alice in Wonderland*)

Unfortunately, many foreign-language students are just as "dreadfully
puzzled" by their assigned reading as Alice was by the Mad Hatter. What they
are attempting to read is *not* English, but some of them treat it as though it
should be; others assume that because it's not English, it couldn't possibly
signify. Some students do not know individual words and grammatical structures; those who do sometimes cannot see meaningful patterns in them.
Moreover, many students neither are interested in assigned texts nor expect to
find sense there. As teachers, we have at times tried little to help students
discover textual meaning—and succeeded less. Today, with a new awareness

of how readers' minds work, we are learning that we cannot simply assign a reading and expect that learners' knowledge of the target language, supplemented by a dictionary, will carry them through it to understanding and concern. We need to teach them how to approach texts and train them to use many skills we have previously assumed they had mastered on their own.

Reading in the Curriculum

We know that reading is an essential skill, the door to empathy with other peoples; understanding and analyzing their literary and cultural writings leads to a greater awareness of both our own culture and those of others (Byrnes 1988). Once acquired, reading can be maintained, requiring only a library, bookshop, newsstand, or generous friend to provide the necessary texts. Within the framework of second-language acquisition theory, reading is regarded as a readily accessible source of authentic language input and valued as an aid to the improvement of writing (Krashen 1984: 4–6). Reading is vital to content-based curricula, where a new language is learned along with other subject matters (Swaffar 1989: 57).

Not surprisingly, then, reading has become the subject of intense research and theorizing; the past two decades alone have seen a much larger volume of research on second- and foreign-language reading than one chapter can hope to encompass. This chapter, in response to the pragmatic needs of foreign-language departments, will consider briefly second-language reading theory and its first-language underpinnings and summarize recommended methodologies for elementary through advanced levels, including the graduate reading course. Specific references to noncognate or "truly foreign" languages (see chapter 8) appear when appropriate. Throughout this chapter the terms *second language* and *foreign language* are used interchangeably, not because they are equivalent but because second-language reading research is generally applicable to the foreign-language teaching central to this book. Finally, to enhance chapter readability, references are limited to key works and summarizing works are cited for the reader curious for more details.

Evolving Views of the Second-Language Reading Process

What most helps readers understand a text in either their first or their second language? Certainly, everything has its importance—vocabulary, syntax, semantics, knowledge of subject matter, expectations about content, aware-ness of the cultural parameters of the text, to name just a few elements. But how important is each item, and how do they relate to each other? In an attempt to answer such questions, researchers generally distinguish between *text-based elements* (components of the text such as letters, spelling, grammar, structure) and *reader-based elements* (reader characteristics such as willingness to take risks and the ability to draw inferences). At first, theorists tended to stress only one of these facets in their analyses, seeing first-language reading as solely a bottom-up process, in which readers derive meaning from examining the text itself, or as basically a top-down process in which what readers bring to a text determines much of what they understand. (On these issues, see Carrell 1988a; Barnett 1989.)

More recently, second-language theorists have been greatly influenced by the belief that first-language reading is an *interactive process* in which both textual elements and reader characteristics combine to create comprehension. Rumelhart, working from an information-processing orientation, hypothe-sizes that "[first language] reading is at once a 'perceptual' and a 'cognitive' process" (Rumelhart 1977: 573; see also Rumelhart, McClelland, et al. 1986); that is, the reader's comprehension depends upon a complex, varying, simul-taneous interaction between the reader's knowledge and strategies and the different hierarchical levels of information received from the text (from the semantic level down through the syntactic, lexical, orthographic, and percep-tual levels). Citing numerous experimental results, Rumelhart shows how knowledge and perception of one level of language can influence those either above or below it: for instance, knowledge of semantics enables a reader to recognize words logically related (e.g., nurse–doctor, bread–butter) more quickly than those not normally related to each other (e.g., bread–doctor, nurse–butter). Thus knowing word meanings helps the reader speed up the text-based ability to perceive letters and recognize words: at all levels of information, "a convergence of top-down and bottom-up hypotheses strengthens both" (Rumelhart 1977: 598).

Closely related to interactive reading process theory, schema theory has inspired much second-language reading research. Originally developed to interpret the first-language reading process, schema theory explains compre-hension as the result of an interaction between the text itself and what the reader knows and expects from the text. Commonly called "background knowledge," existing concepts about the world form the reader's *schemata*. According to schema theory, readers understand a text efficiently by interpret-ing its linguistic elements with respect to their own experiences. To illustrate the role of schemata in readers' comprehension, Carrell and Eisterhold (1983: 577–78) offer reflections on this minitext: "The policeman held up his hand

and stopped the car." A reader who activates the familiar schema of a traffic cop signaling a driver to stop a car imagines the policeman raising his hand and the driver applying the brakes. On the other hand, the reader who has been told that the policeman is Superman (and who knows Superman's powers and usual activities) may well interpret the same sentence to mean that the policeman physically stopped the car, which might have had no driver. The words in themselves allow either interpretation and still others; it is the reader who brings meaning to the text.

Yet a reader cannot effectively apply schemata to comprehend a text unless (1) the appropriate schemata exist in the reader's mind, and (2) the text corresponds fairly accurately to the reader's expectations. Efficient readers possess and activate two types of schemata: *formal schemata,* background knowledge of the rhetorical organization of the text, and *content schemata,* background knowledge about the text topic (Carrell 1988b). Furthermore, both the content and structure of texts are normally bound by the culture in which they were written; consequently, schema theory has especially important ramifications for readers of foreign-language texts. Oriental paragraphs, it seems, are more likely to be circular, whereas English logic is typically linear (Kaplan 1966); English speakers also find specific aspects of Japanese rhetoric difficult (Hinds 1983). Similarly, research directly comparing reader comprehension of texts with familiar and unfamiliar cultural content indicates that readers recall more and make more correct inferences after reading texts set in their own culture than those from another culture (see Carrell 1988a). Students asked to read a text with unfamiliar cultural content may mistranslate or misinterpret according to their own cultural perspective (Bernhardt 1990; Parry 1987).

Interaction of Text-Based and Reader-Based Elements

Looking at foreign-language reading from a schema-theoretic point of view casts new light on some old research issues but does not yet resolve them. The question of whether one feature most determines efficient reading—and, if so, which—remains central to foreign-language reading research and theory. We also wonder about the relationship between first- and second-language reading processes but find this connection hard to study: matching first- and second-language texts for difficulty level is problematic; equating studies in the two areas is troublesome because of varying methodologies, hypotheses, and subjects. Moreover, there are as yet very few reports comparing reading in alphabetic languages and in ideographic languages, like Japanese or Chinese, although they are increasing. Rare is research investigating reading of foreign languages not cognate with the learners' first language, and we would be ill advised to extrapolate results from experiments on cognate languages to noncognate language reading. Also still unresolved are the questions of the relative importance of a reader's linguistic proficiency in reading comprehension and, in particular, the relative weight of different aspects of linguistic proficiency (knowledge of vocabulary, recognition of semantic fields, control of syntax, awareness of text type) in this process (see Swaffar 1988 for a summary). On the topic of whether first-language reading skill transfers to second-language reading, however, there is some consensus despite remaining debate: advanced foreign-language learners regularly use first-language skills to comprehend, and even beginners sometimes transfer these skills. Clearly, readers who encounter unfamiliar or uncontrolled vocabulary and grammar in a foreign language find the going rough; nonetheless, activating various reading skills, cognitive abilities, and appropriate schemata seems to improve their chances of comprehending (see Barnett 1989 for references).

Adolescent and adult foreign-language learners approach a text with not only schemata derived from their life experiences but also already developed cognitive skills and an ability to analyze and evaluate metacognitively what they do as they read. Studied and classified in earnest only since the late 1980s, these skills and abilities, usually termed *reading strategies,* are most often defined as the conscious or unconscious mental operations involved when readers purposefully approach a text to make sense of what they read. A complete inventory of such strategies may prove to be an impossible task, given the complex nature of individual strategy use, but several useful taxonomies have been offered, ranging from practical, hands-on skills to metacognitive awareness of how one approaches a text (Hosenfeld et al. 1981; Sarig 1987). Practical tactics include text-based strategies like skipping unknown words while using other contextual clues to establish meaning, identifying the grammatical category of words to ascertain their function, and recognizing cognates, as well as such extra-text strategies as using knowledge of the world to guide in inferring meaning, continuing to read for further clues when unsuccessful, and evaluating guesses as further meaning is comprehended. Metacognitive awareness involves readers' recognition of how well they understand as they read and of how efficiently they use their various strategies to discover meaning (Carrell 1989; Casanave 1988). Specialists in foreign-language pedagogy commonly recommend training students in strategy use, especially at the elementary and intermediate levels of language study, rather than presuming that all are reading effectively.

Articulating Reading Pedagogies

Research results demonstrating variation in the reading process of learners at different levels reading different types of texts in different languages (Allen et al. 1988: 168–70) imply assorted pedagogies for diverse situations. When teaching cognate languages, we can incorporate these into a logical sequence of goals. In elementary courses, students develop useful reading strategies while improving their linguistic skill for text comprehension. At the intermediate level, students learn to analyze what they have comprehended and to refine their reading techniques. At the advanced level, where foreign-language reading skills begin to approximate native-language skills, teachers and students concentrate on gaining cultural and literary insights from texts. Finally, graduate reading courses, by their very nature, imply a reading-for-information goal. Teaching "truly foreign" languages such as Arabic, Turkish, Chinese, or Japanese normally involves quite different methodologies and sequencing and will be discussed briefly.

Achieving the goal of reading program articulation requires adhering to a set of principles which, by their very existence, give students the sense that they are progressing along a known pathway. First, because learning a language is learning about another culture—in this case, embedded in texts—students need to read authentic materials written by and for native speakers, and to read them within some knowledge framework (Nostrand 1989). Second, prereading activities designed to involve students with the text *before* they read it are essential at all levels, although they necessarily vary in nature. Third, teachers and students should always strike a balance between the cognitive and linguistic aspects of reading; since students must continue to grow in both directions, teachers should endeavor to select texts and exercises appropriate both to students' knowledge of the target language and to students' control of resourceful reading strategies and background knowledge. Fourth, testing of reading at all levels matches teaching methods and grows out of course objectives. Each of these principles appears in the following methodological discussion, with details as appropriate.

Building Reading Skills

College students learning a cognate foreign language can read even as they begin to study the language. They are first-language-literate, have a certain level of cognitive development, and can learn and activate cognitive strategies. Granted, beginning students live with a precarious mix of general cognitive abilities and second-language linguistic skills, the former relatively highly developed, the latter frustratingly less so. But students' lack of linguistic knowledge should no longer stop teachers from presenting authentic texts:

students trained to use their top-down processes (e.g., thinking about similar texts or inferring word meanings in context) can understand much more of a text than their linguistic skill alone would allow (Grellet 1981: 7–8). Students trained in both language structures and cognitive strategies have more ways to negotiate text meaning; and the more they understand, the more likely they are to acquire a yet greater knowledge of vocabulary and grammar from what they read.

How can we best teach language structures to enhance reading comprehension? Most methodologists advise teaching vocabulary in context, both because it is more meaningful, and thus more memorable, and because context offers additional information about what unfamiliar words mean. Context may come from a complete reading text or from activities designed to group words meaningfully: semantic association, semantic mapping, and semantic feature analysis (Barnitz 1985). In all these activities, students (and sometimes the teacher) brainstorm all the words or phrases they can find related to the context, content, or concept of a text; next they organize these in some logical fashion, analyzing the similarities and distinctions among them. In another approach to active vocabulary learning, students consider word derivation and analysis, still preferably in context (Rivers 1981). Closely related to the more cognitively oriented strategy of inferring word meanings from form and context, emphasizing word formation makes vocabulary instruction more meaningful by helping students recognize patterns within words.

Despite the traditional focus on vocabulary for reading comprehension, we cannot ignore the role of syntax. A student who does not realize that a murder *had* taken place before the hero left or who does not gather that the "she" referred to is the heroine risks total misunderstanding. Recognition grammar of this type requires different preparation from that of productive grammar for speaking (Rivers 1981: 267). Moreover, reading comprehension goes beyond "grammar learning" in that it requires the reader to recognize how words in a text relate to each other. Not surprising, then, is the present attention to cohesive language ties, the words and phrases that relate one part of a text to another: reference words such as pronouns and demonstrative adjectives, conjunctions, and repetition of words already used, as well as logical connectives. Pedagogical suggestions center on helping students concentrate on vital cohesive ties, underlining reference words, for instance, and finding their referents (Williams 1983). Such close reading of a text may enter into the reading lesson at different points, depending on the complexity of the text, students' level of expertise, and the reading goal; it is particularly important in classes where reading for information is paramount. A text with a complex start, for instance, requires early syntactical analysis to guarantee readers' immediate comprehension; a text used as a model of logical reasoning requires later detailed exploration of style and structure.

Reading pedagogies vary to meet particular needs also in that text-based strategies, such as those enumerated above, must be integrated with reader-based cognitive strategies. Training in cognitive strategy use is most beneficial at the elementary and intermediate levels of language instruction because careful strategy use can compensate for the relatively poorly developed linguistic skills of many of these students (Kern 1989). The term *training* is used consciously here: individual students are to a greater or lesser degree effective strategy users in English, and even resourceful strategy users are not always naturally adept at transferring their skill to reading in the foreign language. In addition, strategy use in reading comprehension varies greatly from one learner to the next, as readers combine strategies in different ways (Sarig 1987) and prefer different learning styles (Carrell, Pharis, and Liberto 1989). The ultimate purpose of this training is to develop students' ability to activate effective strategies on their own.

When teachers no longer assume that their first-language-literate students necessarily know how to approach a foreign-language text, they choose reading texts and comprehension activities not just for the content they offer but also for their usefulness in strategy training. Authentic texts have been written for authentic purposes, and particular comprehension strategies are more or less applicable to individual texts. To decide which comprehension strategies might be best taught with a specific text, teachers consider each text within its cultural context, asking themselves such questions as: What would a native reader find most important in this text? What are the most productive strategies for understanding the main point of the text?

With a particular text in hand and the relevant answers to these questions, the teacher is ready to begin training in strategy use, taking into consideration both the *global strategies* used to analyze discourse and the *local strategies* used to examine a single word or phrase. Frequently suggested is some minimal training in strategy use within the first language before extrapolating to the second. Hosenfeld et al. (1981) recommend first using native-language texts to practice inferring word meanings before working with second-language texts. Although target-language texts are, of course, the object of study, discussion of strategies is often best undertaken in the first language to ensure that students understand what they are being asked to do.

Global strategies include skimming for the gist, scanning for specific information, predicting forthcoming text, identifying main points, rereading, recognizing text structure. In-class or homework exercises to develop such strategies normally show students how to use a pertinent strategy to obtain requested information. Thus a skimming exercise may ask readers to underline all the phrases relevant to the main theme of "ethics in journalism" and then choose from a list the sentence that best summarizes the text or, at more advanced levels, write the summarizing sentence themselves. Scanning exercises are most productively done in class under a time limit; for these, students look through an unfamiliar text for important information such as dates, personality traits, places. Exercises on predicting upcoming text integrate learners' information schemata with the text already encountered, whether it be paragraphs or simply a title or illustrations. Doing some of these exercises in class as group projects or pair work enables students to learn from their peers, as they also do when the teacher asks for an explanation of how correct answers were found.

Local strategies include examining within a context word meaning, word formation, and grammar; paraphrasing a segment of text in order to clarify meaning; rereading to verify comprehension; writing down key elements in the text; using the glossary or dictionary. Again, exercises to develop local strategy use should be introduced first in class, where the teacher can answer questions and see how well the students understand the procedure. For instance, beginning to read the text itself at the end of a prereading session, teacher and students can share methods of determining the meanings of problematic words or phrases. As appropriate, the teacher asks questions like the following: Does the word resemble a native-language word? Is it a cognate? Does the cognate make sense in the sentence? Is the word most probably a noun, adjective, or verb? How do we know? What words could this pronoun refer to? Do we need to know exactly what this word means? In some cases, certainly, context will be insufficient for inferring word meaning, or a precise meaning will be essential. To prepare students for such situations, teachers instruct them in how to use a dictionary, reminding them that the part of speech is important and that it is crucial to check chosen word meanings in the context of the original sentence.

Training in cognitive strategy use should not only increase efficient strategy use and comprehension but also improve learner traits (Kern 1989; Casanave 1988). That is, students whose minds are open to applying their thinking ability to foreign texts, rather than blundering blindly ahead, are more likely to keep textual meaning in mind, read with the expectation of finding meaning, take chances in order to identify meaning, and employ a wide variety of strategies. They may also be more metacognitively aware of their strategy use, that is, recognize their own cognitive activity and thus control it more consciously. This emphasis on readers' metacognition parallels current attention to language learners' strategy use in general and prompts teachers to encourage students to participate in developing their own learning processes.

The object of all the linguistic and strategy training just detailed being student comprehension of foreign-language texts, the teacher devises means for checking this comprehension. Fortunately, there are numerous options besides the traditional "who, what, when, where" questions. Grellet (1981), in particular, gives numerous samples of a wide range of activity types, each growing from the text it accompanies and each designed to develop a specific skill. At an elementary level, for example, students visualize the vital scene of a story by completing a partial drawing, adding the essential characters or props. To establish the chronology of a narrative, students finish a chart of times, places, and people. To analyze the pro and con arguments of an essay, students decide whether each of a list of statements correctly summarizes different positions. Varying the type of comprehension activities both intrigues students and appeals to varied learning styles. Grellet (1981: 11) also suggests not submerging a text under too many exercises but providing exercises at different levels of difficulty in order to individualize students' work.

Undoubtedly, comprehension exercises, whether used as practice activities or as testing devices, must grow from the real-world purposes of texts. For example, a newspaper article that establishes facts may be followed by a fact-listing activity but not by abundant questions about unessential details. Students who read an editorial arguing in favor of recycling should be asked to summarize the main lines of reasoning, using facts only to support the main thrust of the text. When used as tests, comprehension exercises should require students to read an unfamiliar text, performing the same functions and demonstrating the same skills as they did during the preparatory activities. At the elementary level, activities should, in addition, invite students to comprehend new texts and display control of reading strategies and linguistic elements taught and practiced in class (Lee 1988; Swaffar et al. 1991).

From Comprehension to Analysis

Depending on previous student preparation and departmental goals, the elementary skill-building level is followed more or less directly by a stage in which students refine their comprehension techniques to attain a level at which they are able to engage in deeper analysis of textual meaning. This is not a transition easily made, and traditional intermediate (second-year) and advanced (third-year) courses have not effected it dependably. Too often, teachers have assumed that intermediate-level students could read the target language proficiently. In reality, levels of reading proficiency vary greatly from one student to the next, even at the advanced level; many students continue to lack some basic reading skills. Thus most of the suggestions offered for elementary readers continue to pertain in second-year college courses. At the same time, however, teachers should be able to spend less time on direct strategy training and involve intermediate students in more complex and demanding comprehension checks.

Comprehension exercises must never be a rehashing of the original text. Munby (1979) proposes a pattern of multiple-choice questions that encourage deeper processing of text and that check on whether students can draw inferences dependent upon a thorough comprehension. Munby (1979: 145) successfully argues that "multiple-choice questioning can be used effectively to *train* a person's ability to think" [italics in the original] by showing how incorrect answers can be analyzed to determine the source of error. Multiple-choice distractors are based on common reasons for misunderstanding, including reading too much into the text, misinterpreting the tone, failing to follow relationships of thought, and failing to understand grammatical relations. Although difficult to write, such questions can prove invaluable for postreading discussions in which students explain their answers.

Much easier to devise, but requiring more analysis by the teacher, are recall protocols, in which students write in their first language as much as they can recall of the text read in the second language (Bernhardt 1986). Because readers create their own meaning when they read a text, the teacher's reconstruction of an assigned text may not parallel students' re-creations; recall protocols give the teacher an insight into how individual students processed the text. An analysis of students' recall protocols of short texts can highlight sources of misunderstanding, such as important errors in interpretation of syntax, vocabulary, or cultural information. Equally beneficial can be a class discussion of two different student protocols and what they show about how and what the readers comprehended.

Such postreading exercises can either become part of a standard four-skills course where reading shares the stage with listening, speaking, and writing or provide the groundwork for a specialized reading course for undergraduates who wish to emphasize that skill. Where two such options are offered, it is important that the distribution of students not be hierarchical; students with the highest grades should not be funneled into a spoken language track, making the reading track a ghetto for less proficient students. Like speaking, effective foreign-language reading requires a number of subskills that less obviously proficient students often possess, and students who are less adept at some of these skills can learn from their more successful peers.

Another popular alternate model to the year-long intermediate grammar-review/four-skills course consists of a one-semester grammar review (normally the third semester of a college-level sequence), followed by a fourth semester of intensive reading. Although such clear focus on different language elements may theoretically appear to help some students concentrate, problems with this model include student boredom and dissatisfaction with the lack of functional language use during the grammar review and with the delay in teaching the basic cognitive skills that are developed through reading and listening comprehension exercises. In a system where most students begin their study of the foreign language with the first-year college course, some of these difficulties may be overcome by careful articulation of cognitive skill development within the first-year program. Students will then have a solid base upon which to build during later reading or content-based courses.

Course offerings are typically even more varied at the advanced level, with—too often—another grammar review, conversation and composition practiced together or separately, introduction to literature, and so on (see chapter 2). Articulation is problematic in most institutions because, depending on local conditions, these courses may receive students with various combinations of college and high school instruction (including Advanced Placement status). As at the intermediate level, students still differ in reading competence; but, at this point, they undertake cultural and literary interpretations; happily, the professional literature has begun to offer teachers and curriculum designers ideas about how to train students in these skills, which they may well not have learned in other courses.

Schema theory is quite helpful in considering ways to approach textual analysis, furnishing productive alternatives to lecturing on historical perspective and introducing literary theory too early (Swaffar 1986). As we know, readers bring certain expectations to any text, as evidenced by a child's exclamation, "Oh, you just made that up!" when the story seems unreal because it does not fit known behaviors. In the classroom, once students have demonstrated general comprehension of a literary text, the teacher can generate a dialog by beginning with students' suggestions of what doesn't make sense, what is different from their experience, what is noteworthy, striking, or unusual. Most of the details and reactions thus elicited will figure in a critical evaluation of the text because of the students' natural ability to make value judgments according to society's norms. What students notice as significant points can then be labeled with the teacher's help as symbols, allusions, hyperboles, metaphors, and so on. By waiting until an appropriate time to introduce figurative terms and technical vocabulary—such as *point of view, stanza, antagonist*—the teacher helps students fit new literary expressions into their existing schemata. It is essential that teachers facilitate advanced students' own interpretive strategies in exploring and appraising texts from both a literary and a cultural standpoint. (For instructional models, see Swaffar et al. 1991; Dubin et al. 1986).

Kramsch (1985) integrates schema theory with theories of artificial intelligence and discourse analysis to redefine teacher–learner roles in the discussion of literary texts; her proposal changes the teacher from the normative authority with the final say to a facilitator of group discussions in which students negotiate textual meaning. Using the Hansel and Gretel story as an example, Kramsch describes several practical procedures, including a class dialog to reconstruct the facts, interpretive role-play activities with peer observers to clarify disagreements, alternative rewritings of the text, and a strict time limit on activities to reduce anxiety. Her approach, consistent with reading comprehension theory, "restores classroom students to their full creative role as a community of autonomous and responsible readers (Kramsch 1985: 364).

Byrnes (1988) emphasizes the cultural aspects of schemata in her proposal for presenting to American students second-language texts dealing with America. Recognizing that "reality" is not a given but rather an interpreted and valuated interaction with the cultural phenomena surrounding us, Byrnes suggests studying how people in the target culture look at American culture. In describing the American scene and their reactions to it, authors are actually comparing American culture with their own and expressing their unfulfilled expectations. Byrnes's methodology for leading students to understand the target culture by analyzing and interpreting native speakers' reactions to America includes examining the language used (e.g., indicators of negation), the textual organization, the hierarchy of prominence given to certain observations (e.g., those in titles, captions, pictures), speculating on what is missing from an American perspective, and connecting the underlying target culture constructs. In this way, American students can better perceive some of the subliminal assumptions inherent not only in the target culture but also in their own.

Reading a "Truly Foreign" Language

Recommendations like those given above may be well and good for Western European languages with structures and vocabulary relatively like those of the students' native language, but what of the noncognate and less commonly taught languages like Chinese and Arabic? They pose to students reading them the added problems of special writing systems (e.g., ideographs or completely unfamiliar symbols), linguistic features with no analogy in the first language (e.g., the inflecting derivational suffixes of Japanese), alien linguistic environments (e.g., the lack of socially neutral speech in Japanese), and very distant cultural orientations (Walker 1989). Fortunately, research on reading such languages, which has been very rare in the past, is becoming more readily available. We have as yet, however, little coherent theory and few research results on which to base pedagogical suggestions for teaching students to read with understanding those languages that rank as most difficult in the Foreign Service Institute experience (Walker 1989: 136; see Appendix B).

Because each of the truly foreign languages differs significantly from the others and because investigations necessarily begin with specific research questions, we do not yet have many well-defined pedagogical directives to apply more generally. Studies and methodological suggestions have tended so far to focus on the linguistic aspects of reading, particularly vocabulary (see Hayes 1988; Koda 1989). Researchers investigating reading in Japanese from a broader perspective find, however, that English-speaking readers' knowledge schemata help them understand Japanese texts about a familiar topic (Horiba 1990) and that their first-language reading strategies do transfer to second-language reading (Koda 1987). Teachers of truly foreign languages can probably integrate successfully some of the cognitive skill development activities that have proven worthwhile for the more commonly taught languages.

Reading for Information: The Graduate Reading Course

Frequently graduate students, and occasionally undergraduates, need to learn enough of a foreign language to read texts available only in that language. The so-called graduate reading course, the most common institutional response to that need, emphasizes by definition the extracting of information, bypassing other language skills and, usually, appreciation of style. The cultural orientation of texts is important to students reading for information only insofar as it impinges on their comprehension or their interpretation of facts, as when unfamiliar rhetorical structure prevails. In addition, because students in these courses generally work on understanding texts in their fields of specialization, they know more about text topics than does the teacher. Bringing highly developed and applicable schemata to their task, they need only break the code of the foreign language, as it were. Thus the goals and methodology of such courses differ greatly from those of the standard undergraduate language course.

Rivers (1988; see also Rivers and Nahir 1989) notes that students in specialized reading courses need to be able to recognize rapidly the target-language words that express basic language functions and the most commonly used key vocabulary; they then need to develop skill in using specialized dictionaries for terms in their particular fields. Specific skills necessary to attain these objectives include recognition of grammatical structures in their relationships within the text, knowledge of word formation (including prefixes, suffixes and compound words), and recognition of cognates and false cognates. After suggesting ways to teach these skills, Rivers recommends beginning the reading course by plunging students directly into texts so that they will gain the requisite confidence to seek out meaning without demanding dictionary definitions of all unfamiliar words. For a first lesson, with cognate languages like Germanic and Romance, she suggests arousing student interest in the relationship of the target language and English: eliciting target-language words regularly used in English; discussing the origins of English by comparing words of Germanic origin (e.g., start, end) with those of Latin origin (e.g., commence, terminate); analyzing sentences based on cognates and sentences that show how certain function words operate in the target language; and, in a final exercise, encouraging the class to decipher a passage containing a large number of cognates. During the semester, full-class activities, she suggests, would center on general language problems and discussion of student-selected texts. But, to individualize the class for the specialist student, Rivers advises that small groups of students working in related fields (for example, social scientists, artists) work on specific passages of interest to students in the group. Students should also be encouraged to bring to class the types of reading materials they most want to discuss. Autonomous activities should include group projects on subjects of special interest and sharing information gleaned from articles individuals have read.

Another technique easily adaptable to foreign-language reading is SQ3R, originally designed to teach effective first-language strategies for reading for information (Robinson 1962). First, the student quickly *surveys* a chapter or article by glancing over headings and reading the final summary paragraph. Next, the student rephrases the first heading as a *question*, thus activating background knowledge and creating a personal purpose in reading. While *reading*, the student searches actively for the answer to the question and then, after reading, *recites* the answer, giving an example and perhaps outlining cue phrases. A student who cannot recite the answer is encouraged to reread the section. After treating each section in the same manner, the student *reviews* the notes of the main points and recalls them by reciting the major ideas under each heading without reading the notes.

TOWARD AN INTEGRATED CURRICULUM

Given the wide variety of foreign-language reading courses, the varying place of reading within foreign-language studies, differing student profiles and divergent teacher orientations, designing an articulated foreign-language reading curriculum is difficult. Yet we must make the attempt: only by consciously developing our students' expertise can we hope to offer most of them a usable skill and the opportunity to discern another culture through its written texts. By stretching what students already know, including their general world experience and their cognitive strategies as well as their linguistic skills, teachers give them ways and means of integrating others' perceptions with their own. Finally, telling students what we hope to accomplish and the purpose of our techniques helps them attain a viable level of cross-cultural and literary understanding through comprehension of what they read. It is for each teacher to devise imaginative activities to achieve these goals.

REFERENCES

Allen, Edward D., Elizabeth B. Bernhardt, Mary T. Berry, and Marjorie Demel. 1988. "Comprehension and Text Genre: An Analysis of Secondary School Foreign Language Readers." *Modern Language Journal* 72: 163–72.

Barnett, Marva A. 1989. *More Than Meets the Eye. Foreign Language Reading: Theory and Practice*. Washington, DC: Center for Applied Linguistics.

Barnitz, John G. 1985. *Reading Development of Nonnative Speakers of English*. Washington, DC: Center for Applied Linguistics.

Bernhardt, Elizabeth B. 1986. "Reading in the Foreign Language," pp. 93–115 in B. Wing, ed. *Listening, Reading, and Writing: Analysis and Application*. Report of the Northeast Conference on the Teaching of Foreign Languages. Middlebury, VT: The Northeast Conference.

————. 1989. "A Model of L2 Text Reconstruction: The Recall of Literary Text by Learners of German," in A. Labarca, ed., *Issues in L2: Theory as Practice, Practice as Theory*. Norwood: Ablex.

Byrnes, Heidi. 1988. "Looking behind the Scenes: Images of America in Texts." Paper presented at the ACTFL Symposium on Teaching Foreign Languages to Adult Professionals. Linthicum, MD.

Carrell, Patricia L. 1988a. "Introduction," pp. 1–7 in P. L. Carrell, J. Devine, and D. E. Eskey, eds., *Interactive Approaches to Second Language Reading*. Cambridge, Eng., and New York: Cambridge Univ. Press.

————. 1988b. "Some Causes of Text-Boundedness and Schema Interference in ESL Reading," pp. 101–13 in P. L. Carrell, J. Devine, and D. E. Eskey, eds. *Interactive Approaches to Second Language Reading*. Cambridge, Eng., and New York: Cambridge Univ. Press.

————. 1989. "Metacognitive Awareness and Second Language Reading." *Modern Language Journal* 72: 121–34.

————, and J. C. Eisterhold. 1983. "Schema Theory and ESL Reading Pedagogy." *TESOL Quarterly* 17: 553–73.

————, B. G. Pharis, and J. C. Liberto. 1989. "Metacognitive Strategy Training for ESL Reading." *TESOL Quarterly* 23: 647–78.

Casanave, Christine P. 1988. "Comprehension Monitoring in ESL Reading: A Neglected Essential." *TESOL Quarterly* 22: 283–302.

Dubin, Fraida, D. E. Eskey, and W. Grabe, eds. 1986. *Teaching Second Language Reading for Academic Purposes*. Reading, MA: Addison-Wesley.

Grellet, Françoise. 1981. *Developing Reading Skills: A Practical Guide to Reading Comprehension Exercises*. Cambridge, Eng.: Cambridge Univ. Press.

Hayes, Edmund. 1988. "Encoding Strategies Used by Native and Non-Native Readers of Chinese Mandarin." *Modern Language Journal* 72: 188–95.

Hinds, J. L. 1983. "Contrastive Rhetoric: Japanese and English." *Text* 3: 183–95.

Horiba, Yukie. 1990. "Narrative Comprehension Processes: A Study of Native and Non-Native Readers of Japanese." *Modern Language Journal* 74: 188–202.

Hosenfeld, Carol, et al. 1981. "Second Language Reading: A Curricular Sequence for Teaching Reading Strategies." *Foreign Language Annals* 14: 415–22.

Kaplan, Robert B. 1966. "Cultural Thought Patterns in Inter-cultural Education." *Language Learning* 16: 1–20. [Reprinted as pp. 399–418 in K. Croft, ed., *Readings on English as a Second Language.* 2nd ed. Cambridge, MA: Winthrop, 1980.]

Kern, Richard G. 1989. "Second Language Reading Strategy Instruction: Its Effects on Comprehension and Word Inference Ability." *Modern Language Journal* 73: 135–49.

Koda, Keiko. 1987. "Cognitive Strategy Transfer in Second Language Reading," pp. 125–44 in J. Devine, P. L. Carrell, and D. E. Eskey, eds., *Research in Reading in English as a Second Language.* Washington, DC: TESOL.

_____. 1989. "The Effects of Transferred Vocabulary Knowledge on the Development of L2 Reading Proficiency." *Foreign Language Annals* 22: 529–40.

Kramsch, Claire J. 1985. "Literary Texts in the Classroom: A Discourse." *Modern Language Journal* 69: 356–66.

Krashen, Stephen D. 1984. *Writing: Research, Theory and Applications.* Oxford: Pergamon Institute of English.

Lee, James F. 1988. "An Input Approach to Reading." Paper presented at the ACTFL Symposium on Teaching Foreign Languages to Adult Professionals, Linthicum, MD.

Munby, John. 1979. "Teaching Intensive Reading Skills," pp. 142–58 in R. Mackay, B. Barkman, and R. R. Jordan, eds., *Reading in a Second Language: Hypotheses, Organization, and Practice.* Rowley, MA: Newbury House.

Nostrand, Howard L. 1989. "Authentic Texts and Cultural Authenticity: An Editorial." *Modern Language Journal* 73,1: 49–52.

Parry, Kate J. 1987. "Reading in a Second Culture," pp. 59–70 in J. Devine, P. L. Carrell, and D. E. Eskey, eds., *Research in Reading in English as a Second Language.* Washington, DC: TESOL.

Rivers, Wilga M. 1981. *Teaching Foreign-Language Skills.* 2d ed. Chicago: Univ. of Chicago Press.

_____, et al. 1988, 1989. *Teaching French / German / Spanish / Hebrew: A Practical Guide.* Lincolnwood, IL: National Textbook Company; Tel Aviv, Israel: University Publishing Projects.

Robinson, F. P. 1962. *Effective Reading.* New York: Harper.

Rumelhart, David E. 1977. "Toward an Interactive Model of Reading," pp. 573–603 in S. Dornic, ed., *Attention and Performance VI.* Hillsdale, NJ: Erlbaum.

_____, J. L. McClelland, and the PDP Research Group. 1986. *Parallel Distributed Processing: Explorations in the Microstructure of Cognition.* 2 vols. Cambridge, MA: MIT Press.

Sarig, Gissi. 1987. "High-Level Reading in the First and in the Foreign Language: Some Comparative Process Data," pp. 107–20 in J. Devine, P. L. Carrell, and D. E. Eskey, eds., *Research in Reading in English as a Second Language.* Washington, DC: TESOL.

Swaffar, Janet K. 1986. "Reading and Cultural Literacy." *The Journal of General Education* 38: 70–84.

_____. 1988. "Readers, Texts, and Second Languages: The Interactive Process." *Modern Language Journal* 72: 123–49.

_____. 1989. "Curricular Issues and Language Research: The Shifting Interaction." *ADFL Bulletin* 20,3: 54–60.

_____, Katherine M. Arens, and Heidi Byrnes. 1991. *Reading for Meaning: An Integrated Approach to Language Learning.* Englewood Cliffs, NJ: Prentice-Hall.

Walker, Galal. 1989. "The Less Commonly Taught Languages in the Context of American Pedagogy," pp. 111–37 in H. S. Lepke, ed., *Shaping the Future: Challenges and Opportunities.* Report of the Northeast Conference on the Teaching of Foreign Languages. Middlebury, VT: The Northeast Conference.

Williams, Ray. 1983. "Teaching the Recognition of Cohesive Ties in Reading a Foreign Language." *Reading in a Foreign Language* 1: 35–53.

6
Languages for Career Support

Judith G. Frommer
Harvard University

INTRODUCTION

This chapter is addressed to three groups: those who teach in an institution with professional programs; those who would like to create a professionally oriented course in their institution; and those who are literature- or humanities-oriented and who need to be convinced of the validity, feasibility, and effectiveness in a college setting of language courses related to careers. In any context, language for career support is a complicated issue involving teacher and student attitudes, teacher and student needs, and the exigencies and expectations of the institution in which one is teaching or studying.

"Languages for career support" usually brings to mind LSP courses, that is, courses in Language for Specific Purposes. In fact, apart from general language courses, too often unimaginatively labeled French I, Spanish II, or German III, all language courses can be interpreted as being for a specific purpose or as preparation for a career: a conversation course has a specific purpose, as do literature courses taught in a foreign language, which are often intended specifically for those who will later teach the second language (L2). In the past, especially in the United States, *specific purpose* and *career* with regard to language have been construed narrowly: The only purpose in learning a language was to read its literature, and the only career associated with the foreign language was teaching. With the shrinking of the globe (jet travel and satellite communications) and the recent emphasis on internationalization in many spheres, the emphasis in foreign-language teaching is changing:

> Leaders in foreign-language education have agreed that the funda-
> mental objective of language learning is the ability to use language in
> meaningful ways, that is, to communicate, and that the teaching of
> communication deals with the ability to interact with people in the
> situations of their respective cultures. (Benevento 185: 16)

While most would acknowledge that this shift in attitude has resulted in an emphasis in language courses on communicative competence and oral proficiency, another effect has been the creation of courses that emphasize not only "communication" but "situation" as well. It is these situationally oriented courses that can be classified as LSP courses and that support preparation for a career other than language teaching. Depending on the career needs of students, certain nonoral courses may also be placed in this category.

JUSTIFICATION FOR LANGUAGE
FOR CAREER SUPPORT

Career-related language and LSP courses merit a place in the college curriculum because they meet the needs of students and provide a legitimate academic content. High priority is given to students' motivations for studying the language, and emphasis (except in the case of nonoral courses) is on communicative competence. Content relevant to the career is stressed and this offers a useful context for language learning. When taught appropriately, LSP courses use authentic documents so that students are brought in contact with the culture of the country or group who speak the language and are involved in "language use" rather than "language usage," that is, purposeful use of the language rather than discussions of language structure (Widdowson 1983: 5,6; 1978: 19).

By definition, language courses for career support meet the students' needs by serving a practical purpose; they can help students to "get ahead" or to do their jobs better. Language can be perceived as either a must or a definite asset to students in future work in a number of fields, either continuously or intermittently, depending on the field and the work location. The advantage is evident to the student who has already obtained a job and knows that a specific foreign language will be indispensable for success, as, for example, when the job is overseas or there is a definite contact with speakers of the second language, through either written or oral communication. It is equally evident for students planning a career in a profession that routinely interacts with immigrant and migrant populations. Since there are nonnative-speaking populations and large numbers of foreign visitors in most of the industrialized nations, anyone coming in contact with these groups will be more productive if he or she can communicate with them.

LSP versus ESP

While LSP and ESP (English for Specific Purposes) are often discussed together and seem theoretically similar in purpose, the apparent lack of appreciation of the importance of foreign-language knowledge as a precondition for employment in the United States creates a significant difference between them. Because of the growing role of English as the de facto *lingua franca* for business, scientific research, information transfer, and travel, learners of English, and especially learners of ESP, generally have greater motivation to become proficient in the language they are learning than do native speakers of English. For those who live and work in bilingual and multilingual countries, such as Canada, Switzerland, Belgium, and other Common Market countries, the necessity of acquiring a certain level of communicative competence or reading ability in at least one foreign language is obvious. While native English speakers may envision a career in which a foreign language will be useful, few of them and few employers have the same sense of exigency felt by speakers of other languages. This difference in potential motivation, along with the generally greater availability of English language materials (because of their domination of the media) means that the situation of ESP courses is somewhat different from that of other LSP courses.

Attitudes in the Business World

Although the main reason for creating courses for career support is to help prepare students for future work, the effect of such courses should not be exaggerated (Rivers 1983: 179). In 1978, a survey of American companies involved in international business found that "language ability, as a criterion for selection of personnel for overseas assignments, is scarcely considered by companies doing business internationally" (Inman 1978: 1). In spite of the fact that much has been written since then about the national need in the United States for improved foreign-language capability, the business world in general still considers language ability as a secondary requirement for employment. As one recent graduate in international business wrote: "The foreign language–international trade major should not underestimate the importance of the business part of the curriculum, because it will probably be on the front end of the job placement; language application will come later" (Sullivan 1987: 194). Students who have taken a course in French, German, or Japanese for business will probably find a future employer more interested in their knowledge of business than in their foreign-language proficiency, even when work with non-English-speakers is involved. A survey of "The Foreign Language Needs of U.S.-Based Corporations" found that "while crosscultural understanding was frequently viewed as important for doing business in a global economy, foreign language skills rarely were considered an essential part of this" (Fixman 1990: 25). It would seem important that the government insist on foreign-language proficiency for its overseas representatives, yet even here ability to use another language is not considered absolutely necessary. Beck observes that although "the Department of State does not require a knowledge of a foreign language as a prerequisite for a foreign service position, it is known that knowledge of a language is often useful" (1987: 184–5). Foreign language, then, while not essential, has the possibility of opening doors in the future, and some employers do include foreign-language ability as a job requirement, especially in the health professions.[1]

General Purposes Served by LSP

The fact that future use of a foreign language is not absolutely certain does not lessen the viability of LSP courses. First, as we will show below, the career implied in "language for career support" need not be exclusively practical, and the foreign language may be considered as a support tool for reading, research, or interviewing in a specific field of study or work in which language proficiency, while not crucial, helps the student to become better informed. A well-designed LSP course that provides students with cultural understanding as well as practical skills will be worthwhile, regardless of the ultimate use to which it will be put. If an LSP course increases students' capacity to communicate effectively, going beyond merely providing them with the lexicon corresponding to their field, then it will be fulfilling larger educational aims, rather than serving only as practical training (Widdowson 1983: 16–20).

Language courses created for career support are an asset to a language program that is interested in producing language-proficient students and in meeting the needs of the entire student body.[2] Because of their content, they attract students who would not enroll in traditional language courses conceived with the language, literature, or civilization major in mind. These students may not have an intrinsic interest in languages as such but see the LSP course as being advantageous in relation to future plans. In other cases, students who would not otherwise consider continuing their language study beyond the beginning or low–intermediate level (often the minimum to fulfill a language requirement) will enroll in these courses because of their interest in the course theme. For business or science majors, a professionally oriented language course may be the carrot that attracts them to the language department to fulfill a humanities requirement or to use up elective credits. The LSP format can also serve to motivate students in requirement courses who, otherwise, would just be sitting out the semester. An LSP course, which literature professors often see as a threat because it takes students from their courses into what they perceive as less intellectual ones, may, by offering students subject matter that interests them, help them to learn the language better and thus stimulate them to go on to more advanced courses in the department at a later date.

Language courses taught from a career perspective offer a natural context for transmitting to students certain types of cultural information that would not be transmitted otherwise (Damen 1987: 92–94), for instance, the attitude in the L2 country to the particular career in question or the appropriate linguistic behavior for situations more likely to occur in the context of the career. Some topics considered culturally insignificant by humanists actually reflect contemporary society as well as, if not better than, classical texts. As one professor of business French has written: "the study of the economy of another country, even at a superficial level, necessitates taking into account numerous cultural aspects" (Dugan 1984: 85). The advertising in a foreign country can tell as much about the customs, mores, and underlying values of a country as many sociological studies (Frommer 1990). Literature courses may help students to learn about universal human values and provide them with language skills for discussions of literature or for philosophical discussion, but even contemporary fiction does not always reflect the current sociocultural contexts within which those interested in active communication need to interact. Furthermore, literature need not be absent from LSP courses, as we will see later on.

Another justification for LSP courses is that their rationale and content correspond to recent thinking in foreign- and second-language pedagogy. For example, language courses for career support that emphasize oral communication generally conform to the oral proficiency model; for these, the general situations of the ACTFL Oral Proficiency Interview can be replaced with professional situations that offer models both for practice and for evaluation of communicative competence (Doyle 1988). In a well-designed LSP course, meaning and context predominate over the teaching of discrete lexical or syntactic items. Relating language to a professional situation that students understand and with which they identify provides them with opportunities for meaningful discourse and enhances retention.

FOCUS OF LSP COURSES

The content of LSP courses is as varied as the interests of the students. By far the largest subset of LSP courses in the United States is foreign languages for business and commerce (Grosse and Voght 1990). These courses are of three types:

1. A basic course in the language of commerce to prepare students for communication in a sales setting; a course such as this would be useful in a business situation when dealing with nonnative customers in one's own country

2. A narrowly conceived course to prepare students for international business in which only the rudiments of the business language are taught

3. A more sophisticated course in which students learn about the business and economic environment of the second-language countries (C2s) and culturally determined ways of conducting negotiations

Other fields for which courses have been created are law enforcement and the health professions, including medicine and social work. Special language courses have also been created in universities with schools of hotel management (as at Cornell and the University of Houston). A perusal of college catalogs in 1990 reveals a number of other professions for which some courses exist, such as journalism, law, agriculture, and engineering. Translation and interpretation are offered in some colleges as a subspecialization for language majors.

Certain languages are associated with specific career orientations: sometimes these are inherent in the profession itself (historically originating in a specific geographical area and therefore linked to the language of the area); or they may be determined by the international relationships within the profession (trading partnerships, for example) or the ethnic composition of the area in which work is envisioned. Thus, in certain areas of the United States a common LSP course is Spanish for Health Professionals, while Language for Business courses are offered in French, German, Spanish, and Japanese. The language for which LSP courses are offered at a particular time depends also on contemporary political events; *glasnost, perestroika,* and the opening up of Eastern Europe in the early 1990s have resulted in an interest in Russian for Business courses, while the reunification of Germany has produced a resurgence in the study of German.

Language for career support need not be exclusively practical: the foreign language may be required for reading, research, interviewing, or interacting in a specific field of study that will lead to a future job or will be ancillary to the professional work itself. This type of course, related to academic disciplines, can facilitate communication with foreign colleagues and support international activity in one's field. For example, a French course based on painting would be useful for students studying art history, and there is one college that offers courses in French and German diction for singers.

Given this emphasis on theme, LSP courses have much in common with the content-based instructional (CBI) approach "in which language proficiency is achieved by shifting the focus of the course from the learning of language *per se* to the learning of subject matter" (Leaver and Styker 1989: 270). An illustration of this relationship is a "First Course in Italian for Students of Architecture" that uses the students' professional interest to teach them enough Italian to profit from a study-abroad program, thus creating a variation of an LSP course: language *through* rather than *for* specific purposes (Persi-Haines 1984). LSP courses have three of the four determinant characteristics of CBI: use of authentic texts, learning of new information; and appropriateness to the specific needs of students. The degree to which the fourth characteristic, subject matter core, will be present depends on the level and format of the course. Like CBI, LSP courses also result in enhanced motivation, confidence, L2 proficiency, and cultural literacy (Leaver and Styker 1989: 270–71). Brinton, Snow, and Wesche (1989) observe that "LSP courses . . . often follow a methodology similar to that of other content-based models in which a major component is experiential language learning in context," but they recognize that, while possessing the advantages of CBI, LSP courses also pay attention to elements of language (p. 7).[3]

Whether intended for an actual work situation or as a tool for understanding work-related material, the objectives of a career-oriented course will determine the aspects of language study to be emphasized—reading, speaking, listening comprehension, or writing. In many cases, oral communication is more important than written skills; for example, oral skills are necessary for interviewing for fieldwork in sociology or anthropology or for journalism. Sometimes, only a reading knowledge of the language is emphasized; this is true of fields in which the language is needed mainly for research, such as political science, philosophy, science, and technology. The language studied also influences the approach: many German for Business courses concentrate on reading, implicitly recognizing that German businesspeople can usually speak English, while Americans doing business with German companies will have to read the German business press and understand correspondence and legal documents.

Specific skill courses may be limited to written expression and reading particularly for bilingual students who, although they speak the L2 fluently, often have little knowledge of its structure and are unable to write it adequately or read it at any level of sophistication. Courses upgrading their skills so that they can perform satisfactorily in positions for bilinguals provide career support even when no specific career is mentioned. On the other hand, there are students whose principal concern is understanding authentic native speech (not a problem for most bilinguals), either transmitted by the media, in professional meetings or in actual conversations. As in bi- or trilingual countries, such as Switzerland, where speaking one's native language in a multilingual situation is acceptable, there are many situations in which it is appropriate to understand the languages used by others, without speaking them oneself. A course stressing listening will be useful for any career that involves extensive participation in international meetings or the summarizing in one's own language of L2 radio or television broadcasts.[4]

Two final remarks should be made about the focus of language courses for career support. First, even when centered on a specific career, many LSP courses provide a broader cultural foundation for language study than is found in what are thought to be more "cultural" (i.e., literature-based) courses. Rather than studying isolated authentic texts, the LSP course presents an environment that gives them meaning, and can, therefore, help students to understand the concepts underlying the culture (Nostrand 1989). For example, in business language courses that go beyond simple business transactions and correspondence, students who are examining the sociocultural and political forces that affect the business environment are in effect studying contemporary society. As mentioned above, when advertising and marketing are studied, the mentality and mores of a country are also analyzed. Although an LSP course is for possible future use, its content should always provide a rewarding educational experience for students by enriching their cultural knowledge.

Secondly, in some cases language study for career support may not necessitate a specific course. For some careers, the best language preparation is a firm foundation in the language and familiarity with social customs, so that one can hold an intelligent, polite social conversation, establishing a congenial relationship prior to a professional interchange. Even if, for the sake of accuracy and for legal protection, one prefers to speak only one's native language in official discussions, a working knowledge of the language and the ability to understand native speakers can prove to be of considerable professional advantage. If a department's basic language offerings, especially at the elementary and intermediate levels, are oriented toward communication, students will acquire a language proficiency that can aid them in any career situation. Ensuring this will mean focusing the so-called "general language courses" on content that stresses discourse strategies and intercultural understanding, placing less emphasis on (but not eliminating) literature and minimizing the study of obscure grammar points.

LEVEL AND FORMAT

The professional career and the language skills appropriate to it, the domains and registers of language involved, and both long-range and immediate student needs will determine the format and level of the LSP course.

Prerequisite Abilities

There are a few reasons why LSP courses should ideally be offered at a second- or third-year level, after students have acquired a firm foundation in the language. First, in cases in which the use of the language in a professional context will follow "breaking-the-ice" exchanges requiring basic social skills and cultural knowledge, a career-oriented course will be more effective if taken after some communication-type courses. Secondly, understanding professional content in the foreign language in speech and writing usually requires an understanding of the fundamental structures of the language. In addition, when the language is more difficult for English speakers (as with Russian or Arabic)[5] or the culture and social customs extremely different from the student's own (e.g., Japanese vs. American), it is important for them to become familiar with normal social usage of the language before learning about the demands of a more restricted context; professionals who cannot conduct an introductory conversation will never find themselves in the situation in which more specialized language is used. Finally, restricting initial language use to LSP content may not cover the full range of the language, which is not a problem after the basics have been learned, but may be stifling or limiting if begun too soon.

Most language professionals concur that language for professional purposes should be introduced at the intermediate or advanced level. According to Rivers: "Like many others, the Council of Europe experts believe that a basic course in the language (a threshold level) is essential before language learners concentrate on more specialized expressions related to their tasks" (1981: 473). While valid, this approach assumes that students will take several years of language study in college, which is an ideal rarely attained in actuality.

Introductory Courses

In the real world of students with other priorities and other requirements, a first-year language course with a professional orientation may be the only alternative to no language course at all. In the case of motivated students who are preparing for an internship or fieldwork during which they will have an immediate use for the language, those who are studying while working at a job using the language, or those who have only one course slot available in their schedule for a language course, it is possible to create a first-year profession-ally oriented course or even a one-semester intensive course. In extension or continuing education divisions, with adults already working at a job for which they have an urgent need to acquire basic language skills, a specialized introductory course is also acceptable. In a situation in which students can take only a minimum number of language courses, training for professional lan-guage use involving a single language skill (oral communication, reading, or writing), can be begun in a first-year language course that is geared specifically to known work-related needs. As with reading-for-information courses, stu-dents' knowledge of the field will facilitate their learning, regardless of the approach involved. Some examples of such professionally oriented courses are the following:

1. A course stressing oral communication skills and cultural mores for law enforcement, medical, and social service personnel who need to be able to ask specific questions and understand the answers to these questions, as well as to recognize how people of a particular culture react in certain circumstances. This type of course is intended for those who work in their native countries with immigrant or migrant groups. Students will need experience in comprehending different varieties of the language (e.g., Puerto Rican vs. Honduran Spanish in New York, or Haitian Creole in Massachusetts). It may be necessary to include some simple writing so that students will understand questions put to them in writing and be able to write simple answers in case the pronuncia-tion and intonation make speech difficult to comprehend. Students may also need to learn to read forms and simple documents and be able to help clients complete these appropriately.

2. A reading course for students studying science or technical subjects, so that they can understand international journals in their discipline; reading-for-information courses, which are not new to the college cur-riculum, are often given to complete beginners. (See also chapter 5.)

3. A course for students planning to work in the travel industry involving all four language skills but restricted to specific tasks. Oral and written communication would emphasize telephone and computer use, letter writing, and form completion. Reading would concentrate on foreign travel schedules and tourist brochures. The course could be extended to include tour guides, with a stronger emphasis on aural comprehen-sion of different varieties of the language.

4. A Language for Business course in which little oral use of the language is envisaged, either because the native speakers of the language

engaged in business mostly speak English or because the student does not plan to work at a level at which personal contact would occur; this course would stress only reading and written communication in the form of letters, memos, faxing, or electronic mail (messaging via computer networks).

Content

Depending on the language and career concerned, it is possible to have a first-year LSP course including all four or selected language skills that would bring a student to a level as high as that attained in a general course. In such a course, all activities would focus on career-related materials. For example, a first-year Spanish course for social workers would include typical units on making acquaintance and talking about one's family and oneself, health, and social provisions for care.

The first-year course with a narrowly defined professional objective is more likely to be found in adult education programs or as an in-house course offered by a company to employees who have an imperative work-related need to know the foreign language. In many areas, companies contract with outreach programs at local colleges for such courses. A good example of this is a French course tailored specifically to the needs of cross-Channel ferry crews, as reported by Ball et al. (1984). Such a course illustrates the difference between "training" and "education" made by Widdowson (1983: 17). According to Widdowson, a training course meets students' objectives, or short-range goals, whereas education satisfies their aims, or long-range goals, which are more general in nature. College-level language courses supporting career preparation should be educationally valuable, rather than narrowly technical, so that they will be worthwhile for the student regardless of the ultimate use to which they may be put.

MATERIALS, ORGANIZATION, AND APPROACH

LSP courses should be designed with both "training" and "education" in mind: In the short term, they should provide students with specific skills necessary for performing well-defined tasks; in the long term, they should give them a linguistic and cultural experience that will be long lasting and as intellectually challenging as other courses in their program.

The quality of a course depends on its syllabus, that is, on the order in which the subject matter is presented and on the materials on which it is based. Whereas the creative teacher of an LSP course can, with experience, prepare a logical and motivating syllabus, obtaining materials is a much more difficult problem.

Textbooks

Textbooks are not plentiful and those that are available do not always correspond to the level and format of a particular LSP course. Since LSP courses are, by definition, specific, they usually do not attract the large numbers of students found in general courses and, while becoming more and more common, they are not yet universally present in departmental programs. Therefore, they represent too small a market to warrant publishing materials in the same quantities as traditional textbooks.

The perfect textbook, if it existed, would probably not be sufficient for most courses intended for career support.

Realia

Authentic contemporary documents and realia are essential to these courses, which are reality-oriented. This emphasis on reality adds to the value of career-oriented courses, but it also creates difficulties. Authentic documents must be obtained from the C2 or the local L2 community, often with the assistance of the embassy or consulates of L2 countries; this can pose a problem for the teacher with no contacts in the L2 country or with no funds to go there. Even when the topic does not seem particularly exotic, such as scientific reading in German, finding suitable up-to-date materials presents a challenge for a teacher in a small college far from an urban center. Teachers accustomed to choosing their materials from textbook publishers' brochures will have to become more aggressive when teaching a career-centered course and seek out their own sources for authentic materials. For Language for Business courses, subsidiaries of foreign companies, or business associations like the Chamber of Commerce, may also be contacted, or even the local government of a city in the L2 country.[6]

Either in the context of professional associations and conferences or informally, LSP teachers should form networks to share the authentic materials that are so essential to their courses, so relatively difficult to obtain, and so unlikely to be distributed by commercial publishers because they appeal to a small market and quickly become outdated.[7]

Audiovisual Materials

Audiovisual materials are even more difficult to obtain than printed matter. While not essential to the more limited types of LSP courses, audiovisual supports are a key element for any course that stresses communication and culture. Authentic listening and viewing documents, such as recorded interviews, films, or television news broadcasts, provide students with cultural details, the fifth dimension that often contains the clues to comprehension (Damen 1987). Audiovisual materials related to the content of the LSP course can supply the comprehensible input that, according to Krashen, is essential for language acquisition (Krashen 1987: 20–30).

Not plentiful for general language courses, useful materials of this type are even rarer for specific purpose courses. If necessary, teachers must be prepared to create their own authentic audiotapes or videotapes, using a tape recorder or camcorder. Without leaving home, they can film or record interviews or actual situations using native informants living locally or visiting their area. It is also possible to film or record simulations of professional conversations, such as a social worker advising a client, and to record lectures by visiting experts.

Simulations and Role-Play

An effort to approximate the authentic is the dominant theme of language courses for career support. Aside from those courses concentrating on preparation for academic research or artistic pursuits, LSP courses are generally anchored in contemporary reality. Therefore, simulations and role-playing in the professional context are suitable classroom activities, with variations determined by the career for which the students are preparing. Future nurses can be placed in situations in which they will have to express sympathy and understanding, whereas future hotel employees will be required to give information about accommodations and sightseeing.

Literature

Notwithstanding the emphasis on contemporary reality in LSP courses and the tendency to consider LSP and literature courses to be mutually exclusive, literature can be included in LSP courses when it is appropriate for the career in question. The context of communication in the L2 country includes attitudes to religion and morality, the structure of society, family and community relations, and the conduct of life in general, information readily available only through fictional representation for many countries. Juxtaposing articles from current periodicals with excerpts from novels or short stories on a similar topic is one way of helping students to relate the factual to the abstract and to expand their horizons.

Field Trips

LSP courses can be structured in nontraditional ways to bring out the specificity of the relationship between the language and the profession or discipline. While most students and teachers associate field trips with pre-college education, this type of activity is most appropriate to LSP courses. Especially in the case of language for health professionals or for business, classes can take place in the professional environment with students observing professionals at work. If there is a local community of L2 speakers, students can do fieldwork in the community by serving as volunteers. In many communities volunteer opportunities exist for help in hospitals, with tutoring, or as legal aids; by helping in this way in bilingual neighborhoods, students will get practice in understanding and speaking the language as well as gaining familiarity with the cultural environment.

Guest Speakers

LSP courses can also be made more lively and more relevant by bringing the field into the classroom. L2 speakers involved in the profession can be invited to speak to students in class. Faculty members who speak foreign languages and who are specialists in the area can be invited as guest speakers.

Preparation for guest lectures requires the same care as any other activity: vocabulary and contextual information are necessary so that the input will be comprehensible. A list of questions can be prepared by the class as a group, each student selecting a question in which he or she is particularly interested to ask at the time of the lecture, in addition to any spontaneous questions that may come to mind later. As a follow-up activity, the class can decide if the prepared questions were answered or side-stepped and discuss what the lecture contributed to their knowledge of the field.

LSP courses can also tap student resources as material for class discussions and activities. Students' previous professional experiences can be integrated into the course, whether they result from part-time or summer jobs in the case of undergraduates or, in the case of adults, from permanent employment.

Case Studies

An approach to Language for Business courses that is novel for language courses but not for business school courses is the case-study format. The case-study method is a holistic approach in which business problems are considered in the context of an actual or realistic company. In courses based on case studies, the class works together to solve problems; the content and order of class discussions is determined by the students' proposed solutions rather than by artificially programed activities and exercises. With the case-study approach, the class can follow a single company throughout a semester or can consider a number of cases involving a variety of problems related to the profession. Although usually associated with business, case studies can be used in other professional areas such as the health professions or law enforcement. This method has the distinct advantage of promoting student interaction in an authentic context. The possibility of using the case-study approach depends, of course, on the availability of case materials, but once having mastered the technique, teachers can develop their own hypothetical cases or reuse ones developed by previous classes.[8]

Alternative Approaches

Language for career support can also be envisioned outside of a traditional single-course structure but within the context of the typical college organization. Since students in a liberal arts college often have diverse career goals, it may be difficult with a small student body to offer an entire course for a specific purpose. One solution is to reserve three or four weeks of the regular semester language course for LSP modules, with classes broken into subgroups formed around different interests. For example, art students could prepare reports on cathedrals or museums, business students on the economy of the L2 country; those interested in the health professions could write and enact a health-related skit.

Another option is individualized instruction, which can be facilitated by combining the use of computerized instructional materials, interactive videodisc, and electronic messaging with personal interviews with an instructor or peer tutor. Internships or fieldwork in the local L2 community, as described above, can be encouraged as independent study projects for course credit, with the students' reports on their experiences taking the place of term papers.[9]

Evaluation

Regardless of the format chosen—separate course, modules in an existing course, or individualized instruction—evaluation of student progress and proficiency cannot be confined to traditional testing procedures. Examinations should be adapted to the purpose of the curriculum, actively involving professional activities. This can mean replacing a conventional "end-of-semester" written examination with an actual task of a professional nature, either performed individually or as part of a group project.

In many cases, students will not have an occasion to use the foreign language professionally immediately after the LSP course or program. Even when they do, their oral use of the language may be sporadic. The course should, therefore, include suggestions to students for reviewing in the future what they have learned in the classroom, or for keeping up with changes in professional vocabulary and practices in the target-language context. Students will retain more if they can have an actual experience in the L2 context to consolidate their learning.

Optimally, LSP courses, and especially those for business and health professionals, should be accompanied by the possibility of an internship program after students have completed the course. Groups of colleges should collaborate in establishing such opportunities, as they do for study-abroad programs.

Given the difficulty of obtaining materials, the nontraditional format of LSP courses, and the outside contacts needed to make the language course really *support* career development, LSP courses demand a considerable time investment by teachers. A course that takes advantage of community resources and uses only current materials needs to be reorganized every year. Before embarking on this path, teachers should realize all that is entailed in creating an LSP course that will offer students a truly educational and professionally valuable experience.

CREATING LSP COURSES

LSP courses, although justifiable academically, are not necessarily appropriate for all departments.

Student Considerations

The first consideration in the creation of an LSP course, or for that matter in the creation of any language course, is the needs of students. As Rivers has expressed it:

First, in all teaching, comes the *student*—the raison d'être of teaching. The teacher needs to consider . . . their objectives in studying the language (to communicate orally, for instance; to read specialized texts; to learn about other peoples and cultures; or to prepare for study abroad) without ignoring the political and social pressures (including career opportunities) that are largely determining their motivation. (Rivers 1987: 5)

The success, both in enrollments and in learning, of a course for a specific purpose will depend on the degree to which its purpose corresponds to students' perceived needs or interests. Thus, a course in Spanish for Health Professionals, which might attract a large number of students in an urban university that awards degrees in nursing and social work, would probably not interest students in a small liberal arts college in an area with few or no Hispanic residents.

Faculty Initiative

It would be an error, however, for faculty to wait until students *request* an LSP course. To a great degree the inclusion of LSP courses in a department's offerings depends as much on faculty attitudes and their openness to nontraditional approaches as on specific student needs. In fact, in a study of French for Business courses in 1985, questionnaire respondents indicated that courses were most often created because of a faculty member's initiative rather than as a result of student petition (Frommer 1985). Likewise, college administrations will often accept new courses that are well received by students and will support or initiate programs of which LSP courses are an integral part if a first course has proved successful.

Institutional Compatibility

The type of institution also affects the extent to which a department's language courses will provide career support, that is, will offer courses for specific subgroups of students. Universities and colleges with undergraduate professional schools or majors—such as business, nursing, or social work—will attract students with more clearly defined goals than liberal arts colleges that offer no specific career training. It should be noted that some liberal arts colleges whose language departments disdain courses for career support, finding them incompatible with the institution's mission, actually offer a business major, as a glance at their course catalogs indicates. Even in colleges that have no formal professional departments, students majoring in economics or planning a career in medicine may well be attracted by courses that speak to their interests rather than those limited in content to a traditional presentation of literature, often at a level beyond their intellectual reach.

Determining the Response in Advance

Whether the initiative for an LSP course stems from the enthusiasm of a faculty member or the decision of a department, it is advisable to consult the students before determining the course level, content, and organization. This can be accomplished by a questionnaire aimed at the target audience in order to ascertain the type of course that will, in fact, appeal to students. If the proposed course is to be at the advanced intermediate level, for instance, students currently in intermediate courses should be asked if they would take the course in question and under what conditions; students in lower-level courses should be asked if such an option would interest them in the future. Positive questionnaire results are especially important when an instructor is soliciting departmental or administrative permission to offer an LSP course.

Preparation and Training

In addition, proposers of an LSP course must prepare materials to support the validity of the course in the academic program of their departments. A proposal for creation of an LSP course should consist of a dossier including the rationale, course description, materials description, target audience, and substantiation in the form of student questionnaire results, plus the *curriculum vitae* of the proposer showing that he or she is already or has a definite plan to become qualified to teach the course. It is also important to show that the LSP course will add to departmental enrollments, rather than merely shifting students from existing courses to the new one.

Perhaps the greatest problem in creating LSP courses and in offering them successfully is in finding adequately prepared teachers. Most foreign-language teachers, trained in either literature or linguistics, do not know another area well enough to teach about it in the L2. Even in a reading course in scientific areas, knowledge of the subject matter in one's native language is necessary to be able to make sense of the material in the L2. In such a case, a teacher fully proficient in the L2 could acquire sufficient knowledge to teach a course by spending a certain amount of time translating scientific articles written for laypeople and obtaining verification of the translations from colleagues in scientific departments. In the case of languages for business, a number of courses are available that have as their specific purpose the retraining of language teachers who have little background in the area; these courses are available in France and in Germany. If the LSP course demands a completely different approach, such as case studies, the qualified teacher must rely on further research and experience to gradually adapt himself or herself to the new context.

Establishment of LSP courses is contingent upon a number of factors. Funds are needed so that traditionally trained language teachers can enroll in workshops and courses to prepare themselves for teaching LSP; this often means traveling to an L2 area or attending conferences or workshops in another region of the teacher's own country. Even when there is a faculty member qualified to teach a given LSP course and interested in doing so, course loads are often too high and budgets too low to allow for an innovative departure from the traditional departmental offerings. Once a well-prepared course with a qualified instructor is instituted, there is still the problem of sufficient student registration to ensure its success. The course may not attract enough students because its "purpose" is too "specific" or because potential students cannot fit a language course into their schedules; if adding a language course means eliminating a course from their professional program, there will be opposition from professors in that program.

Successful Models and Existing Courses

In spite of the difficulty of creating and maintaining LSP courses, there are established courses at both four-year and two-year undergraduate colleges and in graduate schools. In a recent survey based on questionnaires sent to four-year colleges and universities in the United States in 1988, Grosse and Voght (1990) found that more than three hundred institutions offer language courses with a career orientation. Compared with previous studies, the most recent results show that "the number and percent of institutions with LSP have remained about the same over the past five years . . . although the overall number of LSP courses has increased by thirty percent. The number of business LSP courses has increased markedly, particularly in French and German, while most other categories of LSP show a decline" (Grosse and Voght 1990: 37).

There is no set pattern for successful LSP courses, but they seem to share some characteristics. The most successful course has the full support of a department or an administration and is perceived by the students as being required or as a desirable and advantageous elective. This will usually be the case in a college or university that awards undergraduate professional de-grees.[10] At the very least, the department has to be supportive enough to allow a faculty member to teach the LSP course rather than a more conventional and more established course offering. The second desideratum is an innovative and interested instructor who is willing to expend time and energy developing and teaching a course that, even if appreciated by students, will not always be respected by fellow faculty members. Thirdly, the course must correspond to the standards and philosophy of the institution. Finally, the content of the course must appeal to students—a factor that may seem self-evident but that adds further complication, since students' interests and attitudes evolve from year to year. Not only can the students' focus change from economics to science to literature, depending on the ethos of the day (relevance was the watchword of the late sixties, whereas economics acquired growing impor-tance throughout the eighties), the languages preferred for study change from year to year according to international relations. Japan's increasing economic importance has sparked student interest in learning Japanese, as *glasnost* and *perestroika* have aroused interest in Russian. These are languages that students now associate with professional opportunities.

The ideal LSP course would be part of a series of language courses, integrated into a coherent sequence as part of a degree program. While this exists at a few American institutions, the more common type of LSP course is an individual offering, tailored not only to a specific purpose, but also to a specific audience. Therefore, it is difficult to propose a model LSP course, and the teacher who wants to create such a course cannot automatically adopt a course from another institution without adapting it to his or her own academic situation. Nevertheless, as a source of ideas, three courses currently taught in American colleges will be described.

The first is a *German for Business* course, an introduction to the language through readings in business and economics. This course combines English and German in an attempt to give students a familiarity with the structure, vocabulary, and sounds of the language without requiring that they speak it. Business majors are advised to take this elective because it provides exposure to international business, with special attention to Germany, and concentrates on written expression. Much of the reading and writing is in English and the students' skills in these areas are improved, which is why the business department appreciates the course. At the same time, the students are intro-duced to German, particularly the reading of pertinent materials, and many continue, taking the regular first-year course subsequent to the LSP course and performing better in it than the average student. The course, taught by a single dedicated instructor, has institutional support and also increases enrollments in the language department, thus meeting three of the criteria for a successful LSP course.[11]

The second example is a general *French for Business* course, taught at the advanced intermediate level. The syllabus of this course is based on topics and language tasks; vocabulary is thematically organized and grammar is considered as it arises from execution of language tasks, such as correspondence, and from the necessity of understanding reading assignments. While following the evolution of a French company, students read current articles on French economy, business, and politics and acquire a general knowledge of the attitudes, customs, and written and unwritten laws that determine the French business environment and with which a foreigner should be familiar in order to interact effectively in a business situation in France. This type of course provides students with a model for developing a general approach to working in any country and culture different from their own, regardless of the language spoken. Students in this course have the option of taking an examination to obtain the "Certificat de français économique et commercial" given by the Paris Chamber of Commerce (la Chambre de Commerce et d'Industrie de Paris). The success of this course is attributable, at least in part, to the support of the CCIP, which provides training for novice teachers and, through the examination, gives it a quasi-official value in the job market.

The final example is an ESP course that uses the *case study* approach, meeting during the summer session in the framework of an important ESL program that attracts foreign students rather than an immigrant population. Using a variety of cases emphasizing different aspects of business, the course prepares students for attending a North American business school or for working in the North American business world. The course replaces traditional language instruction with total involvement in a variety of case studies. Students are challenged to think independently and to assert themselves in class discussions. Rather than being quizzed on grammar, vocabulary, or comprehension, they must analyze cases and propose solutions; they are not graded on right or wrong answers but on the quality of their oral participation and written work (Dow and Ryan 1987).

CONCLUSION: THE FUTURE FOR LSP COURSES

There is cause for guarded optimism with regard to the future of language courses for career support. Grosse and Voght (1990) use the results of their survey to demonstrate the current health and appraise the future prospects of LSP courses in the following terms: "The large number and variety of LSP courses offered at hundreds of colleges and universities lead us to conclude that applied foreign language and cultural instruction has become a wide-spread and permanent aspect of the curriculum in US higher education" (p. 45). There is, however, no clear-cut indication that LSP courses have taken the country by storm, and several factors suggest a less than secure future.

First, as indicated above, most LSP courses are not created as part of a program or integrated into a definite course sequence, but result from the interest and initiative of a single faculty member. These courses risk extinction (which in some cases has occurred) when and if the faculty member loses interest or retires. Secondly, there are not many institutions, regardless of size, in which LSP courses attract more than forty students per semester, and the majority of course enrollments are closer to twenty.

Whether LSP courses are here to stay or are a passing fancy depends on three factors. As in any discipline, a good course will attract students. LSP courses will survive and prosper if they give students the career preparation they want or simply a good language experience. Such courses could be particularly effective on an introductory level in junior or community colleges, in continuing education, or as a framework for individualized instruction.

Research and studies of LSP courses and their effect on language learning are necessary to establish this area with the same expectation of permanence as language for literature courses. Recognition by the language teaching profession of the validity of LSP and establishment of guidelines and standards would ensure a secure place for LSP courses in language programs. Progress has been made in this direction in at least one area: At least three American universities have recently established a faculty position for the teaching of business French (Elton 1990: 5). In addition, the combination of a business or international trade major with a foreign-language minor is gradu-ally becoming more prevalent. Language departments should work closely with other departments to establish more joint concentrations of this type.

Ultimately, the success of LSP will be decided by the marketplace. The changing balance of world power will probably make it necessary for Ameri-cans who want to work in an international context to learn a foreign language, in spite of the prevalence of English as a *lingua franca*. Recently, the U.S. Secretary of Education, citing the increasing ethnic diversity of the population at large, stated that all teachers should learn a foreign language.[12] Those in positions of power are beginning to realize that there is a national need for language proficiency. When this awareness of the importance of foreign-language knowledge is transformed into a condition for employment, students will want to pursue their language study beyond the minimum needed for passing proficiency examinations or fulfilling requirements; in this case LSP courses will offer an attractive alternative to traditional language study.

NOTES

1. In the *New York Times* employment section of July 15, 1990, three offers for managerial or executive positions asked for foreign-language skills, but three positions specifically mentioning international business and foreign exchange did not require any language ability. In contrast, ten offers for jobs in the category Health Professions listed Spanish as required or a plus, and one mentioned Russian also. On July 23, 1990, two job offers requested a knowledge of Russian, but no other language was mentioned in the general employment section. In contrast, at least 30 percent of job offers appearing in a 1990 summer issue of the French magazine, *L'Express,* required English.

2. Departments interested only in having their language sections prepare students for future literature courses will create and assess their language courses based on other criteria. When literature as an intellectual pursuit is the sole interest of the department, students with a reading knowledge of the target language and some writing ability will be adequately prepared.

3. On the other hand, Krashen, disregarding the variations that can exist among LSP courses, distinguishes between the ESP course that "requires a detailed analysis of the syntax, vocabulary, and discourse of a subfield," and "subject matter teaching [which] focuses only on the topic . . ." (Krashen 1987: 170).

4. For a study by the Council of Europe of 44 categories of adults who need another language, setting out the skills they will need in specific situations and to what degree of proficiency, see J. L. M. Trim, R. Richterich, J. A. van Ek, and D. A. Wilkins, *Systems Development in Adult Language Learning* (Oxford, Eng.: Pergamon, 1980), pp. 68–86.

5. The Foreign Service Institute has established categories of language difficulty based on the number of hours needed for the average language learner to arrive at specific levels of proficiency. (See Appendix B.)

6. The Chambre de Commerce et d'Industrie de Paris (C.C.I.P.) is an excellent source of materials, training, and general assistance and support to teachers of French for Business courses. Their "Valise du Français des Affaires" is available for loan to interested teachers from French Cultural Services offices in the United States.

7. Languages and Communication for World Business and the Professions, the annual conference organized since 1981 by Eastern Michigan University, offers the new LSP instructor an excellent opportunity to learn about the field.

8. For a detailed discussion of the implementation of the case-study method, see Dow and Ryan (1987).

9. Professor Stephen Sadow of Northeastern University (Boston) has supervised such projects.

10. These examples reflect the situation in the United States, which is the one most familiar to the author. It is difficult to generalize to other countries because of the difference between the educational system in the United States and that in most other countries. Since university education in the United States is usually more general than in Europe, students take a more varied course load, and it is not unusual for a student to have taken courses in the humanities while concentrating in science, and vice versa.

For example, this discussion of the language courses taken by undergraduate business majors would be irrelevant in France, where those interested in business go to a business school in which foreign-language study is usually required.

11. This course is taught by Dr. Ross Hall at Northeastern University.

12. Reported in an unsigned article, "Cavazos Asks Bilingualism among Teachers," in the July 6, 1990, edition of the *New York Times,* p. A9.

REFERENCES

Ball, R., et al. 1984. "A Venture in French for Special Purposes." *British Journal of Language Teaching* 22,1: 17–22.

Beck, C. 1987. "Foreign Languages and Careers in Government," pp. 183–89 in S. Spencer, ed., *Foreign Languages and International Trade.* Athens: Univ. of Georgia Press.

Benevento, J. 1985. *Issues and Innovations in Foreign Language Education.* Bloomington, IN: Phi Delta Kappa Education Foundation.

Brinton, D. M., M. A. Snow, and M. B. Wesche. 1989. *Content-Based Second Language Instruction.* New York: Newbury House.

Damen, Louise. 1987. *Culture Learning: The Fifth Dimension in the Language Classroom.* Reading, MA: Addison-Wesley.

Dow, Anne R., and Joseph T. Ryan, Jr. 1987. "Preparing the Student for Professional Interaction," pp. 194–210 in Wilga M. Rivers, ed., *Interactive Language Teaching.* Cambridge, Eng., and New York: Cambridge Univ. Press.

Doyle, M. S. 1988. "Business Spanish: Role Playing for Oral Proficiency," pp. 1094–1108 in Gaston des Harnais, ed., *Proceedings of the Seventh Annual Eastern Michigan University Conference on Languages for Business and the Professions.* Ypsilanti: Eastern Michigan University.

Dugan, J. S. 1984. "Foreign Languages for Business: Career or Culture?" pp. 84–88 in Patricia B. Westphal, ed., *Meeting the Call for Excellence in the Foreign Language Classroom.* Proceedings of the Central States Conference on the Teaching of Foreign Languages. Lincolnwood, IL: National Textbook Company. [EDRS ED 262 646]

Elton, Maurice G. A. 1990. "FFBAIT Questionnaire—Preliminary Report." *French for Business and International Trade* 2: 4–5.

Fixman, Carol S. 1990. "The Foreign Language Needs of U.S.-Based Corporations," pp. 25–46 in R. D. Lambert and S. J. Moore, eds., *Foreign Language in the Workplace.* The Annals of the American Academy of Political and Social Science, vol. 511 (Sept. 1990). Newbury Park, CA: Sage.

Frommer, J. G. 1985. "French Business Courses in American Colleges and Universities: Trends and Prospects," unpublished paper presented at the Conference on

Languages and the Internationalization of Business, École Supérieure de Commerce de Lyon, Lyons, France.

————. 1990. "Le français des affaires: cours de langue, cours de civilisation," pp. 105–22 in André A. Obadia, ed., *Premier colloque international sur l'enseignement du français en Chine: communications choisies.* Burnaby, B.C.: Simon Fraser University.

Grosse, C. Uber, and G. M. Voght. 1990. "Foreign Languages for Business and the Professions at U.S. Colleges and Universities." *Modern Language Journal* 74,1: 36–47.

Inman, M. 1978. *Foreign Languages, English as a Second/Foreign Language, and the U.S. Multinational Corporation.* Arlington, VA: Center for Applied Linguistics.

Krashen, Stephen D. 1987. *Principles and Practice in Second Language Acquisition.* Englewood Cliffs, NJ: Prentice-Hall.

Leaver, B. L., and S. B. Styker. 1989. "Content-Based Instruction for Foreign Language Classrooms." *Foreign Language Annals* 22,3: 269–75.

Nostrand, Howard L. 1989. "Authentic Texts and Cultural Authenticity: An Editorial." *Modern Language Journal* 73,1: 49–52.

Persi-Haines, Claudia. 1984. "Subject Matter as Input for Beginners: A First Course in Italian for Students of Architecture (A Working Paper)," pp. 37–49 in Lynne Young, ed., *Carleton Papers in Applied Language Studies,* vol. 1. Ottawa: Centre for Applied Language Studies, Carleton University.

Rivers, Wilga M. 1981. *Teaching Foreign-Language Skills.* 2d ed. Chicago: Univ. of Chicago Press.

————. 1983. *Speaking in Many Tongues: Essays in Foreign-Language Teaching.* 3d ed. Cambridge, Eng., and New York: Cambridge Univ. Press.

————. 1987. "Interaction as the Key to Teaching Language for Communication," pp. 3–16 in Wilga M. Rivers, ed., *Interactive Language Teaching.* Cambridge, Eng., and New York: Cambridge Univ. Press.

————, ed. 1987. *Interactive Language Teaching.* Cambridge, Eng., and New York: Cambridge Univ. Press.

Sullivan, L. 1987. "Foreign Languages and Careers in Exporting," pp. 190–96 in S. Spencer, ed., *Foreign Languages and International Trade.* Athens: Univ. of Georgia Press.

Widdowson, H. G. 1978. *Teaching Language as Communication.* Oxford, Eng.: Oxford Univ. Press.

————. 1983. *Language Purpose and Language Use.* Oxford, Eng.: Oxford Univ. Press.

7

Technology for Language Learning and Teaching: Designs, Projects, Perspectives

Gilberte Furstenberg and Douglas Morgenstern
MIT

INTRODUCTION

In recent years, foreign-language teachers have been presented with an increasingly large array of tools to enhance their teaching. Textbooks, for a long time the sole instructional aid, are now published with an accompanying assortment of "multimedia" tools, such as individual audiotapes, video packages, and computer programs. Language labs, renamed "language learning centers" or "language resource centers" now boast—besides the ubiquitous audio carrels—video monitors, computer centers, and interactive audio and video workstations. The classroom walls are gradually crumbling as satellite communications, teleconferencing facilities, and networking technology allow direct connections with the outside world, domestic and foreign. Technology, it seems, has made its way into the foreign-language arena!

Yet a closer look reveals that the inroads have been rather slow. The role of technology itself is still not well defined and its efficacy is as yet undemonstrated. Teachers, whose education did not include computer or video literacy, have been generally hesitant to use and experiment with technologies with which they are unfamiliar. Involvement in the field brings uncertain professional rewards. The road ahead is still not clear.

What is already clear, however, is that the future of technology in the foreign-language field is inseparable from a certain number of other larger issues, such as theories of language acquisition, the role of technology in the teaching and learning process, the role of the teacher, and the recognition (or lack thereof) given to language teaching.

THE FIELD OF FOREIGN LANGUAGE LEARNING AND TEACHING: A TWENTY-YEAR TRANSITION

Language teachers, applied linguists, and designers of learning and teaching materials have steadily—but perhaps not systematically—ventured into one another's domains. A common thread is the awareness that the field has been "in transition" for at least two decades. In transition to what? Converging and diverging forces complicate the answer.

Expanding Goals

After the preeminence of oral production, there is renewed attention to reading and listening comprehension. Emphasis on the visual, e.g., gestures and kinesics, now complements concentration on verbal aspects of language learning. The entire role of culture is being reassessed. Since instructional contact time is still limited, the crucial question hinges on synergy: will efforts expended on one skill or area of knowledge resonate and yield positive results with the others? Partial solutions sidestep the question and simply reduce goals and expectations. The standard corpus of linguistic structures required for active mastery is pared down. In order to allow learners to benefit from working with authentic texts, tasks are modified; instead of total comprehension, understanding key elements or the gist is considered sufficient.

Extended Learning

Orientations informed by psycholinguistics and cognitive science concentrate on inward expansion. Affect, motivation, learning styles, learning strategies, reflection, and memory and processing considerations all influence language-learning models. Simultaneously, sociolinguistics and discourse analysis extend outward our conception of the learner. Here attention is focused on a community of learners and interlocutors engaged in turn taking, topic control, negotiation for meaning, and other kinds of interactions in natural and classroom settings.

Process and Product

Some methodologies, techniques, and activities concentrate on learning as a process. Experiential learning, such as that found in role plays, simulations, and projects linking students to living members of the target-language community, as well as activities such as introspective reporting and interlocutor negotiation, are all process-based. In contrast, the standardization and accountability promoted by the proficiency movement in the United States focuses on the endpoint, the product: the student's demonstrable use of the language during a series of measurable performances. Fortunately, convergence of these two axes occurs in an important area: the learning of communicative functions—language for use—has now complemented and in some cases supplanted the treatment of language as a system of grammatical rules and examples.

Control and Creativity

Increased reliance on small-group work implies the relinquishing of teacher control. Relationships among the learners themselves become paramount. At times, error detection and correction become secondary considerations, complicating the eternal accuracy vs. fluency dilemma. The effective integration of group tasks becomes vital to the creatively managed classroom.

TECHNOLOGY AND LANGUAGE LEARNING AND TEACHING: AN OVERVIEW

How does technology fit into the field in this period of transition?

Video: The Privileged Technology

Video is the technology that has made the greatest inroads for several reasons. First, videocassette recorders are affordable and readily accessible. With the proliferation of VCRs in the home, video is a medium with which teachers and students now feel comfortable, and with the increasing emphasis on the communicative approach to language learning—which has stressed the importance of authenticity—video has clearly imposed itself as a privileged pedagogical tool for teaching language within an authentic visual and cultural context.

The market for foreign video programing has mushroomed in the last decade: publishers, realizing the importance of the medium, are all producing, with varying degrees of success, videos to accompany their basic textbooks. Video programs from foreign countries are now widely distributed through specialized vendors and associations such as PICS (Project for International Communications Studies), which buy the rights to television programs abroad (ranging from news broadcasts and commercials to games) and then package these programs for classroom consumption. With satellite dishes continuously receiving programs from all over the world through such organizations as SCOLA (Satellite Communications for Learning Worldwide), foreign-language teachers now have at their disposal an enormous choice of programs they can use at any time.

The question that often arises is what to do with all these video and television programs. Even though every language teacher will agree that video is an ideal medium for "teaching culture," few of us know how to utilize it most effectively for that end. This is understandable, since many programs have not been designed for that purpose. A highly paradoxical situation has resulted, characterized by an overabundance of live, cultural materials and a dearth of pedagogical expertise. The materials are consequently often underutilized or misused.

This situation is being partially remedied by the publication of teachers' guides and students' workbooks that now accompany the videos on the market. (PICS also publishes videos on how to teach with video.) An increasing number of workshops are being offered on the use of video in the language classroom to help teachers make better and more appropriate use of the medium. The situation will never be fully remedied, however, until teachers are trained to better understand and master the power of the image. Visual elements are insufficiently integrated into the comprehension process and often ignored. The very specificity of the medium is thus negated; cross-disciplinary training in the interaction of language and image is an urgent necessity.

While video is mostly employed as a viewing device, it is also a recording device and, as such, it is often effectively used for teacher-training purposes. In-house productions by students are also becoming increasingly prevalent, using the potential of the medium profitably as a vehicle for live communication.

Computers and Foreign Languages

With the advent of the microcomputer came CAI, Computer-Aided (or -Assisted) Instruction. CALI (Computer-Aided Language Instruction) soon followed, and software began to be developed in the early sixties. More recently CALL (Computer-Aided Language Learning) materials have sprung up, reflecting a shift in the field from a teacher-focused approach to a learner-centered one, and accordingly from a view of the computer as mainly a teaching aid to that of the computer as essentially a learning aid.

An examination of the computer software currently available reveals, however, that the majority of programs still consists of text-based tutorials and drill-and-practice activities. The computerized exercises are generally mechanical: unscrambling sentences, cloze exercises, fill-in-the-blanks, multiple choice, and sentence completion. Recently, more diversified software has emerged, ranging from programs designed to improve pronunciation to simulations, games, and problem-solving activities.

The predominance of drill-and-practice software can be explained by the fact that it is the easiest to develop. Most authoring systems permit creation of only these kinds of exercises. And when novice teachers (novice in terms of computer familiarity) become interested in developing their own exercises, they tend to create the kind that is the easiest to implement with the authoring system they are using. Perhaps a more important reason for the prevalence of such software is that they present a format with which foreign-language teachers and developers are already familiar. This is creating a paradoxical situation for the profession. Language teaching has shifted powerfully in the last ten years from a structural approach to a communicative one, where language is no longer seen as a set of linguistic rules but as a dynamic process of interaction. Yet most computer programs developed to date do not, in any way, take into account these new approaches and seem increasingly out of synchrony with newer theories and pedagogical practices.

The fundamental question of what role the computer should play in helping teachers and learners in their task is still unanswered. It is a question many people in the profession are asking themselves, sometimes out of skepticism, sometimes out of genuine interest, but it is a question to which no one really agrees on an answer. Most foreign-language teachers will say that the greatest strength of the computer resides in its role as an ever-patient drill master, which gives undivided and individualized attention and feedback to the learner; it is perfectly suited, therefore, for drill-and-practice tasks. Others fear that reducing the computer to this role will signify its demise, as students will soon lose interest and teachers will become disenchanted with the technology. Still others believe that computers can provide learners with a rich, dynamic environment, suitable for communicatively oriented interaction.

TECHNOLOGY AND PEDAGOGY:
PERSPECTIVES BY ESCHER

> We cannot make ourselves smarter by an act of will; we cannot learn a
> new language as fast as we want. . . . To suggest ways of reconciling the
> software of mind with the hardware of brain is a main goal of this book.
> (Hofstadter 1980: 302)

The art of M. C. Escher (in Hofstadter 1980), replete with maddeningly
gradual transmutations (where do the birds end and the fish begin?) and
disorienting perspectives (multiple stairways without an anchoring center)
offers a metaphorical analogue for the relationship between technological
promise (and practice) and the pedagogical flux alluded to previously. A priori
assumptions at first glance often prove illusory.

A fundamental paradox originates in the fluidity of the technological
environment. Advances in computer technology such as greater portability,
audio and video devices, improved display capabilities (greater size, resolution,
capacity to create visual "windows"), enormous leaps of computational power
and speed, and increased interconnectedness (computer networks, satellite
transmission) sometimes fail to result in the expected correlative improvement
in language-learning materials, e.g., software based on current learning principles. There are so many options, and change occurs so rapidly—often accompanied by software/hardware incompatibility—that teachers, administrators,
and language laboratory designers become ambivalent about taking action.
Motivation to enter the fray at any point is counterbalanced by the desire to
wait until the dust settles and a residual inertia from earlier disenchantments,
particularly with the great expectations for the audio language lab that never
materialized.

The predominance of drill-and-practice software, then, has distorted the
general perception of the capabilities of computers and related media. Other
considerations that add to the difficulty include (1) *Logistical issues* and the
practical aspects that arise from these, e.g., the ability and willingness to
incorporate new materials; (2) *Conceptual issues:* how can technology become
truly integrated into the curriculum and not be marginalized? The latter
concern is related to other issues such as teacher receptivity and training and
availability of innovative quality materials that improve both teaching and
learning; (3) *Professional issues,* such as the degree of career incentive offered
for the development of technologically oriented materials, a factor that can
largely determine who creates software and where it is designed and tested. A
related concern, at least in the United States, derives from the traditional
separation of the practitioner of educational design, usually in the School of

Education, from the language teacher/author–designer or even the applied linguist in the Language Department.

Optimism is justified, however, because of the potential match between current technological capabilities and effective learning and teaching approaches. We will categorize these capabilities by isolating four aspects— *presentational, processing, exploratory* and *communicative*—with the full realization that they are in fact closely interrelated.

Presentation

The linking of text, graphics (static or animated), video (single frames, such as photographs, or full motion) and audio of various kinds (voice, music, ambient sound) in a computer workstation represents an extraordinary advance. Only a few years ago, computers offered text, perhaps accompanied by some graphics and simple bell-and-whistle type sounds. The popularization of Apple Macintosh computers featuring HyperCard and SuperCard has placed this new environment within reach of many developers and end users. Rapid, controlled contact with speech, gesture, expression, movement, ambience, and innumerable cultural phenomena is now possible. Learners can now simulate immersion in an authentic environment (exploration of a document, an encounter with a native speaker, a walk down a street), but instead of listening to simplified dialog, they can confront difficult, otherwise impossible tasks by using powerful tools such as instant repetition of segments, retrieval of earlier scenes, and access to hints and reference tools. *Montevidisco,* the pioneering interactive video program developed at Brigham Young University, was *sui generis* in the early 1980s; it is a sign of the times, however, that a project for popularizing video materials at the University of Iowa, PICS, which began distributing videotapes of foreign broadcasts, now also handles videodisc design for the same programs. Interactive video and multimedia seem particularly appropriate for current language-learning goals. Exclusive use of the target language, implicit rather than explicit incorporation of grammar, correction and corroboration through modeling, and a low-anxiety atmosphere are some of the desirable features of this kind of learning environment (Bush and Crotty 1989).

Processing

Computational processing is vital to language-learning technology in a number of areas. It allows tracking of learner interaction with the program and can be extremely useful for research into the cognitive processes involved in second-language learning (Garrett 1987). At present, processing of the learner's input into the system lags far behind presentational capabilities. We can digitize native speech and store it on a CD or floppy disk; we can do the same with the learner's response, but the program, apart from playing it back, can do nothing with it. Voice recognition systems used to interpret commands for business applications are inadequate for language-learning needs.

The alternative to voice recognition is to process what the learner enters via keyboard and mouse. This kind of processing has taken two paths, one permitting relatively controlled input, the other allowing for more freedom by the program user. Controlled input can consist of menu choices (the dominant mode in much extant software) or highly restrictive pattern matching (such as cloze procedures with a set number of words accepted by the program as appropriate to fill in the blanks).

Pattern matching can also be employed with "natural language" input, with sentences freely composed by the learner. The program designer anticipates particular words or phrases, but instead of including them in overt menu choices, programs them as hidden patterns. The computer recognizes these particular fragments of the input and is able to react, responding with something apparently related to what the learner has just entered. The effectiveness of pattern matching depends on the ingenuity of the design, but since only a portion of the input is processed, much is left to chance.

Freely composed learner input can be analyzed instead of matched to preprogrammed patterns. Here there is some attempt at "comprehension." If the computer can generate effective responses to the learner input, a dialog can ensue. Psycholinguistic objectives (increased motivation) and discourse objectives (practice in conversation management, e.g., staying on topic) might be attained in systems offering artificial intelligence (AI) capabilities.

It must be noted, however, that those who have worked on the design and development of AI-based projects for language learning have encountered daunting challenges (Morgenstern 1986; Jehle 1987). An "intelligent" program must convert the raw input—strings of letters, spaces, and punctuation marks—into lexical and morphological units recognizable by a parser. The parser tries out numerous permutations against hundreds of grammatical rules in an attempt (which may or may not be successful) to come up with a set of syntactic probabilities, that is, one or more surface models of the sentence. Meaning is not merely the sum of the parts of the input, unfortunately. Semantic relationships, reference, ambiguity, assumptions, intentions, indirectness, and real-world knowledge are not necessarily explicit in the words and their arrangement. Partial success has been achieved by researchers in extremely limited domains, e.g., within the constraints of a single, specific topic.

Processing failures can be masked by designs that mimic human discourse strategies. For example, when faced with incomprehensible input by the learner, the computer requests clarification or paraphrase. If this additional input still cannot be processed, the computer takes control of the conversation and switches to another subtopic. It is significant that some AI research in natural-language processing has approached the notion of "comprehension" differently, relying on schemata associated with particular topics and situations instead of on syntactic analysis. If the program sees the word *waiter,* it assumes a restaurant situation, so when the word *tip* appears, it assumes it is a gratuity and not the tip of a pencil, a tip of one's hat, the tip of the iceberg, or advice on a racehorse or Wall Street stock. Perhaps the future for natural-language processing lies with a careful integration of parser-based analysis with the ability to match what essentially are patterns in a highly complex web of associations and rules about real-world knowledge and behavior.

Natural-language processing, it must be noted, has other uses besides the creation of learner–computer dialogs. The Intelligent Workbook, in development as a component of MIT's Athena Foreign Language Learning Project, as applied to learning Spanish, combines a parser with a set of situational/functional tasks. The grammaticality of sentences offered in Spanish by the learner is checked and commented upon, but meaning is ignored; it is up to the learner to compare his or her final text to a stored version created by a native speaker.

Finally, AI is not limited to natural-language processing. Expert systems can offer different benefits to the language learner. Since by nature expert systems focus on content (whether in the field of medicine, history, or art) and not on the message itself, they seem especially compatible with the orientation offered by content-based learning. We are not aware of any computer-assisted language-learning project that has utilized this approach, but we would be surprised if none appears in the near future.

Exploration

Exploration of linear print, audio, and video materials is qualitatively different from that of interactive materials. The exploratory component depends on several elements, notably accessibility and control, guidance, and richness of the environment. These design aspects are themselves related to language-learning variables such as motivation, aptitude, and learning style. Discovery learning, sometimes inefficient in a classroom, can be a viable option in explorationally based software.

Hypertext is the computer-mediated arrangement of multiple text sources into branches and nodes that are interconnected in such a way that users can access them without a preordained sequence. In most setups, screen windows can be formed, modified in size, and moved around so that texts or portions of text from different sources may be viewed simultaneously. In some arrangements, learners can add their own text file nodes to the system for others to explore as well. This system is useful for students to communicate with the instructor and with each other. *Hypermedia* combines text materials with those from visual and audio sources and can be thought of as a multimedia environment where exploration (as opposed to presentation and response) is the normal mode of navigation. *Intermedia,* developed at Brown University in the late 1980s under the IRIS Project, is a networked hypermedia system used for research and courseware development, including that for writing and literary studies. At Harvard University, Gregory Crane is directing the *Perseus* Project, an electronic library for use in learning the classical Greek language and civilization. The data exist as text and as images, the latter stored both on videodisc and on compact disc. This HyperCard-based endeavor will contain 100 megabytes of text, including prose and drama in Greek and English, and will feature a morphological parser for Greek. Users can choose a word from a text source and access a definition as well as a list of other locations where the word appears in the text. A "path editor" allows the user to save a set of locations for a subsequent visit. *Perseus* has been employed for reading and archeology courses at several institutions, including Bowdoin College and St. Olaf's College, and will be evaluated at other test sites. Both the *Intermedia* and *Perseus* prototypes are expected to be models for future large-scale hypermedia projects.

Communication

For our purposes, *communication* refers not to a language-learning method but to the technology-mediated connections and networks among learners and teachers. Hypertext (and hypermedia) can also be approached from the perspective of communication, as opposed to individual exploration. The Educational Online System, developed at MIT by Edward Barrett and James Paradis for writing and composition courses, emphasizes the social dimensions of this medium:

> [A] hypertext is fundamentally a linguistic entity that exists to be manipulated, transformed through a series of collaborative acts either between just one user and the original database (that is, the original programmed structure), or among many users performing various operations upon a central core of texts. . . . The programming structures . . . merely support the larger *hyper-context* of social construction. . . . This

virtual environment of the hypertext is most completely evoked within the larger context of a networked, online environment. . . . As space melts away, the collaborative operations of review and re-visioning are expanded. (Barrett, ed. 1989: xvi. Italics his)

Yet, even without an elaborate hypertext apparatus, networked communication can be highly supportive of language learning and research. For example, the TALK function of the MIT's Athena network allows users to engage in a real-time text conversation. All operations performed on the keyboard by both interlocutors are instantly viewed by both (without the need to press "Return" or "Enter") on a split screen. A program can trace and record all interactions, including deleted segments, and play back the episode exactly as it occurred; a printed hard copy is also available. Several long-distance sessions between one of the authors of this chapter and a series of students— engaging in role play in order to provide data for a separate experiment— permitted a privileged view of learner behavior. Since one could see words appear and be deleted or modified, vocabulary choice, morphology and syntax repair, and even topic management behavior (through cursor movement) became transparent.

Networked communication among learners involved in a common task was the basis for another project: students from two French classes, one at Stanford and the other at Harvard, jointly planned and edited a journal.

ICONS (International Communications and Negotiations Simulations) is a project that plans and implements periodic teleconferencing events. Teams of students at various universities within the United States, and in some sessions in other countries as well, are linked by satellite to a central mainframe at the University of Maryland. Each team represents a specific country and tries to model its probable behavior in responding to text messages that simulate events and crises. The designers maintain that "a whole range of foreign languages are brought to life and used both concurrently and communicatively" (Crookall and Wilkenfeld 1985: 258).

In summary, although much of the available technology-based material is predicated on outdated pedagogical assumptions, this is not always the case. Indeed, the contrary may be true in some instances: pedagogical practice and even theory may not be prepared for the opportunities and challenges offered by technology. This is evident with video-related technology, where the availability of materials is far ahead of research. The extent of learner control inherent in highly interactive multimedia software or hypermedia networks far exceeds what is found even in the most learner-centered classrooms or with the most progressive text and tape materials. The range of design implications of the projects described above and in the next section suggests a truly complex intertwining of technology and learning principles.

TYPES OF FOREIGN LANGUAGE SOFTWARE

There are many categories of software; their design tends to reflect the developers' views about the role and uses of the computer in the foreign-language learning process. Briefly stated, there are four broad categories of software available on the market. The ones mentioned below have been generally considered the best of their kind.

Drills and Tutorials

Most commercially available language software still tends to focus, as mentioned earlier, on drilling vocabulary and grammar at the first-year level. Much of it comes attached to a textbook, some is text-independent. The development of these materials is based upon the view that computer-based materials are most appropriately used for such tasks, thereby freeing class time for more communicative types of tasks. An example of a good available grammar tutorial is Spanish MicroTutor (by Frank A. Dominguez, of the University of North Carolina), which won a Distinguished Software award from NCRIPTAL/EDUCOM in 1989. It is meant to be used outside the classroom and help students develop mastery of Spanish grammar at their own pace (Dominguez 1989).

Materials Focusing on Specific Skills

Among the four skills (speaking, writing, reading comprehension, and listening comprehension), speaking takes an obvious back seat, as there is as yet no available speech-recognition system. Speaking is usually introduced by adding a recording device to the computer, but at present this is always peripheral to the task at hand. It is worth mentioning, however, that a number of Macintosh-based programs have been developed for teaching sound perception and production, such as the one developed for German at the University of Texas at Austin. Listening comprehension, reading comprehension, and writing are the foci of an increasing amount of software, and they tend to reflect the new theoretical and pedagogical approaches for the development of those skills.

The following programs are worthy of specific mention:

For the development of writing

- *Système D,* a French writing program (developed by J. Noblitt, D. F. Sola, and W. J. A. Pet), was the recipient of an NCRIPTAL/ EDUCOM award. Combining a word processor with such reference tools as a dictionary, a grammar section, a vocabulary section, and a list of communicative phrases, it allows students to write compositions at the computer with great accuracy and efficiency. The program does not include an error-analysis component, but rather encourages an exploratory approach to language, as it allows students to delve into any aspect of the language they want or need (Garrett 1988).

- *The Graduated Word-Nest Generator* for intermediate Russian, developed by C. Chvany of MIT and S. Paperno of Cornell, uses the same database design as *Système D*. It helps students establish links between words based on common roots, origins, and meaning (Chvany and Paperno 1990).

- *Hanzi Assistant,* used for learning the Chinese writing system, is a program developed by D. Bantz, Director of the Language Resource Center at Dartmouth College. It includes 3500 characters; pen-stroke and brush-stroke images can be accessed along with audio models for pronunciation. Professor T. Graham of M.I.T. is working with the Dartmouth system (which is Macintosh-database, and therefore easily exportable) to create a Japanese *kanji* database, consisting of 2000 characters. Applications include self-study drills for students and the ability to create *kanji* lessons and handouts for class instruction.

For the development of reading comprehension   Most existing software does not go beyond the multiple-choice or fill-in-the-blank exercise. More noteworthy, however, are those programs that attempt to parallel the new pedagogical approaches to reading and have students do prereading activities, scan texts for the gist, and do text reconstruction. The advent of hypertext has enriched the scope of reading activities by providing the student with additional lexical, structural, and cultural commentary.

For the development of listening comprehension   There is a wide range of programs that interface computers with either audiotapes, video monitors, or even videodiscs, depending on the local equipment resources available. Worth mentioning, because it requires only moderate expenditure and allows a great variety of exercises, is FLIS (Foreign Language Instruction System), developed at Northern Illinois University, which allows any recorded utterance to be played under computer software control. A device called Instavox allows almost instant random access to any audio segment, in conjunction with computer-displayed text and graphics. The audio segments may include hints and cultural notes, as well as feedback messages or slower and more distinctive rerecording of the original natural-language segment. FLIS also includes an authoring system. Some of these programs are drills and tutorials, but the most promising ones are more interactive, such as The Interactive Story, based upon the concept of the "Choose your own adventure" stories, which has the reader adopt the role of one of a set of characters and select alternative paths. The Hyper-Speech, another program worth mentioning, gives students a set of instantly available aids to comprehension. These aids can be accessed at will by the students according to their individual learning styles, thus giving the learner a great degree of control and exploratory power (Henry et al. 1989).

An ambitious approach to improving listening comprehension is exemplified by *interactive video programs,* which will be dealt with later in this chapter, under the heading "Interactive Video."

The programs mentioned above are by no means the only ones that deserve mention. A large number of them are not even well known; having been developed by individual teachers, they are used only in their institutions and will not become commercially available. These were chosen to give us a wider view of the potential of the medium.

Communicatively oriented materials   Recently developed computer-based materials are converging with communicative approaches to foreign-language learning and teaching. This trend comes out of the increasingly shared view that the role of the computer need not be limited to that of a patient tutor, but can and should be able to foster communication in the target language. These programs resolutely stay away from the "wrong—try again" format and from the notion that computers are in control of the student's learning. Instead, they are designed in such a way that the computer's role shifts to that of a partner and a resource. They do not involve learners only in simple linguistic manipulations, but rather engage them in meaningful, interactive tasks, where the focus is decidedly on the contextual use of the language. Among this category of programs are simulations and games. *Juegos Comunicativos* offers text-based activities intended to provide as much communicative practice as possible within the constraints of modestly powered standalone microcomputer environments (Sheppard 1986).

Testing materials   An altogether different area of computer use, and a growing one, is in the area of testing. One of the more promising types of foreign-language computer testing is CAT (Computer-Adaptive Testing), which tailors itself to the individual's level of proficiency. ACTFL is currently working on a prototype of such a test for evaluating reading proficiency, based on the same premises as the Oral Proficiency Interview, that is, that the test should move through several levels of difficulty until the candidate's level of proficiency has been evaluated. Some work has also been done on the development of similar texts for listening comprehension by R. Ariew of the University of Arizona and P. Dunkel of the University of Pennsylvania (Dandonoli 1989).

Keeping informed   One of the main difficulties encountered by teachers is finding out what is available and selecting those types of software that best fit into their course curriculum and teaching approach. CALICO-sponsored publications and conferences have sought to remedy this situation since the early 1980s. Other sources of information on currently available software include: *Foreign Language Annals* (journal of ACTFL), which, in a section under the direction of N. Garrett and R. S. Hart, was the first to recognize this crucial dearth of information and has regularly published since February 1985 a review of available software. The *Modern Language Journal* provides the same service, as does the Newsletter of the Northeast Conference on the Teaching of Foreign Languages. The ERIC Clearing House on Languages and Linguistics, housed at the Center for Applied Linguistics, maintains extensive databases of information for teachers. The *Athelstan Newsletter on Technology and Language Learning,* a quarterly publication edited by M. Barlow and S. Kemmer in La Jolla, California, publishes information on software, authoring systems, projects in development, and announcements of books dealing specifically with technology and language teaching.

Authoring Systems

A large number of foreign-language authoring systems have now been developed to help teachers create their own lessons. They offer a variety of designs, from the very structured to the very open-ended, reflecting the assumptions made by the developers on what tools might be useful for language teachers. Among the best known are Dasher for the Apple II, CALIS for the IBM, MacLang and Private Tutor for the Macintosh, and, of course, HyperCard, which is also designed for other fields. The development of HyperCard by Apple and of subsequent hypertext and hypermedia programs such as Course-Builder (for the Mac), IconAuthor, LinkWay, and HyperTies (for the IBM) has generated strong interest. These systems allow a multidimensional, nonlinear approach to learning, which resembles much more accurately the multidimensional nature of language. They also permit traditional barriers to be transcended: the barriers between the four skills, between the different levels of learners, and between such domains as language and literature, language and history, language and sociolinguistics.

INTERACTIVE VIDEO

Clearly the technology that is generating the greatest level of excitement is interactive video. It is the technology that holds the most fascination and the most promise for both the foreign-language teacher and the foreign-language learner. The best source for video access and storage is currently the 12″ optical videodisc, which offers image durability and clarity, ease of manipulation, and instant random access. Even "level one" discs (those without a computer program to control them) are an invaluable teaching tool, since teachers (using a remote control device) can have instant access to a variety of video scenes. Another natural asset of the technology is that it integrates video, audio, texts, and graphics, thus allowing the learner to be truly immersed in the language and to simultaneously develop listening, viewing, and reading skills. Random-access capabilities allow for an unprecedented degree of interactivity.

It must be noted, however, that the word *interactive* is often used indiscriminately to describe many different forms of interaction. Interactive use can mean anything from simply viewing a scene and performing a series of exercises designed to check comprehension to simulating contact with a character on the screen, affecting the course of a story, and manipulating materials.

Now available are videodiscs that retrofit linear materials, such as full-length foreign feature films or television programs. Some are level one discs, others, such as those developed by PICS, come accompanied by interactive lessons. J. Abercrombie of the University of Pennsylvania has developed software for use with inexpensive discs (Garrett 1991).

Another direction is the development of original video materials, which are then transferred to videodiscs. Costly and difficult to produce well, their instructional value can be superlative, as they have been designed specifically for videodisc use and are based on particular instructional and learning goals. Currently available are

- *A Safe Affair,* a level three Hebrew interactive videodisc program developed by E. Coffin of the University of Michigan, which won a Distinguished Software Award in the 1989 NCRIPTAL/EDUCOM competition and which allows the student to investigate a legal problem.

- *Japanese: The Spoken Language,* a complete Japanese videodisc language course consisting of 250 units of instruction, was developed by E. Jorden at the National Foreign Language Center in Washington, D.C. A level one disc, the goal of which is to teach Japanese language and culture, it allows learners to focus on the simultaneous and dynamic interaction of language and culture.

- *The Language Learning Disc* also deserves special mention. It is a two-sided interactive disc accompanied by five diskettes, developed by J. Rubin, whose goal is to help English-speaking adults "learn how to learn" a foreign language (Rubin 1989).

Some other discs are currently being produced, which have been designed in a truly interactive way, so as to ensure a high degree of interaction between user and machine. At MIT, the Athena Language Learning Project, under the direction of Janet H. Murray, has developed communicative-based interactive video programs for French and Spanish (Murray et al. 1989). One goal of this project is to take full advantage of the inherent power of videodisc technology so as to engage the learner in effective communicative activities. The three discs produced so far are based on original productions that have been designed interactively.

The French videodiscs, developed by G. Furstenberg, include an interactive fiction, *À la Rencontre de Philippe,* and an interactive documentary, *Dans le Quartier St. Gervais,* both available for Macintosh-based video workstations. In *À la Rencontre de Philippe,* students interact with the main character in the film and help him solve his problems, particularly his search for a place to live. In *Dans le Quartier St. Gervais,* students explore on their own a neighborhood of Paris by manipulating video, images, and texts. What is at the core of the design of these two programs is the task in which students are engaged, whether it is solving a problem or creating a documentary of a neighborhood. The intention is to immerse the learners in a completely authentic world, giving them tools and tasks to help them understand and interpret the linguistic and cultural reality around them, so that their role shifts from that of an essentially passive reactor to that of an active and creative participant.

No recuerdo, the Spanish program developed by D. Morgenstern, is a simulation combining interactive fiction with documentary segments shot in Bogotá, Colombia. The disc contains an hour of motion video and audio, with another channel devoted to additional audio narration and conversational fragments organized by topic and communicative function. At key points, several paths permit contact with different events, contradictory perspectives, and multiple endings. All language is authentic native-speaker improvisation within story or topic constraints.

The original design plan of *No recuerdo,* linking the video to student natural-language input, has been postponed in order to deliver a more modest version for the Macintosh. In this implementation, the video content (involving amnesia, flashbacks, romantic intrigue, and science fiction) is accessed by students given the role of reporters, who take notes and exchange messages with their "editors" (simulated by the computer program). Since 1988, portions of *No recuerdo* have been used as comprehension and cultural material for third-semester Spanish courseware. Students who use it evaluate the program as well as the design of the Athena video workstation on which it runs, thus providing input for improvement.

Producing one's own videodiscs is both time-consuming and costly, but the benefits to be derived from the learner's point of view, such as high degree of involvement and motivation, make such a venture a worthwhile alternative to other routes.

DESIGN AND EVALUATION: PRACTICAL CONSIDERATIONS

Educational technological design, a field unfamiliar to most language professionals, is undergoing a paradigm shift, with cognitive theory replacing behaviorism as its base (Hannafin and Rieber 1989). A related phenomenon is the proposed reconsideration of a formerly unchallenged assumption, that instructional technological design should imitate human interaction, i.e., computer programs should try to emulate good teachers (Winn 1989). Most technology-based language-learning materials have not been created to adhere to design theory, although in fact there may be some overlapping; what is intuitively appealing to a designer proceeding *ad hoc* may in fact coincide with formal principles.

An exposition of cognitive theory versus behaviorism is beyond the scope of this chapter. We suggest that those in need of judgment criteria for software examine their own theoretical inclinations and look for certain features in the program that reveal its theoretical base (if such a base exists at all). For example, an emphasis on entertaining graphics with no cultural justification, and on the presence of encouraging feedback, rapid correction, and effective reinforcement indicate behaviorist underpinnings. Key concepts of a cognitive orientation include the following: attention to memory encoding and retrieval; the importance of prior knowledge of context; global "top-down" processing of information by the learner; emphasis on authentic motivation (motivation sufficient for users to return to the program voluntarily after the explicit assignment is fulfilled); and the centrality of metacognition, which obliges users to become aware of their own learning processes.

Other aspects of design that should be considered carefully are (1) text design, (2) graphics design, (3) screen layout, (4) sequencing, and (5) pacing. Note that the last two issues may not be relevant to exploratory, hypertext programs. These aspects can be evaluated only in relation to local needs.

Logistics must also be considered. Is the program to be used individually or can it accommodate small groups, allowing learners to benefit from their own interchanges?

Some programs seem technologically driven; they exist because technology makes them possible. Those most useful for language learning are designed by the inverse process, by adapting the technological environment to learning and teaching needs. Teachers and administrators normally begin with perceived needs. Is the software for instruction to be run by the teacher in a class setting or to be used individually by learners? What is needed—grammar tutorials? a linguistic database to explore? Language-specific needs must also be considered, e.g., the need to learn and use a nonroman script or to read and write vertically or from right to left. In some cases, one will have to consider what nontechnological options are available, such as tutoring by native speakers. (This is a necessity for individualized programs in rarely taught languages, like Turkish.) Perceived needs should not, however, be the absolute limiting factor. Technology can present new opportunities to expand or alter course content and organization. To take an example from outside of academia: Did rock-and-roll performers and producers know that they "needed" music videos and MTV before they were created? Yet they are needed now to fulfill audience expectations and achieve success.

Obsolescence is a concern in the evaluation of software and hardware. Unlike successive editions of textbooks, which change minimally (and whose cost is borne by students), technological modifications can be extremely expensive. Systems are changing so rapidly that to give guidance is difficult.

For example, as of the writing of this chapter (summer 1990), there are two types of interactive video workstations. A one-screen system, which is available only as an experimental prototype, digitizes the analog video signal coming from the laserdisc player and allows it to be shown on a high-resolution computer monitor along with text and graphics. The commercial configuration currently available requires two monitors—a standard video monitor showing what is on the laserdisc and a computer monitor for text, graphics, and perhaps a static digitized "snapshot" in black and white from the laserdisc. The industry has already announced that single-screen systems are in development for the market. One-screen configurations are intuitively appealing, and require less space. Do we wait or go ahead and install currently available systems?

The few suggestions we now offer admittedly are influenced by our own pedagogical orientation and experiences in materials development.

For general purposes, multimedia software with a strong video component should be at the top of the list. Within interactive video, look for (1) cultural authenticity and richness, (2) natural native-speaker behavior, both linguistic and paralinguistic, (3) engaging subject material, whether it is documentary or fictional, (4) design elements that permit deep learner interaction, such as multiple paths, and (5) powerful but unobtrusive help tools.

In other kinds of software, we recommend designs that require more than simple mechanical responses. There should be at least some degree of exploratory learning possible, as well as the kind of stimulation that fosters group work and collaborative effort. Authoring systems that by their nature allow teachers to create software to fit local needs can prove more satisfactory than closed designs, but only if the final product is worth the effort expended.

Finally, bring language learners themselves into the evaluating process; age, interests, reactions to technology and to interactivity, and cultural patterns may make them more or less receptive to particular materials than teachers or administrators.

PREDICTIONS

Research

No issue relating to technology and language learning or instruction will be resolved without increased research. The pioneering CALL study conducted by the Center for Language and Crosscultural Skills (Robinson 1989), which indicated some benefits from meaningful and discovery-oriented exercises, was based on junior high school students using an earlier generation of microcomputers. Additional large-scale experiments are needed, as are small but well-conceived studies such as that of G. Brown (1989) on video and information exchange among learners, and the Penn study by R. Young (1988) on group interaction with computers.

The field of instructional design will experience rapid change, moving toward an open system able to incorporate new knowledge into the design process (Merrill et al. 1990). Inversely, the computer's ability to track students' moves provides us with a formidable asset, as it gives us, for the first time, insights into cognitive learning processes. This provides researchers with a great source of invaluable information that can potentially be fed back into second-language acquisition theory and classroom practice.

Materials

AI-based multimedia may be the most useful type of language-learning software (Underwood 1989), but a less labor-intensive approach to the challenges of Artificial Intelligence must be discovered first; each hour of CAI requires 200–300 hours of professional development, but Intelligent CAI currently requires 1500 hours (Lippert 1989). Technologies in development such as CD-I (Compact Disc–Interactive) and DVI (Digital Video–Interactive) will complement the audio and video laserdisc as effective means of audio and video storage, access, and delivery.

In other areas, spatial and conceptual boundaries will continue to fade; even now some classrooms are designed with enough technological support for their functionality to overlap with that of the language laboratory. Modality divisions (text / computer / audio / video / telephone) will also continue to fade, subsequently blurring the traditional separation between speaking, writing, reading, and listening. For example, digitization will allow smaller workstations to run motion video. These video images will become transmittable just as text and audio are transmitted today via fax and phone. The unsolicited catalogs of software and foreign candy that language teachers now receive by mail will arrive by electronic mail (e-mail) and, in time, by videophone.

People

Current hierarchies and relationships among learners, teachers, and publishers may change. Rather than the authoritative central source of knowledge and practice, some teachers will become courseware designers and adapters, their task being to guide students as much as instruct them. While Open and Distance Learning may save the vestiges of humanism from the cultural fragmentation of the postmodern era (Fox 1989), issues of greater import concern us: In foreign-language departments, anxious novice T.A.'s may well be handed digital video interactive discs on registration day and be expected to plan their courses. Nevertheless, language teachers will *not* be replaced by machines.

CONCLUSION

Need it be said that technology per se will not solve anything? It is only a vehicle and it will be only as good as its design, its methods, its underlying pedagogical principles and its pedagogical applications. Yet, as a tool, it has the power to significantly change the language teaching and learning process if a certain number of requirements are met:

1. If the development and use of foreign-language software is based upon solid theories of language acquisition, is congruent with the new pedagogical approaches, and is built upon the best features of the technology

2. If technology is fully integrated into the curriculum. This will never occur until teachers are really convinced that technology can enhance their teaching. This in turn can happen only when the value of the software available has been demonstrated and more teacher training has focused on the integration of technologies into the teaching and learning process. Otherwise, technology will continue to be seen as an adjunct to be used in the language lab, for and by students only, and its marginality will be perpetuated.

3. If the development of technologically based materials is ultimately recognized as a valid intellectual endeavor, worthy of professional rewards, so that the most talented of our instructors can afford to devote time to this undertaking

REFERENCES

Barrett, E., ed. 1989. *The Society of Text: Hypertext, Hypermedia, and the Social Construction of Information.* Cambridge, MA: MIT Press.

Brown, G. 1989. "Making Sense: The Interaction of Linguistic Expression and Contextual Information." *Applied Linguistics* 10,1: 97–108.

Bush, M. D., and J. Crotty. 1989. "Interactive Videodisc in Language Teaching," pp. 75–95 in Wm. Flint Smith, ed., *Modern Technology in Foreign Language Education: Applications and Projects.* The ACTFL Foreign Language Education Series, vol. 19. Lincolnwood, IL: National Textbook Company.

Chvany, C. V., and S. Paperno. 1990. "Word-Nest Generator." *AATSEEL Newsletter* 32,5: 6–9.

Crookall, D., and J. Wilkenfeld. 1985. "ICONS: Communications Technologies and International Relations." *System* 13,3: 253–58.

Dandonoli, Patricia. 1989. "The ACTFL Computerized Adaptive Test of Foreign Language Reading Proficiency," pp. 291–300 in Wm. Flint Smith, ed., *Modern Technology in Foreign Language Education: Applications and Projects.* The ACTFL Foreign Language Education Series, vol. 19. Lincolnwood, IL: National Textbook Company.

Dominguez, F. A. 1989. "Spanish MicroTutor," pp. 327–31 in Wm. Flint Smith, ed., *Modern Technology in Foreign Language Education: Applications and Projects.* The ACTFL Foreign Language Education Series, vol. 19. Lincolnwood, IL: National Textbook Company.

Fox, S. 1989. "The Production and Distribution of Knowledge through Open and Distance Learning." *Educational and Training Technology International* 26,3: 269–80.

Furstenberg, Gilberte. 1988. "Quand une pédagogie rencontre une technologie." *Le Français dans le monde: Nouvelles technologies et apprentissage des langues,* Août–Septembre, 158–66.

Garrett, Nina. 1987. "A Psycholinguistic Perspective on Grammar and CALL," pp. 169–96 in Wm. Flint Smith, ed., *Modern Media in Foreign Language Education: Theory and Implementation.* The ACTFL Foreign Language Education Series, vol. 18. Lincolnwood, IL: National Textbook Company.

————. 1988. "Computers in Foreign Language Education: Teaching, Learning and Language-Acquisition Research." *ADFL Bulletin* 19,3: 6–12.

————. 1991. "Technology in the Service of Language Learning: Trends and Issues," *Modern Language Journal* 75: 74–101.

Hannafin, M. J., and L. P. Rieber. 1989. "Psychological Foundations of Instructional Design for Emerging Computer-Based Instructional Technologies: Part I." *Educational Technology Research and Development* 37,2: 91–101.

Henry, G. M., J. F. Hartmann, and P. B. Henry. 1987. "Computer-Controlled Random-Access Audio in the Comprehension Approach to Second-Language Learning," *Foreign Language Annals* 20,3: 255–64.

————. 1989. "FLIS: Random-Access Audio and Innovative Lesson Types," pp. 227–33 in Wm. Flint Smith, ed., *Modern Technology in Foreign Language Education: Applications and Projects.* The ACTFL Foreign Language Education Series, vol. 19. Lincolnwood, IL: National Textbook Company.

Hofstadter, D. R. 1980. *Gödel, Escher, Bach: An Eternal Golden Braid.* New York: Vintage.

Jehle, F. 1987. "A Free-Form Dialog Program in Spanish." *CALICO Journal* 5,2: 11–22.

Lippert, R. C. 1989. "Expert Systems: Tutors, Tools and Tutees." *Journal of Computer-Based Instruction* 16,1: 11–19.

Merrill, M., Z. Li, and M. Jones. 1990. "Limitations of First Generation Instructional Design." *Educational Technology* 30,1: 7–11.

Morgenstern, Douglas. 1986. "Simulation, Interactive Fiction and Language Learning: Aspects of the MIT Project." *Bulletin de l'ACLA / Bulletin of the CAAL (Canadian Association of Applied Linguistics)* 8,2: 23–33.

Murray, Janet H., Douglas Morgenstern, and Gilberte Furstenberg. 1989. "The Athena Language Learning Project: Design Issues for the Next Generation of Computer-Based Language-Learning Tools," pp. 97–118 in Wm. Flint Smith, ed., *Modern Technology in Foreign Language Education: Applications and Projects.* The ACTFL Foreign Language Education Series, vol. 19. Lincolnwood, IL: National Textbook Company.

Robinson, Gail L. 1989. "The CLCCS CALL Study: Methods, Error Feedback, Attitudes and Achievement," pp. 119–34 in Wm. Flint Smith, ed., *Modern Technology in Foreign Language Education: Applications and Projects.* The ACTFL Foreign Language Education Series, vol. 19. Lincolnwood, IL: National Textbook Company.

Rubin, Joan. 1989. "LLD: The Language Learning Disc," pp. 269–75 in Wm. Flint Smith, ed., *Modern Technology in Foreign Language Education: Applications and Projects.* The ACTFL Foreign Language Education Series, vol. 19. Lincolnwood, IL: National Textbook Company.

Sheppard, M. 1986. "Juegos Communicativos—A Review." *Foreign Language Annals* 19,4: 333–36.

Underwood, J. H. 1989. "On the Edge: Intelligent CALL in the 1990's." *Computers and the Humanities* 23: 71–84.

Winn, W. 1989. "Toward a Rationale and Theoretical Basis for Educational Technology." *Educational Technology Research and Development* 37,1: 35–46.

Young, R. 1988. "Computer-Assisted Language Learning Conversations: Negotiating an Outcome." *CALICO Journal* 5,3: 65–83.

8
Broadening Our Traditional Boundaries: The Less Commonly Taught and the Truly Foreign Languages

Eleanor H. Jorden
The National Foreign Language Center at The Johns Hopkins University

THE LCTLs AND THE TFLs

There was a time not too long ago when the foreign languages taught in American schools were identified in terms of four varieties—Spanish, French, German, and Other. In the real world, the native speakers of Other comprised most of the world's population and laid claim to most of the world's territory, but foreign-language study usually stayed carefully close to home, limited to the "Big Three." The increase in international involvement and mutual dependence that extends far beyond traditional boundaries, occurring during a period when general interest in foreign-language study has been on the rise, has resulted in dramatic changes in attitudes toward Other: in fact, it is some of the languages within this category that are currently showing the most marked increase in enrollments.

Since interest in languages other than the "Big Three" has grown, we rarely encounter Other as a broad language identification any more. Those formerly lumped in this category are now included in the "less commonly taught languages" (LCTLs). While the least commonly taught languages are easily identified, however, it isn't clear exactly which languages comprise the LCTLs. It is important to note that, regardless of where the line is drawn, this is an administratively motivated designation. More important is the fact that the

LCTLs include among their members languages that present special problems for English speakers because they are not cognate with English. These are the Truly Foreign Languages (TFLs). To add a TFL to a curriculum—whether one that attracts low or one that attracts high enrollments—presents challenges vastly different from those that arise when one adds Dutch or Italian to a curriculum of European languages.

In fact, it is when we come to grips with TFLs that our linguistic chauvinism becomes evident. How many of our most basic assumptions about language stem from the specialized evidence furnished by a closely related set of European languages? With such limited data we assume that number distinctions (singular versus plural), tense distinctions (past, present, future), and pronominal reference distinctions (first, second, and third person) are to be identified as the norm and function similarly in all languages. It is only following the study of TFLs that a different taxonomy for the language universe seems more accurate: The commonly taught, linguistically related languages are no more than a subset of a major unit that also includes the TFLs. While the designation "TFL" is itself chauvinistic—truly foreign for whom?—this broader taxonomy avoids the pitfall of suggesting that the TFL group is somehow strange and beyond the bounds of the normal. Actually, when our analysis extends to cover the significant features of the TFLs adequately, the European languages are still accommodated, of course; but to consider the European languages as generic is contrary to linguistic reality.

Categories of Difficulty

The Foreign Service Institute of the Department of State has defined four categories of foreign languages on the basis of the difficulty they pose for native speakers of English—i.e., the length of time required to achieve comparable, specifically defined levels of proficiency (see Appendix B). It is significant that the most commonly taught languages—Spanish and French—are both Category I languages, both cognate with English and among the easiest for English speakers to learn. The LCTLs, on the other hand, are to be found in all categories, with Category IV, the most difficult, composed entirely of LCTLs that are also TFLs: Japanese, Chinese, Korean, and Arabic.

According to FSI figures, it takes 1320 hours of instruction in a Category IV language to bring a student of average aptitude to a level of proficiency achieved in only 480 hours of instruction in Category I languages. A difference of this kind has important implications for curriculum design. Are students majoring in a TFL to be required simply to take the same number of credit hours as other language majors or are they expected to reach the same level of proficiency? The unfortunate decision in some programs has been to try to say yes to both alternatives, rushing students through materials at a pace that makes internalization and control impossible.

Languages not cognate with English may contrast with English to varying degrees, with those of Category IV most markedly contrastive. These are languages that have phonologic, morphologic, and syntactic features, to say nothing of vocabulary items, not matching up at all with those found in the cognate languages of Europe. What is more, the basic analyses of these languages are still being developed. Whereas word classes, verb tenses, and the pronominal systems of the Big Three have long since been generally agreed upon, the linguistic analyses of the TFLs show no such general agreement.

FOREIGN WRITING SYSTEMS

A further difficulty is encountered in the learning of the writing systems of these Category IV languages. In studying French and Spanish, the learning of reading skills matches well with learning to read English. In contrast, the reading of a Category IV language requires the mastery of a totally new, nonalphabetic writing system.

Japanese, for example, involves the mastery of two syllabaries (of which each symbol represents a syllable with no reference to meaning) and several thousand characters borrowed from Chinese (each one representing pronunciations that have particular meanings). Most characters have at least two pronunciations, one (or more) of which is native to the Japanese language and the other(s) borrowed originally from Chinese. While the various pronunciations usually have related meanings, in any given context only one pronunciation is correct. It is as if we used, for writing English, a symbol X that in isolation was read 'year', but when compounded with a following *-al* or *-ally* was read 'annu-al/ly' and when compounded with a following *-ly* was read 'year-ly'. As basic a character as 人, all of whose readings have meanings related to 'person', is read *hito* 'person' as an independent word, as *-zin* in the compound *nihon-zin* 'Japanese person(s)', as *-nin* in *san-nin* 'three people', and as *-ri* in *huta-ri* 'two people'. Obviously knowledge of the spoken language is an extremely important aid in the development of Japanese reading skills. But even for the fluent speaker, countless hours are required simply to memorize symbols.

For Chinese, multiple readings for characters are not a problem, but many more characters are in current use than for Japanese, for which characters in everyday use have been cut in number to 1945. Korean uses an extremely sophisticated syllabary, but again, for advanced reading, students are required to handle characters which, as for Japanese, were borrowed from Chinese. The Arabic writing system is totally different, not involving characters, but rather a collection of phonologic symbols with complicated rules for arriving at appropriate accompanying vowel sounds depending on the neighboring consonants. In the case of all four languages of Category IV, learning to read presents a further complication, even beyond the difficulties of the spoken language.

BEYOND THE LINGUISTIC CODE: CULTURE

But the linguistic code of noncognate languages—challenging though its mastery may be—is only one part of the difficulty: How these languages are used within their social contexts—the pragmatics—comprises an even greater problem for the learner.

The pairing of language and culture as a course designation, or references to a cultural component within a language course, usually refers to a sampling of aesthetic culture (literature, art, music, etc.), informational culture (facts about the society: What is the population? What is the present form of government? What are the major industries? and so forth), and skill culture (such aspects as cooking, wrapping packages, sawing wood, and the like). The shared characteristic of all these types is that they are consciously learned, by cultural natives as well as foreigners.

But there is another kind of culture, which natives acquire subconsciously as they are socialized within their native society. This deep-level mindset might be called acquired culture in contrast with learned culture, paralleling the distinction between acquired language (one's native spoken language gained outside of awareness) and learned language (a foreign language or a writing system consciously studied).

Acquired culture is the driving force that determines attitudes toward time and space, styles of analysis and interaction, and identification of self, among others, as the determinant of appropriate behavior. Japan, for example, has a culture in which context plays an important role in determining generally approved behavior, including language: In other words, conformity is highly valued and rules and regulations are expected to be followed by the majority. This contrasts with the United States, a culture in which individualism and originality are highly valued: Most Americans resent being called conformists even in situations in which they are in fact conforming. These behavioral and attitudinal features that comprise the native mindset seem so natural and normal to cultural natives that they often mistakenly assume them to be universal human behavior rather than culture-specific.

It is the TFLs, through the striking contrast they provide, that demonstrate the crucial importance of this type of culture for determining appropriate linguistic usage. Rather than language *and* culture, it is language *in* culture that should be our concern, for acquired culture, the deep culture of the native, is the dominant force that drives all behavior, including linguistic behavior.

As suggested above, a taxonomy more representative of reality would show the closely related languages of Europe as a subset of the languages of the world including the TFLs; and every language would be seen as one type of manifestation of acquired culture. Even among the native speakers of the cognate languages of Europe there is variation in acquired culture—not as great as the contrast with TFLs, to be sure, but worthy of much greater attention than is usually directed to it in language programs. The study of TFLs makes evident the crucial importance of the behavioral aspects of culture, which are often ignored when culture is mistakenly identified with only its learned aspects, as is the case for many teachers of foreign languages.

THE TARGET NATIVE INSTRUCTOR AS A REFLECTION OF CULTURE

When foreign-language teachers are themselves native speakers and cultural natives of the language being taught—i.e., target natives—they bring to the classroom the target mindset. The amount of their training in and of their experience with the culture of the learners—the base natives—will affect the degree to which behavior stemming from their native heritage has undergone change, but many target natives continue to follow their native pedagogical paradigm to the letter. Here again the TFLs offer a sharp contrast that suggests that the influence of acquired culture in the language classroom should be carefully examined, even in cases where the differences may be less extreme.

Currently, our own emphasis in foreign-language pedagogy is focused on the learner. The expectation is that the quality and quantity of what the learner learns—the output—should guide our teaching. This requires sophisticated evaluation procedures that measure students' ultimate ability to function meaningfully in the target language. It is not surprising to us when students are vocal in expressing their goals and their reactions to a course curriculum. But imagine cultures in which teachers are recognized as absolute authorities, are expected to transmit knowledge down to their students, are not to be questioned or challenged, and are certainly not subject to evaluation by the learners. What happens when such teachers face a class of American students?

The native paradigm of teachers of Chinese and Japanese, for example, invariably involves strong—if not exclusive—emphasis on the written language. Target natives remember their own schooling, which stressed reading and writing from the beginning, forgetting that they arrived in the first grade already fluent in the language for which they would now learn a written representation. The failure to mark word division, a regular feature of Chinese and Japanese writing, is no problem for native speakers but poses a major hurdle for a learner unfamiliar with the spoken language. And for the foreigner eager to learn to speak and understand as well as to read and write, the downplaying of instruction in the oral language can be extremely annoying. What is more, teaching a spoken language is much more difficult than teaching reading, particularly for native speakers, who acquired their oral competence subconsciously. Without specialized training, they are poorly qualified for the task of *explaining* pronunciation, accent, intonation, pitch, volume, self-correction, amplification, turn-taking, and the like. Having a skill and teaching a skill are very different indeed.

Attitudes toward language in general, and one's native language in particular, reflect one's acquired culture. When target natives insist on teaching foreigners a special variety of their language that is never used by natives, this may not be simple linguistic tampering but rather may be reflecting attitudes of broader cultural significance having to do with territoriality.

Consider this scenario. A class of Americans with experience in the Big Three begins a TFL and expects a rapid move to free conversation practice. The English language and American cultural filters that were in operation when, with considerable success, they experimented intuitively with European languages suddenly are totally useless. Not only is there no guarantee that the lexicon and the morphologic and syntactic patterns they are using are appropriate in the new context, but beyond the linguistic code there is the further question of what message they should be trying to convey in the particular setting within which they are operating.

For many language learners the initial brush with a TFL provides the first insight into what foreign-language learning really is. The widespread notions that vocabulary is the major problem, that the careful, close translation of a conversation in one's base language will produce normal conversation in the target, that "a smile means the same all over the world" must be abandoned. It is only because of the close relationship among the languages of Europe that such attitudes have persisted.

THE TEAM TEACHING APPROACH

For the TFLs, orientation of students to the new language is an absolute requirement, but it is all too often lacking, particularly when instructors are target natives. After all, the target linguistic and cultural behavior is the norm for them, foreign only to the students, and they often do not recognize where and how it is foreign. But such instructors are absolutely essential if students are to have an authentic model, linguistic and cultural, of their target. The solution adopted in some programs is team teaching, an approach that calls for a team of trained target natives and trained base natives who teach the language cooperatively. They complement each other's work, each filling the role that only he or she can fill. The target native concentrates on those parts of the program that actively use the language (the "act" component), with students and teachers interacting in the target language. Base native instructors, on the other hand, who know what it is to learn the target language as a foreign language and who know what it is to be a foreigner in the target culture, talk *about* the target language and culture using the base language (the "fact" component), with emphasis on the challenges of the particular mix created by *this* target and *this* base. Needless to say, many hours of act instruction are required for each hour of fact.

The value of the team becomes particularly obvious in dealing with TFLs. The question is not simply which foreign language is being learned, but also by whom. I am reminded of the difficulty encountered by a Japanese who enrolled in a Dutch course at an American university. The other students were all Americans, many of whom had already studied German. But even without a knowledge of German, the shared knowledge, both linguistic and cultural, was so great that the barest of explanations was sufficient for all except the Japanese, who was constantly baffled. What was lacking was an instructor who understood the specific Japanese-plus-Dutch mix and could provide appropriate explanations. Teaching Chinese to Americans is very different from teaching the same language to Koreans or to Thais or to Finns, even though the target is identical. Again there is the distinct possibility that this fact, so striking in reference to the TFLs, may in fact have relevance for the Big Three.

When a team approach is impossible, that is, when the only instructor or all instructors are either target natives or base natives, compensation for the missing member becomes important. If a target native is lacking, the base native instructor should make available recordings made by native speakers and arrange for class visits by target natives residing in or visiting the area, to provide an opportunity for students to hear and interact with authentic models. Conversely, if the teaching staff includes no base native representation, target native instructors should search out linguistic and cultural explanations appropriate for these particular students, who are not and never will be target natives.

But regardless of the makeup of the staff, the courses in any one language must be organized as a unified program, directed by a manager who guarantees continuity and coordination among the courses, all of which will be taught according to a methodology consistent with a definable philosophy of language instruction. Since the learning of a language involves the cumulative gaining of a skill and the progressive ability to use this skill in interactive ways, anything that destroys continuity, by which each level builds on what was previously learned, is surely counterproductive.

RESIDENCE AND STUDY ABROAD

Given the difficulty of the TFLs and the administrative problems associated with the LCTLs in general, study abroad is frequently offered as a solution. In fact, a widely held notion is that, if not the only way, at least the best, fastest, and easiest way to learn a foreign language is to go to the country where the language is spoken natively. For the TFLs this is far from the truth. There is no question that advanced proficiency in one of these languages does indeed require residence abroad, with serious application to increased acquisition. But rank beginners, who without any orientation assume they can pick up the language simply by living in the target society, encounter many problems. In some cases, virtually none of the foreign language is acquired at all. In many other cases, a special variety of the TFL develops, which has been aptly labeled "abominable fluency." The term is self-explanatory. Uninitiated students proceed by making judgments and generalizations based on their native language, unaware of the fact that the TFL simply does not function in a parallel way.

Another alternative is for the beginner to go abroad and enter a formal language program there. In such cases, students are well advised to check on the efficacy of the native paradigm for teaching the native language as a foreign language, particularly at the beginning level. Is there a tradition of teaching only the written language or of teaching a special prescriptive, used-only-by-foreigners spoken dialect? Are countless nationalities indiscriminately combined in classes to form an impossibly confused base native component? Do the instructors know anything of the students' base language and culture, so that their pedagogy can be relevant and productive? At the advanced level, students are beyond the stage where such considerations become crucial. Using private tutors, they can progress according to their own interests, without the constraints of a lockstep program, only portions of which meet their needs. It is for this level of study that residence abroad is most productive.

ADMINISTRATIVE PROBLEMS WITH THE LCTLS

Administratively, all the LCTLs, including the TFLs, pose three major problems. There is the question of low and fluctuating enrollments, the lack of professional staffs to teach them, and the need for appropriate teaching materials.

Low Enrollments

The enrollment figures that are regularly published are, of course, composite figures for the nation as a whole. But when the foreign-language enrollments at one particular institution are examined, an LCTL may have higher enrollments than even one of the Big Three. Japanese is a case in point. The study of Japanese is currently increasing more rapidly in the United States than that of any other foreign language: almost 45 percent between the years 1983–1986, according to the Modern Language Association's (MLA) survey of colleges and universities. Comparable overall figures for the period following 1986 are not yet available from the MLA, but examination of enrollments in 171 institutions in 1989–90, gathered in an independent, National Foreign Language Center survey, shows an increase of about 70 percent over 1986 enrollments in these same schools. When we take into account the fact that at many schools Japanese enrollments are limited by the administration, thus denying acceptance to many students hoping to study the language, the numbers actually become conservative indicators of the current interest in Japanese language study.

While the total national figure continues to require its designation as an LCTL, this is not true when we look at individual institutions. In some cases the introduction of a Japanese program can attract enrollments that swell so quickly as to require staff additions almost annually. Justified requests for more class hours per week and for smaller class size than for the Big Three, based on the difficulty of the language, are often met with opposition from staffs of entrenched language programs, particularly if they themselves are suffering enrollment shrinkage. The "new kid on the block" may be viewed with suspicion and resentment as a truly foreign LCTL that is being too commonly taught within what has been a traditional, Europe-oriented curriculum.

But these are special cases. Usually, the administrative challenge posed by LCTLs, including TFLs, relates to low and fluctuating enrollments. Can an institution be persuaded to add to its regular faculty an instructor in a language that will attract only a few students at best and, in some years, none at all? Clearly, for most schools the answer is no, unless there is special outside financial support for a particular program.

Some institutions have elected to move to a different learning environment to handle highly fluctuating, low-enrollment languages. For example, the National Association of Self-Instructional Language Programs (NASILP)[1] makes it possible for its member schools to offer a broad range of LCTLs through programs in which students with tapes, textbooks, and a few group contact hours per week with an untrained native speaker, who serves as a resource person, are able to study LCTLs that are not offered on their campus in regular language programs. NASILP headquarters has prepared a number of instructional orientation videos, hosts an annual conference for administrators, and recommends available materials that are particularly appropriate for the NASILP mode. Program quality is maintained through its examination system, whereby instructors in regular, established programs in the languages being offered travel to NASILP schools and administer individual examinations to each student participant. Grades are determined by the visiting examiner.

Individualized instruction is another format that lends itself to the LCTLs. In this mode, students proceed individually at their own pace, using specially designed materials aimed at the learner working alone. An instructor is available for consultation as needed and for evaluation to judge student readiness to progress to more advanced material. With its provision for flexible credit, this format makes it possible to accommodate with minimum staff a range of students unable to meet at regularly scheduled hours or to advance at a prescribed rate.

In step with the rapid development of modern technologies, many new, still experimental approaches to language learning are appearing. Thus far, the hardware has advanced more rapidly than the software. It is the unpredictability of language that will undoubtedly continue to make live teachers irreplaceable for a long time to come, although the routine features of language learning can increasingly be handled by machines. Good computer programs can be used to teach *about* a language and its culture, to introduce a writing system, to provide electronic dictionaries, and to check on comprehension, oral and written. But as long as "conversation" with an interactive computer involves participation by the student only through typed language or matched templates of limited speech, a vital component of language learning, namely speaking, must be provided through other means. Typed responses become even more inappropriate when they involve control of a foreign writing system. If the "conversation" breaks down, is it because the student does not know the appropriate response, or simply does not know how to write it?

Video, with its ability to present the visual image of language in action—including paralinguistic features, gestures, proxemics, and appropriate settings—is a powerful learning tool, provided the linguistic material is natural and the acting and filming are of professional quality. It is particularly useful when the language is a TFL. Television programs produced for target natives serve as useful and interesting teaching material for advanced students, but for the beginner videos must be specially prepared. Their scripting requires professional linguist–language teachers and their production professional actors and technicians.

In spite of the proliferation of these new teaching tools, the usefulness of well-designed audiotapes does not diminish. They provide the learner with a means of developing good pronunciation through careful practice with native models, structural control, and fluency—again, provided the taped material is prepared by experienced professionals and the recorded tapes are themselves of premium quality. Good tapes are particularly important for students of LCTLs, since such students are less apt to have frequent opportunities to meet with native speakers.

The Shortage of Trained Instructors

For the institution that is ready to move into adding an LCTL to its curriculum, the major hurdle is finding an appropriate instructor. The temptation to insist on a native speaker of the target language, even if untrained, is strong, particularly for the TFLs. The assumption seems to be that even for a native speaker to have acquired one of these so-called mysterious, exotic, weird languages is remarkable; who could be better equipped to teach it than the native?

Of course, nothing could be further from the truth. The wife-of-the-local-wrestling-coach syndrome, by which any native speaker who happens to be in the area is hired as an instructor, has resulted in many a tragic course. Nor is experience alone the answer. Experience without training and added linguistic and cultural sophistication can result in no more than a bad teacher's becoming truly good at being bad. The more TF the TFL is, the more the would-be target native instructor requires training in how base natives learn and analyze; what requires explaining and how to explain; how to evaluate; and how to pace, grade, interact with students and colleagues, and so forth.

On the other hand, while even base native instructors who have proficiency in the target language may encounter fewer of these latter problems, again, without training they do not know how to analyze a language or transfer a language skill to students. To know something of a language is very different from knowing how to teach it.

The third category is the target-language specialist in literature or theoretical linguistics, academic disciplines that have little to do with foreign language learning or teaching. While such specialists can make excellent language teachers provided they have relevant training, few have actually studied foreign-language pedagogy. In most cases, their teaching is heavily influenced by the way in which they themselves were taught, often resulting in the preservation of outdated, less effective methodologies.

The pedagogy courses offered in most colleges of education and language departments usually prepare instructors to teach cognate languages, particularly the Big Three and English as a foreign language. The curricula of such courses pay little attention to the acquired culture of target languages or to contrastive pragmatics, so central to the teaching of a TFL. What attention *is* paid to language-specific pedagogy tends to take the form of meetings or workshops of extremely limited duration (three days to a week), which amount to little more than show-and-tell presentations by individuals promoting a broad range of approaches to language teaching. The growing awareness of the critical need for trained TFL teachers is, however, having results. Meaningful programs—particularly summer intensive programs—are beginning to be offered in increasing numbers, in some cases in conjunction with summer intensive language programs.[2] This kind of coordination of teaching and teacher training offers instructor-trainees a unique opportunity to observe directly the results of the training they are receiving.

The Shortage of Appropriate Teaching Materials

It is sometimes suggested that our third problem, the lack of appropriate teaching materials, can also be addressed during summer intensive programs. This suggests one of the "quick and easy" approaches—for example, the preparation of a target-language passage with a glossary, which unfortunately has for so long been the standard format for materials preparation. On countless campuses, such materials are in constant development; it is a cottage industry whose products are rarely used beyond the walls of their production site. We need more than this ad hoc, patched-up process. Many of the LCTLs are lacking well-designed materials even for elementary instruction.

The production of such materials, with accompanying audiotapes and videotapes, workbooks, and computer programs that are linguistically and culturally valid, requires years of work by thoroughly trained and experienced teams of target and base natives. Only materials like these become widely used and stand the test of time. However, working against their production are the lack of specialists in materials preparation for many of the LCTLs and the dearth of financial support for projects and publications relating to the least commonly taught languages. This is a problem that needs special attention.

RELATED AREA STUDIES

When an LCTL does become part of an institution's curriculum, the question of related area studies inevitably arises. For some LCTLs, courses covering the general area will already be in place: for example, within an undergraduate curriculum that offers area courses related to the Big Three, the addition of Dutch, Norwegian, or Portuguese may introduce only the need for a slight expansion of courses that are already being offered. A TFL, however, may be totally lacking in area backup; for some institutions, this very fact gives rise to resistance against offering the language. Concerns over courses in learned culture (the history, anthropology, sociology, literature, and art of the area) with accompanying library requirements weigh heavily on budget makers. Nevertheless, for some TFLs, the area in which they are spoken is of sufficient importance to warrant a new look at budget allocations and the need for major new initiatives. The amazing increase in Japanese language programs, for example, not only in undergraduate colleges and junior colleges, but even at the K–12 level, is a clear reflection of Japan's emergence as an economic power of enormous proportions. This has propelled the demand for well-developed Japanese language and area programs in spite of their expense.

For any individual LCTL not apt to cross over to the more-commonly-taught category, clearly a pyramid of programs will be needed to satisfy national needs. At the broadest, base level will be a number of programs like NASILP that offer courses requiring only a minimal commitment by an institution. At the peak of the pyramid, a limited number of truly comprehensive language programs with appropriate area support—in some cases, even only one—should be developed, to which aspiring specialists will ultimately transfer regardless of where they begin their studies.

CONCLUSION

As we examine LCTL courses and programs throughout the country, we find the worst and the best in foreign-language pedagogy. In too many institutions, instructors with no training in how to teach a language proceed by individually developed methods based on assumptions, intuitions, and myths that have no basis in fact and have never stood up to the test of empirical research. At the other end of the spectrum are the programs taught by trained professionals, whose underlying philosophy, goals, methodology, and classroom techniques are coordinated in the teaching of an organized curriculum, in which everything fits together to produce learners with meaningful competence.

While the LCTLs can create administrative problems insofar as they represent a tremendous multiplicity involving comparatively few learners, the

TFLs within the group furnish the wherewithal for a more objective view of language. We are already beginning to see the mainstreaming of some of the TFLs, particularly Japanese and, to a lesser extent, Chinese, requiring that we come to grips with linguistic and cultural problems never faced in teaching cognate languages. It is the examination of the truly foreign that can suggest a fresh look at the truly familiar: Have assumptions of similarity somehow led us to ignore differences, some of which may be more significant than we realize? And have actual points of similarity among a group of closely related languages led us, without justification, to assume universality? Answers to these questions can lead to improvement in the teaching of all languages.

NOTES

1. The headquarters of NASILP is located at Temple University, TV 022 38, Philadelphia, PA 19122; Dr. John Means, Executive Director.

2. One such program is a nine-week summer intensive training course for target natives on the teaching of Japanese as a foreign language, offered at Bryn Mawr College, under the auspices of the *Exchange: Japan* Program of The Hokkaido International Foundation (U.S. headquarters: Box 3434, Ann Arbor, MI 48106). Each summer, approximately fifty teachers are trained prior to teaching at colleges and universities throughout the U.S. and Canada, where, in most cases, they simultaneously pursue graduate studies leading to a Master's degree. Their summer training includes practice teaching with a group of beginning language students.

REFERENCES

Hall, Edward T., and R. Mildred. 1983. *Hidden Differences: How to Communicate with the Germans.* Hamburg, Ger.: Stern Magazine, Guner & Jahr AG.

————. 1987. *Hidden Differences: Doing Business with the Japanese.* Garden City, NY: Anchor.

Jorden, Eleanor H. 1984. "Language Training *in situ:* The Optimal Option or a Risky Route?" *Publications in East Asian Languages.* Vol. 1. Honolulu: University of Hawaii.

————. 1985. "Japanese Language Education: A New Wave?" *Japan Quarterly* 32,2: 145–50.

————. 1986. "On Teaching Nihongo." *Japan Quarterly* 33,2: 139–47.

————, and A. Ronald Walton. 1987. "Truly Foreign Languages: Instructional Challenges." *Annals of the American Academy of Political and Social Science.* Vol. 490. Newbury Park, CA: Sage.

Walker, Galal. 1989. "The Less Commonly Taught Languages in the Context of American Pedagogy," pp. 111–37 in H. S. Lepke, ed., *Shaping the Future: Opportunities and Challenges*. Report of the Northeast Conference on the Teaching of Foreign Languages. Middlebury, VT: The Northeast Conference.

Walton, A. Ronald. 1989. "Chinese Language Instruction in the United States: Some Reflections on the State of the Art." *Journal of the Chinese Language Teachers' Association* 24: 1–42.

9
Latin and Classics in the College Curriculum: Something New under the Sun

Richard LaFleur
University of Georgia

*A*LL OF US IN LANGUAGE TEACHING WHO HAVE EVER REFLECTED UPON the history of our profession are aware that it has been characterized by shifts and fitful swings of national mood and pedagogical mode, of enrollment peaks and valleys, of challenges varied, to be sure, but unremitting. This has certainly been true of the classical languages as much as of the modern. Ever since the founding of the Boston Latin School in 1635 and of Harvard College the following year—both of them institutions with an almost exclusive academic focus on Greek and Latin—and throughout the next two and a half centuries or so in which classical studies virtually dominated the humanities curriculum, the field has been praised by some as educational panacea and damned by others as the irrelevant puffery of an antidemocratic elite. (For some glimpses of the latest, unlovely round in this affray, see Culham and Edmunds 1989.)

Even at the turn of this century, when both the number and percentage of public schoolers enrolled in Latin classes had risen to all-time highs (over 50 percent of our public secondary school students were taking Latin in 1900—figures for 1890–1978 are reported by Parker 1957 and Hammond and Scebold 1980: 11), debates continued to rage over the value of the discipline, over the methods and materials with which it was taught, and over the position it ought to occupy in the curricula of schools and colleges (West 1917; Reinhold 1984, 1987; LaFleur 1987). As the classics have been valued, and then devalued, throughout this century, enrollments—and the morale of the profession—have risen, and fallen, and risen again (although, in terms of the percentages rather than the raw numbers, the trend until the 1980s was steadily downward). Materials and methods have been revised and revived, packaged and repackaged (viz., book jackets have been artfully redesigned and the pictures within ingeniously shuffled), and invented and reinvented (the "conversational" and oral–aural activities increasingly—and felicitously— popular again in Latin classes of the 1980s and 1990s hark back not just to Oerberg's *Lingua Latina* series of the 1960s but all the way to Roger Williams's experiments with the "direct method" in the seventeenth century; see Advisory Committee 1924: 233–35; Gummere 1963: 60). Thus the position and status of the classical languages have alternately advanced, as with Latin during this past decade and a half, and more often, more precipitously, alas, receded.

My point is certainly not to preach the sermon of *nihil sub sole novum* and thus relativize our prospects in a siren's song to professional inertia. In fact, though I have colleagues who seem to believe (or even to hope!) that the discipline is inexorably doomed (an assemblage of them are represented among the essayists in Culham and Edmunds 1989), it is my own firm sense that the prospects for the classics in American education are sunnier than they have been in quite some time, and that there is much in our thinking and teaching that is both new, or at least wholesomely refreshed, and vigorous. Ed Phinney, past president of the American Classical League (ACL), has aptly referred to the latest chapter in the history of classics in America, from the late 1970s to the present, as a "halcyon period," following the stormy days of the 1960s and early 1970s (Phinney 1987: 2). But, as Phinney would agree, it is as much an axiom of the history of classical studies as it is of meteorology that a calm may precede a storm as well as follow one.

The message of what follows then is neither a call to complacency, nor a doleful (or spiteful) eulogy for the classics, but rather a hale and hearty *carpe diem!* There have been some highly significant advances in classics teaching in recent years. We need to build on those advances, and, in some instances, we need first actually to catch up with them, so rapidly have new or revitalized texts, materials, methods, technologies, and scholarly perspectives on teaching been developing. And with the increased challenges that the academic as well as the fiscal economies of the twenty-first century are certain to present, classicists must become increasingly dedicated, versatile, and aggressive politi-cal animals, in the profoundest Aristotelian sense.

With only the very limited compass of a single chapter in which to survey the many issues of vital importance to the teaching of college classics, what I have to say will be brief and suggestive; readers interested to know more will be assisted by the appended list of references, in which most of the topics touched upon here are elaborated. My choice of topics is also necessarily selective:

while the chapter focuses, like others in the book, upon the undergraduate curriculum, considerable attention is given to the schools, whose teachers our colleges must prepare, whose graduates enter our programs, and with whose objectives and curricula, therefore, our own must articulate, if we are to maximize the effectiveness of our instruction. Some attention is given as well to graduate training, in particular to the preparation of graduate assistants for their responsibilities in teaching undergraduates in our college classes and, ultimately, in their own. Latin figures far more prominently in the chapter than does Greek, partly due (and this is merely an *apologia,* not an *excusatio*) to the limitations of my own experience and specialization, and partly as a reflection of the higher interest and enrollments in Latin in the United States and the more dramatic acceleration of efforts in developing texts, curricula, methods, and technologies for Latin instruction in recent years. Finally, much of the discussion is devoted to classical humanities courses, which occupy an even more significant position in most classics programs than literature and culture courses do in departments of modern languages.

FROM RELEVANCY TO BASICS AND BEYOND

During the late 1980s a flurry of important publications appeared, which scrutinized the role Latin and classics have played in American education, particularly during the past generation, and which offered some prognoses and prescriptions for the future. In 1985 the American Philological Association (APA) contributed a chapter entitled "Current Problems Related to Teaching the Classics" (North 1985) to the volume submitted to Congress in connection with reauthorization of the National Endowment for the Humanities (NEH). Ed Phinney's survey (1987), "The Current Classical Scene in America," was lead article in the autumn 1987 issue of the British *JACT Review.* Phinney's article capture the attention of British classicists alarmed at the displacement of classics from their new National Curriculum (see Janko 1989 and articles in the *JACT Bulletin* and the *JACT Review* from the late 1980s to the present), as did *The Teaching of Latin in American Schools: A Profession in Crisis* (LaFleur, ed. 1987), which discussed the renaissance of interest in Latin that had begun in the United States in the late 1970s, focused on the serious Latin teacher shortage that became one of its unfortunate consequences, and detailed a number of actual and proposed responses to the shortage (see the review by Baldock 1987 and "Editorial" 1987).

Appearing almost immediately afterward were, first, a report by Burns and O'Connor (1987), which presented the recommendations of a joint APA / ACL conference funded by NEH in 1986, dealing with the whole range of

Latin and classics teaching in grades K–12, and then a *Helios* special issue by Santirocco (1987). This contained the proceedings of another 1986 national colloquium, the Wethersfield Conference, entitled "Latin in Today's World," and surveyed the history of Latin teaching and its role in American education. In 1989, a very different "crisis" volume appeared, *Classics: A Discipline and Profession in Crisis?* (Culham and Edmunds 1989); aptly termed by one review "an *olla podrida* of a book in which the gloomy reader can fish for what bits he or she finds appealing or appalling" (Sullivan 1990: 35), the collection's 37 essays peer, some of them through a rather dark and distorted lens, at the current status of classics and sundry issues in teaching, research, and professionalism (or its absence) in, primarily, college- and university-level classics programs.

One major focus of these publications (the Culham and Edmunds volume excepted) and the two national conferences was the resurgence of Latin that had occurred in the United States over the previous decade. Following a decline of nearly 80 percent, from more than 700,000 in 1962 to only about 150,000 in 1976, public secondary school Latin enrollments (in grades 9–12) had risen to approximately 152,000 (1.1 percent of the public secondary school population) in 1978, 170,000 (1.3 percent) in 1982, and 177,000 (1.4 percent) in 1985. College Latin had also dropped from nearly 40,000 in 1965 to about 24,000 in 1977, and then risen slightly and stabilized at just over 25,000 in 1986. College Greek, conversely, after doubling to nearly 26,000 during the period 1960–77, declined steadily to less than 18,000 in 1986. These are unfortunately the latest national figures available, as of this writing: see Dandonoli 1987, Brod 1988, LaFleur 1991, and Appendix 9A to this chapter.

The decline of the 1960s and 1970s had been one manifestation of complex changes in American education and society generally during that period. Mathematics and science became more important than languages, and modern more important than classical, in the face of the "red menace" of the late 1950s and early 1960s. As the decade progressed, language requirements were being dropped by colleges around the country, and during the 1970s even modern-language enrollments were falling sharply (LaFleur 1991). Not surprisingly, Latin, that unloved relic of the ancient past ("first it killed the Romans, and now it's killing me"), held even less appeal for those whose taste for "relevance" dictated the fare served up in the cafeteria-line curricula of those "do-your-own-thing" years. Latin had been dealt another blow when it was dropped from the Catholic liturgy in 1963 and, subsequently, from the college preparatory requirements of many parochial schools (Kovach 1968: 390–92); and during the Vietnam years the Latin curriculum, with its continued emphasis on such texts as Caesar's *Gallic Wars,* drew the enmity of some for seemingly "enshrining the militaristic values of the Roman dictators and emperors"(Phinney 1987: 2). The sluggishness of classicists (despite the efforts of the ACL: Latimer 1968) in developing improved curricula and methods and materials better suited to the changing times also contributed, one should hasten to add, to the language's near demise.

A Profession Mobilized

The reasons for the subsequent renaissance were likewise numerous and many-faceted (see LaFleur, ed. 1987; Phinney 1987, 1989). One important factor was the mobilization of the profession: with ACL and its president Gil Lawall in the lead, APA, the Classical Association of the Middle West and South (CAMWS), and other regional and state classics groups joined forces during the late 1970s under the umbrella of the National Coordinating Office for the Promotion of Latin in the Schools (NCOPLS, now the National Committee for Latin and Greek, NCLG) and undertook a vigorous and enormously successful promotional and networking campaign (Barthelmess 1982). NCLG affiliated with a political action group, the Joint National Committee for Languages, and established an intricate Classics Action Network; state classical associations and newsletters were established or revived; state placement services and committees on teacher training and the promotion of classics were instituted across the country. The ACL's National Latin Exam Committee was set up during this same period (see National Latin Exam 1984–85), and with its energetic publicity campaigns has increased participation from 9,000 in 1978 to over 71,000 in 1990 (Appendix 9A).

New Texts and Materials

Both cause and effect of Latin's continuing renewal, new and livelier classroom materials have been developed, including most notably the North American revisions of the Scottish *Ecce Romani* textbook series (Lawall et al. 1984–90) and the British *Cambridge Latin Course* (*CLC,* Phinney, ed. 1988–89). Other new materials proliferated as the 1980s progressed, not least a variety of computer software programs, whose growing importance to the classroom (as well as for research) prompted the institution of ACL and APA standing committees, several new publications on computer applications for classics, and the introduction in 1989 of a new computer department, "Random Access," in the ACL's journal, *The Classical Outlook.* As part of a project developed by the American Council on the Teaching of Foreign Languages (ACTFL) and funded by the U.S. Department of Education, a committee compiled exhaustive annotated lists of textbooks, computer software, audiovisuals, and other resources for the teaching of both Greek and Latin published between 1975 and 1988 (Lawall et al. 1988a, supplemented by the periodic textbook and audiovisual surveys in *The Classical World*).

Back to Basics: Back to Latin

The Back to Basics movement of the 1970s was unquestionably also a major factor in Latin's comeback. With our high-schoolers' SAT scores and other indicators of verbal and general academic competence in steady decline, the broad dissemination, ultimately in the popular media, of persuasive reports on the positive correlation between Latin study and improved English verbal skills in students from the elementary grades through the college level captured the public's attention (Masciantonio 1977; Mavrogenes 1977, 1987; Sussman 1978; Lehr 1979; Wiley 1984–85). Particularly successful and well-publicized were the Foreign Language in the Elementary Schools (FLES) Latin programs established during the 1970s in Washington, Indianapolis, Philadelphia, and Los Angeles (the last two still flourishing), in which youngsters studying the language for only 20 minutes a day, three times a week, consistently demonstrated significant gains in English vocabulary and reading comprehension. An NEH-funded program of the early 1980s, the Latin Cornerstone Project in New York City (Polsky 1986, 1987), led ultimately to the publication in 1987 of the first textbooks available from a major publisher for elementary school Latin, Longman's *First Latin* by Marion Polsky, materials that have contributed substantially to a revitalization and expansion of FLES Latin around the country. Polsky's *First Latin,* David Florian's *Phenomenon of Language* (newly revised in 1990), and the *CLC* and *Ecce* texts are also being used increasingly in middle school programs (grades 6–8), where enrollments in language exploratory courses involving Latin likewise seem to be on the upswing (Strasheim 1983, 1990). Other NEH-funded programs of the late 1980s, including summer institutes on Homer's *Odyssey,* Vergil's *Aeneid,* and Ovid's *Metamorphoses* for elementary school teachers, have further boosted interest in the classics in the lower grades and were a major stimulus to organizing the Elementary Teachers of Classics, a new ACL subgroup, and their journal *Prima.*

    Publicity these programs have received nationally continues to have very positive consequences for Latin and classics, keeping before the public's eye the valuable cultural, historical, and literary perspectives as well as the language-building skills that Latin and classical studies can impart to our students. (See most recently Germani 1990; Goode 1990; Hakim 1990; Mydens 1990.) The Latin/English learning-transfer phenomenon in particular remains, despite occasional protestations (e.g., Strasheim 1990; Wyatt 1990), a compelling argument for Latin at all levels, whether in discussions with pragmatic officials in government and education or with practical-minded students and their parents. The Latin-Spanish connection, it might be added, has also been useful in demonstrating the value of Latin in school districts like Los Angeles and Miami with large Hispanic populations (Baca et al. 1979). As Hispanics constitute the most rapidly growing minority in the United States, this factor warrants closer attention in the future, when we may hope to see school and even college texts and materials that build upon the myriad connections that exist between the Latin and Spanish (and other Romance) languages and cultures.

The Carter Commission and the Classics

Latin has benefitted too from the exhortation to increase foreign-language and international studies generally, issued first in the Carter Commission report, *Strength through Wisdom* (President's Commission 1979), and subsequently repeated in *A Nation at Risk* (National Commission 1983) and other national education reports of the 1980s (see Lawall 1980; LaBouve et al. 1982). The down side to the subsequent rehabilitation of foreign-language study and the restoration of foreign-language requirements in the United States over the past decade is that the phenomenon has been motivated more by political and economic considerations than by humanistic ones. As one consequence, the less commonly taught languages such as Japanese, Chinese, Arabic, and Russian are gaining a stronger foothold in schools and colleges (Draper 1989), a felicitous development in and of itself, but, given the inevitable constraints of time and budget, one that presents Latin again with the risk of being crowded out of schedules and budgets.

Although there have been continuing increases in both national Junior Classical League memberships and participation in the National Latin Exam (Appendix 9A), there are some indications that the upward trend in secondary school Latin has slowed since the 1985 ACTFL enrollment survey (see Kitchell et al. 1989: 137–38). The rise of the less commonly taught and the other "strategically and economically practical" languages is very likely a factor in the flattening growth (as is the complex of problems associated with the Latin teacher shortage, an issue addressed later in this chapter). The grievously weakened status of Latin and classics under the new National Curriculum in England, a society so long a bastion of the classics, should serve as a reminder of the vulnerability of the discipline and of the imperative for ensuring the viability and vitality of the classical languages, alongside the modern, from the elementary grades straight through to the doctoral seminar. The case can and must be made for the role of the classics in "multicultural, global education," as the framers of the 1989 ACTFL statement on the classics have asserted (see

Abbott 1991 and Appendix 9A to this article), and here the challenge of the 1990s and beyond is for ever closer cooperation with colleagues in the modern languages and in the colleges and state departments of education.

Classics and the
General Studies Curriculum

The typical undergraduate classics program consists of general studies courses for lower-division (freshman–sophomore) students and advanced courses for minors and majors. General studies offerings ordinarily include a variety of classical humanities or "classics in translation" courses, as well as the elementary–intermediate Latin and Greek sequences, which until the 1960s comprised its content almost exclusively. While not wishing to preach for the "cult of philology" (Bernal 1989: 68), I should think that most classicists still regard the elementary to intermediate Greek and Latin sequences as being at the heart of our departmental offerings. With the growth in high school Latin, greater numbers of students are entering college with two or more years of the language and more freshmen are enrolling in advanced courses; nevertheless, the elementary classes remain a vital offering for most classics departments, enrolling hundreds of students per term in the larger universities and constituting potentially the single most important pool of prospective majors.

The "Quick-Fix Mentality" and the Rise of the LCTs

While the renaissance of Latin at the secondary level assuredly has had a salutary effect on college programs, the impact has not proven as significant as one might have expected. Throughout the 1970s and up to 1986 at least, overall college Latin enrollments remained fairly steady. It seems clear that while some departments were gaining ground, others were losing it; there was certainly no enrollment growth of the proportions that were seen in the schools. One factor has been the "quick-fix" mentality: increasing numbers of students have enrolled for two years of Latin in high school, but a great many of these have felt that "two years is enough," and so prospective college enrollments have been lost. Growing interest in the less commonly taught languages (and renewed interest in German, with the phoenix of a reunified Germany on the rise) seems to be having an impact on Latin in college, as well as in the schools, exerting a pressure that is almost certain to intensify as we move into the twenty-first century.

School–College Articulation and Curriculum Goals

School–college articulation—or rather the lack of it—has also had a limiting effect on college Latin. Though the problems are not as severe as with the modern languages, where bright high school graduates with four years of proficiency-based training frequently have very negative experiences at college with traditional placement exams and grammar / literature-oriented curricula, we most certainly do need to improve the situation for Latin. College classicists need to be far more aware of what is taught in the schools, of what methods and materials are used, and why. They need to be more involved in the development of curriculum generally and in coordinating their own curricula with those of the schools, so that a strong student with three years of high school Latin will be able to progress directly and with reasonable facility into a fourth-semester college course. Classics departments should familiarize themselves with the Latin Achievement Test and the Advanced Placement exams, establish their own institutional norms for these tests, employ them for advanced placement and course credit, and communicate this information to the schools. The College Board, for its part, needs to continue its efforts to improve these exams and accommodate them to curricular change.

The challenge of articulation is an enormous one, as texts and methodologies are changing, placement tests need further revision, and, a consequence of our national aversion to standardization, no standard national curriculum for Latin exists. Although any curricular guidelines we establish should be flexible and free of connections to particular textbooks or methodologies, we need to catch up with our colleagues in the modern languages and design national proficiency guidelines for Latin posthaste. The ACL / APA Joint Committee on Classics in American Education, organized in 1988, has already made important progress in this direction and has plans for publishing a full report on this issue. A general agreement on the principles and goals such a curriculum should reflect can be seen in the recommendations of the 1989 ACTFL position paper (see Appendix 9B below) and in the 1990 statement on curriculum goals for Latin and Greek in the schools and colleges published by the Classical Association of New England (see CANE; Appendix 9C). An admirable model already exists in the New York syllabus, *Latin for Communication* (see Gascoyne 1986), which describes general proficiency levels for the language and specifies learner outcomes associated with each.

Recruitment and Requirements

A strong program of outreach, collaboration, and articulation with the schools is one important means of attracting students into our lower-division programs. Recruitment efforts even more obviously should focus on the freshman and sophomore students already on campus and, just as importantly, on their advisors. Meetings during orientation with student groups and annually with lower-division advisors, and the regular distribution of fliers and other promotional materials (available from the ACL's Teaching Materials and Resource Center), can be especially effective. If the institution lacks foreign-language admissions and graduation requirements, established or reinstated by increasing numbers of colleges in recent years (Brod and Lapointe 1989; Draper 1989), classicists should collaborate with their modern-language colleagues to lobby for their introduction, as a means of both strengthening the college's degree programs and encouraging student enrollment.

"A teacher affects eternity" (Henry Brooks Adams)—And So What Do We Do with TA's?

The most effective recruiting device, quite obviously, is a strong instructional program, and this means, above all, that instructors assigned to teach the elementary–intermediate sequence should be highly competent and committed. Ideally these classes, with a limit of 25–30 students, should be assigned to senior faculty, or to junior faculty only after thorough orientation and with an ongoing program of mentoring. Where the economics of a graduate program mandate the use of teaching assistants, the first recourse should be to employ them in a supporting role, as proctors, graders, or tutors or to lead drill and review sessions.

Where graduate assistants are to be given sole responsibility for their own classes, the department should provide and require (for course credit) structured teaching apprenticeships involving extensive observations, formal instruction and discussions on methodology, and group-monitored practice teaching. (See Azevedo 1990; Waldinger 1990.) Once the teaching assistant has been assigned his or her own class, regular observations and mentoring should continue. The graduate coordinator may be responsible for directing the apprenticeship, or, in larger departments, the task may fall to a director of the elementary language program (as, for example, at the University of North Carolina at Chapel Hill, where program director Cecil Wooten has authored comprehensive handbooks for in-house distribution to graduate assistants teaching elementary Latin).

Texts and Materials

Besides assigning our most competent faculty, not our least, to teach the elementary language courses, and abandoning laissez-faire policies in the supervision of graduate assistants, classics departments need to pay increasing attention to developments in methods and materials for elementary language teaching. In general, there has been more innovation in the schools over the past decade than in the colleges. While traditional grammar-translation texts like *Latin for Americans* (Ullman et al. 1965) and the Jenney series (Jenney et al. 1990, recently revised, but not altogether happily received: see Howard and Montross 1990–91) are still widely used in the schools, there has been a steady increase in adoptions of such grammar-in-context primers as *Ecce Romani* and the *CLC,* which employ the sort of four-skills approach to language teaching encouraged in the ACTFL and CANE position papers and the Burns-O'Connor report (for descriptions of the texts, see Phinney 1981b; Palma 1984–85).

From the very opening chapters these texts emphasize oral reading and listening skills and include Latin comprehension and *responde Latine* questions. While classes are generally not conducted exclusively in Latin, and the texts do incorporate a variety of supplementary exercises and cultural material in English (unlike the Englishless *Lingua Latina* texts, which enjoyed more limited popularity during the 1960s and 1970s [Oerberg 1965]), conversational and other oral–aural activities are regularly included and encouraged and can be readily supplemented by TPR—total physical response—exercises that build on students' right-brain, kinetic learning skills and make for a livelier classroom environment (Salerno 1987). Morphology and rules of syntax are introduced more gradually than in traditional courses, although many teachers supplement the texts with their own more formal, accelerated instruction in grammar. Students trained in these more inductive programs appear to develop strong reading comprehension skills sooner than those using traditional texts. As important, the readings in *Ecce, CLC,* and similar programs focus on interesting and significant *realia* of Roman culture, daily life, and politics; they even include some unadapted classical Latin, both prose and verse, and such "authentic materials" as graffiti and funerary inscriptions— another emphasis that, like the use of TPR and the four-skills approach, has been influenced by the modern-language classroom (Strasheim 1982–83).

Some college faculties are beginning to adopt these newer texts: the University of Massachusetts has used the *CLC* with considerable success (Phinney 1980), for example, and both Richland College, a two-year Dallas County community college, in its innovative "Classics Cluster Project" (Pascal 1988–89), and the University of Maryland have employed *Ecce* with good results. Whichever textbook is used, however, a great deal more ought to be done with listening, speaking, and reading comprehension activities. "Latin is a language," as William Wyatt (1990: 30) has reminded us, "and all those who teach it should be constantly aware of that fact." In reality, however, very few classics professors employ a four-skills approach to elementary language teaching, and Frederic Wheelock's (1963) flinty and weathered grammar-translation text, *Latin: An Introductory Course Based on Ancient Authors,* originally published in 1956, appears still to be the textbook most widely employed in college classrooms (as it was at the time of the last APA textbook survey in 1982: see Taylor and Lawall 1984). Two supplementary readers designed specifically to accompany Wheelock were published in the 1980s, *Auricula Meretricula* (Cumming and Blundell 1981) and the more successful *Thirty-Eight Latin Stories* (Groton and May 1989), and these have compensated somewhat for only one of the texts' more grievous deficiencies, the lack of continuous reading passages for each chapter.

At the time of the 1982 APA survey, the other most frequently adopted primers included Moreland and Fleischer's *Latin: An Intensive Course* (1977) and the sorely dated *College Latin* (De Witt et al. 1954), as well as the livelier *Latin via Ovid* (Goldman and Nyenhuis 1982). Since then other new elementary texts aimed primarily at the college level have appeared, among them *Latin Plus* (Lacey 1985); *Latin for Reading* (Knudsvig et al. 1986), the latest in a series of structural texts from the University of Michigan (see Seligson 1981); the British *Learning Latin* (Randall et al. 1986) and *Reading Latin* (Jones and Sidwell 1986); Robert Ball's *Reading Classical Latin* (1987); and Johnston's *Traditio* (1988), none of which has as yet had the reception in the colleges that *Ecce* and the *CLC* have enjoyed in the schools. On the Greek side, the British Joint Association of Classical Teachers' excellent *Reading Greek* (JACT 1978), which employs an inductive, culture-focused approach, led the adoption list in the APA survey, but a number of professors were and still are using outdated texts like the stark Chase and Phillips (1961—first edition 1941) or even Crosby and Schaeffer (1928)—the old "war-horse" of Greek texts, as Ball and Ellsworth term it (1989: 7), which assumes students already have a grasp of Latin, a safer assumption sixty years ago than it is today. Encouragingly, some new primers have been published very recently, including Ellsworth's *Reading Classical Greek* (1982), Hansen and Quinn's *Greek: An Intensive Course* (1987), and a very user-friendly North American revision of Balme's *Athenaze* (Balme and Lawall 1990).

The question of what to read at the intermediate level and how intermediate textbooks should be designed is continually debated (see Taylor and Lawall 1984). By the third and fourth college courses students can be reading generous selections of unadapted classical Latin prose and verse, as they continue to review grammar and sharpen their general comprehension and translation skills, but they most certainly should be provided with modern texts with ample commentary and vocabulary aids. Happily, new and better equipped editions, including both individual works and anthologies, are appearing with remarkable frequency (just another sign that the classics are alive and well!), most of them reviewed or listed in the journals (particularly

The Classical Outlook; the ACTFL listings in Lawall et al. 1988a; and *The Classical World's* periodic textbook surveys).

My own sense is that anthologies with briefer readings are a far better choice for the early intermediate level than taking third-semester students on a forced march straight through a Ciceronian oration or two (cf. Daugherty 1990–91 on the use of Latin epistles in intermediate classes). Excellent anthologies are: the new Cambridge series, Themes in Latin Literature, which includes four separate texts (Bell and Whalen 1988–89), each focusing on a particular topic ("Amor et Amicitia," "Multas per Gentes," "Urbs Antiqua," and "Imperium et Civitas"), with selections from a variety of prose and verse authors, and furnished with brief introductions, facing vocabulary, and discussion questions (reviewed by Hamilton 1990); and the six Longman Latin Readers (Lawall et al. 1988b), each with generous selections of unadapted Latin from Cicero, Vergil, and other authors, and amply equipped with introductory material, facing notes, reading comprehension questions, grammar exercises, and vocabulary (reviewed by Allan 1989). Of the latter the Catiline reader is especially well done, integrating excerpts from both Cicero and Sallust into an overall history of the conspiracy and its background. Those preferring to read complete works might consider the excellent editions with commentary in the Cambridge Greek and Latin Classics series, as well as the inexpensive Bryn Mawr Greek and Latin Texts, most of which (though rather dreary in format) have notes well suited to the intermediate reader.

In 1985 the APA/ACLS report concluded that "new texts that employ modern approaches to language study and are realistic in their expectations are . . . among the greatest needs of classical teaching today" (North 1985: 77). There are so many more good texts to choose from now than there were just 10 or 15 years ago, or even at the time of the APA report, that departmental curriculum or textbook committees ought to make systematic review and evaluation of the latest publications an ongoing activity.

Computers in the Language Classroom

Another development of growing importance is the production of increasingly sophisticated software for computer-assisted instruction (CAI) in Latin (there is a desperate need for comparable materials for Greek), including both generic and text-specific programs designed to run on a variety of microcomputers (for useful surveys see Hughes 1987; Latousek 1989a; Culley 1989; and the "Random Access" columns, Latousek 1989b, 1990a–b; many of these programs can be purchased from the ACL's Teaching Materials and Resource Center). While early CAI programs were hardly more complex than flashcards (Culley 1978, 1984; Waite 1970), and some could be run only on mainframe computers, which were available on only a limited number of campuses, the most recent programs are much more interactive and are compatible with a variety of the most commonly available microcomputers. Scanlan's PLATO program, which includes extensive vocabulary, morphology, and translation drills to accompany Wheelock's *Latin,* is still used on a number of university campuses (Scanlan 1980, 1981). Of the newer software packages, one of the best is Culley's *Latin Skills,* which runs on both Apple and IBM micros and is available in versions keyed to several of the most widely used textbooks (including Wheelock, Jenney, Ullman, Goldman and Nyenhuis, and *Ecce*—see Culley 1984–85 and reviews by Scanlan 1985–86 and Phillips 1987); the Wheelock version can be employed along with syllabus, audiotapes, and a complementary computer program from the University of Delaware entitled *Individualized Latin Curriculum,* to provide a wholly auto-tutorial course.

Other packages, such as *MacLang* for the Apple Macintosh, provide drill formats with editing and authoring functions that permit instructors to design programs customized to their own syllabi. Hypertext programs, like the Macintosh *HyperCard,* which are now available or under development and which have applications for both intermediate and advanced classes, permit students who are reading texts from Latin literature on the computer monitor to ask for and receive responses to questions on vocabulary, forms, syntax, or historical context, for example, as an aid to comprehension and translation. Interactive simulation games are available that will interest both classics and Latin students, including *Annals of Rome,* a war game in which players can control tax rate, army salaries, and troop movement and in effect rewrite history (Latousek 1990a: 88), and Culley's *Saltus Teutobergiensis,* in which the player, taking the role of a Roman soldier in the Teutoberg Forest, plots tactics for his survival by carrying on a conversation with the computer exclusively in Latin (Culley et al. 1986; Culley 1989; Braidi 1988–89; Latousek 1990a).

Classical Humanities Courses

Classical humanities (or "Classics-in-Translation") courses, especially Greek and Roman civilization and mythology, were offered with increasing frequency during the 1960s and 1970s, not least as a defensive response to declining enrollments in Greek and Latin, and now they often constitute two-thirds or more of a department's enrollments. Such courses will remain vital to the discipline's well-being for a number of very sound reasons. The maintenance of a high overall enrollment as a counterbalance, for number-conscious administrators, to the relatively low numbers typical of advanced Greek and Latin classes is certainly one consideration (forthrightly defended by Sussman 1989), though philosophically it is the least important.

More crucial is the issue of access: if we wish to expose as many of our undergraduates as possible to the inestimable benefits that the Greek and Latin classics have to offer, then classical humanities courses will continue to represent our most realistic opportunity. As British classicist Michael Grant has remarked of his own efforts at popularizing the classics for the general reader, "non-classicists who want to know about the classical world . . . are numerous, and it is imperative to meet their intelligent and questioning needs. Indeed, in the long run, I imagine that the whole future of the classics depends on doing so—since otherwise the subject will sink into something entirely esoteric, recherché and peripheral" (Grant 1990: 1).

One very positive consequence of the scrutiny to which American education has been subjected over the past decade is the renewed (though not unchallenged) emphasis we have seen on the great books and traditional curricula, including the classical humanities (e.g., the model undergraduate core curriculum described in Cheney 1989). Without subscribing to the most extreme premises or conclusions of Bloom (1987), Hirsch (1987), and Bennett (1984), on the one hand, or of the most vehement canon-bashers in the Stanford debate, on the other, it seems to me reasonable that classical culture not only should, but very likely will, continue to occupy a significant position in the core curricula of our strongest baccalaureate programs, not to the exclusion of non-Western cultures and subcultures but rather with attention to the "commonalities" among the world's cultures, the "transcendent truths," as NEH Chairman Lynne Cheney has recently termed them, that "go beyond the accidents of birth and individual circumstance" (Cheney 1990: 8). While Edmunds and others take a less optimistic view (Culham and Edmunds 1989: xii; and, in the same volume, Konstan and Richlin), Helen North (1985) remarks that "classical studies constitute the very heart of the Humanities" (p. 30) and most classicists today would still agree with her premise. Certainly every Classics department should work to ensure a place for its offerings among courses that students may elect to satisfy core literature, humanities, religion, social studies, and even fine arts requirements. In programs where such requirements do not exist, classicists ought to be in the forefront of those faculty lobbying for their institution. Besides the general Greek and Roman civilization and mythology courses that are most often taught by Classics departments (useful discussions and bibliography for the teaching of these subjects can be found in Galinsky 1983; Morford 1983, 1984; and O'Connor and Rowland 1987), and the Western Civilization sequences in which classicists sometimes team-teach, numerous special focus courses may be designed as general studies offerings, as courses related to the major in other departments, in interdisciplinary programs, or even in other schools or colleges of the university. Courses on women in antiquity, for example, first widely developed in the 1970s, continue to have considerable appeal, particularly in larger colleges with women's studies programs; the bibliography is now quite substantial and has been enhanced by the perspectives of feminist criticism of the past two decades (see, e.g., Perkell 1984; Skinner 1989). With interest in the role of blacks in the ancient world recently rekindled by debates around publication of Martin Bernal's *Black Athena* (Bernal 1987; Levine and Peradotto 1989), it may be hoped that courses on blacks in antiquity will likewise be offered on more campuses—perhaps with the salutary effect of attracting additional minority students into a discipline in which they are grossly underrepresented at all levels (see Haley 1989).

Depending on the interests and expertise of the classics faculty and on the special needs of cooperating departments and schools, courses might be offered on ancient religion and philosophy, art and archeology, or the classical tradition. Courses dealing with ancient science or medicine, including medical, or bioscientific, terminology, can be especially valuable to students in premedical and other science majors, although "med-terms" should never be reduced to a mere "words" course but should include generous dosages of historical and cultural material. In universities that have colleges of agriculture, a course in ancient agriculture might be an excellent humanities offering, and, besides including readings from Homer, Hesiod, Aristotle, Varro, Cicero, Vergil, Pliny, and a host of others, would serve to introduce students to art, daily life, politics, and other aspects of ancient society; with the emphasis broadened to include issues of industry, commerce, and the ancient economy in general, business students might also find the course an appealing humanities option. Likewise, in colleges with strong prelaw programs, an offering on ancient law (see Vaughn 1984) can readily earn a place as a program requirement and, like the other special topics courses suggested here, might also be credited, if taught at an intermediate level, toward a minor or major in classics. With the return of the Olympics to the United States in 1996, courses on ancient athletics, like the enormously popular one taught for many years by Waldo Sweet at the University of Michigan, should prove increasingly attractive; extensive resources are available for teaching this subject and for introducing students to the wide range of art, literature, and religious thought that bear on the subject of athletic competition in antiquity (Tebben 1984).

In view of the interdisciplinary character of classical studies, the possibilities for other special-topics courses focusing on issues of contemporary interest are nearly limitless. With the growing attention given to international education, there are likewise countless opportunities for defining and ensuring a place for the classics in the internationalized curriculum—opportunities that the profession will be wise not to ignore. Offering an array of interesting classical humanities courses that are taught by knowledgeable faculty (Mellor's cautions [1989: 102–5] on this point are well founded), in moderately sized classes (not, via the "myth for the masses approach," in sections of

100–200 or more students), and that are accessible to, and satisfy requirements for, undergraduates throughout the Arts and Sciences college and even beyond it, will bring the benefits of our discipline to the broadest possible audience, assure the value of our programs to colleagues across the campus, and serve also as a means of attracting a wider range of students to consider a major or minor in classics.

MAJOR–MINOR PROGRAMS IN CLASSICAL LANGUAGES AND CIVILIZATION

Classics programs (sometimes with as few as two or three faculty— sometimes, *horribile dictu!*, with only one) typically offer majors in Greek and Latin, or a Classics major that combines the two; at least 8–10 advanced courses are required, of which most should be in the language(s), others in classical civilization or the related areas discussed below. The language courses may focus on a single author or genre, but often examine special topics via a variety of texts ("Party Politics of the Late Republic," "Heroes and Heroines in Latin Literature"). In the case of Latin majors who are working toward teacher certification, the department needs to coordinate its require- ments carefully with those of the Education department.

Somewhat less common is the Classical Civilization major, an attractive humanities option for students who desire a strong liberal arts major concen- trating on the ancient world, but who have little interest in the classical languages and do not plan to do graduate work in the field. The civilization major should also include a minimum of 8–10 courses, in classical humanities and related areas. Many of the topics mentioned earlier in discussing the general studies curriculum (such as women and blacks in antiquity, ancient science and law, or religion and philosophy) could also serve as the focus of advanced courses, for which at least one or two introductory classical civiliza- tion courses should be prerequisite. Ronald Mellor has remarked (1989: 101) that the increased popularity of this major "has produced the most intellec- tually exciting curricular changes in recent years: the growth of specialized courses on antiquity for students without Greek or Latin." The possibilities are practically endless, limited only by the interests and qualifications of the faculty. Our own department, for example, has designed numerous 400-level culture courses, sometimes as split-level offerings that also enroll Master's students, on such topics as "Ancient Comedy," "The Etruscans and Early Rome," "Homer and the Epic Tradition," "Ancient Sanctuaries and Festivals" (team taught by an archeologist and a specialist in Greek literature and semiotics), and "Ancient Cities," which regularly draws a large enrollment, not just from our majors, but also from the School of Environmental Design. Study of Greek and Latin should obviously also be encouraged and credited toward the major.

Courses available to the civilization major (some of which should also be credited toward the majors in Latin or Greek) can be supplemented by offerings from outside the department. There should, in fact, be close liaison with other programs whose faculty can enrich, and be enriched by, the major offerings in classics or who, in cooperation with a very small classics faculty, can staff an interdisciplinary Ancient Studies major. There is much to be gained by networking with colleagues in art, history, philosophy, religion, English, linguistics, comparative literature, women's studies, and so many other fields represented on our campuses. A recent example in our own department is the proposal for a course on "Gender Issues and Greek Religion" that we expect to be crosslisted with our Religion department and that will count toward the major in both Classics and Women's Studies. Classics is the quintessential interdiscipline; as North has so eloquently observed (1985: 74), "classical studies by their very nature require the synthesis of independent modes of investigation and thus provide a model for the intellectual life as an ideal." It is crucial to the intellectual well-being of our students and the profession that we enact this model; indeed, our nexus with other programs should be so intimate that the classics are seen, not as a "frill" (the perspective of some administrators and even some other faculty) but as quite indispensable to the vitality of the college's humanities curriculum.

In addition to the major (or, in the case of very small programs, in lieu of the major), minor programs, requiring a minimum of four or five advanced courses, ought to be offered in Greek, Latin, and, if possible, Classical Civilization. The opportunity for a minor concentration in classics has in our own institution attracted students from such disparate majors as biology, political science, mathematics, and computer science, as well as the more closely related areas of English, comparative literature, and the modern languages. Where these minor programs are not already in place, their implementation should be a top priority for any undergraduate department.

PHILOLOGY IS ALIVE, BUT IS SHE WELL AND WHERE DOES SHE RESIDE?

Philology may be imagined as a middle-aged but still handsome woman of stern visage but gentle demeanor who lives in an over-large house with insufficient electricity and plumbing in a decaying section of town. She is known familiarly as "Phil" by neighborhood urchins, and is regarded with amused contempt. She is not "with it." (Wyatt 1983: 27)

The major programs in Greek and Latin, while introducing and refining the more advanced skills of literary and textual analysis and interpretation, must emphasize continued development of basic language skills, including not only grammatical analysis and translation, but also reading comprehension and oral–aural skills. One issue that runs through several of the essays in Culham and Edmunds (1989), and which is relevant to our major/minor curricula as much as to our graduate programs, is the Culture vs. Philology debate. As Edmunds succinctly states in defining the sides in this controversy over the degree of importance philological training ought to have in classical studies (1989: xiii): "The elitist position insists on the primacy of the languages; the egalitarian says that it is more important to democratize the classics, even if that means abandoning the languages."

Surely the reasonable position is somewhere between the two: philology is essential to classical studies, just as linguistic proficiency is essential to the study of modern cultures by nonnatives. But our definition of and approaches to philology should be broad, sensible, academically (not ideologically) motivated, and, in sum, humanistic, as they sometimes, unfortunately, are not. To insist on anything less for our students or ourselves than a constant striving toward mastery of the classical languages (just as our modern-language colleagues strive toward a "Superior" on the ACTFL Proficiency Scale), not as an end in itself, but as one essential means of fully appreciating classical antiquity and its relation to the whole phenomenon of human culture, would surely be to weaken and ultimately undermine the discipline.

Classicists should not need to be told that Horatian "balance" is what we properly seek in our programs and in our students. Undoubtedly there are departments—and individual faculty—that are out of balance academically, that indulge in overspecialization, whether of a philological or other sort. Some of the worst violations occur in departments that give highest priority to their doctoral programs and treat their undergraduate curricula like deformed and unwanted stepchildren. Besides ensuring that our majors acquire solid linguistic skills, our curricula must also provide them with a strong grounding in Greek and Roman culture, in social as well as political history, and in literature and the arts. Traditional philological and historical approaches provide a variety of perspectives on these subjects, as do the more recent findings of anthropology, psychology, semiotics, structuralism (Peradotto 1989), deconstructionism, and feminist research, to mention only a few of the rich intellectual resources available to us as we advance classical studies into the twenty-first century.

These are ambitious goals, but they are approachable, if departments will only persist in the systematic and rigorous development of their curricula and provide a strong program of student advising. We can assure as least a degree of well-roundedness in our majors through judiciously selected course requirements, including survey courses and sequences. We can also provide reading lists (quite common in graduate programs but lamentably rare in major–minor curricula) that include a realistic selection from ancient litera-ture, some to be read in the original, some in English translation. We can make available as well a few basic handbooks on history, literature, and the other major subfields of the discipline.

The Undergraduate Proseminar

Also helpful to a program's integration (and again a *rara avis*) is the under-graduate proseminar, offered once or twice a year, carrying one or two hours of course credit, and required of all majors and minors, who should be enrolled in the class as soon as possible after entering the program. The proseminar may begin with an overview presented by the undergraduate advisor; students then meet once a week for an hour or two, with members of the classics faculty as well as with faculty from ancient history, comparative literature, philosophy, religion, women's studies, and other related fields, each of whom introduces ideas, issues, and bibliography for a major area within, or an approach to, classical studies. There might, for instance, be sessions introducing the field of classical archeology on the one hand, and new criticism, structuralism, and other branches of literary theory on the other. At least one session ought to focus on such professional matters as employment opportunities, trends in pedagogy, minority concerns, the prospects for graduate education, and professional organizations and journals; even undergraduates should be encouraged to join those groups that offer low student rates for both member-ship and subscription, like the ACL, which publishes *The Classical Outlook,* and CAMWS with its *Classical Journal.*

Not only can the proseminar serve the obvious purpose of providing every major with a broad overview of both the content of and approaches to classics, but it also brings together all the department's majors at once and ensures their introduction to the department and associated faculty early in their program of study. Other means of promoting the sort of communication, collegiality, and esprit de corps that characterize a healthy undergraduate major–minor program include: providing majors and minors with a gathering place—a departmental library or lounge and reading room—and with their own mail-boxes in the departmental office for quick communication of the latest news, special lectures, advising appointments, and other such happenings; inviting them, along with faculty and graduate students, to the department's social as well as academic activities; and supporting a Classics Club, or, better yet, a Senior Classical League or Eta Sigma Phi chapter. These provisions are just nuts and bolts, to be sure, but they are among the many considerations that build an academically and spiritually vigorous major–minor program.

Other Nuts and Bolts: Texts and Technologies

Little need be added here to what has already been said on the subject of textbooks (except, please, once they are majors, and not merely lower division students, let's not just hand them a Teubner and the occasional stern lecture to prod them through our language courses—even graduate students should have modern texts with sound introductions, ample commentaries, and whatever other resources we can provide to facilitate and accelerate their learning). To be sure, more classicists need to commit their energies and expertise to the production of improved texts; in the meantime, many of our programs and the students in them would benefit enormously if departments would only appoint standing textbook committees to examine and offer objective evaluations of the excellent texts that have already appeared over the past decade or so, as well as of the many new texts and other classroom resources that are published every year.

In addition to the CAI and other computer materials for elementary language instruction described earlier, there are several resources, either now available or in various stages of planning and development, that will prove valuable to advanced undergraduate instruction (see Crane 1989; Mylonas 1989; Culley 1989). As observed by Theodore Brunner (1988), director of the NEH-funded *Thesaurus Linguae Graecae* (TLG) project, which has produced an electronic data bank of all 61 million words of Greek literature from Homer to A.D. 600, "the next generation of Classics undergraduates, who have little awe of computers, will be able to perform at an academic level previously reserved for graduate students" (p. 12). Undergraduates certainly regard as user-friendly the IBYCUS PC system, which allows, among other more complex tasks, word-searches via compact disc (CD-ROM), at the rate of one million words per second, through the entire corpus of classical Greek literature in the TLG bank, as well as the now nearly complete data bank of Latin literature and a variety of papyrus and other late texts. Other available materials include: the database on videodisc and CD-ROM from the Perseus Project, which ultimately will provide at the computer monitor an interactive word and image encyclopedia for study of the entire classical Greek world (Harward 1988; Heath 1990); and a variety of applications for advanced multimedia compact discs that can store "text, audio, and still-frame and motion video on the same medium [and] accommodate up to 350,000 pages of text, or 16 hours of audio, or 7,000 color stills, or more than 10,000 pages of color graphics or computer animation" (Culley 1989: 29).

Computer technology is changing rapidly and the classics profession has truly been in the forefront of humanities disciplines in developing valuable applications for both instruction and research. As noted earlier, both the ACL and APA have committees on computing and the classics, and *The Classical Outlook*'s "Random Access" department keeps readers up to date on instructional applications in particular. The challenge for classicists, however, is not merely to keep ourselves informed, but also, as Mylonas has emphasized (1989: 143–45), to ensure that our students have the opportunity to become computer literate, and that our campuses and our students have readily available to them the resources necessary to take full advantage of this revolutionary new bridge to learning.

Teacher Shortages and the Imperative for Teacher Training

There can be little doubt that the resurgence of interest in Latin in the United States since the late 1970s has had a salutary effect on the whole discipline of classical studies. If we are to maintain and even improve our current state of health, Classics departments need to give their utmost attention to the shortage of qualified Latin teachers and to the very serious consequences of that shortage (LaFleur, ed. 1987; Yom 1990). While total college Latin enrollments remained fairly constant from the mid-1970s through the mid-1980s, the number of students preparing for teacher certification during that period failed to keep pace with the demand for new and expanded high school programs. Although it now appears that college Latin enrollments may have risen over the last few years and the teacher shortage seems to have abated somewhat, positions still outnumber fully certified candidates, and in some instances we find even well-intentioned administrators simply giving up on Latin. In other cases teachers without Latin credentials continue to be hired or reassigned to teach the language. One very recent report noted, for example, that of the 110 Latin teachers in Maine, "50% do not have the 18 college hours of Latin needed" for certification (Wooley and Wiencke 1990: 6). The consequences for such underprepared, "back-door" teachers and their students will inevitably be less than gratifying: the teacher does poorly, so do the students; enthusiasm wanes; the program languishes or is dropped; an opportunity is lost.

Successes, however, have outnumbered failures, and the classics profession has responded creatively and energetically to the problems associated with the teacher shortage. College departments are giving more attention to teacher preparation programs for their undergraduate Latin majors and Master's students. Latin teacher placement services have been improved and new services established, usually by college Classics departments. Summer degree programs and institutes designed to provide in-service training to new and prospective Latin teachers have multiplied, some of them funded by generous grants from NEH and other federal and state agencies. Courses specially scheduled in the evenings, on weekends, on satellite campuses, and via correspondence have served similar purposes. Some university departments (including those at Georgia, Maryland, Tufts, and Virginia) have appointed secondary school master teachers as adjunct faculty in their summer seminars and institutes. In the most beneficial of these courses and workshops, ample time is allotted for discussion of methods, materials, and other professional issues, as well as for working with the language itself and with vital aspects of classical literature and civilization. Scholarship programs for persons working toward Latin certification have been instituted by ACL, under the auspices of its Teacher Training Committee, and by CAMWS, likewise under the administration of an active scholarship committee; and competitive teacher fellowship programs for summer study, notably those funded by NEH, the Rockefeller Foundation, and the Council for Basic Education, have been steadily growing (LaFleur 1990). Some Classics departments have established their own teacher scholarship programs and arranged for tuition waivers or reductions for teachers.

Assessing the Major

A word might be said about assessment, as that term (and its companion, accountability) now comes up almost daily in higher education, particularly in connection with evaluating the effectiveness of our undergraduate major programs. Professors occasionally seem terror-stricken at the prospect of inquisitors descending on the academy, nationally normed examinations in hand, extirpating faculty and entire departments whose students fail to meet the standards their bureaucracies have established according to some mystical set of learner outcomes. In reality, if reasonably managed, assessment is neither sinister nor mystical, and it is an activity in which virtually every academic department is to some extent involved already every day. The tests and final exams and the student and peer evaluations that we routinely administer, the curriculum review and revision that we periodically conduct, and the annual reports that we dutifully organize and write each year are all a part of this assessment.

What accrediting agencies typically seek in addition is an assessment plan, with at least some component that is broader in scope than course evaluation (a senior exit interview and questionnaire or a senior comprehensive exam, for example) and some provision for extramural standards by which a program's students might be measured (this might involve a visit and full-scale report by an external evaluation team, of the sort that can be provided by the APA's Campus Advisory Service or, for teacher candidates, the Latin certification exam that is mandated in some states, or it might be something as simple as periodically tracking the success of graduates via alumni questionnaires). The "assessment movement" is not intrinsically evil, and, indeed, is essentially sensible and well-intentioned. At least two caveats, however, should be applied: first, that departments insist upon the freedom to design their own assessment plans for approval by the college and not have arbitrary plans or "instruments" thrust upon them, and second, that the results of assessment be employed as they are properly intended, i.e., analyzed and evaluated by the departments themselves as a basis for the ongoing improvement of their own programs.

POSTSCRIPT: ORGANIZATION AND ALLIANCE

Much of the foregoing rather optimistically presupposes Classics departments that are well organized, and faculties that are motivated to improve the academic enterprise. While many college and university classics programs have been strengthened and enriched in a great variety of ways in recent years, others have languished. Most departments, it is probably safe to say, would benefit from a more systematic and energetic approach to program development, and most faculty will respond to the challenges such program development presents, provided the department has, not just the resources it needs from the Dean, but effective, communicative leadership and a democratic process of faculty involvement. Fundamentally, this means that the chairperson's responsibility amounts to a great deal more than simply minding the store: energy, the vision for long-range planning as well as a tolerance for day-to-day detail, and an ability to deal openly with colleagues and tactfully but aggressively with administrators are all prerequisite. In the case of classics programs that are housed in a foreign-language department or some other academic unit, there ought to be a Classics section head, who must likewise be politically astute.

The administrative organization of larger departments should include not only capable and efficient undergraduate and graduate coordinators, but also, in the case of programs employing graduate teaching assistants, a faculty member specifically charged with their supervision. Traditionally we have failed to provide sufficient pedagogical training for our graduate assistants, either for their teaching or assistance in our courses or in preparation for their own subsequent careers in the college classroom. The demographics—including, among other factors, both the next baby boomlet's advance to college age beginning in the mid-1990s (high school graduates in 2004 are expected to exceed the 1988 level by more than 5 percent, according to the Western Interstate Commission 1988) and the "graying of the professoriate"—suggest an improving job market for Ph.D.'s into the next century (Bowen and Sosa 1989), a circumstance that should favorably affect Classics Ph.D.'s as well as others in the humanities. With the ever-growing diversification of classics curricula, it is imperative that we train our graduate students not just for research, but also for teaching, and for teaching not only Greek and Latin but especially the culture, civilization, and interdisciplinary courses that they are increasingly likely to be assigned (see Mellor 1989).

Every classics program (indeed, every college department that has counterpart programs in the schools) should also designate a schools liaison—again, a *rara avis* in our departments (though see "Oxford" 1990). The schools liaison should have responsibility for coordinating the department's articulation efforts and its collaborative activities with public and private school teachers K–12 and with the college's school or department of education, as well as for working with undergraduates preparing for teacher certification. The possibilities for school–college collaboratives are practically limitless. Exchanging classroom visits and presentations (professors can learn from observing teachers teach just as much as the opposite is true), co-editing state classics newsletters, cooperating in classical association activities, assisting in placement and promotional efforts, supporting Junior and Senior Classical League functions, and sponsoring "Latin Days" are all activities that will reward both the schools and the colleges that contribute to them. All of a department's faculty, however, and not just the schools liaison, should be encouraged to support such activities, to affiliate with local and state classical and foreign-language associations, and to join, attend the meetings, and read the journals of such organizations as ACL and ACTFL, whose principal concern is with improving what goes on in language teaching. Sad to say, in 1990 only about 12 percent of ACL's nearly 4,000 members were college professors.

In smaller programs (and the average Classics department in this country includes no more than half a dozen or so faculty), the functions of undergraduate coordinator and schools liaison might be combined, as might those of the graduate coordinator and the supervisor of teaching assistants in a program with only 10 or so graduate students. The functions of these offices, however distributed, are absolutely essential to a vital and progressive department; consequently, exemplary service in these support and advising positions ought to be credited in tenure and promotion decisions, as well as compensated by released time from at least one course per academic year, as is done, for example, at the University of Maryland (see Hallett 1990).

The APA and the ACL: Scholars and Teachers Together

Among the positive outcomes of the difficulties besetting our discipline over the past several years have been the vigorous efforts of "many university/ college level professionals . . . to rebuild the foundation of the American classical establishment" (Phinney 1989: 79) and the renewed attention given by the traditionally research-oriented American Philological Association to pedagogical issues, to concerns of the classroom as well as of the study. Its program of awards for Excellence in the Teaching of Classics, its Committee on Educational Services, and its series of pedagogical pamphlets, were all instituted or bolstered during the 1980s. APA has of late collaborated more and more closely with ACL, not only in responding to the teacher shortage but in promotional and developmental efforts as well. The NEH-funded *Teaching of Latin* (LaFleur, ed. 1987), for example, was co-sponsored by the two organizations, which also contributed to the costs of distributing the book to selected colleges of education and to every Classics department and state foreign-language consultant in America. APA was a charter member (along with CAMWS and other regional and state organizations) of the ACL-initiated National Committee for Latin and Greek. As a consequence of the 1986 APA/ ACL-sponsored Conference on the Classics in American Schools, the two groups are further affiliated in the Joint Committee on Classics in American Education, which has already taken the first steps toward ensuring the intensified collaboration between university professors and school teachers that will be essential to the profession's vitality through the 1990s and into the new millennium.

In general the prospects for Latin and the classics in America are bright. In the lower and middle grades, Latin and classical humanities are being taught with splendid new materials to growing numbers of students as FLES programs are being revived. In the high schools, improved and livelier methods and texts and a wealth of computer resources and other new materials are being used by an increasing number of teachers. Most of the conditions seem right for continued growth—unless, of course, we allow a diminution of our energies in the preparation of well-qualified teachers, in curriculum and materials development, and in the promotion of our programs. In the colleges, enrollments seem at least to be holding; vastly improved texts, computer resources, and other classroom materials are available, or under development, and are gradually being adopted; school collaboratives have received encouragement; and it even appears that we have succeeded in encouraging at least a few more of our students to enter the profession of Latin teaching in the schools. And we are assessing, not only the shape of our curriculum, but even—as we confront serious questions about the relevancy of traditional canons and of classical versus modern—its character and the bases for our attitudes toward it.

The one circumstance that we can predict with certainty in American education is its unpredictability, and this is true not least of the shape and status of the teaching of classics, the history of which has been marked, not just in recent generations but over the centuries, by the ebb and flow of challenge and response and renewed challenge. If there is any approximate solution to such uncertainties, it must come, first, from an absolute confidence in the worth of classics as a discipline whose lessons can be made valuable to our society, no matter how the society itself may be transformed. Next, we must commit ourselves with greater vision, determination, and energy to sharing those lessons with the broadest range of students in the most humane and effective ways, actively evaluating the methods, materials, and technologies at our disposal, diversifying our curricula, and keeping our own minds ever alert to the myriad connections, many of them yet undiscovered, that the ancient world has with the one in which we and our students live. And, finally, we must hold to the conviction that communication and collaboration—between advocates of both modern and classical languages, between humanists and professional educators, between teachers in the schools and professors in the colleges, and among fellow classicists, whose academic perspectives and values may vary widely—are quite indispensable to the vitality of our discipline and, more importantly, to the spiritual and intellectual well-being of the students we educate.

REFERENCES

Abbott, Martha. 1991. "Critical Instructional Issues in the Classics for American Schools." [See Appendix 9A.]

Advisory Committee of the American Classical League. 1924. *The Classical Investigation, Part One: General Report.* Princeton, NJ: Princeton Univ. Press.

Allan, Charlayne. 1989. Review of Lawall, et al. *Classical Outlook* 67: 35–36.

Azevedo, Milton M. 1990. "Professional Development of Teaching Assistants: Training versus Education." *ADFL Bulletin* 21,1: 24–28.

Baca, Albert R., et al. 1979. "Language Transfer Project of the Los Angeles Unified School District." *Classical Outlook* 56: 74–80.

Baldock, Marion. 1987. "Latin in the High Schools." Review of LaFleur, ed. 1987. *JACT Bulletin* 75: 3.

Ball, Robert J. 1987. *Reading Classical Latin: A Reasonable Approach*. Lawrence, KS: Coronado.

————, and J. D. Ellsworth. 1989. "Teaching Classical Languages: A Reasonable Approach." *Classical World* 83: 1–12.

Balme, Maurice, and Gilbert Lawall. 1990. *Athenaze: An Introduction to Ancient Greek*. 2 vols. Oxford, Eng., and New York: Oxford Univ. Press.

Barthelmess, James A. 1982. "A National Public Awareness Campaign for Latin and Greek." *Classical Outlook* 59: 107–10.

Bell, Patricia E., and Paul Whalen. 1988–89. Themes in Latin Literature series. 4 vols. Cambridge, Eng., and New York: Cambridge Univ. Press.

Bennett, William J. 1984. *To Reclaim a Legacy: A Report on the Humanities in Higher Education*. Washington, DC: National Endowment for the Humanities.

Bernal, Martin. 1987. *Black Athena*. New Brunswick, NJ: Rutgers Univ. Press.

————. 1989. "Classics in Crisis: An Outsider's View In," pp. 67–74 in Phyllis Culham and Lowell Edmunds, eds., *Classics: A Discipline and Profession in Crisis?* Lanham, MD: University Press of America.

Bloom, Allan. 1987. *The Closing of the American Mind: How Higher Education Has Failed Democracy and Impoverished the Souls of Today's Students*. New York: Simon and Schuster.

Bowen, William G., and Julie Ann Sosa. 1989. *Prospects for Faculty in the Arts and Sciences*. Princeton, NJ: Princeton Univ. Press.

Braidi, Susan M. 1988–89. "In Ancient Rome: A Computer Game Uses Artificial Intelligence to Instruct Language Students." *Enquiry,* Winter 1988–89, pp. 16–21.

Brod, Richard I. 1988. "Foreign Language Enrollments in US Institutions of Higher Education—Fall 1986." *ADFL Bulletin* 19,2: 39–44.

————, and Monique Lapointe. 1989. "The MLA Survey of Foreign Language Entrance and Degree Requirements, 1987–88." *ADFL Bulletin* 20,2: 17–41.

Brunner, Theodore F. 1988. "Overcoming 'Verzettelung': A Humanistic Discipline Meets the Computer." *Humanities* 9,3: 4–7. Reprinted in 1988 *Classical Outlook* 66: 10–13.

Burns, Mary Ann T., and Joseph F. O'Connor. 1987. *The Classics in American Schools: Teaching the Ancient World*. Atlanta: Scholars Press.

Chase, Alston H., and Henry Phillips. 1961. *A New Introduction to Greek*. 3d ed. Cambridge, MA: Harvard Univ. Press.

Cheney, Lynne V. 1987. *American Memory: A Report on the Humanities in the Nation's Public Schools*. Washington, DC: National Endowment for the Humanities.

————. 1989. *50 Hours: A Core Curriculum for College Students*. Washington, DC: National Endowment for the Humanities.

————. 1990. "A Conversation with College Board President Donald Stewart." *Humanities* 11,4: 4–8.

Crane, Gregory. 1989. "Computers and Research in the Classics: The Evolution of the Electronic Library," pp. 117–31 in Phyllis Culham and Lowell Edmunds, eds., *Classics: A Discipline and Profession in Crisis?* Lanham, MD: University Press of America.

Crosby, Henry L., and John N. Schaeffer. 1928. *An Introduction to Greek.* Boston: Allyn and Bacon.

Culham, Phyllis, and Lowell Edmunds, eds. 1989. *Classics: A Discipline and Profession in Crisis?* Lanham, MD: University Press of America.

Culley, Gerald. 1978. "Computer-Assisted Instruction and Latin: Beyond Flashcards." *Classical World* 72: 393–401.

————. 1984. *Teaching the Classics with Computers.* APA Committee on Educational Services Papers, no. 1. New York: American Philological Association.

————. 1984–85. "The Delaware Latin Skills Project." *Classical Outlook* 62: 38–42.

————. 1989. "CAI in Classics: An Assessment." *Classical Bulletin* 65: 17–31.

————, et al. 1986. "A Foreign Language Adventure Game: Progress Report on an Application of AI to Language Instruction." *CALICO Journal* 4,2: 69–87.

Cumming, Ann, and Mary W. Blundell. 1981. *Auricula Meretricula.* Cambridge, MA: Focus Classical Library.

Dandonoli, Patricia. 1987. "Report on Foreign Language Enrollment in Public Secondary Schools." *Foreign Language Annals* 20: 457–70.

Daugherty, Greg. 1990–91. "Teaching Roman Epistolography as a Threshold to Literature." *Classical Outlook* 68: 41–44.

De Witt, Norman J., et al. 1954. *College Latin.* Glenview, IL: Scott, Foresman.

Draper, Jamie B. 1989. *The State of the States: State Initiatives in Foreign Languages and International Studies, 1979–1989.* Washington, DC: Joint National Committee for Languages.

"Editorial." 1987. *JACT Bulletin* 75: 1.

Ellsworth, J. D. 1982. *Reading Ancient Greek: A Reasonable Approach.* Lawrence, KS: Coronado.

Florian, David. 1990. *The Phenomenon of Language.* 2d ed. White Plains, NY: Longman.

Galinsky, Karl. 1983. "The Challenge of Teaching the Ancient World," pp. 1–41 in Douglas M. Astolfi, ed., *Teaching the Ancient World.* Chico, CA: Scholars Press.

Gascoyne, Richard C. 1986. "Latin for Communication: The New York State Syllabus." *Classical Outlook* 63: 115–16.

Germani, Clara. 1990. "Schools Dust Off Classical Studies," *Christian Science Monitor,* 16 July 1990, p. 12.

Goldman, Norma, and Jacob E. Nyenhuis. 1982. *Latin via Ovid.* 2d ed. Detroit: Wayne State Univ. Press.

Goode, Stephen. 1990. "'Dead' Tongue Shows Signs of Life." *Insight,* 14 May 1990, pp. 56–57.

Grant, Michael. 1990. "One View of the Classics." *CA News* 2: 1–2.

Groton, Anne H., and James M. May. 1989. *Thirty-Eight Latin Stories*. 3d ed. Wauconda, IL: Bolchazy-Carducci.

Gummere, Richard M. 1963. *The American Colonial Mind and the Classical Tradition*. Cambridge, MA: Harvard Univ. Press.

Hakim, Joy. 1990. "Classics Are for Kids." *American Educator,* spring 1990, pp. 35–40.

Haley, Shelley P. 1989. "Classics and Minorities," pp. 333–38 in Phyllis Culham and Lowell Edmunds, eds., *Classics: A Discipline and Profession in Crisis?* Lanham, MD: University Press of America.

Hallett, Judith P. 1990. "Public Programs, Private Initiatives: Latin Day at the University of Maryland." *Classical Outlook* 68: 3–8.

Hamilton, Richard. 1990. Review of Bell and Whalen 1988–89. *Classical Outlook* 67: 99–100.

Hammond, Sandra B., and C. Edward Scebold. 1980. *Survey of Foreign Language Enrollments in Public Secondary Schools, Fall 1978*. New York: ACTFL.

Hansen, Hardy, and Gerald M. Quinn. 1987. *Greek: An Intensive Course*. Rev. ed. New York: Fordham Univ. Press.

Harward, V. Judson. 1988. "From Museum to Monitor: The Visual Exploration of the Ancient World." *Academic Computing* 2: 16–19, 69–71. Reprinted in 1989–90 *Classical Outlook* 67: 42–48.

Heath, Sebastian. 1990. "The Perseus Project." *CD-Rom Professional* 3,6: 66–70.

Hirsch, E. D., Jr. 1987. *Cultural Literacy: What Every American Needs to Know*. Boston: Houghton Mifflin.

Howard, Peter, and Linda Montross. 1990–91. Review of Jenney, et al., 1990. *Classical Outlook* 68: 73–74.

Hughes, John J. 1987. *Bits, Bytes, and Biblical Studies: A Resource Guide for the Use of Computers in Biblical and Classical Studies*. Grand Rapids, MI: Zondervan.

JACT. 1978. *Reading Greek*. Cambridge, Eng., and New York: Cambridge Univ. Press.

Janko, Richard. 1989. "Dissolution and Diaspora: Ptolemy Physcon and the Future of Classical Scholarship," pp. 321–31 in Phyllis Culham and Lowell Edmunds, eds., *Classics: A Discipline and Profession in Crisis?* Lanham, MD: University Press of America.

Jenney, Charles, et al. 1990. *First Year Latin* and *Second Year Latin*. Rev. ed. Englewood Cliffs, NJ: Prentice-Hall.

Johnston, Patricia. 1988. *Traditio: An Introduction to the Latin Language and Its Influence*. New York: Macmillan.

Jones, Peter V., and Keith C. Sidwell. 1986. *Reading Latin*. Cambridge, Eng., and New York: Cambridge Univ. Press.

Kitchell, Kenneth F., et al. 1989. "Promoting Latin in the CAMWS Area: Present Progress and Future Concerns." *Classical Journal* 84: 137–61.

Knudsvig, Glenn M., et al. 1986. *Latin for Reading.* Rev. ed. Ann Arbor: Univ. of Michigan Press.

Konstan, David. 1989. "What Is New in the New Approaches to Classical Literature," pp. 45–49 in Phyllis Culham and Lowell Edmunds, eds., *Classics: A Discipline and Profession in Crisis?* Lanham, MD: University Press of America.

Kovach, Edith. 1968. "Classics: The Teaching of Latin and Greek," pp. 389–414 in Emma Birkmaier, ed., *Britannica Review of Foreign Language Education,* vol. 1. Chicago: Encyclopaedia Britannica.

LaBouve, Bobby, et al. 1982. "Classics and the Report of the President's Commission on Foreign Languages and International Studies." *Classical Outlook* 59: 104–13.

Lacey, Douglas N. 1985. *Latin Plus.* Reynoldsburg, OH: Advocate.

LaFleur, Richard A. 1987. "Perpetuating the Renaissance: A Challenge for Latin in the Coming Decade," pp. 141–46 in Matthew S. Santirocco, ed., *Latinitas: The Tradition and Teaching of Latin.* Lubbock: Texas Tech Univ. Press.

————. 1988. "The ACL/UGA/NEH National Latin Institute." *Classical Outlook* 65: 109–16.

————. 1990. "Empowering the Teacher of Latin: Rockefeller Fellowships and the Classical Languages." *Classical Outlook* 67: 116–19.

————. 1991. "The Classical Languages and College Admissions." *Classical Outlook* 68: 124–32.

————, ed. 1987. *The Teaching of Latin in American Schools: A Profession in Crisis.* Atlanta: Scholars Press.

Latimer, John F. 1968. *The Oxford Conference and Related Activities: A Report to the National Endowment for the Humanities.* Oxford, OH: American Classical League.

Latousek, Robert B. 1989a. *Survey of Latin Instructional Software for the Computer.* Oxford, OH: American Classical League.

————. 1989b. "Random Access." *Classical Outlook* 67: 22–23.

————. 1990a. "Random Access." *Classical Outlook* 67: 88–89.

————. 1990b. "Random Access." *Classical Outlook* 68: 30–31.

Lawall, Gilbert. 1980. "The President's Commission and Classics: Recommendations and Strategies for Their Implementation." *Classical Outlook* 57: 73–79.

————, et al. 1984–90. *Ecce Romani.* 2nd ed. White Plains, NY: Longman.

————. 1988a. *ACTFL Selected Listing of Instructional Materials for Elementary and Secondary School Programs: Latin and Greek.* Yonkers, NY: ACTFL.

————, et al., eds. 1988b. Longman Latin Readers series. 6 vols. White Plains, NY: Longman.

Lehr, Fran. 1979. "Latin Study: A Promising Practice in English Vocabulary Instruction?" *Journal of Reading* 22: 76–79. Reprinted in 1980 *Classical Outlook* 57: 87–88.

Levine, Molly Myerowitz, and John Peradotto, eds. 1989. *The Challenge of "Black Athena."* [Special issue of *Arethusa.*] Buffalo: State Univ. of New York at Buffalo.

Masciantonio, Rudolph. 1977. "Tangible Benefits of the Study of Latin." *Foreign Language Annals* 10: 375–82.

Mavrogenes, Nancy. 1977. "The Effect of Latin on Language Arts Performance." *Elementary School Journal* 77: 268-73.

————. 1987. "Latin and Language Arts: An Update." *Foreign Language Annals* 20: 131–37. Reprinted in 1989 *Classical Outlook* 66: 78–83.

Mellor, Ronald. 1989. "Classics and the Teaching of Greek and Roman Civilization," pp. 99–105 in Phyllis Culham and Lowell Edmunds, eds., *Classics: A Discipline and Profession in Crisis?* Lanham, MD: University Press of America.

Moreland, Floyd L., ed. 1981. *Strategies in Teaching Greek and Latin: Two Decades of Experimentation.* APA Pamphlet, no. 7. Chico, CA: Scholars Press.

————, and Rita Fleischer. 1977. *Latin: An Intensive Course.* Rev. ed. Berkeley: Univ. of California Press.

Morford, Mark, ed. 1983. "Teaching Courses in Greek and Roman Civilizations and Classical Mythology," pp. 151–83 in Douglas M. Astolfi, ed., *Teaching the Ancient World.* Chico, CA: Scholars Press.

————, ed. 1984. *Greek and Roman Civilization: Essays on the Teaching of Four Aspects of Classical Civilizations.* Columbus: Ohio State Univ. Press.

Mydans, Seth. 1990. "Latin Redux: A 'Dead' Language Finds New Life," *New York Times,* 30 December 1990.

Mylonas, Elli. 1989. "Universes to Control: Classics, Computers, and Education," pp. 133–46 in Phyllis Culham and Lowell Edmunds, eds., *Classics: A Discipline and Profession in Crisis?* Lanham, MD: University Press of America.

National Commission on Excellence in Education. 1983. *A Nation at Risk.* Washington, DC: Government Printing Office.

National Latin Exam Committee. 1984–85. "The National Latin Exam: 1978–85." *Classical Outlook* 62: 45–47.

North, Helen F. 1985. "Report of the American Philological Association," pp. 74–81 in *A Report to the Congress of the United States of America on the State of the Humanities.* New York: American Council of Learned Societies.

O'Connor, Joseph F., and Robert J. Rowland, Jr., eds. 1987. *Teaching Classical Mythology: The 1986 APA Panel.* APA Committee on Educational Services Papers, no. 5. New York: American Philological Association.

Oerberg, Hans H. 1965. *Lingua Latina Secundum Naturae Rationem Explicata.* 4 vols. 3rd ed. New York: Nature Method Language Institute.

"Oxford Appoints Schools Liaison Officer in Classics." 1990. *JACT Bulletin* 84: 7.

Palma, Ronald B. 1984–85. "*Ecce Romani:* A Preview of the North American Revision." *Classical Outlook* 62: 42–44.

Parker, William R. 1957. *The National Interest and Foreign Languages*. Washington, DC: UNESCO.

Pascal, Nanette R. 1988–89. "Integrating the Classics into General Education: The NEH / Richland College Classics Cluster Project." *Classical Outlook* 66: 38–42.

Peradotto, John. 1989. "Texts and Unrefracted Facts: Philology, Hermeneutics, and Semiotics," pp. 179–98 in Phyllis Culham and Lowell Edmunds, eds., *Classics: A Discipline and Profession in Crisis?* Lanham, MD: University Press of America.

Perkell, Christine. 1984. "Women in Classical Literature," pp. 11–31, 51–52 in Mark Morford, ed., *Greek and Roman Civilization: Essays on the Teaching of Four Aspects of Classical Civilizations*. Columbus: Ohio State Univ. Press.

Phillips, Oliver. 1987. "Two Years with 'Latin Skills.'" *Classical Outlook* 65: 32.

Phinney, Ed. 1980. "Cambridge Latin Course at the University of Massachusetts." *Classical Outlook* 57: 102–6.

———. 1981. "Revision of the Cambridge Latin Course: An Update." *Classical Outlook* 59: 6–7.

———. 1987. "The Current Classical Scene in America." *JACT Review* 2d series 2: 2–7. Reprinted in 1989 *Classical Outlook* 66: 119–25.

———. 1989. "The Classics in American Education," pp. 77–87 in Phyllis Culham and Lowell Edmunds, eds., *Classics: A Discipline and Profession in Crisis?* Lanham, MD: University Press of America.

———, ed. 1988–89. *Cambridge Latin Course*. 3d ed. Cambridge, Eng., and New York: Cambridge Univ. Press.

Polsky, Marion. 1986. "The NEH / Brooklyn College Latin Cornerstone Project, 1982–84: Genesis, Implementation, Evaluation." *Classical Outlook* 63: 77–83.

———. 1987. "The New *First Latin* Program," pp. 147–53 in Matthew S. Santirocco, ed., *Latinitas: The Tradition and Teaching of Latin*. Lubbock: Texas Tech Univ. Press.

President's Commission on Foreign Language and International Studies. 1979. *Strength through Wisdom: A Critique of U.S. Capability*. Washington, DC: Government Printing Office.

Randall, John G., et al. 1986. *Learning Latin: An Introductory Course for Adults*. Liverpool, Eng.: Francis Cairns.

"A Recommendation from the Classical Association of New England on the Teaching of Latin and Greek." 1990. *New England Classical Newsletter and Journal* 17,3: 7–8.

Reinhold, Meyer. 1984. *Classica Americana: The Greek and Roman Heritage in the United States*. Detroit: Wayne State Univ. Press.

———. 1987. "The Latin Tradition in America," pp. 123–39 in Matthew S. Santirocco, ed., *Latinitas: The Tradition and Teaching of Latin*. Lubbock: Texas Tech Univ. Press.

Richlin, Amy. 1989. "Is Classics Dead?" pp. 51–65 in Phyllis Culham and Lowell Edmunds, eds., *Classics: A Discipline and Profession in Crisis?* Lanham, MD: University Press of America.

Salerno, Dorsey P. 1987. *Latin in Motion.* Oxford, OH: American Classical League.

Santirocco, Matthew S., ed. 1987. *Latinitas: The Tradition and Teaching of Latin.* Lubbock: Texas Tech Univ. Press.

Scanlan, Richard. 1980. "Computer-Assisted Instruction in Latin." *Foreign Language Annals* 13: 53–55. Reprinted in 1980–81 *Classical Outlook* 58: 44–45.

————. 1981. "Computer-Assisted Instruction in Latin and in English Vocabulary Development." *Studies in Language Learning* 3,1: 11–22.

————. 1985–86. Review of Gerald Culley, Latin Skills (computer software). *Classical Outlook* 63: 70, 72.

Seligson, Gerda. 1981. "Reading Latin: A Progress Report," pp. 11–16 in Floyd L. Moreland, ed., *Strategies in Teaching Greek and Latin: Two Decades of Experimentation.* APA Pamphlet, no. 7. Chico, CA: Scholars Press.

Skinner, Marilyn B. 1989. "Expecting the Barbarians: Feminism, Nostalgia, and the 'Epistemic Shift' in Classical Studies," pp. 199–210 in Phyllis Culham and Lowell Edmunds, eds., *Classics: A Discipline and Profession in Crisis?* Lanham, MD: University Press of America.

Strasheim, Lorraine A. 1982–83. "Latin in the Total School Curriculum: Reaching toward the Twenty-First Century." *Classical Outlook* 60: 37–40.

————. 1983. "Latin and Emerging Adolescent Education." *Prospects* 1983: 1–4. Reprinted in 1984–85 *Classical Outlook* 62: 55–58.

————. 1990. "Latin in the 1990s and Beyond." *NASSP Curriculum Report* 20,1: 1–4.

Sullivan, J. P. 1990. Review of Culham and Edmunds. *Classical Outlook* 68: 35–36.

Sussman, Lewis A. 1978. "The Decline of Basic Skills: A Suggestion So Old That It's New." *Classical Journal* 73: 346–52.

————. 1989. "The Research, Publication, Advancement Triangle and the Teaching of Classical Civilization Courses," pp. 107–15 in Phyllis Culham and Lowell Edmunds, eds., *Classics: A Discipline and Profession in Crisis?* Lanham, MD: University Press of America.

Taylor, Martha C., and Gilbert Lawall. 1984. "American Philological Association: Greek and Latin Textbook Survey." *Classical Outlook* 61: 108–10.

Tebben, Joseph. 1984. "Greek and Roman Athletics," pp. 63–87 in Mark Morford, ed., *Greek and Roman Civilization: Essays on the Teaching of Four Aspects of Classical Civilizations.* Columbus: Ohio State Univ. Press.

Ullman, B. L., et al. 1965. *Latin for Americans.* New York: Macmillan.

Vaughn, John. 1984. "Roman Law," pp. 89–117 in Mark Morford, ed., *Greek and Roman Civilization: Essays on the Teaching of Four Aspects of Classical Civilizations.* Columbus: Ohio State Univ. Press.

Waite, Stephen V. F. 1970. "Computer-Supplemented Latin Instruction at Dartmouth College." *Computers in the Humanities* 1: 313–14.

Waldinger, Renée. 1990. "Training PhD Students to Teach in College." *ADFL Bulletin* 22,1: 20–23.

West, Andrew F., ed. 1917. *Value of the Classics.* Princeton, NJ: Princeton Univ. Press.

Western Interstate Commission for Higher Education. 1988. *High School Graduates: Projections by State, 1986–2004.* Boulder, CO: WICHE.

Wheelock, Frederic M. 1963. *Latin: An Introductory Course Based on Ancient Authors.* 3d ed. New York: Barnes and Noble.

Wiley, Patricia D. 1984–85. "High School Foreign Language Study and College Academic Performance." *Classical Outlook* 62: 33–36.

Wooley, Allan, and Matthew I. Wiencke. 1990. "Highlights of the November Meeting on the Establishment of Norms in the Teaching of Latin and Greek." *New England Classical Newsletter and Journal* 17,3: 5–7.

Wyatt, William F. 1983. "Philologia Rediviva." *Classical World* 77: 27–32.

————. 1990. "Latin Is a Language." *New England Classical Newsletter and Journal* 17,3: 30–32.

Yom, Sue-Sun. 1990. "Shortage of Latin Teachers Threatens to Undermine Resurgence of Subject." *Wall Street Journal,* 6 November 1990, page C15.

APPENDIX 9A:
LATIN ENROLLMENTS, CLASSICAL ASSOCIATION MEMBERSHIPS, AND LATIN/GREEK EXAM PARTICIPANTS (1960–1990)

Year	H.S. Latin[1] 9-12	College Latin[2]	College Greek[2] (Ancient)	NJCL	NSCL	ACL	APA	CAMWS Area[3]	CAMWS Total[4]	CAAS	CAPN	CANE	AIA	CAC	Natl. Latin Exam	Latin AT	Latin AP	Natl. Greek Exam	Natl. Myth Exam
1960	654,670[5]	25,700[5]	12,700[5]	72,280		4622		2192	4363			892	2746	560		10,048	208		
1961	695,297			84,070		5497	1568	2296	4577			930	3014	518		13,474	352		
1962	702,135			101,416		5613	1685	2378	4696	950[5]		933	3404	582		16,980	439		
1963	680,234			105,238		5936	1784	2541	5027			929	3693	580		17,788	677		
1964	590,047			107,086	213	6252	1855	2591	5143	953		921	3868	619		20,244	862		
1965	591,445	39,600[6]	19,500[6]	101,810	448	6120	2053	2649	5184	956		934	4202	636		22,297	885		
1966				106,990	694	6064	2175	2736	5239	860		954	4520	667		20,670	984		
1967				98,201		5855	2355	2698	5112	841		973	5173	547		19,561	882		
1968	371,977	34,981	17,516	88,727		5812	2468	2768	5244			906	5996	562		18,462	971		
1969				51,437	766	5209	2586	2682	5205			904	6446	554		15,920	1208		
1970	265,293	27,591	16,697	52,339		4465	2770	2606	4816			841	6753			12,777	1046		
1971				43,741	674	4118	2765	2600	4618			780	6867			7,460	975		
1972				39,772		3872	2837	2512	4449			730	6889			5,425	853		
1973				36,890		3444	2861	2231	3968		124	752	6695			4,231	705		
1974	167,165	25,167	24,391	32,918	610	3562	2900	1991	3524		127	724	6202			3,049	611		
1975				28,894		3469	2928	1916	3443		129	714	5752			1,433	624		
1976	150,470	24,403	25,843	30,532	632	2970		1872	3535	750[5]	125	651	6063			1,555	745		
1977				28,870	543	2814	2864	1834	3357	685	132	641	6999	548		1,734	841		
1978	151,782			29,010		2771	2855	1754	3100	787	122	576	7601	542	9,000[8]	1,725	880		
1979				31,152		2890	2847	1654	3071	734	125	616	7923	559	16,497	1,649	1016		
1980		25,035	22,111	32,026	600	2880	2932	1618	2915		141	606	8758	557	20,710	2,060	1122		
1981				33,924		3006	3025	1657	2881		120	645	9680	559	27,602	2,258	1261	310	
1982	169,580			37,017	659	2995	3025	1575	2753	643	109	662	8981	548	33,336	2,587	1311	415	
1983		24,224	19,350	40,574	643	2980	3087	1611	2757	630	107	712	8717	530	35,604	2,455	1529	597	
1984				44,452	550	3061	3093	1651	2805	682	99	756	8645	535	46,565	2,685	1704	545	
1985	176,841			48,350	525[5]	3088	2890	1613	2682	675	120	777	8739		53,505	2,865	1929	639	
1986		25,038	17,608	49,489	478	3472	2925	1637	2809	781	106	810	8668		60,026	3,140	2104	752	
1987				46,902	485	3649	2970	1669	2865	656	124		7545		60,758	3,227	2545	957	
1988				48,416	562	3626	3018	1646	2707	652	132		7230		63,750	3,617	2630	813	
1989				51,320	522	3896	2966	1623	2741	678	128		7560		69,205	3,452	2688	779	
1990				52,562	534	3844		1657	2711		135		8505		71,457	3,338	2712	795	3208

Abbreviations: NJCL, National Junior Classical League; NSCL, National Senior Classical League; ACL, American Classical League; APA, American Philological Association; CAMWS, Classical Association of the Middle West and South; CAAS, Classical Association of the Atlantic States; CAPN, Classical Association of the Pacific Northwest; CANE, Classical Association of New England; AIA, Archaeological Institute of America; CAC, Classical Association of Canada; Latin AT, the College Board's Latin Achievement Test; Latin AP, the College Board's Latin Advanced Placement Exam.

[1]Source: ACTFL. [2]Source: MLA. [3]Includes only members in the thirty CAMWS states and two Canadian provinces. [4]Includes members, subscribers to the *Classical Journal* (the association's journal) from outside CAMWS territory. [5]Estimated. [6]Rounded to the nearest hundred by MLA.

Table updated from R.A. LaFleur, ed., *The Teaching of Latin in American Schools: A Profession in Crisis* (Atlanta, GA: Scholars Press, 1987; 1989 rpt. available from ACL, Miami University, Oxford, OH 45056).

APPENDIX 9B:
CRITICAL INSTRUCTIONAL ISSUES IN THE CLASSICS FOR AMERICAN SCHOOLS (ABBOTT 1991)

Summary and Recommendations

The Classics profession made great strides during the 1980's as enrollments in Latin increased and classicists at all levels developed innovative collaborative efforts. Because of the important benefits that students derive from the study of the Classics and Latin, the coming decade must see a renewed commitment by the profession to build on the strengths and new directions of the 80's, to secure the place of these important classical studies in the curriculum of all American schools, and to develop innovative and practical ways to face the challenge of a shortage of qualified Latin teachers. In addition, classicists must redefine curriculum and pedagogy for the Classics and Latin in the schools in relation to the needs of the students of the 90's and the current focus on international education.

In light of the above, classicists at the ACTFL Conference have identified the following priorities with accompanying recommendations:

Work to ensure a vital role for the Classics and Latin in the curriculum of all American schools.

- Formulate a rationale for the Classics and Latin, in both the elementary and secondary curricula, which would take into consideration the diversity among students and the need for a curriculum that supports multicultural, global education.

- Seek to make the teaching of the ancient world, classical literature in translation, and mythology an integral part of the school curriculum.

- Make Latin instruction available as widely as possible and as early as possible to all students.

- Promote a role for Latin in exploratory language courses.

Adapt Latin pedagogy so that Latin instruction focuses on teaching Latin as a language including development of proficiency in all four language skills with primary emphasis on reading.

- Formulate a broad and flexible set of norms regarding the balance between instruction in language and culture, the pace of instruction, and the rate at which levels of mastery of elements and structures of the language should be expected and achieved.

- Develop measurable standards of proficiency in students' ability to read Latin at set levels of achievement, accompanied by measurable proficiency standards in listening, speaking, and writing.

- Continue research and development of computer-assisted instruction, interactive video, and distance learning to facilitate development of language skills and to enable Latin instruction to be offered to more students.

Encourage active recruitment of teachers of Latin while ensuring that there are high quality training programs and staff development opportunities for in-service teachers.

- Increase efforts to recruit new teachers and to retrain current teachers as Latin teachers.

- Develop a variety of in-service training programs and summer institutes to acquaint teachers with all available methods, pedagogical strategies, and materials.

Promote collaborative efforts within the Classics profession and with modern language organizations to achieve strength through working toward shared goals.

- Improve articulation between school and college/university instruction in Latin.

- Increase efforts in the area of public awareness and promotion of the study of the Classics, Latin, and Greek in the schools.

- Renew commitment to networking both within the classical language profession and with the modern language profession to identify purposes in common and areas of cooperation and mutual support.

APPENDIX 9C:
A RECOMMENDATION FROM THE CLASSICAL ASSOCIATION OF NEW ENGLAND ON THE TEACHING OF LATIN AND GREEK ("RECOMMENDATION" 1990)

There is currently a nationwide call for statements of educational goals and purposes in teaching of every academic subject, including Latin and Greek. The Classical Association of New England, representing the teachers of Classics in the secondary schools and colleges of New England, is in an excellent position to make such a statement on instruction in Latin and Greek. This recommendation is made to the end that instruction in ancient languages be more broadly understood and appreciated by the public, by schools, by accrediting agencies, and by state and local departments of education. It is offered with the further hope that excellent instruction in Latin, a language fundamental to our culture, may become available to every student in school and college.

I. What is the aim of instruction in Latin and Greek?
   A. The use of Latin has varied broadly over the centuries. In the present age the purpose of teaching Latin in schools and colleges should include the following:
      1. To read Latin literature, because of its intrinsic value and its continuing, unbroken influence on the literature and thought of our culture;
      2. To understand better how language works in general, to facilitate the learning of other languages, and to improve the mastery of the English language; and
      3. To understand and appreciate better the history and culture of the world.
   B. Instruction in Latin should reflect the preceding purposes in the following:
      1. Stress upon the elements of the language (grammar, syntax, and vocabulary) should be strong enough to allow students to understand at sight passages from Latin authors with some assistance in the form of commentary on rarely-seen vocabulary and sentence-structures. Understanding may be expressed through translation, parsing, summarization, paraphrase, and responses to questions on the passage. Intermediate college courses expect the ability to translate and analyze grammar and syntax.

2. Conversation and composition in Latin should be designed to help students learn to read Latin literature, since they offer an opportunity for active rather than merely passive use of the language.

3. Motivation to read Latin literature should be instilled and increased by the presentation and assessment of Roman culture and history. This presentation may be varied but should be initiated and elaborated through Latin texts where possible.

C. The study of Greek should continue, as it has been since the Renaissance, for the purpose of reading Greek literature. The prior study of Latin is helpful in learning Greek. The benefits from the study of Greek literature are the same in kind as from the study of Latin literature. Students of Latin should be encouraged to study Greek both in the secondary schools and in colleges, since Greek and Roman literature are closely related.

II. For what pedagogical conditions is this recommendation intended?

A. The pace of instruction may vary from class to class and school to school, but it is more affected by the amount of class time than the age or maturity of the student. Completion of "intermediate secondary school Latin" should be understood to mean that the student will have completed the essential elements of grammar (morphology), syntax (sentence-structure), and vocabulary of the Latin language, and will have read some Latin literature. This stage of achievement has traditionally been attempted by approximately the end of the second year of instruction in the secondary school and by the end of one year in college. "Intermediate college Latin," traditionally completed in two years of study in college, should be understood to include the reading of both Latin prose and Latin poetry.

B. Higher levels of Latin should include with the reading of Latin literature a systematic review of grammar and syntax.

C. Latin and Greek, like all foreign languages, should be taught with maximum efficiency so as to instill in the students the greatest interest and motivation to learn. Students should be encouraged to begin the study of Latin as early and to continue as long as possible. School schedules should allow students to study as least two foreign languages.

III. How should the results of instruction in ancient languages be evaluated?

A. There is a wide variety of tests that teachers may use to evaluate the progress of their students. Among these are the National Latin Exam, the CEEB Achievement Test, the Advanced Placement Tests (AP), and various tests of the individual states.

B. It should be recognized that these tests may be based upon a syllabus of readings different from that of individual programs. To the extent possible such "standardized" tests should attempt to reflect rather than control the actual curriculum of Latin instruction.

C. One measure of results is the ability of secondary students to continue their study of Latin and Greek in college. To this end colleges should make clear, if possible through their catalogues, the preparation required for their intermediate courses.

10

Testing as a Guide to Student and Teacher: Placement, Achievement, Proficiency

Rebecca M. Valette
Boston College

TESTING AS A GUIDE TO STUDENT AND TEACHER

The main role of testing in a university foreign-language program is to provide information about how students are doing, for themselves as well as for their instructors: what courses they should take, how they stand in relationship to one another, and whether they have completed course or diploma requirements.

Testing also plays an important role in determining the nature of the university language program. Whether we like it or not, students study for tests and are motivated by obtaining good grades. The way in which we assign grades and the types of tests we use in effect determine the objectives of our courses and influence the way in which students study. Through our tests, we are able to encourage the types of learning activities most conducive to successful language acquisition.

Most college language departments do not have a testing specialist on their faculty. In fact, the great majority of foreign-language professors are unfamiliar with psychometrics and uncomfortable with statistics. This chapter, therefore, constitutes a brief and simplified introduction to the complex field of foreign-language testing and evaluation. In order to make additional source material available to faculty and teaching assistants, it would be useful to establish a departmental reference library containing a few of the following basic language testing manuals: Valette 1977; Finocchiaro and Sako 1983; Carroll and Hall 1985; Madsen 1983; Underhill 1987; Henning 1987.

PURPOSES OF
LANGUAGE TESTING AND EVALUATION

College and university language programs generally use tests and other forms of evaluation for three purposes:

- To determine *placement* in the departmental course sequence

- To measure *achievement* in a given course, including proficiency-oriented goals

- To measure overall *proficiency* in relation to exterior norms or as part of undergraduate or graduate degree requirements

The name of a given test, however, does not necessarily reflect its purpose. Certain "achievement" tests may function as placement instruments or measures of overall proficiency. Some "proficiency" tests may be incorporated in language courses to measure the achievement of specific objectives.

It should be noted that in recent years the term *proficiency* has been widely used to describe the students' ability to use a second language for communication. In a "proficiency-first" program, emphasis is on creative language use, often with a high tolerance for inaccuracy of expression as long as messages are considered comprehensible. In a "grammar-oriented" or "accuracy-first" program, emphasis is on having students learn to manipulate the second language correctly with the expectation that they will then be able to use the language for effective communication. Most universities are turning to "grammar-supported proficiency-oriented" programs, which combine a concern with building a solid linguistic foundation with frequent opportunities for creative self-expression.

SOME BASIC MEASUREMENT CONCEPTS

Although college language teachers do not need to be experts in measurement and evaluation, they should be familiar with three basic concepts; reliability, validity, and standard error.[1]

Reliability

The *reliability* of a test refers to the dependability or consistency of its scores. In other words, if a student receives a B+ or 88 on a test, that score should provide a reliable reflection of the student's ability. Test reliability depends on four factors: standard tasks, multiple samples, standard conditions, and standard scoring.

Standard tasks   All students are answering the same (or equivalent) questions.

In single-section courses with written examinations, this requirement is easily met. There is sometimes a problem, however, with multisection courses where each instructor prepares a different examination for his or her classes. In this event, an "A" on a test given in one section may not reflect the same type or the same level of performance as an "A" on a test in a parallel section. Reliability can be improved by having all those teaching in a multisection course share in the construction of tests and the establishment of the grading system.

Multiple samples   The examination consists of numerous questions that reflect the many aspects of the subject being tested.

Most elementary language exams meet this criterion because they are composed of many short-answer questions. In literature or culture courses, however, it may happen that the final exam questions focus on only one or two aspects of the course. For example, if the main question on an exam in nineteenth century French poetry deals only with Victor Hugo, it will not be a reliable measure of how well students are acquainted with Musset, Lamartine, Baudelaire, or Verlaine. It will also penalize students who spent most of their time studying the latter poets. From the reliability point of view, it is better to have an exam that, in addition to some longer essay questions, also contains a broad sampling of short-answer questions drawn from the many topics of the course.

Standard conditions   All students take the test under the same conditions. For the well-known standardized tests, such as the College Board Achievement Tests and the Graduate Record Examinations, this means that all students take the test on the same day and are allotted exactly the same amount of time to answer the questions. In reality, however, standardizing the conditions is more complex. For example, if a student has the flu on the day the test is given, the resulting score may not be a reliable reflection of his or her true ability. A student with dyslexia or one who is a slow writer might need more time than other students to complete an equivalent examination. In a rare case at Boston College several years ago, there was a beginning language student who was clearly an "A" student in class but who was consistently getting "D's" and "F's" on tests: it turned out that she had such a fear of tests that she simply froze when the word was mentioned. The solution was to excuse her from all tests (because they simply were not reliable measures of her ability) and have her spend the equivalent amount of time on extra reading or listening comprehension activities; her final grade was based on her classwork.

Standard scoring   All tests are scored according to the same standards so that if the same test were scored by someone else, the result would be the same.

Multiple-choice items and questions where there is a single correct answer (such as a verb form needed to complete a sentence) provide highly reliable scores. Essay questions are much less reliable, for not only may different teachers score an essay differently, but even a single teacher reading a pile of essay questions may become more lenient (or more severe) as the task of grading wears on. The scoring of less structured tests, such as oral interviews and written compositions, can be made more reliable through the establishment of precise scoring guidelines.

Validity

The *validity* of a test concerns what the test measures and how effectively it does so. For instance, in the area of *content validity,* a vocabulary test that has students give the foreign-language equivalents of a list of English words measures the ability to pair words in the two languages but does not necessarily indicate whether students can use these words appropriately in a conversation or composition. A placement test has high *predictive validity* if its scores allow the department to place incoming students correctly in the language sequence.

In the area of foreign-language testing, there is an ongoing tug-of-war between maintaining good reliability and establishing high content validity. For example, a written final examination in a beginning language course may be quite reliable because it contains many short-answer questions, but it may be of limited validity because it does not evaluate the communicative aspects of the program: namely, the students' ability to express themselves orally and in writing, to understand authentic speech, and to read for personal meaning. An oral interview, if administered by teachers with some evaluation training, can be quite valid but provide scores that are not as reliable as those of a multiple-choice test. The art of testing in the foreign-language classroom is one of selecting a combination of measurement instruments that permits a reasonably reliable and valid evaluation of the students' progress, while encouraging course activities that help students develop effective and accurate communication skills. (For a more extensive discussion of validity in second-language tests, see Stevenson 1985.)

Standard Error

Standard error is a crucial concept that is frequently ignored or misunderstood. Simply stated, standard error means that even if a test were extremely reliable and completely valid, most student test scores would still fluctuate somewhat, except for those at the extremities of the scale. For example, three B– language students of equivalent ability may end up with different grades on a given test: one may get a few unexpected questions right and be given a B, the second may make some "stupid" mistakes and be given a C+, and the third will perform at his or her "true" level and get a B–. The A+ student who has studied is likely, however, to continue getting A+ grades, while the F student who has not studied will always get an F.

While for most students the score on any given test is open to some interpretation, given the element of standard error, the average of many such test scores across the semester offers a more precise picture of the student's ability. A potentially unfair situation can arise when a single test score is used to make a crucial academic decision, as has traditionally been the case in European higher education, where a student's future orientation could be determined by performance on the *Abitur* or the *concours* of a *Grande École*. A similar unfair situation may obtain in U.S. colleges when a graduation language requirement is made to depend on performance on a single test.

APTITUDE TESTING

Much of the research in foreign-language aptitude was conducted in the 1950s and 1960s leading to the development, for adult students, of the Carroll-Sapon *Modern Language Aptitude Test* or MLAT (Carroll and Sapon 1959). Thirty years later various government agencies are expressing a renewed interest in predicting success in second-language learning (Parry and Stansfield, eds. 1991). In particular, they have classified the world's languages into four categories of difficulty and have determined minimum aptitude scores for each category (Lett and O'Mara 1991: 224; see also Appendix B at the end of this volume).

In general, American colleges and universities do not use aptitude tests for selection purposes. A few schools, however, do use scores on the MLAT to determine whether a student's measured aptitude is so low that he or she should be exempted from a language requirement. (There is a potential problem here in that students may intentionally score poorly in order to gain an exemption.)

For universities offering instruction in a variety of languages, it might be appropriate to adopt an aptitude instrument for counseling purposes. Students wishing to study the more difficult languages, such as Chinese or Japanese, could determine in advance whether their aptitude level was such that they could expect to perform well in an academic language-learning environment.

PLACING STUDENTS IN
THE APPROPRIATE COURSE SEQUENCE

One of the annual challenges of departments of French and Spanish—and to a lesser extent German, Italian, and Russian—is how to place incoming students into a basic language sequence. One can no longer reliably equate numbers of years of prior study with specific college courses because students come from such varying backgrounds. In two years of Spanish one high school may "cover" twice as much material as another school. One French program may stress oral communication while another stresses grammatical accuracy and vocabulary building. One student may have had German in 11th and 12th grades and then continue with the language in the freshman year of college, while another student from the same program may wait until senior year to take another German course, having certainly forgotten a great deal of material in the intervening three years.

Basically each foreign-language department must tailor a placement procedure to correspond to its own course sequence. The most common systems are self-placement, College Board (CEEB) Achievement Test scores, and local placement instruments. In addition to the above, there are the innovative placement tests in the CAT (computerized adaptive testing) format. (For a survey of placement procedures in university Spanish departments, see Wherritt and Cleary 1990.)

In *self-placement,* students are given a description of each course accompanied by suggested prerequisites. These prerequisite statements relate directly to the course content, for example:

Elementary Spanish 101 (A). No prior study of Spanish.

Elementary Spanish 101 (B). Students can talk and write about daily-life activities using the present. (Typical background: two years of junior high Spanish or one year of high school Spanish.)

Elementary Spanish 102. Students can talk and write about daily-life activities using the present and the preterite. (Typical background: three years of junior high Spanish or one or two years of high school Spanish.)

The course descriptions and their prerequisites are mailed by the department to incoming freshmen in May, together with an explanatory letter advising students to discuss their placement with their most recent high school language teacher. Students mail back a form indicating their choice of courses. The advantage of self-placement is not only that faculty do not have to be mobilized for placement testing during orientation week, but also that the department has had the summer during which to place students into classes and to arrange for the required number of sections, classrooms, and teachers.

Other departments use *College Board Achievement Tests,* which provide scores ranging from 200 to 800. Since many incoming students may not have taken language achievement tests in high school, the college then administers retired forms of these tests during fall orientation as part of the placement procedure.[2] Because these tests are scored by machine, the results are usually available from the college testing center within a day or two of administration. Each language department then establishes its own system of placement cutoff scores as a function of past experience.

Still other departments have established their own *local placement tests* that correspond directly to their course sequence. Since these tests are also administered during fall orientation immediately before classes begin, it is important that their results be available within 24 hours. They are, therefore, usually either machine-scored multiple-choice tests or fill-in-the-blank written tests that can be rapidly scored by hand. These tests may or may not have a listening comprehension portion.

The *CAT placement tests* (Henning 1987: 136–140; Stansfield 1990: 398–399) are administered individually with a microcomputer, which may be used in conjunction with an interactive tape recorder or videodisc. The computer analyzes the results of each item as the test proceeds, estimates the student's level of proficiency, and then selects additional items to confirm that estimate. The test is terminated once the student's level has been ascertained. Therefore, the CAT test takes less time than the typical placement test because students are not asked to answer questions far above or below their ability level. Such a placement test in Spanish (S-CAPE: Spanish Computer Adaptive Proficiency Exam) has been developed at Brigham Young University and is available through CALICO.[3]

The goal of the placement procedure is to place the largest possible number of students appropriately from the outset, but no system is perfect. Whether a school adopts self-placement (where some students may misestimate their ability) or a placement instrument (where scores may be affected by the imperfections in the test and the factor of standard error), there will always be 5 percent to 10 percent of the students who are misplaced and who need to be changed from one course to another during the first week of classes. An effective short global test, which can be administered on the first day of class, is the *dictation* (Oller 1979: chapter 10). Students who score significantly above or below the class average can be sent to the coordinator for an interview and possible transfer to another course.

Some instructors, especially in more advanced language courses, prefer to base their judgment on an interview or a writing sample. The important consideration is that during the drop–add period all instructors continue to monitor student performance carefully so as to advise those who should be moved up or down to a more appropriate level.

One serious placement problem is that of students with prior foreign-language experience who insist on enrolling in an elementary course. These "false beginners" often claim to have forgotten what they learned in high school or may insist that their previous instruction was inadequate. While this may be true in some cases, often these students mainly want to be assured of a high mark for little effort in order to pull up their overall grade point average. Placement testing does not solve the "false beginner" problem, for such students will purposely perform poorly in order to be placed down. An effective solution is to adopt a departmental policy (published in the university catalog) whereby students who offer two high school language credits for admission may only audit but cannot receive college credit for the first-semester elementary course. Similarly, students who offer three high school credits are informed that they cannot receive college credit for the first- and the second-semester elementary courses.

ACHIEVEMENT TESTING AND EVALUATION

Basic Language Courses

The largest enrollments in most college language programs are found in the elementary and intermediate courses. If these courses are free electives, most of the students who enroll are eager to improve their command of the second language. As more colleges reinstate language requirements, however, these courses are increasingly populated by students whose main motivation is academic survival as demonstrated by maintaining a reasonable grade point average. The way in which progress is assessed and grades are calculated, consequently, can have a significant impact on how students study and by extension how much they learn from the course. This is particularly true now, at a time when students, even those motivated to acquire a second language, find themselves under great pressure to do well in their courses.

Drawing up the syllabus and establishing the grading system   In the commonly taught languages, most colleges offer several sections at each of the basic levels. Typically all sections use the same textbook and follow the same syllabus. In many cases, there are also common tests. The syllabus and grading system are established either by a course coordinator or by a committee of all those teaching the class. Since in many institutions this syllabus is considered a "legal contract" for which teachers and students may be held accountable, it must often be filed with the chairperson, if not the dean.

A well-worded syllabus will clearly indicate the objectives of the course and will describe how performance is to be evaluated. If a syllabus mentions only two midterms and a final exam, there is nothing to prevent a student from cutting classes and failing to hand in homework as long as he or she passes the required tests. On the other hand, a carefully structured syllabus can reward regular class participation and encourage meaningful preparation. The following description is taken from a syllabus for a beginning language course:

Elementary French:
second semester

Course emphasis:
The emphasis of the course is on language *acquisition* and interpersonal communication. The course requires regular classroom participation and approximately 2 hours of outside preparation (listening, writing, and grammar study) for every hour of class.

Grading:
Grades will be determined as follows:

preparation and participation (30%)

workbook: 15 assignments @ 5 points each	75
compositions: 15 assignments @ 3 points each	45
laboratory listening: 15 assignments @ 5 points each	75
reading selections: 5 assignments @ 5 points each	25
participation	80

tests and quizzes (70%)

unit tests (listening and writing): 50 points each	250
pronunciation tests (recorded dialogs): 4 @ 25 points	100
speaking tests: 2 @ 50 points	100
final examination	250
TOTAL (to be divided by 10)	1000

Grading of outside preparations:	compositions	other work
complete, correct, and on time	3 points	5 points
1 or 2 days late	2 points	3 points
3 to 7 days late	1 point	2 points
over 7 days late	½ point	1 point

(points may be subtracted from the above for work poorly done)

Participation grade:
3 absences tolerated
10 points off for each subsequent absence

With a syllabus of this type, students quickly realize that by doing regular homework and coming to class they earn 30 percent of their final grade. This allows the instructor to spend most of the class hour on oral communication activities because the students have prepared the lesson. The written assignments can be corrected in small groups during the last five minutes of the period. (Since students realize that they will lose points for errors that have not been corrected, they are careful in checking their work and asking the instructor for assistance when necessary. Thus motivated, they learn from their mistakes. Subsequently, the instructor only needs to record the points in the grade book and spot-check the homework, because most corrections have been made by the students prior to handing in their papers.)

Adapting commercial tests   The publishers of most basic language textbooks, especially those in the commonly taught languages, offer their users free test programs or test banks. It is important to look at these test programs carefully, analyzing the types of items and determining which ones fit the aims of the departmental program. While occasionally these tests may be adopted in their entirety, it is much more common that course coordinators will use portions of the commercial test and add sections that they and their colleagues have developed. The most important goal is to maintain an effective balance between skill-getting items, where accuracy is essential, and skill-using segments, where the emphasis is on communication first. (In addition to the testing handbooks mentioned above, coordinators may also wish to consult Omaggio 1986: chapter 8 and appendix C; Rivers et al. 1988: chapter 10; Rivers and Nahir 1989: chapter 10).

Emphasizing the importance of listening comprehension   By including a heavy listening comprehension component in regular unit tests, instructors of elementary courses can encourage students to strengthen both their listening skills and their speaking ability. In addition to traditional brief listening items (is a sentence logical or not? does the sentence refer to a past event or a future event? where is the speaker?—in a restaurant? a train station? a furniture store?

etc.), oral cues can also be used for the grammar and vocabulary sections of the test.

For example, students hear: *Dites à Pierre de se reposer. (Tell Pierre to rest).* They write: *Pierre, repose-toi.*

In order to produce the right response, students must first understand the spoken cues, which are read only twice. (At first, students will complain that such listening / writing items are too difficult, but they soon learn to study with cassettes, thus acquiring a sense of what the new language sounds like and a feeling for what is correct.)

At the intermediate and more advanced levels, it is important that the listening comprehension tests not become exercises in memory and retention. The most effective listening comprehension tasks are those that parallel real-life situations in which students know in advance what specific information they are interested in. For example, before hearing a railroad station announcement, the students are told what to listen for:

You are at the train station and want to meet a friend who is coming in from Munich. What time is the train due and on which track is it arriving?

Then they hear a recording announcing several trains, including the one from Munich. This approach is much more valid than one in which the students first listen to the entire announcement and only then are asked to recall specific information.

Encouraging accurate pronunciation   Recorded pronunciation tests encourage students to pay close attention to how the language is spoken. Students are given an instruction sheet telling them which passage to practice, how to make their recordings, and how their performance will be graded. If the grading system is challenging, students will be very conscientious in preparing their cassettes, often making many recordings until they are satisfied they have done their best. For example, in the French course described in the above syllabus, students are informed that the recorded pronunciation tests are graded as follows:

25 points
Accurate intonation and pronunciation:
Text recorded at conversational speed (as on tape program)
Rhythm and intonation are natural (as on tape program)
No unnatural pauses between words; phrases are linked (as on
     tape program)
Almost no mistakes of pronunciation

23 points
Near-accurate intonation and pronunciation

20 points
Generally correct and comprehensible, but with several errors

17 points
Generally correct, but with quite a few errors

15 points
Difficult to understand; many errors

(5 points subtracted from grade if cassette is handed in late.)

Assessing oral proficiency   One of the challenges of large multisection classes is how to schedule and administer oral tests. One would want to have at least two such tests per semester, if at all possible. With beginning classes in the first semester, it is usually most effective for the teacher to interview students individually: often two minutes per student is sufficient and the entire class can be rapidly tested in one period. Grades are assigned according to a holistic scale, such as the following:

A+
Student understood everything said and did not ask for repetitions.
Student speech was fluent.
All questions answered and relevant information given.
All statements were structurally correct.
Native speaker would understand everything that was said.

A
Student understood almost everything and only asked for clarification
    once.
Student speech had no unnatural pauses; almost effortless.
All relevant information was given.
Only minor structural problems.
Native speaker would understand almost everything said.

B
Student understood most questions and if questions were repeated, stu-
    dent understood them easily the second time.
Student speech had hardly any unnatural pauses.
Most of the relevant information was given.
Many correct statements, but some structural problems.
Native speaker would understand most of what was said.

C

Student asked for clarification on about half the questions.

Student speech had some unnatural pauses; sometimes halting.

Only half the relevant information was given.

Some correct statements but many structural problems.

Native speaker would understand with difficulty what was said.

D

Student had trouble understanding over half the questions.

Student speech was frequently halting and fragmented.

Less than half the relevant information was given.

Few statements were structurally correct.

Native speaker would understand only small parts of what was said.

F

Student had trouble understanding most of the questions.

Student speech was very halting.

Very little or no relevant information was given.

Native speaker would not be able to understand what was said.

By the second semester, students can be tested in twos, allowing about three or four minutes per pair. In pair testing, the two students act out a role play or ask one another questions about a given topic. (For additional suggestions, see Gonzalez-Pino 1988.)

For more advanced classes, oral interview tests can be structured according to a "modular ladder." For each topic, the instructor prepares a series of four questions of increasing complexity. Students are graded according to how accurately and fluently they can respond at each step of the "ladder" (Goldfus and Rosenbluth 1988: 52–54).

General Format	**Example**
Topic:	*Topic:* The family
Question 1: General factual information When? where? who? which? how many? why?	*Question 1:* To whom do you feel especially close? your parents or your brothers and sisters? Why?
Question 2: Comparison In what ways is it similar/different?	*Question 2:* Would you like to be an only child? Why or why not? Do you think children are better off in large families or in smaller families?

Question 3: Definition
   What characterizes. . . ? (What
   makes up, determines, defines,
   makes it unique?) What is. . . ?

Question 3: How would you define a
   family? In many families a family
   tree has been worked out. Have you
   ever thought about your own family
   tree? Tell me about it. Why are people interested in their family trees?

Question 4: Generalization
1. *Present* (attitudes)
   How do people view this issue
   today?
2. *Past* (attitudes)
   In what way is the attitude of your
   generation different from that of the
   previous generation?
3. *Future* (attitudes)
   What change in attitude might be
   anticipated in the future?

Question 4: Is the family as a unit still
   as important in today's society as it
   used to be? Explain yourself. Give
   alternatives to the family unit as we
   know it.

Assessing writing proficiency   Although students in basic language courses
usually perform many writing tasks (homework assignments, written exercises, guided written tests), they often have very little practice in writing for
communication. If writing proficiency is a course goal, it is important to have
students write frequent short creative compositions and to include similar
activities in the written examinations. (See Terry 1989.)

Here is a sample communicative writing segment from an elementary
French test:

Describe an event you recently witnessed: an accident, a mishap, a
sports event, etc. Write a short paragraph in which you use:

5 verbs in the passé composé
5 verbs in the imperfect

You may consider the following points: date? time of day? weather?
what were people doing? what happened? what did you do then?

Scoring: 25%   correct use of verbs
           25%   overall accuracy of expression
           25%   breadth of vocabulary
           25%   organization and fluency

The above scoring system encourages originality and creativity by
rewarding breadth of vocabulary and fluency, while at the same time emphasizing correct use of language.

Administering multisection common final examinations   Many universities give common final examinations in beginning and intermediate language classes. These are typically scheduled on the same date and at the same time in several large classrooms or lecture halls across campus. As a result, the exams are often proctored by teachers who do not know all the students in the room to which they are assigned. A key concern, consequently, is to maintain academic integrity. The following guidelines can help minimize the possibility of cheating.

1. Prior to administration, keep all exams under lock and key in the department office.

2. If more than one section is assigned to a large classroom, combine students from two different courses and seat them in alternate rows, perpendicular to the front of the classroom. For example, the first row on the left from front to back seats elementary Italian students one behind the other; the second row seats intermediate Italian students; the third row elementary students again, and so on. In this way, students tempted to look across at the papers of those next to them will see only the exams from another course.

3. If there is a concern that students may ask a more talented friend to take the exam in their place, require all students to present picture IDs as they sign in and out of the examination room.

4. Instruct proctors to keep moving around the room during the whole examination.

Advanced Courses

In most university language departments, the advanced undergraduate and graduate courses—language, literature, and culture—are taught by full-time faculty who have the responsibility of preparing their own syllabi and developing their own assessment measures. Traditionally these may include one or more of the following: a midterm, an oral or written final exam, a class presentation, or a research paper.

The main question to be raised with respect to advanced language courses relates to the matter of reliability: how sure can one be that the grades assigned are a reliable reflection of the students' achievement? As we have seen above, reliability is a function, among other factors, of multiple samples. This means that a course grade is more reliable if it is based on several evaluations rather than one or two. The reliability of an essay test will be improved if it includes a section consisting of many short-answer questions.

Clarifying the syllabus   The way to develop a more reliable grading system for an advanced course is to establish in advance how the final grade is to be determined. (In this era of potential litigation, many universities now require that such descriptions be part of the syllabus.) It is also advisable to include some type of short-answer test that covers at least a portion of the material being taught. In addition, it is often effective to have a simple objective measure of class preparation and participation.

The formula for the determination of the final grade is usually presented numerically. Here are three samples from different types of courses:

A participatory language course: French phonetics

Memorized dialogs (best 18 out of 22) @ 10 points each	180
Phonetic dictations (best 4 out of 5) @ 30 points each	120
Recorded pronunciation tests (5) @ 60 points each	300
Listening logs (5) @ 30 points each	150
Final written examination on phonetics	250
Total (to be divided by 10)	1000

Notes: Classroom participation and preparation are evaluated through frequent in-class recitations of memorized dialogs. The oral tests, which represent the primary goal of the course, namely the improvement of pronunciation, are weighted most heavily and spread across the semester. Since extensive listening to natural French speech (in the form of films, videos, and radio recordings) is an important component in the acquisition of native speech patterns, students keep a log of the 50 hours of outside listening they are expected to do. Because the university requires a written final exam, the written phonetics test, which consists of many short-answer items, is scheduled during the exam period. In reality, a version of the test is given during the last week of classes. Students who are not satisfied with their performance have the opportunity to retake an alternate form of the test during exam week. This test–retest approach encourages students to master the key concepts of the course.

A lecture (and discussion) course meeting twice a week: literature or culture

One-minute papers (20)	20%
Midterm exam	20%
Term paper	30%
Final examination	30%
Total	100%

Notes: The "one-minute paper" is a simple system of ongoing assessment of class participation (Light 1990: 36–38). At the end of each class, the teacher allows a minute or two for the students to write brief answers to two questions:

1. What is the big point you learned in class today?

2. What is the main, unanswered question you leave class with today?

These responses can be quickly graded with either a "check" (for adequate answers) and a "check-plus" (for particularly insightful answers). An added benefit of the system is that the professor can react to the responses rapidly at the beginning of the next class and clarify any misinterpretations.

In the above syllabus, the weighting given the various components indicates that the students' original contributions (the one-minute papers and the term paper) are as important as the set examinations.

A seminar meeting once a week: literature or culture

Reaction papers (10)	30%
Class presentation(s)	30%
Final examination (or term paper)	40%
Total	100%

Notes: This is a course for which there are regular assigned readings. Each week the students write a one-page reaction paper in which they reflect on one or two salient points arising from what they have read. Depending on the course, students may give either one longer class presentation or several shorter contributions. (Often several shorter presentations are more effective pedagogically since students have the opportunity to refine their presentation techniques across the semester. Also the shorter presentations are usually more meaningful to the rest of the class and one avoids the potential problem of a class period filled with a single presentation during which a student drones on at length.) The final examination, in order to be a reliable test, could contain two essay questions and a section of short-answer questions consisting either of definitions of terms or identifications of names, works, events, or quotations. In some seminars, the final examination is replaced by a term paper based on original research. These papers may be discussed in the final class session so that the students can share their research findings with one another.

Fighting plagiarism   The grade on a term paper is valid only if the paper represents the student's original work. Sometimes the question arises whether a paper might have been plagiarized from another source or heavily edited by an unacknowledged assistant. A simple procedure to verify whether there has been plagiarism is to use a cloze test (Buckingham 1984). The teacher selects a representative passage or combination of passages from the paper adding up to about 300 words. This passage is retyped and every fifth or sixth word of running text is deleted. Then the student, under supervision, is asked to fill in the blanks. If the student cannot provide 70 percent of the missing words (or acceptable replacements thereof), it is highly unlikely that he or she has written the paper alone. According to Buckingham, in almost all cases, students who have trouble completing the cloze passage will readily admit to plagiarism or unauthorized assistance.

New approaches to language testing and evaluation   As university language departments expand their program offerings and broaden their course content, many instructors are beginning to experiment with new approaches to testing and evaluation at the higher levels of instruction. Intermediate and advanced conversation courses may produce video or radio programs, with students writing the script, editing a final corrected version, and participating in the recording. In commercial language courses, teams of students may interview foreign business representatives in the second language and report their findings back to the class. Literature classes may plan videotaped panel discussions in which groups of students talk about a literary work as if they were contemporaries of the author. In each of these instances, the instructors develop rating scales to evaluate the students on the effectiveness of their participation.

DEPARTMENTAL COMPREHENSIVE EXAMINATIONS

Comprehensive or general examinations form a part of all Ph.D. programs, most Master's programs, and, in some colleges, even the undergraduate major. These comprehensive exams may be entirely written, entirely oral, or, most frequently, partly oral and partly written. As proficiency examinations, these differ from course examinations in that they are administered by a committee of several faculty members and are graded on a pass/fail basis. (Frequently, the passing grade is further subdivided into categories such as high honors, high pass, and pass.) As their name suggests, these examinations are "comprehensive" or "general" in that they commonly include not only material studied in specific courses but also other material outlined in a reading list or a departmental list of questions.

In order for these comprehensive examinations to be valid assessments of whether students have reached the objectives of our programs, faculty must be careful to provide appropriate preparation for the tests, and not simply erect them as "hurdles" to be surmounted. To this effect, it is important to recall the Florida case of *Debhra P.* v. *Turlington* (cited in Shohamy 1990: 391), in which the U.S. Court of Appeals ruled that Florida students could not be denied diplomas because of a test whose contents they had not been taught. Departments who are not already doing so might profitably introduce a system of "dry-run" tests for candidates, especially if the comprehensive contains an oral component. Another useful practice is to establish a library of audio or video cassettes of oral exams (if these are open to the public) so that previous comprehensive exams can be reviewed by prospective candidates.

It is also important to ensure that comprehensive examinations provide reliable scores. This means that during the oral portion, examiners need to take into account temperamental differences among candidates. Some students exude self-confidence while others are reserved and even quite timid. Moreover, certain American students may feel intimidated by the more aggressive or sarcastic interrogation styles of some nonnative professors. In order to ensure "standard" testing conditions, it may be advisable to have new faculty sit in on a couple of oral examinations as observers and then discuss the conduct of the examination with their colleagues once the candidate has left. Similarly, after the new faculty member has actively participated in a comprehensive oral exam, his or her colleagues could review the conduct of the test and make suggestions for improvement. (If the examinations are videotaped, this type of test analysis can be done on a separate day while watching the video.)

EVALUATING LANGUAGE PROFICIENCY

During the 1980s, there has been significant professional interest in defining and evaluating overall second-language proficiency. The main proficiency tests used in American colleges and universities are of two sorts:

- Those based on the ACTFL Proficiency Guidelines

- Those originating abroad and administered through foreign government agencies such as the Goethe Institute and the French Chamber of Commerce

Tests Based on the ACTFL Proficiency Guidelines

The most widely publicized United States effort in this area has been spearheaded by the American Council on the Teaching of Foreign Languages (ACTFL), which published the *ACTFL Provisional Proficiency Guidelines* in 1982. This booklet contained generic guidelines in the areas of speaking, listening, reading, writing, and culture, accompanied by language-specific guidelines in French, German, and Spanish. In 1986, ACTFL published an updated version of the generic guidelines for the language skills (but not the cultural component) under the title *ACTFL Proficiency Guidelines* (ACTFL 1986; see Appendix A to this volume). Since then, teams of linguists have drawn up language-specific guidelines in Chinese (ACTFL 1987a), Japanese (ACTFL 1987b), Russian (ACTFL 1988), Arabic (ACTFL 1989), Hindi (ACTFL 1990), and Hebrew (ACTFL 1991).

OPI (Oral Proficiency Interview)   Among American language teachers, the best-known proficiency test is the OPI or Oral Proficiency Interview (Liskin-Gasparro 1987). This test, which was developed by ACTFL and ETS (Educational Testing Service), is based on the interview technique developed by the Foreign Service Institute and the Defense Language Institute over several decades.[4] Student performance is reported according to the ACTFL Proficiency Scale and may range from Novice–Low to Superior. The OPI is administered to candidates by certified testers on an individual basis. Many colleges and universities either have certified testers on their faculties or are encouraging faculty members to become certified by participating in the ACTFL–OPI training institutes, which are offered regularly around the country.[5]

As the profession becomes more familiar with the ACTFL Proficiency Guidelines, these ratings are beginning to figure in descriptions of minimum competence. For example, the Commission on Professional Standards of the AATF (American Association of Teachers of French) recently published a report entitled "The Teaching of French: A Syllabus of Competence," which proposes two competency levels for prospective teachers of French. At the "basic level of competence," teachers should be able to perform at the Advanced level of the ACTFL scale in Speaking and Writing and at the Advanced High level in Listening and Reading. To reach "superior competence," teachers should perform at the Superior level in all four skills (Murphy and Goepper 1989: 11–13). It should be pointed out that at this time the only available proficiency tests for the commonly taught languages are the Oral Proficiency Interviews, which measure speaking ability. Research is being carried on to develop instruments to evaluate proficiency in listening, reading, and writing.

Some universities are beginning to include statements of minimum levels of oral proficiency in their degree requirements. At Boston College, for example, all entering graduate students must take the Oral Proficiency Interview. Before being allowed to take their comprehensives, MAT candidates must demonstrate speaking proficiency at the Intermediate–High level, while M.A. and Ph.D. candidates must demonstrate oral proficiency at the Advanced level. It is expected that students will exceed these levels, and that, with experience, the minimum standards will be raised.

ACTFL-based proficiency tests in the less commonly taught languages
The Center for Applied Linguistics has been active in developing semidirect tests of oral language proficiency (also known as SOPI: Semidirect Oral Proficiency Interviews), which are now available in Chinese, Hausa, Hebrew, and Indonesian (Stansfield and Kenyon 1989). In addition, a similar test in Hindi has been developed at the University of Pennsylvania (Rocher 1987). These tape-mediated tests, which are scored according to the ACTFL/ILR Proficiency Guidelines, are usable in situations where face-to-face testing is financially or administratively unfeasible (Clark 1986).

Proficiency tests of reading and writing comprehension based on the ACTFL/ILR guidelines have also recently been developed in Chinese (Wang and Stansfield 1988), Hindi (Rocher 1985), Japanese, and Russian (Educational Testing Service 1986a; 1986b).

Proficiency Tests from Abroad

Goethe Institute   The German government sponsors three proficiency tests that are administered by the regional Goethe Institutes. The most widely used test is the *Zertifikat* (Deutscher Volkshochschul-Verband 1985), which measures basic proficiency across the four skills. More advanced students can take the *Sprachdiplom* test, which, if passed, permits them to study in German universities. There is also a new test of business German, *Prüfung Wirtschaftsdeutsch International,* given annually in April, which measures proficiency in handling German in a commercial context and replaces the former *Diplom Wirtschaftsdeutsch.* These proficiency tests are more widely recognized by German-owned American companies than the ACTFL Oral Proficiency Interview (Britt, Roessler, and Schutte 1989).

La Chambre de Commerce et d'Industrie de Paris   The French Chamber of Commerce sponsors two proficiency tests in commercial French given annually at American universities[6] as well as at the regional centers of the Alliance Française. Students who pass the basic-level test, consisting of a four-hour written section followed by an oral interview, receive the *Certificat Pratique de Français Commercial* attesting to their ability to use French in a business context. At a more advanced level there is a second proficiency test leading to the *Diplôme Supérieur de Français des Affaires*.

CONCLUSION

This chapter has presented a brief overview of some key testing questions as they relate to foreign-language programs in colleges and universities. When properly used, tests and other evaluation techniques can help us guide our students more effectively, strengthen our programs, and translate our course aims into attainable goals. The challenge is to select, and if necessary to develop, measurement instruments that reflect the various aspects of our course offerings as well as our overall objectives.

NOTES

1. For an expanded introduction addressed to the lay reader, see Valette 1977: chapter 4. For a detailed psychometric presentation, consult Henning 1987.

2. Retired achievement tests in French, Spanish, German, and Latin are available for rental through MAPS (Multiple Assessment Programs and Services). For order information, contact Director, MAPS, The College Board, 45 Columbus Avenue, New York, NY 10023.

3. CALICO, 3078 JKHB, Brigham Young University, Provo, UT 84602.

4. The ACTFL proficiency levels were derived from the FSI/DLI or ILR (Interagency Language Roundtable) scale, as follows: Novice–Low, Novice–Mid, Novice–High (corresponding to 0 and 0+ on the ILR scale), Intermediate–Low, Intermediate–Mid, Intermediate–High (corresponding to 1 and 1+), Advanced, Advanced–High (corresponding to 2 and 2+), and Superior (corresponding to 3, 4, and 5). See Appendix A to this volume.

5. For information on OPI training programs, contact ACTFL, 6 Executive Blvd., Yonkers, NY 10701; phone (914) 963-8830.

6. For information about how to administer these tests on an American campus, contact: Direction de l'Enseignement, Relations Internationales, Chambre de Commerce et d'Industrie de Paris, 42 rue du Louvre, 75001 Paris, France.

REFERENCES

ACTFL. 1982. *ACTFL Provisional Proficiency Guidelines.* Hastings-on-Hudson, NY: ACTFL.

―――――. 1986. *ACTFL Proficiency Guidelines.* Hastings-on-Hudson, NY: ACTFL.

―――――. 1987a. "ACTFL Chinese Proficiency Guidelines." *Foreign Language Annals* 20: 471–87.

―――――. 1987b. "ACTFL Japanese Proficiency Guidelines." *Foreign Language Annals* 20: 589–603.

―――――. 1988. "ACTFL Russian Proficiency Guidelines." *Foreign Language Annals* 21: 199–97.

―――――. 1989. "ACTFL Arabic Proficiency Guidelines." *Foreign Language Annals* 22: 373–92.

―――――. 1990. "ACTFL Hindi Proficiency Guidelines." *Foreign Language Annals* 23: 235–52.

Britt, C. W., H. R. Roessler, and L. E. Schutte. 1989. "The Demand for German Language Proficiency in German-Owned Companies in the United States." *Die Unterrichtspraxis* 22: 186–90.

Buckingham, T. 1984. "Cloze to the Truth." *TESOL Newsletter* 18: 6.

Carroll, Brendan J., and P. J. Hall. 1985. *Make Your Own Language Tests: A Practical Guide to Writing Language Performance Tests.* Oxford, Eng.: Pergamon.

Carroll, John B., and S. M. Sapon. 1959. *Modern Language Aptitude Test.* San Antonio, TX: Psychological Corporation.

Clark, J. L. D. 1986. "Development of a Tape-Mediated, ACTFL/ILR Scale-Based Test of Chinese Speaking Proficiency," pp. 129–46 in C. W. Stansfield, ed., *Technology and Language Testing.* Washington, DC: TESOL.

Deutschen Volkshochschul-Verband. 1985. *Das Zertifikat: Deutsch als Fremdsprache.* Munich: Goethe Institut.

Educational Testing Service. 1986a. *Japanese Proficiency Test: Test Manual.* Princeton, NJ: ETS.

―――――. 1986b. *Russian Proficiency Test: Test Manual.* Princeton, NJ: ETS.

Finocchiaro, M., and S. Sako. 1983. *Foreign Language Testing: A Practical Approach.* New York: Regents.

Goldfus, C., and P. Rosenbluth. 1988. "The Oral Bagrut: Testing the Interview and the Monologue." *English Teacher's Journal (Israel)* 37 (June): 52–59.

Gollan, Ruth, et al. 1991. "Hebrew Proficiency Guidelines." *Bulletin of Higher Hebrew Education* 4,2: Supplement 1–47.

Gonzalez-Pino, B. G. 1988. "Testing Second Language Speaking: Practical Approaches to Oral Testing in Large Classes." *Northeast Conference Newsletter* 24: 14–16.

Henning, G. 1987. *A Guide to Language Testing: Development, Evaluation, Research.* Cambridge, MA: Newbury House.

Horwitz, E. K., and D. K. Young. 1991. *Language Anxiety: From Theory and Research to Classroom Implications.* Englewood Cliffs, NJ: Prentice-Hall.

Lett, J. A., Jr., and F. E. O'Mara. 1991. "Predictors of Success in an Intensive Foreign Language Learning Context: Correlates of Language Learning at the Defense Language Institute Foreign Language Center," pp. 222–60 in T. S. Parry and C. W. Stansfield, eds., *Language Aptitude Reconsidered.* Englewood Cliffs, NJ: Prentice Hall Regents / Center for Applied Linguistics.

Light, R. J. 1990. *Explorations with Students and Faculty about Teaching, Learning, and Student Life.* Harvard Assessment Seminars: First report. Cambridge, MA: Harvard University Graduate School of Education.

Liskin-Gasparro, Judith E. 1987. *Testing and Teaching for Oral Proficiency.* Boston: Heinle and Heinle.

Madsen, H. S. 1983. *Techniques in Testing.* New York: Oxford Univ. Press.

Murphy, J. A., and J. B. Goepper. 1989. "The Teaching of French—A Syllabus of Competence: The Report of the Commission on Professional Standards of the American Association of Teachers of French." *AATF National Bulletin* Special Issue 15.

Oller, John W., Jr. 1979. *Language Tests at School: A Pragmatic Approach.* London, Eng.: Longman.

Omaggio, Alice C. 1986. *Teaching Language in Context: Proficiency-Oriented Instruction.* Boston: Heinle and Heinle.

Parry, T. S., and C. W. Stansfield, eds. 1991. *Language Aptitude Reconsidered.* Englewood Cliffs, NJ: Prentice Hall Regents / Center for Applied Linguistics.

Rivers, Wilga M., et al. 1988. *Teaching French / German / Spanish: A Practical Guide.* Lincolnwood, IL: National Textbook Company.

————, and M. Nahir. 1989. *Teaching Hebrew: A Practical Guide.* Tel Aviv, Isr.: University Publishing Projects.

Rocher, R. 1985. *Hindi Proficiency Test: Test Information and Score Interpretation Manual.* Philadelphia: Univ. of Pennsylvania Dept. of South Asia Regional Studies.

————. 1987. *Hindi Oral Proficiency Test: Test Information and Score Interpretation Manual.* Philadelphia: Univ. of Pennsylvania Dept. of South Asia Regional Studies.

Shohamy, E. 1990. "Language Testing Priorities: A Different Perspective." *Foreign Language Annals* 23: 385–94.

Stansfield, C. W. 1990. "Some Foreign Language Test Development Priorities for the Last Decade of the Twentieth Century." *Foreign Language Annals* 23: 395–401.

————, ed. 1986. *Technology and Language Testing.* Washington, DC: TESOL.

————, and D. M. Kenyon. 1989. *Development of Semi-Direct Speaking Tests for the Less Commonly Taught Languages.* Final Report to the U.S. Dept. of Education. Washington, DC: Center for Applied Linguistics.

Stevenson, D. K. 1985. "Pop Validity and Performance Testing," pp. 111–18 in Y. P. Lee, et al., eds., *New Directions in Language Testing*. Oxford, Eng.: Pergamon.

Terry, R. M. 1989. "Teaching and Evaluating Writing as a Communicative Skill." *Foreign Language Annals* 22: 43–54.

Underhill, N. 1987. *Testing Spoken Language*. Cambridge, Eng., and New York: Cambridge Univ. Press.

Valette, Rebecca M. 1977. *Modern Language Testing*. 2nd ed. New York: Harcourt Brace.

Wang, L. S., and C. W. Stansfield. 1988. *Chinese Proficiency Test: Test Interpretation Manual*. Washington, DC: Center for Applied Linguistics.

Wherritt, I., and T. A. Cleary. 1990. "A National Survey of Spanish Language Testing for Placement or Outcome Assessment at B.A.-Granting Institutions in the United States." *Foreign Language Annals* 23: 157–65.

11
Authentic Contact with Native Speech and Culture at Home and Abroad

Robert Frye
Regis College

Thomas J. Garza
The University of Texas at Austin

MATERIALS FOR AUTHENTIC CONTACT IN DOMESTIC PROGRAMS

In recent years, as the communicative and proficiency movements have placed increased emphasis on the *performance* factor in foreign-language learning, much of the literature and many professional workshops on teaching foreign languages and cultures at the university level have focused on the use of authentic materials and cultural realia in the classroom. Such materials bring the "real" spoken and written language to the students as a needed supplement to the patterned dialogs, one-sided conversations, and grammar substitutions so frequently used to develop grammatical competence. One of the most obvious ways to facilitate increased contact with native language and culture in the domestic foreign-language classroom is to incorporate current print and audio or video materials into the basic curriculum. By using a variety of materials originally produced by and intended for native speakers of the target language rather than for learners (i.e., "authentic" in our usage), students are exposed to language that reflects contemporary usage and standards as opposed to artificially formulaic, contrived, or inappropriate language that conforms to the lexical and grammatical specifications of a given lesson syllabus.

Print

Authentic print materials and documents may include any sources in which a written text—often including photographs or illustrations—is meaningful and relevant to a native speaker of the language in which the text is written. Such texts may range in length from the quite extensive (excerpts from literature, newspaper or journal articles, or personal letters) to the brief (product advertisements, classified advertisements, product labels, forms, pamphlets, and so on). Regardless of length, or even complexity of language, such texts allow the student to work with language in a natural and culturally bound printed format and setting, offering—upon in-class examination—much important nonlinguistic information relevant to cultural values clarification for nonnative readers of the target language. As Collie and Slater (1987: 3) contend, authentic print documents expose learners to language that is "as genuine and undistorted as can be managed in the classroom context."

Audio

Similarly, authentic audio materials are drawn from obvious sources, such as radio and commercial recordings (advertisements, news broadcasts, discussions with prominent personalities, and popular songs), as well as from more diverse sources, such as prerecorded telephone messages, subway, train, or airport messages for passengers, and recordings of "overheard" conversations made *in situ* in various situational settings. As with authentic printed text materials, these audio texts provide students with current language in use; additionally, they provide native speech models of pronunciation, intonation, and phrasing that printed representation cannot match. Especially for university settings that do not provide ready access to a native speaker of the target language, such materials are essential for developing both aural comprehension and oral production skills.

Video

Authentic video materials, drawn from film, television, and commercial or documentary videos, add a dynamic visual modality to the foreign-language script that contributes significantly to the instructional value of the materials as a source of information on the native culture. Well-chosen authentic video materials, effectively exploited in the classroom, can provide a "slice-of-life" quality to the semi-immersion atmosphere of domestic language programs, offering our students a glimpse into the real-life usage of the target language within the context of the sights and sounds of the target culture (Lonergan 1984).

Criteria for selecting appropriate video segments for language teaching purposes are well documented in the literature (Altman 1989). Garza (1986) lists the following: (1) useful video material must contain linguistic material that is current, accurate (though not prescriptive), and appropriate for a corresponding real-life situation; (2) video materials for language teaching must be thematically interesting and relevant to the target audience; (3) the video segment should be multilayered, encouraging—if not requiring— repeated viewings of the segment for complete understanding; and (4) the video portion of the material should provide visual contextualization and clarification of the language of the audio track.

Of course, for maximum benefit to the learner, even scrupulously selected video materials should be used in an interactive classroom setting in such a way that students do not merely sit back and watch a foreign film while frame after frame of "comprehensible input" washes over them—but rather, they should discuss it, act it out, rewrite it, and rerecord it. To make authentic contact with the target language and culture, learners (and instructors) need to develop active viewing skills (Lavery 1983), in order to reap the linguistic, paralinguistic, and cultural information that is intricately layered within a given segment of authentic video.

Realia

In conjunction with the use of authentic print, audio, and video materials in the foreign-language classroom, appropriate realia from the target culture should be incorporated whenever and wherever possible. Integration of such materials is possible for all languages at all levels of instruction. For example, as a prelistening activity for a Mexico City radio broadcast on the Mexican national presidential elections, a Spanish class might examine and describe (or discuss, depending on the proficiency level of the given group) some genuine preelection posters or propaganda leaflets, obtained from in-country sources, on the various parties and candidates.

In some cases, authentic materials and realia can be effectively combined in a multiple-part language use activity: a follow-up activity to a reading from a commentary column of the Russian weekly publication *Literaturnaja gazeta,* strongly criticizing the negative portrayal of a particular character in a current Soviet film, might be coupled with the viewing of a segment of the film in question, followed by an elicitation from the students of opinions of the character. Such activities with authentic materials and realia allow the students to remain in contact with engaging topics of current interest to native speakers of the language they are learning while gaining exposure to the media, sources, and artifacts of the relevant culture.

THE ROLE OF THE NATIVE SPEAKER FOR AUTHENTIC CONTACT IN DOMESTIC PROGRAMS

Another option for increasing the "authenticity factor" of foreign language and culture instruction while still in a domestic university setting is the use of a native resource teacher from the target-language/culture country. There are several categories of resource teachers, each possessing inherent pluses and minuses. The first and most common category for American university programs is the émigré native speaker of the target language who, in the best-case scenario, is well-educated and has an academic background in foreign-language teaching pedagogy and methodology. Such personnel, because of their diverse interests and backgrounds, often play critical and essential roles in enhancing the curricular diversity of domestic foreign-language programs. Furthermore, they provide invaluable linguistic support as active speakers of the foreign language, demonstrating correct pronunciation and intonational models, commenting on lexical choice and appropriateness, and providing current cultural and sociological information on situational and functional use of language, as well as on the attitudes and values of those who speak the language natively.

The cavil here is that, in some cases, even highly qualified and talented émigré instructors may not maintain regular contact with their native countries and cultures. As a result, their language and cultural knowledge may become "fossilized" at the standard norm (linguistic and cultural) for the period of their last contact with their native country. Their lexical use, especially of neologisms, slang, and colloquialisms, may become dated; cultural changes that reflect the political, social, and philosophical transitions of their society may even be unknown to the isolated émigré native informant. It is not accidental that the Foreign Service Institute of the Department of State, which provides a semi-immersion environment for U.S. diplomatic personnel training in foreign languages by having only native speaking instructors, maintains a "recency" requirement in its hiring policy for new language and culture instructors, stipulating that they must have resided in their home country during at least two of the previous ten years.[1]

A second option for using native informants to enhance the linguistic and cultural authenticity of programs in the United States is the active recruitment of visiting language specialists from academic institutions in the target-language country for short-term appointments (one to two semesters) in American foreign-language programs. Such appointments may even take place as bilateral exchanges. Such exchanges offer the opportunity for an American teacher to teach English in the host institution while reimmersing himself or herself in the language and culture, so that both institutions can benefit from the expertise offered by a trained native speaker of the respective target language. This system has particular relevance in countries with a dearth of convertible currency to finance regular exchange of specialists with Western countries. This is the case for some Third World nations, most Central and Eastern European countries, and the Soviet Union.

An example of a bilateral exchange of resource teachers in one of the critical language areas for the United States is conducted under the aegis of the American Council for Collaboration in Education and Language Study (ACCELS) in Washington, D.C. Under the terms of this exchange, trained specialists in the teaching of Russian as a foreign language from the Soviet Union are placed in various U.S. universities and colleges for semester or academic-year appointments to teach language and culture courses in Russian and to provide consultation on materials development and curriculum design. Concurrently, American specialists of English as a Second Language (ESL) provide similar service in Soviet pedagogical (teacher training) institutes or universities. The host institution provides each resource teacher with room and board, while transportation costs and salaries are covered by governmental and private funding sources in the two countries.[2]

Yet a third and quite innovative option for the "native informant" role in stateside programs is the inclusion of student veterans from in-country study-abroad programs as peer counselors and informants for more novice students of the foreign language and culture. Recent works by Bruffee (1981) and Gaies (1985) document the contributions and successes in peer involvement in foreign-language learning at the university and secondary school level. Fraser (1989) describes a model program at Brown University that allows for the collaboration of veterans of study-abroad programs in Germany with regular faculty in the German department, and Dartmouth College involves such program veterans as apprentice teacher (ATs) in language drill sessions (Rassias 1971). Through programs like these, students and faculty alike can benefit from the veterans' experience abroad in the target culture and language, and the veterans themselves have the opportunity to "maintain fluency in their chosen language and to pass on their unique perspective of the culture" of the country from which they have returned (Fraser 1989: 34).

Authentic Contact at Home:
The Immersion Concept

Language Houses

For students unable to study abroad, numerous opportunities for immersion-style contact with a foreign language already exist in the United States, on campuses and frequently in the larger urban setting where clusters of ethnic groups who maintain their cultural and linguistic heritage can be found. On many college campuses, language houses have been established where residents pledge to speak only in the target foreign language. If such houses are monitored or managed by native or near-native speakers, the day-to-day immersion experience can be enormously beneficial. The foreign-language-theme house can be a marvelous environment for students working on perfecting their language skills on a daily basis in a relaxed, more natural milieu than the formal classroom. But the environment created here cannot be left to chance, since what goes into the preparation will be reflected in the progress made by the residents. The culture of every language house depends on the target language and the chemistry of the students chosen to live there, but certain guidelines are essential:

1. The language house must have full, enthusiastic support—demonstrated by the participation and frequent on-site presence—of the affiliated academic department.

2. Because faculty are not trained residence counselors, the cultural and educational components must remain distinct from the normal administrative and living aspects of this on-campus housing arrangement.

3. If the house is to have a cultural program, a faculty director in conjunction with a team consisting of some faculty, residential support advisor(s), and representative residents must work together to ensure participation in and commitment to the goals of the house.

4. Native-speaking resident advisors should be selected on the basis of their ability to inspire enthusiasm about the linguistic and cultural mission of the house and to infuse energy into the program. Accepting resident advisors solely because of their participation in an exchange program should be avoided.

5. Student residents, chosen on a competitive basis, must understand the conditions of their residency, including: (a) an inviolable pledge to speak and use only the target language in the house; (b) an agreement to participate daily in house activities, such as taking meals together, attending house events, and organizing house activities.

6. The associated language department, beyond the involvement indicated above, should further support the endeavor whenever possible by organizing on the premises lectures, conferences, seminars, films, luncheons or dinners with guest speakers, colloquia, and musical and theatrical events that incorporate the target language and culture into the life of the house.

Everyday Opportunities

Students may be encouraged, through establishing partnerships or clearly defined projects, to befriend international students in other parts of the university (business, medical, or law schools), using them as linguistic sources while helping them adapt to American life. In addition, virtually all campuses offer other opportunities that ought to be taken advantage of: foreign films, videotapes, cable networks, satellite transmissions, records, audiotapes, lectures by visiting scholars, inviting to lunch the interesting German woman married to the American physics professor, student coffee hours with the language teaching faculty, or attending Spanish table every Tuesday in one of the residence halls or the student union. All this and more can promote language proficiency and interest in foreign languages, as well as acting as a source of genuine contact with a foreign culture.

The St. Lambert Model

The Canadian government has institutionalized immersion programs into its educational system for some twenty years. The St. Lambert experiment in the Montreal suburbs was the prototype for later programs that provided tens of thousands of Anglophone students at the elementary and secondary levels with some part of their daily instruction in French. The results have been impressive, showing that immersion students develop significantly higher levels of proficiency in French than do students in nonimmersion, skills-based courses. Consequently, the number of children in immersion programs in Canada has risen from 37,000 in 1980 to 240,000 in 1990.[3] Some attempts have been made to adopt the immersion model in the United States, particularly in California, Ohio, and Maryland, almost all programs being at the elementary or secondary level. Recently, however, an immersion and multiliteracy program has been undertaken at the University of Utah, with impressive early results (Sternfeld 1989). The goal in Utah has been a blending of language and area studies, that is, basic background knowledge of the culture coupled with immersion in the language.

The Dartmouth Model

Other language models have had their successes as well. The Dartmouth Intensive Language Model (DILM), with the dynamic John Rassias and a team of drill instructors (ATs), prepares students in three-hour-a-day programs for immersion in the target country upon completion of the course (Rassias 1971). The notion of parachuting students into completely unfamiliar surroundings without any support network, as in the "village drop" program, is not to everyone's liking, however. Less ambitious, perhaps, but equally encouraging are efforts to revitalize existing programs in ways that respond to students' needs while engaging faculty in the essential task of rethinking the courses they teach, in terms of both content and process. One small private college in Maryland has shown such resilience with the introduction of intensive foreign-language instruction in French. Word of their program has reached prospective freshmen who, since the inauguration of the intensive program, are inquiring in far greater numbers about the possibility of majoring in French (Cippola 1984).

Some foreign-language departments have begun to introduce mini-immersion programs for majors and other interested students as well. Perhaps the best-known stateside model of such mini-immersion programs is the summer school experience at Middlebury College where students, usually graduate degree candidates, live together and study under contract to use only the targeted foreign language.

Immigrant Communities

For most Americans, the Middlebury experience is beyond their ability and perhaps their means. On a more practical level, there are opportunities for contact with transplanted cultures and their languages. Some question the "authentic" nature of such contacts, asking, for instance, whether the Italian spoken in Boston's North End is the standard Italian one would find taught in the college classroom or spoken on the streets of Rome, Florence, or Milan. The reality of dialects evolving along unpredictable lines within the confines of an American *vase clos* are real and soon distinguish the dialect markedly from whatever evolution the mother tongue may be undergoing thousands of miles away. Hispanic, Portuguese, Acadian, and Haitian communities come to mind in this context as well. Does second-generation bilingual speech conform to the linguistic norms most foreign-language instructors are seeking to promote, that is, the standard language students will need later in the international arena? Be that as it may, opportunities such as these provide a level of authentic contact that can be richly rewarding and ought to be exploited to the maximum, to increase understanding and appreciation of these communities in our midst.

AUTHENTIC CONTACT
IN THE STUDY-ABROAD CONTEXT

In spite of claims of "total immersion," foreign-language learning environments in university, private, and commercial programs offered in the United States, even those that maintain target-language-only rules in classroom, dining, and housing facilities, must still acknowledge that the outside English-speaking world is never far away and even the best-motivated students will encounter the occasional local newspaper, receive the occasional telephone call, or make the occasional trip into town for supplies. The only genuinely "total" immersion programs are those offered *in situ* at established language and culture training institutions abroad. Indeed, for truly authentic contact with the target language and culture, in-country training is clearly the best option for students in search of a totally native experience. It is essential to emphasize that our discussion concerns only established study-abroad programs that can provide quality instruction, guidance, and evaluative feedback as the student proceeds with the study of the target language, preferably while living together with native representatives of the culture. As Kubler (1987: 131) emphatically contends: Just living overseas for a period of time is not enough!

Very disconcerting is the commentary of Judkins (1989) in his recent survey of study-abroad opportunities; he observes that "a significant number of faculty are skeptical of study abroad, particularly if the program you attend is not directly related to the graduate work for which you will apply" (p. 13). He was also struck by the motley variety of programs and arrangements for study abroad,

> an incongruous variety of individual programs offered by private companies, nonprofit institutions (some based in the United States and some based abroad), colleges and universities in foreign countries but accredited in the United States, foreign universities with specifically designed U.S. study programs, individual entrepreneurs in American universities, departments, or schools in American universities, and finally programs offered under the full auspices of an American college or university. In short, study abroad seems wide open, resembling the days of the California gold rush with individuals and organizations pushing forward to stake a claim. (p. 5)

Barriers

If specialists are confused, how must the typical undergraduate feel when considering the possibility of undertaking a semester or year of foreign study? When one adds to this the additional costs likely to be incurred by international travel, residency in a foreign land, the limited opportunities to work overseas, and the fact that many colleges and universities will not allow scholarships or grants to be applied toward the costs of study off campus, the scope of the barriers becomes ever more apparent. Sadly, too, the geographical isolation of the United States may encourage parochial and provincial thinking. One foreign student advisor relates the experience of fielding a query about graduate study in philosophy at a Russian university from an "inquirer (who) stated unabashedly that he did not know a single word of Russian!" (Baumann 1975: 31). The French government has been moved to remind foreigners coming to study that instruction in French universities is given entirely in French (Baumann 1975: 3). In other words, a desire to study abroad and preparation for that experience must go hand in hand.

Study Abroad: An "American Ghetto"

A complaint frequently voiced by Americans who study abroad is that, after traveling thousands of miles at considerable expense to arrive at their destination, they spend an astonishingly large part of their foreign experience with other young Americans and nonnative speakers of the target language. In too many study-abroad programs, Americans are selected (or self-selected in commercially oriented programs) despite their having little or no ability in the target language. For students engaged in the study of truly foreign languages (see chapter 8), this is somewhat understandable because the learning of the language has been begun at college level. All too often, however, foreign study programs in the commonly taught languages accept candidates with practically no proficiency in the target language at all. This inevitably leads to frustration, disappointment, and ultimately resentment toward the sponsoring program or home institution—as well as toward the foreign culture, on the part of the disgruntled students. Demographic reports tell us that the college-age population will steadily decrease over the next few years.[4] As a consequence, admissions offices at colleges and universities will get caught up in the frenzy of recruiting from the dwindling pool of graduating high school seniors, taking in students with a lower level of preparation. In view of this trend, we can hardly expect the standards of acceptance of existing programs that hope to survive financially to become more demanding.

    The case of an American student who studied during the fall semester of 1989 in Paris may be symptomatic of what many of our college students experience in a typical study-abroad pattern. The student, Christina, a young woman attending a private Eastern college, had acquired a solid foundation in French language skills before venturing across the Atlantic. Her much-anticipated study-abroad experience among the French "degenerated" (her word) into a ghettolike existence with other Americans and foreign students. The *lingua franca* outside the classroom was English. Courses were populated largely by other Americans; the fact that she came to know students of French from other countries in courses for foreigners provided no compensation for Christina, who felt that such contacts were something she could as easily have accomplished at home. Her living arrangement was the bright spot in her daily life, although she complained that her Place de Clichy neighborhood had more of a North African ambience than a Parisian one. The widow in whose apartment she rented a room was the *only* native French person with whom she actually spoke French outside of her classes. Their twenty-minute exchange over breakfast, the only meal she took with her landlady, was her single authentic linguistic exchange of the day. By the end of the semester, Christina felt cheated overall, angry at her American compatriots for refusing to speak French among themselves, and more than a little duped because of the gulf separating her expectations from the reality of her study-abroad semester. Other individual cases one could document anecdotally speak of personal disappointments that ought never to have occurred. With proper planning, they can be avoided.

Preparation for Study Abroad

Of paramount importance in incorporating a study-abroad program into a university language training cycle is the necessary preparation of the participants in two specific aspects: linguistic and cultural. While there is no debate that experiencing the sounds, sights, and smells of the country in which the target language is used is valuable for the student at any stage of study, the greatest linguistic and cultural returns on a student's investment (of time and money) come when he or she is already adequately prepared in knowledge of the target language and culture to benefit fully from the experience. In other words, the immersion environment and intensive exposure to life and language in the foreign culture have greater value *after* the student has a reasonable base on which to build more advanced skills.

This position is well argued by Kubler (1987: 131–2), who asserts that for the student with a solid grammatical and lexical base, progress in the target-language environment can proceed faster than in any other setting. Lambert (1986: 117–19) not only concurs with this contention, but adds that additional support from both governmental and private sources should be provided to encourage study-abroad programs specifically to improve advanced proficiency. Brecht, Davidson, and Ginsberg (1991) report that, among the students studying Russian in Leningrad, those who had the strongest preparation in the structure of the language made the greatest gains in spoken language proficiency during their stay.

While this emphasis on language competence is of great importance, insufficient attention has perhaps been paid in the past to an adequate preparation in understanding and appreciating the target culture. If a domestic language program makes extensive use of authentic source materials in its curriculum, students will have had many opportunities as a natural part of the classroom agenda to discuss intercultural and crosscultural issues, both in the native language and in the target language. A high level of competence that embraces both "big 'c'" Culture (literature, the arts, history, folklore, institutions, traditions) and "little 'c'" culture (current societal norms, popular culture, fads, and so on) is essential to appropriate and accurate language use and comprehension, especially at the advanced level, and this is acquired most fully in the authentic environment of the foreign country. Through authentic contact with native speech and culture abroad, the inherent relationship of language and culture becomes apparent. International study may certainly be considered the most effective means of training for intercultural communication (Bourque 1974: 329).

Program Planning and Evaluation

As with an on-campus foreign-language-theme house, great care must be taken when weighing whether to organize a program abroad and, once the decision is taken in that direction, how to monitor and assess the program's success in terms of its own goals and the mission of the supporting institution. Each college is unique and needs to determine its own priorities. Attention to the following guideline questions should help foreign-language instructors and administrators arrive at an informed decision before embarking on a foreign-language study-abroad program:

1. Is the affiliated department capable of supporting a study-abroad venture in terms of enthusiastic and willing faculty volunteers for the on-site director's position?

2. Is there a sufficient student pool to justify the program, or will outside recruiting be necessary (possibly of both director and participants)?

3. Does the college administration fully understand the venture in light of foreseeable enrollment trends and the possible need to recruit on-

campus and on-site directors, as well as replace or restaff courses normally taught by faculty who will be abroad?

4. Given the broad array of existing programs noted in Judkins (1989), especially in Western Europe, serving as they do from as few as five to as many as several hundred students in varied time combinations (semester, year, summer, short course during winter or spring breaks), is the proposed program a significant addition to existing curricular offerings, or is it essentially redundant?

5. Could the program succeed and be strengthened if it were co-sponsored by several departments within the same system (state college, for example) or affinity groups (junior colleges, women's colleges, colleges that share geographic location, or colleges with common interest in an overseas location for linguistic, political, economic, or academic reasons)?

6. In what ways do the academic and extracurricular offerings ensure the overseas program's success and integrity (courses that do not repeat stateside offerings, selection and retention of highly qualified on-site faculty who have familiarity and experience working with American students), as well as meet the students' desire for integration into the target culture (by providing opportunities for meaningful interchanges with native speakers, access to clubs, youth groups, sports, hobbies, religious and other affinity groups, service/volunteer activities, internships, teaching in the schools, and so forth), without which the study-abroad experience will most likely be limited to life in an American ghetto or almost exclusive contact with other nonnative speakers of the target language?

7. What are the criteria for site selection? Will this program be but one of many, and not the first, competing for limited faculty, classrooms, and resources in a generally favored metropolitan center? Is the local city and region able to provide a strong and varied cultural life that enhances its attractiveness to potential participants? Are there existing faculty and administrative links with the new campus to facilitate the arrival and integration of this program into the university and local communities?

8. On what basis will student participants be chosen? Academic record, personal profile, interview, linguistic ability?

9. Will the students be fully, partially, or not at all integrated into the local university courses, and will this reality be clearly reported to all applicants?

10. What kinds of student support services—academic, social, and health—are available?

11. What kinds of assessment vehicles will be established to help the program, the supporting department, and the college administration determine how well the operation is going, where it needs strengthening, and the kinds of strategies to develop for long-range planning?

12. What housing options are available: families, dormitory, rented rooms, apartments? Do these options reflect the desires of college-aged students and the program's academic goals? For example, will placing three Americans in the same apartment significantly enhance the linguistic competence of these students? How are native-speaking host families to be matched with guest students? And what are the residency requirements of the current and future on-site directors and their families: house versus apartment, removed from campus (the privacy factor) or easily accessible to students, rented or purchased, furnished or unfurnished, available for sublet in the summer or not?

Research on Benefits of Study Abroad

For over two decades, qualitative and quantitative studies have attempted to give empirical backing to the conventional wisdom that time spent in a study-abroad program enhances significantly, more than does an equivalent period of home study, not only the student's linguistic and cultural competence in the target language, but also his or her motivation to pursue further study of the language and culture. The existence of such a program, it is believed, also provides an incentive for other students to engage earnestly in foreign-language study with a view to joining the overseas program (Bourque 1974: 332). Probably the most significant of the earlier studies is that of Carroll (1967) who not only contends that even a brief period of time spent abroad has a marked impact on a student's language competence, but also asserts that often students who do not participate in an in-country study program do not excel in the study of the foreign language.

Cox and Freed (1989), in their study, also confirm the notion that students who spend time in a study-abroad immersion program become more proficient in the target language. Another study by Brecht, Davidson, and Ginsberg (1991), which employs the only existing longitudinal database of American students of Russian studying in various in-country programs under the auspices of the American Council of Teachers of Russian, reveals significant gains in language proficiency attained by a wide variety of university-level students of Russian as a result of their in-country immersion experience. Of particular note in the study were the gains in listening and oral proficiency based on pre- and postprogram testing. Both studies, however, also demonstrate the role played in final achievement by differences in learning styles, temperament, and sex, insofar as they increase or limit the degree of close contact with native speakers, in and out of formal classes, during the in-country experience.

MISGUIDED PRIORITIES AND AN AGENDA FOR THE FUTURE

The current situation regarding foreign-language education and study-abroad programs in the United States is rather grim; a discussion of how best to educate our students to prepare them for the global village McLuhan and Fiore envisioned (1967: 67) must be prefaced by a consensus that the study of *any* foreign language is a nationally valued pursuit—a consensus that at present does not exist. The status quo is "unbalanced" in terms of our national needs and represents a "bewildering potpourri of international exchange and training programs" (Lambert 1987: 142). While acknowledging the rich diversity of study-abroad opportunities, Lambert argues that this array of options, "seen cross-sectionally (. . .) borders on chaos": "each of these programs doubtless has its own rationale and mandate, but surely some overall planning articulating the various programs would not be out of order" (p. 142). The paltry percentage of Americans engaged in preparing for present and future international needs is sorely inadequate: "We need an overseas (agenda) aimed precisely at the need of raising the language competency of a substantial portion of the American public" (p. 147), without which the United States will move increasingly toward "parochialism and isolation" (p. 153). The May 1990 report of the National Task Force on Undergraduate Education Abroad is equally categorical: "Our citizens are not well prepared for the international realities ahead," they say; "we as a people are poorly educated to deal with the political, economic, and social issues which we will face in a new global era" (Burn and Smuckler, eds. 1990: 1).

Ambassador Barbara Newell echoes many of Lambert's concerns and notes that American businesses and the military are "experiencing critical deficiencies in international expertise" (Newell 1987: 134). Recalling the 1979 report of the President's Commission on Foreign Language and International Studies, which concluded that foreign-language instruction in the United States was in a shambles, Newell deplores the drastic reduction in federally and privately sponsored fellowships for training and research in international affairs and foreign studies, concluding that "the urgency for a world perspective has so accelerated that we can no longer afford to be satisfied by small, incremental change. (. . .) Human survival, as well as business competitiveness and defense capability, depends on the speed with which American educational institutions incorporate an international perspective." The problem, as she sees it, is that "curricula have yet to recognize how small and interdependent our satellite has become" (p. 139).

Similar concerns have been voiced by the Advisory Council for International Educational Exchange in their report, *Educating for Global Competence* (Bartlett 1988). They recommend: (1) increasing to at least 10 percent (more than quintupling from the current level) the number of college students who study abroad; (2) identifying and encouraging students with leadership ability to incorporate study abroad in their academic programs, and to do so in a greater range of subjects (i.e., not only language and literature study *per se*); (3) giving special attention to study abroad in developing countries and those outside the traditional Anglo-European settings; and (4) accepting responsibility for implementing increased internationalization at the highest educational levels (p. 5). Once the goal of 10 percent of undergraduates studying abroad has been met by their target of 1995, the ACIEE considers "a realistic goal would be an increase to 20–25 percent by 2008—with a continuing increase into mid-century" (p. 11). This report concludes on a familiar refrain: "Internationalization of higher education including studying abroad is no longer merely desirable; it is a necessity. We can no longer view the world with the same detachment as an interesting and diverse place where we inevitably exercise political leadership. . . . Our standard of living, our security and our nation's prestige are all at stake" (p. 21).

There is no question that established study-abroad programs can address both the issue of internationalizing our academic community and the necessity for increased foreign-language proficiency among our students. Significantly, authentic contact with the target language and culture in the native environment facilitates the attainment of both goals. In-country foreign-language training can provide the best possible combination of both structured and informal presentation of language material by educated native informants, unlimited opportunities for crosscultural contacts, and firsthand information on the country, culture, and people of the target language, all in a total immersion environment.

For the many cases in which travel and study abroad are not possible for the foreign-language student, semi-immersion environments may employ the many and varied types of authentic materials and interactive classroom techniques presently available in order to approximate the target-language setting, and thus serve as effective substitutes for "being there." Such learning environments in the home country can be very effective in empowering the student with the necessary linguistic tools to make optimum use of the in-country experience should the opportunity arise in the future. In either case, whether the student is able to enjoy the benefits of a solid in-country experience or participate in a carefully planned classroom simulation at home, the benefits of providing authentic contact with the target language and culture cannot be underestimated. Foreign-language proficiency and cultural literacy are no longer simply matters of curricular importance: they are issues of national and, indeed, global significance.

NOTES

1. Foreign Service Institute Language and Culture Instructor Qualification Standards, January 20, 1988. The exact text of point 5 reads: "Recency of Linguistic and Cultural Experience: Has lived and / or worked in the specified language and cultural environment for at least 24 months in the past ten years, with at least 12 months continuous residence."

2. For more information on this bilateral program model for the exchange of foreign-language resource teachers and curriculum consultants, contact ACCELS, 1619 Massachusetts Ave. NW, Washington, DC 20036.

3. *Dialogue* 6, 1 (June 1990): 1. Publication of the Council of Ministers of Education, Ottawa, Canada.

4. See *The Chronicle of Higher Education,* May 4, 1988, p. 28A, as reported by the Western Interstate Commission for Higher Education.

REFERENCES

Altman, R. 1989. *The Video Connection: Integrating Video into Language Teaching.* Boston: Houghton Mifflin.

Bartlett, T. 1988. *Educating for Global Competence.* Report of the Advisory Council for International Educational Exchange. New York: CIEE.

Baumann, C. C. 1975. *Advisor's Guide to Study Abroad.* CIEE Occasional Papers, No. 19. New York: CIEE.

Bourque, J. 1974. "Study Abroad and Intercultural Communication," pp. 329–51 in Gilbert A. Jarvis, ed., *The Challenge of Communication.* The ACTFL Foreign Language Education Series, vol. 6. Lincolnwood, IL: National Textbook Company.

Brecht, R., D. Davidson, and R. Ginsberg. 1991. "The Empirical Study of Proficiency Gain in Study Abroad Environments among American Students of Russian: Basic Research Needs and a Preliminary Analysis of Data," in A. Barchenkov and T. Garza, eds., *Proceedings of the First Soviet–American Conference on Current Issues of Foreign Language Instruction.* Moscow: Vysshaja shkola.

Bruffee, K. A. 1981. "The Structure of Knowledge and the Future of Liberal Education." *Liberal Education* 67,3: 181–85.

Burn, B., and R. Smuckler, eds. 1990. *A National Mandate for Education Abroad: Getting On with the Task.* Washington, D.C.: National Task Force on Undergraduate Education Abroad.

Carroll, John B. 1967. "Foreign Language Proficiency Levels Attained by Language Majors near Graduation from College," *Foreign Language Annals* 1: 131–51.

Cippola, W. F. 1984. "Building from the Bottom Up," pp. 224–27 in C. Gaudiani, ed., *Strategies for Development of Foreign Language and Literature Programs.* New York: Modern Language Association of America.

Collie, J., and S. Slater. 1987. *Literature in the Language Classroom: A Resource Book of Ideas and Activities.* Cambridge, Eng., and New York: Cambridge Univ. Press.

Cox, R., and B. Freed. 1989. "The Effects of Study Abroad on Form and Function: A Comparison of the Differences in the Language of Students Who Have Studied Abroad and Those Who Have Not." Unpublished manuscript.

Fraser, C. C. 1989. "Collaborating with Veterans of Foreign Study Programs to Teach Language and Culture." *Northeast Conference Newsletter* 26: 34–37.

Freed, Barbara F. 1990. "Language Learning in a Study Abroad Context: The Effects of Interactive and Non-Interactive Out of Class Contact on Grammatical Achievement and Oral Proficiency," pp. 459–77 in J. E. Alatis, ed., *Linguistics, Language Teaching and Language Acquisition: The Interdependence of Theory, Practice and Research.* Georgetown University Round Table on Languages and Linguistics. Washington, DC: Georgetown Univ. Press.

Gaies, S. J. 1985. *Peer Involvement in Language Learning.* Language in Education: Theory and Practice, No. 60. Washington, DC: Center for Applied Linguistics.

Garza, T. 1986. "Foreign Language Teaching and Video: Providing a Context for Communicative Competence." Unpublished qualifying paper. Cambridge, MA: Harvard Graduate School of Education.

Judkins, D. 1989. *Study Abroad: The Astute Student's Guide.* Charlotte, VT: Williamson.

Kubler, C. 1987. "Training for High-Level Language Skills," pp. 125–36 in R. Lambert, ed., *The Annals of the American Academy of Political and Social Science,* vol. 490. Newbury Park, CA: Sage.

Lambert, Richard D. 1986. *Points of Leverage: An Agenda for a National Foundation for International Studies.* New York: Social Science Research Council.

————. 1987. "Durable Academic Linkages Overseas: A National Agenda," pp. 140–53 in Nathan Glazer, ed., *The Fulbright Experience and Academic Exchanges.* The Annals of the American Academy of Political and Social Science, vol. 491. Newbury Park, CA: Sage.

Lavery, M., et al. 1983. *Active Viewing Plus.* Canterbury, Eng.: Pilgrims Language Courses.

Lonergan, J. 1984. *Video in Language Teaching.* Cambridge, Eng., and New York: Cambridge Univ. Press.

McLuhan, Marshall, and Q. Fiore. 1967. *The Medium Is the Massage.* New York: Bantam.

Newell, B. 1987. "Education with a World Perspective," pp. 134–39 in Nathan Glazer, ed., *The Fulbright Experience and Academic Exchanges.* The Annals of the American Academy of Political and Social Science, vol. 491. Newbury Park, CA: Sage.

President's Commission on Foreign Language and International Studies. 1979. *Strength through Wisdom: A Critique of U.S. Capability.* Washington, DC: Government Printing Office.

Rassias, J. A. 1971. "New Dimensions in Language Training: The Dartmouth College Experiment." *ADFL Bulletin* 3: 23–27.

Sternfeld, S. 1989. "The University of Utah's Immersion/Multiliteracy Program." *Foreign Language Annals* 22: 341–54.

12
The Excitement of Literature: A Lifelong Pursuit

Verónica Cortínez
University of California at Los Angeles

*A*cademics are students who never grow up—people who wish to
remain students for the rest of their lives. Is this not one way to express a
love of learning?   —HENRY ROSOVSKY (1990: 88)

The general debate about teaching has a wavelike quality: It remains calm
for a while but it strikes with force when you least expect it. Although it
basically addresses similar questions everywhere, the debate has different
nuances in each country. In the United States, in the last decade or so, there has
been an important change in the attitude of many professors toward teaching,
literature professors among them. According to Henry Rosovsky, former Dean
of the Faculty of Arts and Sciences at Harvard University: "Scholars in
research universities tend to think of themselves first as members of a
particular discipline—economics, English literature, physics—and only sec-
ondarily as teachers" (1990: 93). Although this may be accurate from one point
of view, it is no less true that many professors today—tenured or not—seem
proud to assert their commitment to teaching.

It is no longer acceptable in academic circles for professors explicitly to
state that they do not care about teaching. Specifically within the literary
profession, some encouraging examples of this development come to mind.

Two major collections of essays emphasizing the teaching of literature were published during the last decade. The first of these, *The Pedagogical Imperative: Teaching as a Literary Genre* (Johnson, ed. 1982), was, surprisingly, an issue of the *Yale French Studies,* a journal that is normally devoted almost exclusively to contemporary literary theory; in fact, this book includes articles by scholars better known for their contributions to literary theory than to pedagogy: such leaders in the field as Paul de Man, Jacques Derrida, and Barbara Johnson. The second, *Teaching Literature: What Is Needed Now* (Engell and Perkins, eds. 1988), collects personal essays by such scholars as Harry Levin, J. Hillis Miller, and Helen Vendler; its editors state: "the essayists do not wish to conceive teaching as one activity, and research and criticism as a separate activity, each with its proper method and aim, but to unite the two" (p. vii).

Even institutions normally associated with quality in research rather than quality in teaching have experienced a change. The Harvard-Danforth Center for Teaching and Learning (now the Derek Bok Center), for instance, established a campus-wide orientation session for anyone interested, however slightly, in teaching. Even in its first experimental year its success was obvious: graduate teaching fellows and instructors from all disciplines came in large numbers; experienced faculty shared their views; some of the university's most popular professors (including several literature professors) gave informal talks; and President Derek Bok participated in a round table discussion with Dudley R. Herschbach, winner of the Nobel Prize in Chemistry, among others.

Interestingly enough, many of the professors speaking or writing about teaching do not seem to be acquainted with what others have recently said on the subject. Many of them seem to be speaking or writing in a vacuum as far as the profession is concerned, drawing entirely on personal experience, and one could easily accuse others of borrowing ideas, at times, without due acknowledgment. But it is precisely this spontaneous approach that reflects how widespread their concerns are.

Two questions reappear almost in ritualistic fashion: Is enthusiasm the way to excellence in teaching? Or is experience the answer? Some favor the former: "A surprising number of students, when asked, will regularly say that what they value most in a lecture is enthusiasm" (Dubrow and Wilkinson 1982: 32; see also Segerstråle 1982: 69; Garber 1987: 37; Perkins 1988: 115). Others stress the latter: "All the reading and reflection in the world cannot teach the instructor as much about teaching as experience can" (Fraher 1982: 122). But what about those people who are neither experienced nor overtly "enthusiastic" in their approach, and yet are considered excellent teachers? And what about those who obviously have both virtues, and yet still regard teaching as a challenge that requires a special kind of effort? As we shall see, enthusiasm and experience are important, but teaching literature effectively depends also on other factors.

TEACHING AS SHARING IGNORANCE?

One cannot but wonder why so many experienced literature professors have recently decided to meditate on teaching. What do they have to gain from this reexamination? Can it be that they have not mastered their own profession yet? The obvious (if partial) answer that comes to mind is that they want to pass on the knowledge they have gained through experience to new, inexperienced teachers. But why, then, this sudden generosity?

Obviously such questions have a complex historical dimension that can hardly be addressed in this paper. But we can at least ask the new theorists themselves what they think their motives are; and, if we do this, we get some rather surprising answers. Perhaps the most penetrating is that given by Johnson in her preface to *The Pedagogical Imperative.* Following up on Socrates' comments in the *Phaedrus,* she asserts that "teaching is a compulsion: a compulsion to repeat what one has not yet understood" (1982: vii). In her article in the same book, she refers once again to Plato, quoting from the *Meno:* "You see, Meno, that I am not teaching . . . anything, but all I do is question" (1982: 181). (Incidentally, the same quotation, including the ellipsis, reappears in S. Felman's article in the same book, 1982: 24). Finally, Johnson reaches the following conclusion: "Positive ignorance, the pursuit of what is forever in the act of escaping, the inhabiting of that space where knowledge becomes the obstacle of knowing—*that* is the pedagogical imperative we can neither fulfill nor disobey" (1982: 182).

The teacher then, paradoxically, strives for a kind of virtuous and self-conscious failure. But is there not also another sort of failure, a more simple, involuntary one? As J. F. Lyotard bluntly asks: "How can you make others understand what you haven't really understood?" (1982: 73). In this sense, all teachers of literature have a guilty conscience of sorts: perfect understanding of a text is unattainable; there are days when discussions fail; there are writers that we prefer and understand better than others; there are simply too many complexities that inevitably escape us all. Moreover, no matter how well prepared teachers are, they must take into account the diverse and ever-changing needs and expectations of students, their moods, their unpredictable reactions and interpretations. Teachers of literature know well that no book is a finished product and that the process of teaching depends as much on what you do not know as on what you know.

TEACHER AS LEARNER

Although perhaps fewer now than before, there are still some teachers that can be described as "playback professors": They read the same notes every year;

they alone have the right to speak in class; and they are secure in their conviction that they already know everything. Often they might as well be talking to themselves. At the opposite extreme, I recall a former professor of mine who used to modify his ideas on a certain Spanish classic poem with each new class lecture, greeting his class with: "Forget what I told you last week. I've thought more about it and now realize that I was wrong." Students who expected clearcut "right answers" felt angry and frustrated, while others appreciated his endless ruminations and benefited tremendously from his differing and often conflicting views on the same text. This may have been an extreme case, but professors who incorporate into their teaching their own changes of interpretation as readers are normally more exciting for students than those who offer a single perspective.

If professors are lovers of truth, as Plato would demand, they need to be constantly searching for knowledge. The most stimulating professors are often those who are actively engaged in research and are looking for ways to combine teaching and research effectively. This is particularly true in literary studies. Literature teachers, as opposed to, say, language teachers, face the challenge of ambiguity. Whereas the subjunctive in Spanish will probably not change tomorrow (although the linguistic description of it may), literary texts, by their very nature, are open to an infinity of interpretations. No matter how many times one teaches the same text, it always reveals new possibilities for insights, depending on one's shifting of emphases, the particular historical moment, or simply the changes in the audience.

We may ask ourselves: Do we need to teach in order to keep learning about the literature we teach? As Muyskens puts it: "One of the benefits of literature is the multiplicity of viewpoints it offers its readers" (1983: 419). Many teachers, however, are unable to assimilate this lesson and project an inflexible attitude in their classes. One may wonder how anyone could possibly teach in a dogmatic fashion a text such as *Don Quijote,* with its potential for so many diverse interpretations. Different people see the world in different ways and every point of view is entitled to tolerance and respect (Bok 1990: 83); in order to do justice to literature, we have to learn how to listen carefully to others, not only to authors and critics, but also to students. If a teacher comes into class with all the answers, the students will not realize the need to develop their own perspective on what they are reading but assiduously take notes that they will serve back to the teacher on the next examination. Perhaps our most difficult task is to liberate ourselves from ready-made answers and keep an open mind. Otherwise, students will doubt the importance of their own thoughts and interpretations. Above all, we need to admit honestly that we do not know everything, but are eager to learn with and from our students. As Gadamer puts it: "When two persons are engaged in true conversation, the relation between them does, of course, represent a complete inversion of the master–slave relationship, for neither is seeking to dominate the other: on the contrary, each is seeking to be fully *open* to and to *listen* to the other" (quoted by Scott 1988: 60; italics in the original). Thus, as we teach we learn.

DESIGNING COURSES

The main goal of literature professors should be to convey to their students the informed love for literature that they themselves feel and, consequently, to help them develop a love for literature as well. As Borges once pointed out, we don't teach books, but the love of them (see also Vendler 1988: 17). This is where enthusiasm comes in. Before designing a course, however, one has to be aware of the way one's own preferences will necessarily interfere in most decisions about content. A professor's choice of texts is always a personal matter. It is very improbable that any two professors will come up with exactly the same syllabus for the same course. It is not so much a question of choosing the "right" books, as of justifying to oneself and one's students the selection that has been made. This need to valorize the works one has chosen acts as an impetus to interpret them in ways that will arouse the enthusiasm of the students.

Professors of foreign literatures are usually required to teach several types of courses. Some of these have been partially or totally structured in advance by someone else: survey courses, general education requirements, and the like. Others can be designed by the instructor according to personal interests: special topic surveys, undergraduate and graduate seminars. This second type of course leaves more room for creativity, but it also demands more careful planning. Generally speaking, students who are not majors or concentrators ignore elective courses in a foreign literature: courses in computers and studio arts seem more enticing. Trivial as it may sound, the title given to a course and the course description can play a crucial role in attracting students. In phrasing these, one should try to make the course sound interesting to students, while taking care not to promise, as sometimes happens, something one will not be able to deliver.

It is essential in the description to make clear the types of students to which each course is directed. Some courses are more appropriate for a specialized audience, while others will make scared newcomers feel at ease. If we ignore the particular needs of each group, while serving our own convenience, we may end up satisfying very few students. This does not mean, however, that students taking the same course should be a homogeneous group, but rather that differences in interests and abilities must be taken into consideration in our planning.

Although professors tend to value their independence from their colleagues, it is important to keep the entire curriculum of the department in mind when planning a course. Taking into account what other professors teach will eliminate duplication and provide students with greater choice, particularly those who would like to stay with the department longer. Students sometimes wonder whether there are any other good novels in Spanish besides García Márquez's *One Hundred Years of Solitude,* or in French besides Stendahl's *Le Rouge et le Noir.* Watchfulness in this regard can entail painful sacrifices. If a favorite writer has been taught in an earlier course by a colleague, one should not succumb to the temptation of including her again (unless there is a very good reason to do so).

Regardless of experience, selecting the most suitable works for study is always difficult. Choosing is, by definition, excluding. Moreover, there are various dangers involved in selection; Brooks et al. warn that "one should not assume that courses on new materials are innovative and courses on traditional materials are conservative" (1989: 19–20). By the same token, fighting the traditional canon simply for the sake of fighting will lead us "to convert modest geese into overvalued swans" (Levin 1988: 38). It has become fashionable to assume that the accepted canon of leading works should be replaced by marginal texts. In the case of foreign literature courses, however, this can result in a misrepresentation of the culture. Whereas American high school students may know something of Shakespeare and Emily Dickinson, they normally do not know Dante, Racine, or Goethe. Once one does move beyond the canon to encompass wider literary interests, it becomes necessary to take into consideration the interests of students, rather than imposing from year to year our own preconceived ideas. On the East Coast, for example, students interested in contemporary literature may be more curious about Puerto Rico or Haiti, while on the West Coast, Mexico may arouse more concern, especially among those of Hispanic descent. In either case, student interest should be the determining factor, not a stereotypical conviction that a certain group will only be attracted to the literature of its native region or a neighboring one.

The more specialized a course is and the more homogeneous its student body, the easier it becomes to set its goals. A junior seminar designed exclusively for concentrators or majors, for example, allows the teacher to make certain assumptions: if nothing else, one can presume that all students share a similar sophomore background. In such courses, it is possible to choose fewer works and to study them in detail (in the original language, of course), rather than to apply the too often superficial field-coverage principle (Graff 1989: 7). Since these classes are usually smaller than those for general education requirements, the teacher can devote more individual attention to each student. The small seminar presents an ideal opportunity to focus on a very common problem: the deficient writing skills of students (particularly in the second language, although often problems remain with native-language written expression as well). Everyone complains about this deficiency (Hillis Miller 1988: 90), but few teachers are willing to take the necessary steps to remedy it (Dubrow 1982: 102). There are, fortunately, a number of ways to improve students' writing, if teachers will take the trouble.

One proven approach is to assign one long (perhaps even publishable) paper on a subject of the student's choice. During the term, students turn in various drafts of the different sections (e.g., the introduction, first paragraph, or conclusion), and these are reviewed with them in great detail. One should expect these papers to be interesting and original, but above all clear. Unfortunately, confusion is too often equated with complexity. As Brooks et al. put it: "The problem is to identify how much of the impenetrable jargon is merely self-indulgent and fuzzy-minded, how much a necessity of complex argument" (1989: 38; see also Levin 1988: 42; Lott 1988: 8).

Other preferred approaches are to request several short papers on a variety of topics; reaction papers about given texts; collaboration papers among a group of students; or even creative writing for those who are interested. Some teachers also involve students in the correction process. Reading other people's work can often teach students how to judge their own.

The large required literature courses for nonconcentrators (general education courses or surveys) are designed to cover much ground. They introduce students to a foreign literature by selecting some representative works from different periods and genres. The key to this type of course is careful choice: trying to include "everything" (all major writers, texts, schools of a particular period) will probably lead to failure. While it is naturally important to study the "major writers," one should also try to include some younger noncanonical writers, whose work is more easily accessible to their contemporaries. For instance, a survey on Latin American literature does not need to stop with Gabriel García Márquez and disregard Manuel Puig or Isabel Allende. Nor do survey courses need to present works in chronological order; the unfamiliar language of earlier texts can often discourage students approaching a national literature for the first time. A way to prevent this is to teach the course in reverse, from the twentieth century backwards, thus moving from the relatively familiar to works requiring more effort to extract meaning. In introductory literature courses, where reading in a foreign language can be arduous for the students, it may be useful to assign some works in the original language and other works (by the same writer) in translation. As Lindenberger has pointed out: "To agree that it is better to read works in the original than in translation does not mean that all one's reading of foreign literature must be in the original" (1986: 36). In this way, students are able to get a broader view of a particular author's ideas, which will enrich their interpretation of those texts read in the original.

There are endless ways to motivate students to enjoy a subject, and this may be especially necessary in literature courses that are being taken to satisfy a requirement. One way to motivate students that is too often forgotten is by making the subject matter relevant to their personal lives (Segerstråle 1982: 59; Di Pietro 1987: 111). This does not mean, of course, substituting personal anecdotes for serious work. Vendler, for example, encourages her students to react personally to the poems they read: they can write an alternative beginning or ending or recount a similar experience of their own. Others favor the writing of original poems "in the style of " for publication in an undergraduate literary journal or for circulation to the class and parallel sections. Actually, the production of a "literary journal" containing the best written undergraduate papers can be a successful incentive technique. We should also allow time for consideration of the "big questions" students want to discuss—questions that many instructors, unfortunately, suppress because they do not fit in an obvious way into the day-by-day syllabus.

Team teaching, though largely unexplored in many colleges, is potentially a very exciting class structure. Much has been written about the positive traces that a mentor can leave on a student (Levin 1960: 4; Jedrey 1982: 115; Johnson 1985: 10; Vendler 1988: 17; Rosovsky 1990: 137), but having two professors share the limelight results in other benefits. Contrary to natural instincts, there are advantages in choosing a partner with ideas and approach as different from one's own as possible. Students can indeed learn from conflicting perspectives: in fact "learning seems to take place most rapidly when the student must respond to the contradiction between *two* teachers" (Johnson 1982: 179).

GETTING TO KNOW STUDENTS

In order to help students learn, teachers need to have some basic information about them as soon as possible. In preparing the course, we will have clarified our goals; it is now essential to find out about theirs, in order to ensure compatibility and make any desirable adjustments. As Wolcowitz rightly observes, the student–teacher contract starts on the first day of class (1982: 10–24). One can collect factual details by asking students to answer in writing appropriate questions, and give, for instance, their background in the field, their interests, and their expectations (much of this information can now be obtained through computer programs of student term schedules, especially with HyperCard). Unless the course is unduly large, teachers should then also conduct short personal interviews in their offices. It is easier to personalize teaching when we know something about our students (Kasulis 1982: 40; Perry 1985: 17).

Regular office hours can provide another opportunity for fruitful communication; if the instructor does not set his or her hours for Fridays at 5 P.M. and does not just talk about the weather, students will take advantage of them. Interaction with a selected few of the students outside the academic setting, even if well-meaning, entails certain risks, such as the charge of favoritism (Nash 1982: 81); students notice and resent the slightest hint of unfairness.

Brooks et al. (1989) optimistically report that "most evidence suggests that professors in the humanities remain close to undergraduates and their academic concerns" (p. 25). This may be true, but too often it applies only to the good students. It remains a fact in undergraduate education that professors tend to care less about the not so talented or the obviously poor students, not to mention the ones with real problems. It is a pleasure, of course, to have highly motivated and intelligent students, but it can be more rewarding, in the long run, to educate those who would not make it without our help. As Levin writes about Babbitt, we have to judge students "by final causes, not beginnings but ends" (1960: 15).

INTERACTION

If T. S. Eliot's only piece of advice for aspiring critics—to be as intelligent as possible (quoted by Levin 1988: 47)—were thought sufficient, there would probably be no need for teachers. Moreover, in an age when lectures can be videotaped so easily, one has to justify the presence of both teacher and students face-to-face in a classroom setting. The transmission of knowledge alone is not a good reason, for learning can also be achieved through books, journals, computers, and even photocopies (there are colleges where professors' notes are sold in advance to students). The classroom is useful only if it fosters true communication (Rivers 1990: 11).

Generally speaking, students perceive literature courses (as opposed to language courses in which they are required to participate extensively) as lectures, which they must attend and where they simply take notes. Professors are expected to know their material well, and there is little room for further exploration. Students are often not encouraged to think critically or even to listen to each other. It is hard to gauge whether this is really education and whether the perceptions of students are being refined in any way at all. Garber (1987), for one, dislikes the type of situation where the professor's voice dominates: "It's not good for anyone (for me, for the teaching fellows, or for the students) if my views go unchallenged, or, at least, unexamined" (p. 37).

Literature professors are searching for alternatives to the old teacher-as-prophet lecture system. Instead of lecturing three hours a week, a professor can incorporate student presentations and workshops; assignments may also include watching video interviews with writers being studied (there are some excellent interviews with Isabel Allende, Simone de Beauvoir, and others) and films based on the works covered in class (Puig's *Kiss of the Spider Woman* and Thomas Mann's *Death in Venice* are prime examples). Films provide much material for in-depth study of the text, as the students examine the changes, deletions, and rearrangements made by the scriptwriter and discuss the degree to which the author's original text has been represented. More and more all over the country, the number of lectures is being reduced to allow for small discussion sections, and question-and-answer periods are frequently provided at the beginning or end of class or at suitable intervals during the class. Incorporating student perceptions into the class does not necessarily require absolute control by the instructor. Although some still believe that "the driving and directional energy of any good discussion class comes from the teacher's questions" (Rosmarin 1985: 37), others are willing to allow more freedom to the students. One alternative is to divide the class into small groups that develop a viewpoint and then defend it against other viewpoints in a full class discussion. One can very successfully promote discussion in class by providing indirect guidance.

There are a few risks inherent in more "participatory" literature classes. The most obvious danger is when professors accept all student comments regardless of their validity. This is not, as some think, a generous gesture, but a condescending one. Students usually know when they can get away with anything they say, but if we expect (and demand) from them reflective observations, they will rise to meet our expectations (Marius 1988: 181). Taking all student comments seriously (Jedrey 1982: 111) does not mean that one must justify nonsense. On the other hand, pretending to be open-minded without really listening to the student's viewpoint is not enough either. Students soon realize when the teacher's comments are the only ones that are really taken into account, whether it be because of dogma or insecurity. Students may then shape their answers according to what they think the teacher wants; they call this "mind reading" and are quite experienced at playing the game. As Garber asserts: "Above all, I would say that teachers—all teachers—gain authority by not insisting on it. Giving authority away—allowing one's students to articulate and argue for their own positions, rather than asking them to fill in the blanks of one's own premeditated argument—is a way of producing excitement and inspiring confidence" (1987: 37; see also Kramsch 1985: 358; Johnson 1988: 70; Perkins 1988: 113).

A second potential problem is that a few extrovert students may monopolize discussions while the shy ones never get to speak. Teachers need to develop a feel for the right balance, using every means they can to promote participation and cooperation among students. Moreover, in many foreign literature courses there are native speakers as students as well as nonnatives. One must watch carefully to ensure that one group does not silence the other. With experience teachers will learn how to profit from this diversity.

Class time, quite obviously, is extremely limited and should be exploited to the utmost. With proper guidance, students can learn a great deal outside of class. A carefully prepared syllabus is the first step toward saving time; rather than wasting precious minutes dictating the bibliography or discussing bureaucratic matters, one can include these in the syllabus. Even a twenty-page syllabus is not necessarily too long. A list of assignments thought out in advance can save much time. Students can search for detailed factual information with the help of computers or in the library. In principle, nothing justifies going over a writer's biography, the historical background of a text, or even other critics' views on a certain subject when students can discover this information for themselves.

It is not that material of this kind is unimportant, but simply that it is usually unnecessary to use class time to explain what can be easily understood by students on their own. Moreover, students will find this type of information more useful and remember it better if they are the ones responsible for researching it. The same applies to articles and books written on the subject by the instructor; students can read these on their own, leaving class time free for discussion of further implications of the ideas they contain. Class time should be devoted exclusively to what students cannot do by themselves: listening to new ideas, presenting their own interpretations in a supportive atmosphere, and, above all, engaging in an exchange that will further stimulate their own reflection.

Since teachers cannot actually force students to do assignments conscientiously, their main task is stimulating motivation (see chapter 19, Principle 2). In the case of literature, students will approach a new text with more enthusiasm if the instructor has previously introduced some of its more interesting elements. This is particularly true in the case of works in a foreign language. The point is not, of course, to summarize the plot or to present a list of topics, but rather, through prereading discussion, to prepare them to observe and understand those aspects that they might otherwise pass over, and in which, to a great extent, lies the pleasure of the text. Students of classical Greek literature, for instance, may tend to overlook the chorus. A prereading discussion of the construction of Greek tragedy in relation to the situations in which it was experienced will sensitize students to the significance of this feature. By handing out questions in advance of the reading of the text, one can focus student attention and facilitate their reading. At the same time, one must be careful not to overload students with an unrealistic number of assignments.

Asking them to read one story by Maupassant is certainly less ambitious than requiring the reading of an entire collection of stories, but the chances are that more students will begin the short assignment than the long one and that the reading will be more careful and thoughtful. Overwhelming students can often lead to paralysis. Moreover, it is easier to enforce required readings when they are easily manageable, and the overall quality of student work will be higher.

An additional benefit, and a very great one, of reading shorter texts with greater care, is that one can thus try to ensure that students read them in the original language. In the exam for a survey course, it is not fair to ask pointed questions about stylistic matters. But when the assignments are smaller, a student need not be shocked by questions about exactly what, for example, Carlos Germán Belli borrowed from Quevedo or why Ovid's couplets seem "smoother" than those of Propertius. It is obvious that students who are taught to anticipate such questions will also have been taught to enjoy the foreign language itself (see also Milosz 1981: 74–75). Although one can never make sure that students read canonical texts in the original language, the small group discussion approach can provide a better opportunity to motivate students into doing so by carefully showing them the differences (and disadvantages) of any translation. As Lindenberger observes: "Even more fundamental is the cultivation of an attitude among all those who teach literature that the experience of reading these texts in the original is something that matters, an experience, in fact, essential to a literary education" (1986: 37–38).

There is no single prescription on how to become an effective literature teacher overnight. Experience, as emphasized by so many writers on the subject, plays an essential role. As Eck (1987) states:

> Learning to teach in a discussion context is not easy. It involves a delicate balance between being in control and letting go. It involves being prepared without being dominating. It requires the discernment to answer questions germane to the discussion, to refer other questions to the reading or after-class consultation, and to return constantly to the discussion of the text. (p. 35)

According to Rosovsky, "Education in its deepest sense will always retain an element of mystery" (1990: 130). Just as the classroom is not where learning starts, it is not where it ends either. Literature can be considered a lifelong pursuit and an intensely rewarding one. Perhaps less important than the poems, plays, and novels that our students examine in class are the ones they will read later on. An enthusiasm for other literatures than their own can be an inexhaustible gift. The important thing is not that they read Tolstoy or Borges now, but that they remain interested and careful readers for the rest of their lives.

REFERENCES

Bok, Derek. 1990. *Universities and the Future of America.* Durham, NC: Duke Univ. Press.

Brooks, Peter, et al. 1989. *Speaking for the Humanities.* American Council of Learned Societies Occasional Papers, no. 7. New York: ACLS.

————, S. Felman, and J. Hillis Miller, eds. 1985. *The Lesson of Paul de Man.* Yale French Studies, no. 69. New Haven, CN: Yale Univ. Press.

Di Pietro, Robert J. 1987. *Strategic Interaction: Learning Languages through Scenarios.* Cambridge, Eng., and New York: Cambridge Univ. Press.

Dubrow, H. 1982. "Teaching Essay-Writing in a Liberal Arts Curriculum," pp. 88–102 in M. M. Gullette, ed., *The Art and Craft of Teaching.* Cambridge, MA: Harvard-Danforth Center for Teaching and Learning (now Derek Bok Center).

————, and J. Wilkinson. 1982. "The Theory and Practice of Lectures," pp. 25–37 in M. M. Gullette, ed., *The Art and Craft of Teaching.* Cambridge, MA: Harvard-Danforth Center for Teaching and Learning (now Derek Bok Center).

Eck, Diana L. 1987. "The Role of the Section Leader," pp. 34–36 in *Manual for Teaching Fellows in the Core.* Cambridge, MA: Faculty of Arts and Sciences, Harvard University.

Engell, J., and D. Perkins, eds. 1988. *Teaching Literature: What Is Needed Now.* Cambridge, MA: Harvard Univ. Press.

Felman, S. 1982. "Psychoanalysis and Education: Teaching Terminable and Interminable," pp. 21–44 in B. Johnson, ed., *The Pedagogical Imperative: Teaching as a Literary Genre.* Yale French Studies, no. 63. New Haven, CT: Yale Univ. Press.

Fraher, R. 1982. "Learning a New Art: Suggestions for Beginning Teachers," pp. 116–27 in M. M. Gullette, ed., *The Art and Craft of Teaching.* Cambridge, MA: Harvard-Danforth Center for Teaching and Learning (now Derek Bok Center).

Garber, Marjorie. 1987. "The Role of the Section Leader," pp. 36–38 in *Manual for Teaching Fellows in the Core.* Cambridge, MA: Faculty of Arts and Sciences, Harvard University.

Graff, G. 1989. *Professing Literature.* Chicago: Univ. of Chicago Press.

Hillis Miller, J. 1988. "The Function of Rhetorical Study at the Present Time," pp. 90–109 in J. Engell and D. Perkins, eds., *Teaching Literature: What Is Needed Now.* Cambridge, MA: Harvard Univ. Press.

Jedrey, C. M. 1982. "Grading and Evaluation," pp. 103–15 in M. M. Gullette, ed., *The Art and Craft of Teaching.* Cambridge, MA: Harvard-Danforth Center for Teaching and Learning (now Derek Bok Center).

Johnson, Barbara. 1982. "Teaching Ignorance: *L'École des Femmes,*" pp. 105–82 in B. Johnson, ed., *The Pedagogical Imperative: Teaching as a Literary Genre.* Yale French Studies, no. 63. New Haven, CT: Yale Univ. Press.

————. 1985. "In Memoriam," in P. Brooks, S. Felman, and J. Hillis Miller, *The Lesson of Paul de Man*. Yale French Studies, no. 69. New Haven, CN: Yale Univ. Press.

————. 1988. "Deconstruction, Feminism, and Pedagogy," in J. Engell and D. Perkins, eds., *Teaching Literature: What Is Needed Now*. Cambridge, MA: Harvard Univ. Press.

————, ed. 1982. *The Pedagogical Imperative: Teaching as a Literary Genre*. Yale French Studies, no. 63. New Haven, CT: Yale Univ. Press.

Kasulis, T. P. 1982. "Questioning," pp. 38–48 in M. M. Gullette, ed., *The Art and Craft of Teaching*. Cambridge, MA: Harvard-Danforth Center for Teaching and Learning (now Derek Bok Center).

Kramsch, Claire J. 1985. "Literary Texts in the Classroom: A Discourse." *Modern Language Journal* 69: 356–66.

Levin, H. 1960. "Irving Babbitt and the Teaching of Literature." The Irving Babbitt Inaugural Lecture, Harvard University, Cambridge, MA.

————. 1988. "The Crisis of Interpretation," pp. 29–47 in J. Engell and D. Perkins, eds., *Teaching Literature: What Is Needed Now*. Cambridge, MA: Harvard Univ. Press.

Lindenberger, H. 1986. "Teaching Literature in the Original or in Translation: An Intellectual or a Political Problem?" *ADFL Bulletin* 17,2: 35–49.

Lott, B. 1988. "Language and Literature." *Language Teaching* 21: 1–13.

Lyotard, J. F. 1982. "Endurance and the Profession," pp. 72–77 in B. Johnson, ed., *The Pedagogical Imperative: Teaching as a Literary Genre*. Yale French Studies, no. 63. New Haven, CT: Yale Univ. Press.

Marius, R. 1988. "Reflections on the Freshman English Course," pp. 169–90 in J. Engell and D. Perkins, eds., *Teaching Literature: What Is Needed Now*. Cambridge, MA: Harvard Univ. Press.

Milosz, C. 1981. *Native Realm*. Berkeley: Univ. of California Press.

Muyskens, Judith A. 1983. "Teaching Second-Language Literatures: Past, Present, and Future." *Modern Language Journal* 67: 413–23.

Nash, L. L. 1982. "The Rhythms of the Semester," pp. 70–87 in M. M. Gullette, ed., *The Art and Craft of Teaching*. Cambridge, MA: Harvard-Danforth Center for Teaching and Learning (now Derek Bok Center).

Perkins, D. 1988. "Taking Stock after Thirty Years," pp. 111–17 in J. Engell and D. Perkins, eds., *Teaching Literature: What Is Needed Now*. Cambridge, MA: Harvard Univ. Press.

Perry, W. G. 1985. "Different Worlds in the Same Classroom," pp. 1–17 in M. M. Gullette, ed., *On Teaching and Learning*. Cambridge, MA: Harvard-Danforth Center for Teaching and Learning (now Derek Bok Center).

Rivers, Wilga M. 1990. "Interaction: The Key to Communication," pp. 7–17 in M. A. K. Halliday, J. Gibbons, and H. Nicholas, eds., *Learning, Keeping, and Using Language*. Amsterdam, Neth., and Philadelphia: John Benjamins.

Rosmarin, A. 1985. "The Art of Leading a Discussion," pp. 34–39 in M. M. Gullette, ed., *On Teaching and Learning*. Cambridge, MA: Harvard-Danforth Center for Teaching and Learning (now Derek Bok Center).

Rosovsky, H. 1990. *The University. An Owner's Manual*. New York: Norton.

Scott, Nathan A. 1988. "On the Teaching of Literature in an Age of Carnival," pp. 49–64 in J. Engell and D. Perkins, eds., *Teaching Literature: What Is Needed Now*. Cambridge, MA: Harvard Univ. Press.

Segerstråle, U. 1982. "The Multifaceted Role of the Section Leader," pp. 49–69 in M. M. Gullette, ed., *The Art and Craft of Teaching*. Cambridge, MA: Harvard-Danforth Center for Teaching and Learning (now Derek Bok Center).

Vendler, H. 1988. "What We Have Loved," pp. 13–25 in J. Engell and D. Perkins, eds., *Teaching Literature: What Is Needed Now*. Cambridge, MA: Harvard Univ. Press.

Wolcowitz, J. 1982. "The First Day of Class," pp. 10–24 in M. M. Gullette, ed., *The Art and Craft of Teaching*. Cambridge, MA: Harvard-Danforth Center for Teaching and Learning (now Derek Bok Center).

13
Linguistics in the
Language Department

Marguerite Mahler
Framingham State College

THE SITUATION

To an outsider linguistics, whatever it is, most naturally belongs in a language department; a judgment very likely inspired by etymological considerations. To members of traditional language and literature departments linguistics, whatever it is, best belongs elsewhere. Whatever the reason for this attitude— a close analysis would reveal misgivings on both sides—it has far-reaching consequences for the general education of our students. Departments are turning out language majors and literary experts dismally ignorant about language and languages. The level of practical knowledge among our students has improved notably with new approaches, techniques, and technologies, but their theoretical knowledge of the subject has remained practically nonexistent.

Commenting on the social responsibility of the university, Stern (1981) highlights this neglected role. The university is there to provide "the most advanced, and most specialized training available anywhere in a community. . . . Indeed, one could go further and say that universities have the power to give shape and substance to the view a society takes of the field of learning in question" (p. 213). If such is the case, then language departments have something to think about. In *Language—The Loaded Weapon,* the linguist

Dwight Bolinger (1986) inveighs against the medieval views and sentiments of those in the community who set themselves up as experts-at-large on questions of language: "Some are abysmally ignorant, others with a rich fund of practical knowledge" (p. 1). The "shaman," as Bolinger calls the less innocent, is most dangerous when legislating on language. It is clear that a wider knowledge of linguistic matters is badly needed.

Modern linguistics has been with us for over a century, yet few of its findings seem to have permeated the educated masses. For example, one topic that is continually harped on is the "decline" of the English language. Critics, writers, teachers of writing, and editors appear on public broadcasting or write columns remonstrating with the public on how they should stop being instruments of corruption and help save the language. Why language soothsayers are unable to correlate contemporary changes with the changes that have unremittingly occurred in the language over the years seems to indicate a closed-mindedness or ignorance difficult to reckon with. One thing that our beloved literary texts reveal, if we go back far enough, is that languages change despite the autocratic dictates of grammarians and teachers.

Sunrises have been praised in song, painted, and described. But a study of the sun, as an object, immediately leaves the realm of illusion. The sun does not go around the earth—the opposite is true; the objective description often bears little resemblance to what one sees and feels. We accept the findings of the physicists, even if they prove to be inaccurate or wrong at a later date. When a similar enterprise is undertaken for language, the public resists. Modern linguistics states that the business of the grammarian is not to prescribe usage but to describe the present state of the language as it is used. It also tells us that writing is secondary to speaking (not all languages exist in written form); that the word is not the basic unit of investigation; that sounds, morphemes, and sentences emerge from a deeper level of representation, and that the principles that regulate language may be part of the biology of the brain. It is perhaps this new attitude toward norms and the rejection of long-accepted attitudes that has disturbed the traditionalists the most. Emotions have overpowered curiosity and precluded meaningful debate.

In our departments, literature students are not taught to become authors but to appreciate literature. Courses are set up so that the student may gain a better understanding and appreciation of the world in which that student lives and learn about what other people think and value. The same option ought to be given to those who want to know more about the nature of language and the behavior of particular languages. The student who in the past has indicated such an interest has often been directed to seek instruction in the linguistics department. Where there is none, the student has been "reeducated" to want what the department offers. Unfortunately for this student, courses offered in linguistics departments are usually oriented toward a particular linguistic theory and aim to equip students with the working tools necessary to become specialists in the field. Much time is spent on problem-solving, with instruction in the theoretical implications of this or that method. Language students are often disenchanted with the dry, piecemeal approach they find in these courses and claim they need to go through an array of courses before getting the general picture and answering some of the questions that piqued their curiosity in the first place.

Language departments can satisfy the legitimate curiosity of their students by offering linguistic courses with a humanistic bent, that is, with fewer problem sets and wider, more comprehensive readings. Linguists also have become more community-minded. Several prominent linguists have written books that explain with a minimum of technical terms the organization of grammar, the current thinking on grammatical theory, and recent findings on language and languages. Chomsky (1986) has made an excellent contribution in this domain; in his *Knowledge of Language,* he introduces the nonspecialist to his ideas on syntax and how he differentiates *language* from particular languages. Many linguists are realizing the need to interest the general population and students from other disciplines in relevant findings from their field.

The purpose of this chapter is to introduce the noninitiated to some of the basic issues and topics in the field of linguistics and propose curriculum changes that will enlighten the language lover and give credible knowledge and skills to the future language specialist. The field is vast and developing rapidly. Linguistics departments more than ever need the research input and teaching of individuals from particular languages to support the testing of their theoretical models. In an age of interdisciplinary learning and global awareness, language departments, at the crossroads of so many disciplines, can no longer ignore the advances made in the most closely related field, linguistics. The intellectualization of language studies could enhance the prestige of a language concentration in a college or university and, at the very least, inform future commentators in public debate on many important language-related matters.

SOME MISCONCEPTIONS

I wish now to take up comments and questions I have heard over the years from concerned language students and others. I have chosen for discussion those topics that are no longer contested in the field of linguistics and are normally dealt with at an introductory level. I hope to show some of the ideational contributions that even an elementary study of linguistics can bring to language learners and language concentrators.

Difficult vs. Easy Languages

"Is it true that language X is the most difficult language to learn?" or "What is the most difficult (or easiest) language to learn?" The assumption behind these statements is that languages differ considerably in terms of level of complexity, some being inherently difficult while others are inherently easy, and that a linguist would know which belongs to which category. Studies in language universals have shown that all languages display the same intricacy, or the same simplicity, depending on how one looks at it. Children all over the world acquire their first language at the same pace, follow the same developmental stages, and have developed control of the language at about the same age. What children have mastered by the age of five pretty well demonstrates the structural intricacy of particular languages.

The individual who asks the above questions is generally focusing on one aspect of the language, for example whether this language has an elaborate case or tense system. A language encompasses more than word endings. It involves various elements and components: sounds, syllable structure, prosody such as stress and tone, morphemes, syntactic phrases, sentences and rules for their combinations, semantic structure. One language may indeed be more complicated than another in some areas yet simpler in others. English, for instance, has a simple morphological structure but a complex sound and syllable structure. Overall, relative complexity averages out.

Primitive vs. Highly Developed Languages

One still hears people qualify languages as "primitive" or "highly developed." If primitive means a simpler precursor of language, then there is no historical record of such a language. Lyons (1984) states:

> no correlation has yet been discovered between the different stages of cultural development through which societies have passed and the type of language spoken at these stages of cultural development. For example, there is no such thing as a Stone Age type of language; or, as far as its general grammatical structure is concerned, a type of language that is characteristic of food-gathering or pastoral societies, on the one hand, or modern industrialized societies, on the other. (p. 28)

There is no "native speech" in the process of becoming a language any more than there are apes turning into humans. If by primitive is meant a limited form of expression, the same applies. The language of so-called "primitive" people is like any other, a complex rule-governed system capable of expressing generalities and subtleties.

An ancillary speech called *pidgin* often develops when speakers of various languages need to communicate. Pidgin is not a full language in that it does not have the power to express the full scale of human wants and interests. It has a marginal grammar and a vocabulary limited to specialized situations such as selling and buying. When after a period of isolation pidgin becomes the only speech available to children, these children, without anyone's help, fill in the missing elements of grammar and vocabulary and turn pidgin speech into a full language called *creole*. The grammars of creole languages are as complex and complete as that of any other language.

The Number of Languages

"How many languages are spoken in the world today?" The answer people give to that question is revealing. American speakers give a number that falls between 70 and 250. The reasoning is the following: the same language is shared by several countries yet several countries have more than one language, so the number must compare to the number of countries in the world, somewhere around 150. The reasoning of a student from the Philippines is similar: there are a couple of thousand languages spoken in my country, the same is true in surrounding countries, so there must be hundreds of thousands of languages spoken in the world today. The answer is somewhere in between these two extremes.

People are said to speak two different languages if speakers of one group cannot understand speakers of another group. How many "Chinese" languages are spoken in China? Eight or two hundred? Some varieties within one language are as diverse as the Romance languages. The language continuum is not always easy to segment. Thus the estimation of the number of languages varies between 4000 and 8000, nearly 200 of which are spoken in the Americas.

Language vs. Dialect

When asked about the number of languages spoken in the world today, most ask whether they should include "dialects." For some, dialects mean nonofficial languages; for others, languages with no written tradition; for still others, languages spoken by "primitive" groups, and so on. The linguistic definition of a language ignores political, social, or technological considerations. There is no such thing as a speaker who does not speak a full language, so an account must include them all. Linguistically, a *dialect* is a systematic variation by a group within a language. We all speak some dialect, in that our speech does not include all the variations of the language. Oftentimes, the speech variety from one region or from one social class acquires a status not given to others and becomes the standard for others to follow. This variety is labeled the *prestige dialect*, but it has no intrinsic linguistic claim to superiority over other dialects of the same language.

The Development of an International Language

Different parts of the world are coming closer together through modern communication and education. "Isn't it possible that sooner or later the number of languages will significantly diminish, perhaps to the point of there being only one 'universal' language?" Worldwide communication is too recent a phenomenon to comment on its effects. What we know from the past and present is that lingua francas have never contributed by themselves to the disappearance of a language. Brosnahan (1963) examined historical cases of language imposition, in particular, the cases of Latin, Greek, and Arabic. He observed that for each successful imposition, the language "was originally imposed on its area by military authority, and . . . once imposed, it was maintained for at least several centuries by similar authority" (p. 15). The freely chosen learning of a "foreign" international language, like English, is unlikely to have a similar effect. Societies searching for their own identity almost always proclaim their native tongue as the official language, forgoing the choice of adopting a more international one, while sometimes retaining a colonial language for intercommunal use, as in India or Sri Lanka. Motherland and mother tongue are two emotionally charged phenomena inextricably linked in the minds of most.

Writing and Language

Educated people tend to visualize languages. Most equate the number of sounds with the number of letters in their alphabet. Thus speakers (and even teachers) of English, Spanish, and French all claim that there are five vowels in their language. If it is true for Spanish, it is far from being the case for English or French. In the following English examples, the words are all identical except for the vowel sound: *beat, bit, bait, bet, bat, bite, bot, bout, boat, bought, but, boot.* Writing systems have more to do with civilization than with the language itself. The examples above show the ingenuity of the medieval scribe trying to transcribe a language with an alphabet fit for another. What was an adequate approximation some 700 years ago is hardly the case today. Similarly, it is not uncommon for people to think that Chinese and Japanese are related just because they share some features of their writing system. Japanese is as different from Chinese as it is from English. All three belong to different language families.

Corruption in Language

Individuals, usually speakers of the prestige dialect, lament the "corruption" or the "degradation" of the language. The drifting of forms and meanings is an inevitable manifestation of living languages. Only dead languages do not change. Persistent common "errors" must be looked at as normal developmental changes—the errors of today are the norms of tomorrow. Linguists estimate at 500 to 800 years the period it takes for a language to be transformed to the point where speakers at each end of the spectrum would be unable to communicate. Insistence on standards and norms retards the process but cannot stop it. The question is whether one wants to keep working at this sisyphian task. Energy might be better spent teaching about the nature and behavior of language, so that people will understand change and the reasons for it.

Grammar

"I don't know my grammar." Neither did Homer, if we mean the ability to label words and explain their relationships. Plato was among the first to isolate lexical categories. He identified noun and verb. Aristotle recognized tense. Once the present inventory was complete, intellectual impetus declined and grammar became an idealized repertoire of what should be rather than what was.

All languages are rule-governed. The forms and the rules for their combination is what we call the grammar of that language. Any native speaker knows implicitly, if not explicitly, all the rules of that speaker's language, therefore of that language's grammar. It is this intuitive knowledge that linguistic grammars try to characterize, and the task has proved to be extraordinarily difficult. Knowledge of and knowledge about are two different types of knowledge. We are still seeking complete answers to questions about grammar.

The Critical Age

"I'm too old to learn a second language." It was thought for a long time that only prepubescent children could learn a second language completely. Studies by Snow and Hoefnagel-Höhle (1978) have challenged this belief. In fact, in their study, motivated adults tended to learn more quickly than young children. In no case was there a natural turning point beyond which progress became impossible. Adults are, however, more likely to abandon the activity once a comfortable level of communication has been reached. Psychological factors more than physiological ones seem to play a determining role in second-language learning. First-language acquisition is different in that it is linked with the maturation of the brain in a situation in which there is strong motivation to communicate.

Language and Thinking

One often wonders whether the language a person speaks influences the way that person sees the world. This question was much debated in the nineteenth century but abandoned when linguists became more attentive to the similarities among languages. Bolinger (1986) expresses the prevailing position when he says that the differences among languages are of

> no more real importance than that between the use of wood to build shelters by forest-dwellers and the use of adobe by the inhabitants of the desert. It will hardly do to assume that speakers of Chinese are telegraphic in their thinking just because a literal translation from Chinese sounds a bit like a telegram. (viii–ix)

The same can be said about the so-called "logic" of word order. Is the subject-verb-object order of English and Chinese more or less logical than the subject-object-verb of Japanese and the verb-subject-object of Arabic?

Linguists

"I'm a linguist." "Oh, then how many languages do you speak?" Most people have never heard the term *linguist* as an occupational category; to them it can mean only someone who is interested in languages and therefore speaks many of them. This elementary view of linguistics has led to various forms of criticism particularly among learned colleagues: "linguists try to describe languages they do not speak." How many poems has the critic written? How many planets has the astronomer visited? This is not to say that scholars would not like to see or practice what they write about. The difference between theory and practice is too well known to elaborate. A linguist is concerned with the structure of languages and can sort, analyze, describe, extract rules, and predict certain behavior from the data produced by native speakers. The linguist's hypotheses are then tested by fellow linguists who either accept, reject, or incorporate these findings after consultation with native informants, who may or may not themselves be trained linguists.

ELEMENTS OF LINGUISTICS

The past thirty years have seen an explosion in linguistics research. This section is a brief nontechnical account of the various components of language and the specialized branches of linguistics that language and literature specialists should become familiar with. The sequence of topics follows the conventional order found in "introduction to linguistics" textbooks. Unfortunately, many native speakers of English think that all languages closely conform to the English model, in that most languages follow a similar word order, form their words in similar fashion, and use the same devices to express grammatical categories and relations. Though the current research in linguistics focuses on the similarities among languages, the purposes of this exposition are better served by concentrating on the diversity across languages.

Phonetics and Phonology

Phonetics is the study of the distinctive sounds used to differentiate words. Excluded from this definition are screams, cries, grunts, and whistles, though these may have important communicative significance. The number of distinguishable sounds human speech organs are capable of producing seems to be physiologically unlimited. The number of contrasting sounds found in the many languages of the world, however, is rather small, about one hundred, and their organization is fairly constrained. The average sound inventory of a typical language is about thirty-five.

Phonology is concerned with sound patterns. In sound production there is a convergence of two simultaneous competitive forces; one that seeks to maintain the highest contrast possible between sounds, and a second that seeks to minimize the physical effort by keeping the number of vocal maneuvers to a minimum. The need for clarity is fundamental, as seen in languages with a small sound inventory. All three-vowel systems are composed of the same three vowels—those sounds located at the vertices of what is called the oral triangle: high front /i/, low central /a/, and high back /u/. A five-vowel system, which is the norm, is made up of the basic three vowels, /i/, /a/, /u/, plus two others located halfway between /i/ and /a/ and /u/ and /a/, that is /e/ and /o/. All languages with five or more vowels share the basic five. Languages then begin to diversify by filling in the spaces between these sounds: series are extended or doubled by changing the position of the tongue or the velum or the shape of the lips. The larger the number of sounds, the greater the sounds' similarity, which reduces proportionally the effort needed to produce these sounds.

Japanese is said to have a smaller-than-average sound inventory. The language makes use of other means to distinguish meaning: vowel length and consonant length. Thus *biru* 'building' and *bi:ru* 'beer'; *tsuji* 'a proper name' and *tsu:ji* 'moving the bowels'; *saki* 'ahead' and *sakki* 'before.' Most languages of the world are tone languages—for example, Chinese, Thai, a great number of languages in Africa, and some native American languages—which contrast meaning by changing the pitch of individual syllables. The Thai sound string *naa* takes on five different meanings depending on the vowel pitch. It can mean 'a nickname,' 'rice paddy,' 'young maternal uncle or aunt,' 'face,' or 'thick' (examples from Fromkin and Rodman 1988). The average tone distinction is four, while some languages have as many as nine.

In every language, rules operate to block certain sequences while favoring others. Well-formed English strings, for instance, exclude initial sequences like *ps, pn, lb* and *sgl,* which are natural in a variety of other languages. Some languages allow only the basic CV syllable type—that is, a vowel (V) preceded by a single consonant (C), while others admit only certain sounds in word-final position. Speakers restructure syllables in loan words to conform to their native rules. Speakers of Spanish tend to add an *e* before an initial consonant cluster beginning with *s,* while Japanese speakers simplify complex clusters by inserting a vowel between contiguous consonants, as in *sotoresu* for English *stress,* thus making a series of CV syllables.

Traditionally, phonology has focused on the way sounds interact. Sounds can be inserted, deleted, changed, or reordered depending on the phonological environment. Consider the French example *film russe* 'Russian film.' The undesirable sequence *lmr* is resolved either by dropping one consonant, the *l,* or adding the vowel *e,* resulting either in *fim russe* or *filme russe.* More frequently, sounds copy a feature from a contiguous sound. In the word *observe,* English assimilates the voiceless *s* to the voiced *b,* changing *s* into *z, o***bz***erv,* while French assimilates *b* into *s* to produce a voiceless *p, o***ps***erv.* The number of phonological rules is limited, but the selection and the manner of application accounts for variety in languages.

Morphology

A morpheme is the smallest linguistic unit with meaning. Languages can be classified according to the way they form their words from morphemes. At one extreme of the continuum, we find languages that are said to have little morphology. These languages do not mark number, gender, case, tense, or mood with special morphemes (as in English *walks, walked*). Words consist mainly of single morphemes and characteristically are monosyllabic. Vietnamese and Chinese are examples. The sentence 'I asked her to buy me books to read' is rendered in Chinese in contrast to English in this fashion: *I* (no case) *ask* (no person, no tense, no mood) *he* (no gender, no case) *buy* (no mood) *I* (no case) *book* (no number, no case) *read* (no mood).

Languages that make use of inflectional morphemes vary in the manner in which the process is achieved. In Latin, a single form stands for several meanings. The final vowel in the verb *amo* 'I love' represents simultaneously person, number, tense, and mood. The boundaries in other types of languages are more clearly delineated. Turkish is one such language. The rendition of the seven-word expression 'to be made to love each other' is a single five-morpheme word *sev-is-dir-il-meh* which corresponds to 'love-reciprocal-causative-passive-infinitive.' Japanese shows a similar organization: *kakaseare-tai* 'wants to be forced to write' or 'write-causative-passive-volitive.' The number of morphemes per word is at its highest in the so-called polysynthetic languages, in which a whole sentence is rendered by one word. Typical of this category are the native American languages. The Greenlandic equivalent of 'I bought myself a fishing pole' is *Aulisa-ut-isaR-siwu-nga* or 'fishing-instrument-suitable-obtaining-my' (example from Sapir 1949).

Fusion is characteristic of the Semitic languages, where words are commonly constructed from consonantal roots and grammatical meaning conveyed through the syllable structure and the vowel quality. In Classical Arabic the verb 'to write' corresponds to the three consonants *ktb*, unpronounceable as such. The syllable structure CVVCVC indicates 'reciprocal.' A vowel *a* in the syllable skeleton indicates 'perfective active,' thus 'we wrote to each other' is *kaatab*.

English is said to be inflectionally poor, and this makes certain other inflectionally rich languages seem "difficult" to anglophone learners. Below is a partial list of the inflectional categories across languages:

Number marking: singular, dual, triple, plural

Gender marking: masculine, feminine, neuter

Noun marking: common, proper, animate, inanimate, single, distributive, collective

Case marking: (up to fourteen, as in Finnish) nominative, genitive, accusative, dative, instrumental, locative, ablative, vocative

Tense marking: present, imperfect, preterite, aorist, experiential perfect, gerundive

Aspect marking: progressive, momentaneous, durative, continuous, inceptive, terminative, iterative

Mood marking: indicative, imperative, jussive, subjunctive, potential, dubitative, optative

Voice marking: active, passive, causative, reflexive

Style marking: formal, informal

Sex marking: male, female

Distance marking: near, median, far

Subjective marking: hearsay, inferred, witnessed

No language has all of the above, fortunately.

Syntax

Words come together to form sentences. Syntax is the study of sentence structures and the rules that govern their organization. A native speaker's knowledge of structures is illustrated in the classical Chomskyan examples *(1a) John is easy to please* and *(2a) John is eager to please,* where the distinction in meaning goes beyond the lexical differences of *eager* and *easy.* A simple transformation reveals the structural dissimilarity of the two sentences: *(1b) It is easy to please John* is an acceptable paraphrase of (1a), while *(2b) *It is eager to please John* is not for (2a). Sentence (2a) can be rephrased as *(2c) John is eager to please anyone.* How in (1a) *John* is both the subject of *is easy* and the direct object of *please* is what syntax has to explain.

Languages vary in the manner in which they order their constituents in sentences. English is basically a subject-verb-object language in which *John sees Mary* is different in meaning from *Mary sees John.* This SVO order is far from canonic. There are as many languages with an SOV order as an SVO order and a significant number with a VSO order. The position of the object (O) (the complement) with respect to the verb (V) (the head of the complement construction) yields interesting generalizations. In SOV languages not only does the object precede the verb but all other complements precede their head: the relative clause precedes the noun, the noun precedes the preposition, and so on. We illustrate with Japanese sentences featuring a possessive construction, a relative clause, a prepositional phrase, and a comparative construction: (1) 'Taro saw his neighbor's dog' is rendered as *Taro [[neighborhood man] dog] saw.* (2) 'Taro saw the dog that ate the meat' gives *Taro [[meat ate] dog] saw.* (3) 'Taro saw a dog from the window' becomes *Taro [[window from] dog] saw.* And (4) 'The dog is bigger than the cat' as *Dog [[cat] than] big.* As they learn another language, students have to adapt to and assimilate different ways of assembling their sentences.

Semantics

Meaning can be analyzed from various perspectives: grammatical, referential, and cultural. Grammatical meaning originates in the acceptable ways in which words can be combined in a particular language. A sentence such as *Punctuality ate an intelligent tree* is nonsensical. Part of knowing the meaning of the verb *to eat* is to know that its subject must be animate and its object concrete. Similarly, a knowledge of the words *intelligent* and *tree* also will prevent their association. The unacceptable sentence **John seems Peter to talk* presents a different problem. There, structural rules have been broken, thus rendering the interpretation of the sentence impossible. Other sentences are structurally ambiguous; the reader is invited to consider the two interpretations of one of the classic examples of ambiguity: *Flying planes can be dangerous.*

"I understand what you are saying but I don't know what you mean" illustrates another way in which meaning is derived, namely, from context. *Did you see them there on that day?* requires some previous information regarding *them, there,* and *that day.* Someone with a watch who is asked *Do you have the time?* is expected to answer something other than *yes* or *no.* Discourse analysis examines the flow of given and new information, illocutionary force, relevance, and so on. Social roles and social kinships are systematically reaffirmed through greetings, apologies, and formal and informal styles. The functional use of language is complex. "Even coldly dispassionate scientific statements, whose associated expressive meaning is minimal, usually have as one of their aims that of winning friends and influencing people" (Lyons 1984: 143).

Historical Linguistics

Historical linguistics analyzes the ways in which languages change over time. Findings in this domain have contributed much to our understanding of how languages change, the rate at which they change, and the factors involved in language change. One of the main activities of historical linguistics has been to classify languages into genetic families. An outstanding accomplishment in this domain has been to relate Japanese to Turkish and possibly to Hungarian and Finnish (Miller 1971). Comrie (1981: 194) warns about some of the problems in attempting to relate languages. Similarities may be due to chance, to borrowing, to a universal tendency, or to a true genetic affiliation. He points out that languages with no written tradition are difficult to categorize and that, for these languages, which account for more than half of the existing languages, a typology based on morphology or word order might be more appropriate.

Sociolinguistics

Interest in language has given rise to several subfields, among which we find sociolinguistics. Sociolinguistics examines those aspects of language that have social significance, for instance, the stigmatization of some speech varieties; styles of speech such as formal and informal, male and female; the use of slang; sexism; racial epithets; taboo subjects and euphemisms; the question of bilingualism; manipulative propaganda; and so on. An often heated social issue in America is the recognition of English as the official language. In previous debates, the kind of English that was taught or should be taught in school was the issue. Changes in attitude are reflected in the language: new words have been coined to avoid favoring one sex over the other, and gratuitous racial and ethnic references have almost disappeared from public broadcasting in the United States. These are all interesting sociolinguistic questions.

Psycholinguistics

Language is involved in the development of the human brain itself. Any physical disruption in brain mechanisms can impair the ability to acquire or use language. Psycholinguistics deals with language acquisition and cognition. The process of acquiring a first language is well documented, but the theories explaining the process are far from satisfactory. The idea that a child learns by imitation and correction is disputed on the grounds that children make creative mistakes and that the quality and quantity of correction and coaching have little effect on the acquisition process. Chomsky presupposes specialized biological structures for language. The fact that deaf children learning from signing parents go through the same stages of development as their talking counterparts supports his "innateness hypothesis." Second-language learning is even more poorly understood. Is learning a second language fundamentally the same as acquiring the first? If so, why does it appear to be different? If not, what is it? Studies in second-language learning are linked to other topics, such as memory and forgetting, attention, motivation, and perceptual strategies. There is much to be learned from current research in these areas.

To the above subfield, we can add a new and expanding discipline, *computational linguistics,* in which computers are programmed to simulate the comprehension and production of human language. This extraordinary enterprise requires both a clear understanding of the way the human mind learns and thinks and a precise description of the way human language is produced and used. Psychologists, linguists, and computer scientists all work together to unravel the great mystery of language and intelligence.

LINGUISTICS IN THE LANGUAGE CURRICULUM

Why should language students study linguistics? Perhaps foremost is the fact that knowledge of linguistic facts raises the level of professional awareness and competence. Part of knowing the world around us is understanding where things come from and how they work, and distinguishing the unique from that which is general. Most disciplines dealing with natural phenomena see to it that their specialists get a fundamental understanding of the object they study. Language is not only a natural phenomenon but the means by which we build and transmit our knowledge about the world.

Related to professional competence is social responsibility. It is reasonable for society to turn to language graduates with questions about language. Decisions about social policy in this domain should be made on a more general basis than a practical knowledge of a second or third language and personal impressions. The language specialist should have information and a historical, cultural perspective from which enlightened decisions can be made.

A teacher with a global understanding of language behavior and change is likely to be a more interesting, patient teacher. Rather than dismissing legitimate questions with "That's just the way it is," the teacher may pique the curiosity of the student. Students do not need long expositions, but informative tidbits can perk the interest of the class. For example, a brief explanation of where a particular exception comes from could do much to foster the learner's appreciation of a second language and give patience to the learner when later confronted with yet another exception. One thing a language teacher should do is raise the level of tolerance and appreciation for language in general and prepare the students for learning and using third or fourth languages.

Finally, as in any field, having a wider knowledge than just that which is necessary to do the job at hand enhances self-image and personal satisfaction. Language specialists should not go through their career with the nagging awareness that a large part of their field of expertise is a complete mystery to them.

We now turn our attention to how best to prepare our students in foreign-language departments. Linguistics is not a seasoned field. As late as the 1960s, the teaching of linguistics was mainly at the graduate level in linguistics departments. Now, several of the former graduate core courses have been introduced at the undergraduate level, and various subfield courses are offered in related departments: aspects of sociolinguistics in the department of sociology, aspects of psycholinguistics in the department of psychology, verbal art in the department of education, and so on. In the following discussion, the term *major* designates the study of a specific language and the term *concentration* refers to a particular option within the major such as literature, culture and civilization, or linguistics.

The courses proposed are grouped in four categories: a foundation course, core courses for the concentrators, recommended optional courses, and courses for graduate-level concentrators. Many language departments already offer several of the courses recommended; these departments can provide experience and guidance for others.

Foundation Course

This course, which should be required of all undergraduate language majors, could be addressed to students of various languages and disciplines. It would survey the topics discussed in the previous section of this chapter, that is, phonetics, phonology, morphology, syntax, semantics, and the major subfields such as historical linguistics, sociolinguistics, and psycholinguistics. Where there is more than one language department as well as a department of linguistics, this course could be hosted by the linguistics department and taught by a linguistics professor either from one of the language departments or from the department of linguistics, the latter selected by the language departments. Sections for discussion of applications to specific languages would be taught by members of that specific department. This team-teaching approach economizes on faculty effort and avoids unnecessary duplication.

Linguistics can easily become abstract and technical. As in any other discipline, the success of an introductory course depends on the competence of the instructor and that instructor's ability to adapt to the needs of the students. This course, intended for humanists, would favor expository readings and the plain statement of findings over problem-solving. Several introductory textbooks are available, and section leaders would add their own readings from studies of their own languages. A title for this course could be Understanding Language and Languages.

Graduate students also need a basic understanding of language and linguistics. An introductory course at this level could focus on the various theories of language, past and present, with particular attention given to contemporary findings and practices. The course could be entitled Language Theories and Linguistics. Here again, students of different languages could combine for a lecture series, with sections for particular languages taught by specialists of those languages. One section could well be allocated to literature concentrators and emphasize aspects of linguistics used in literary criticism. This would be a valuable course, not only for students of foreign literatures, but also for students of comparative literature.

Core Courses for Concentrators

These courses, offered in the language department for advanced undergraduates and graduate students as well as interested students from the linguistics department, would deal specifically with the structure of a particular language or a language group. To ensure adequate coverage of the four traditional components (phonology, morphology, syntax, and semantics), a sequence of two such courses would be advisable. How the material is divided between these two courses will depend greatly on the framework used to study them. For example, a generative approach will favor a course in phonology and another in syntax (where the latter absorbs morphology and semantics).

Some principles of corrective phonetics can be presented in conjunction with the phonology course. The individual practices sounds with exercise tapes. Recordings by the student, on which the instructor makes comments, is extremely effective. Other possibilities might be a theoretical study of the language followed by a practical course, or a historical followed by a synchronic study, or even a synchronic study followed by a historical overview from the point of view of the evolution of the language.

Optional Courses

The choice at this point depends to a large extent on what is available in other departments. The following five options would be useful. A history of the language, or of a group of languages, would pay particular attention to the dynamics of change. Another course would deal with language universals presenting the results of both the Greenberg approach and the Chomsky approach; this course could be entitled Studies in Language Universals. A third and fourth category of optional courses would involve language acquisition and language in society; appropriate are First and Second Language Acquisition and Language and Society. A course on approaches and methods in second-language teaching should be required for all graduate teaching assistants and future teachers of language. These optional courses can be designed to meet the needs of both undergraduate and graduate students, in which case there should be separate sections for the two levels of students to ensure reflection of an appropriate depth.

Graduate Seminars for Concentrators

Topics for graduate seminars would depend on the field of expertise and availability of the professors concerned. It is highly recommended that graduate students concentrating in the linguistics of a particular language take graduate courses in the linguistics department. Advanced theoretical courses provide a solid basis from which to conduct future research.

Most students who earn a graduate degree in a language and literature department teach that language sooner or later; in fact, depending upon factors such as the size of a department and seniority, most of these individuals teach language courses for a large part of their career. That these teachers be well versed in the literature and culture of that language is widely accepted. This, however, is no longer sufficient. The linguistics perspective can supply something of what is presently lacking. Not only does it provide important insights that enrich a humanistic education, but it broadens and deepens the knowledge of language of future professors and teachers of language, literature, and culture in ways that can lead only to better teaching and understanding of their specialties.

REFERENCES

Bolinger, Dwight L. 1986. *Language—The Loaded Weapon: The Use and Abuse of Language Today.* New York: Longman.

Brosnahan, L. F. 1963. "Some Historical Cases of Language Imposition," pp. 7–24 in J. Spencer, ed., *Language in Africa.* Cambridge, Eng.: Cambridge Univ. Press.

Chomsky, Noam. 1986. *Knowledge of Language: Its Nature, Origin, and Use.* New York: Praeger.

Comrie, B. 1981. *Language Universals and Linguistic Typology.* Chicago: Univ. of Chicago Press.

Fromkin, Victoria, and R. Rodman. 1988. *An Introduction to Language.* New York: Holt, Rinehart and Winston.

Lyons, John. 1984. *Language and Linguistics.* Cambridge, Eng.: Cambridge Univ. Press.

Miller, Roy A. 1971. *Japanese and Other Altaic Languages.* Chicago: Univ. of Chicago Press.

Sapir, Edward. 1949. *Language.* New York: Harcourt Brace.

Snow, Catherine E., and M. Hoefnagel-Höhle. 1978. "Age Differences in Second Language Acquisition," pp. 333–44 in E. M. Hatch, ed., *Second Language Acquisition. A Book of Readings.* Rowley, MA: Newbury House.

Stern, H. H. 1981. "Language Teaching and the Universities in the 1980s." *Canadian Modern Language Review* 37,2: 212–25.

14
Languages and International Studies

Richard D. Lambert
The National Foreign Language Center at The Johns Hopkins University

ONE OF THE MOST REMARKABLE EDUCATIONAL INNOVATIONS IN RECENT years has been the development on campus after campus of a major initiative to introduce what is called an international dimension to undergraduate education or, more generally, international studies. The locus of these initiatives usually lies in the social sciences, or sometimes in the applied and professional schools. Hence, foreign-language departments, whose base is most often in the humanities, frequently do not play as central a role as they might in these important initiatives. As I will note below, foreign-language study is an important part of international studies. Moreover, colleagues engaged in international studies can be important allies within the college and university community in the promotion of foreign-language instruction. The foreign-language community would be well advised to seek out ways to make common cause with international studies more generally.

The purpose of this chapter is to inform members of the foreign-language community about the various components of international studies and the ways in which their own activities might most fruitfully articulate with those larger initiatives. The issues discussed emerged in the course of a large number of interviews and analyses of aggregate data in the course of a national review of undergraduate international studies (Lambert 1989a). Scattered around the country there are many examples of innovative programs addressing these issues. I will deal mainly, however, with the challenges facing foreign-language department faculty as they relate to the growing field of international studies. I will discuss briefly the following main components of undergraduate international studies: (1) general education requirements; (2) substantive international studies courses; (3) internationally focused majors, minors, and concentrations; (4) study abroad; and (5) preprofessional and other occupationally oriented international studies.

General Education

I take general education to mean that portion of the curriculum whose purpose is to provide all students with a shared basic intellectual experience independent of the specialization represented in the major or concentration. Introducing students in an intellectually orderly fashion to the rest of the world is an obvious objective within general education. Viewed in these terms, foreign-language instruction is an integral part of international studies. If one takes, as part of the purpose of international studies, the broadening of students' perspectives by exposing them to a culture other than their own, then this is a goal of both foreign-language instruction and international studies.

Indeed, on most college campuses foreign-language courses comprise the majority of the internationally focused courses being offered.[1] For the largest number of students, they represent the only international exposure those students will receive during their college years. Further, the most common required course in international studies is a foreign-language course. Our national survey (Andersen 1988) showed that 69 percent of American universities and 40 percent of the four-year colleges had a language requirement for graduation for at least some students. And where there is a foreign-language requirement it is rarely for just one course, but most often for two years of study (57 percent) or at the very least two semesters (33 percent). While most four-year institutions (77 percent) in their general education requirements specify a nonlanguage international studies course, this is usually a single course in western civilization (47 percent), or a world history or civilization course (35 percent). Other international studies requirements in the general education core curriculum usually comprise a melange of unrelated internationally focused courses from which the student may choose, these often being lumped in with courses on ethnic or women's studies under the overarching rubric of diversity education (Lambert 1989a: 108–10).

Language and Other Requirements

What is odd about this pattern of general education requirements is that only on a very few campuses is there any link between the foreign-language requirement and other internationally focused courses in the general education requirement. They usually operate in total isolation. Surely the two could be linked in some imaginative fashion. For instance, courses can be constructed that combine foreign-language instruction and use with these other internationally focused general education requirements.[2] Indeed, in this age of easy transnational travel and communication, there is something disturbing about a pattern that limits what students get in their general education either to elementary or intermediate instruction in a foreign language or to courses on other countries that have no foreign-language component. Can we not generate general education courses in which at least part of what is taught actually requires the use of a foreign language?

Aside from the traditional divides that separate international studies from foreign-language departments, one limiting factor in carrying out such a proposal is the low level of foreign-language competence that students bring to college from high school. The shackles of English at the postsecondary level are a direct consequence of this low level of competence, which makes impossible any solution that demands the use of a foreign language in the college curriculum. This situation may be changing, however. Most students now enter college with at least two years of foreign-language study. For instance, in 1987, the proportion of freshmen entering universities who had taken at least two years of foreign-language instruction in high school was 88.6 percent (Astin et al. 1987: 47). Colleges and universities have a major stake in increasing both the length and the effectiveness of precollegiate training, if only to make more feasible the use of foreign languages in general education courses. Even now, however, a beginning might be made by moving some of the general education requirements to the senior year after the collegiate language courses have been taken. There is no reason why all required general education courses need be taken only in the freshman and sophomore years. A capstone general education course in the senior year would make it more likely that a substantial portion of the student body would have a high enough foreign-language competence to use it in a substantive internationally focused course.

Since all of this is unlikely to happen in the short run, and since foreign-language courses—particularly the lower level courses that are the only ones that most students take in college—serve as the de facto core curriculum in international studies, it is useful to ask how these courses in and of themselves may best serve the general international studies goal of broadening students' perspectives beyond the narrow confines of their own society. I leave aside as irrelevant for present purposes whether foreign-language study makes a more general intellectual contribution to the students' education,[3] or teaches them something about their own language. Here I will concentrate on the role of the foreign-language course in giving the student a general international perspective.

The Cultural Component of Language Study

Under a somewhat different rubric, a substantial amount of attention is already being paid to the matter of foreign languages and international understanding. It takes the form of a debate about the proper mix of language and culture in foreign-language education (Kramsch 1989). There is, of course, a contribution to be made just by having the student participate, through learning the mechanics of a foreign language, in the intellectual processes of another people. It is by and large the culture part of the language–culture mix, however, that is of interest in this discussion.

It is commonplace that language and culture cannot be separated but, for the language teacher, there is clearly a choice to be made between two ultimate goals in the inclusion of culture in language instruction, a choice with important consequences for how much and what kind of cultural materials are introduced. The first concentrates on the ability of the learner to comprehend and produce the language as the desired outcome of language study, the other concentrates on what the student learns about another society as a byproduct of studying its language. These two goals dramatize the difference between the current orientation of much of basic language instruction toward producing as much communicative competence as possible and what might happen if, as an alternative, the international studies goal of promoting intercultural understanding were chosen as the principal objective. The two are, of course, interrelated, but the emphasis on one or the other leads to different curricular designs. The first, and by far the most common, conception of the proper mix of language and culture asks the question how much and what kind of cultural knowledge should be intertwined with linguistic skills to make language competence most effective. Proponents of this approach vary in how far beyond language behavior they are willing to go in drawing in cultural materials. The de minimis solution selects cultural items closely tied to speech acts, that is, the teacher introduces those bits of culture that are relevant to the particular linguistic feature and language communicative act being performed. At the other extreme, there is an attempt to characterize the culture more broadly and on its own terms, with only a minimal attempt at tying it to specific linguistic features. The cultural features selected in this approach usually comprise very general, "deep" themes that are believed to epitomize the culture in which the language is spoken. In its extreme manifestation, this takes the form of separate lectures or materials on the cultural features themselves semi-independently of the linguistic features that the student is trying to master, or even a kind of a reincarnation of the old "civilization" courses taught by foreign-language professors.

Both approaches lend a general education/international studies aspect to foreign-language instruction, but the greater the attempt to emphasize the cultural context the more the approach resembles other parts of the international studies enterprise, particularly when all discussion is in the native language of the student. One of the things that makes emphasis on international studies objectives in foreign-language instruction desirable is that many students stick with language learning for so brief a time that any hope of providing even a minimal level of communicative competence is slim. The typical attrition rate in both high school and college between first and second year and between second and third year language classes is about 50 percent, so that half of the students who take any foreign-language courses at all take only one year or less, and most of the rest only two years (Fetters and Owings 1984; Lambert 1989a: 66). It is difficult to make much headway toward genuine communicative competence in this time, or for that matter to take students very far into the cultural mindset of the country through low-level instruction in the mechanics of the language. Tilting the goal a little toward international studies objectives may make a more achievable contribution to the general education of most students.

What is clearly needed is a major national discussion among language teachers of how these general education goals might best be served. This includes a careful analysis of what cultural content is currently contained in language texts and courses and what should be contained from the perspective of international studies. The challenge of creating fresh instructional patterns to reflect this perspective brings to the fore another major agenda item for foreign-language teachers.

The Need for Collaboration

Particularly at the postsecondary level, international studies is heavily disciplinized, that is, most courses are given from one or another disciplinary perspective. While to some extent this disciplinary tendency is restrictive, it also provides a series of organized intellectual frameworks within which student appreciation of other societies can be fashioned. A significant expansion of the international studies role of foreign-language instruction would benefit from the introduction of other disciplinary perspectives, taken both from the humanities and the social sciences. Most foreign-language teachers, however, have a professional level of competence in only one or perhaps two disciplines—usually literature and history—relating to the country or countries where the language they teach is spoken. Hence, the creation of such multidisciplinary courses provides an opportunity for collaboration, perhaps through team teaching, where language and nonlanguage faculty work together on common pedagogical tasks. Another opportunity would be in the orientation of students preparing to go abroad, with both language and nonlanguage faculty instructing them on how to learn the most from their overseas stay.

SUBSTANTIVE INTERNATIONAL STUDIES COURSES

So far we have been talking about foreign-language courses per se, particularly with respect to general education at the college level. It is not much of a shift in perspective to redirect attention from how to enrich language courses by introducing a set of international studies objectives to how to enrich international studies courses by introducing foreign-language components. A perusal of the catalog of almost any four-year institution will show a surprising number of internationally oriented courses being offered in a variety of disciplines. For instance, in our recent American Council on Education national survey of undergraduate education (1989a), we counted 1478 such courses in just 13 research universities and 1729 in 13 baccalaureate institutions. They dealt with 45 countries and 9 different disciplines.

The Monolingualism Problem

As part of that survey and in an earlier review of college and university catalogs (Lambert 1981) we found very few courses outside the language departments that indicated any use, let alone requirement, for the use of a foreign language. This is a continuing national disgrace.

As noted earlier, this situation, is, in part, a product of the low level of language competence of nonlanguage faculty and students. What may be surprising to some is that this situation is evident even in literature courses, the language faculty's own substantive courses. A detailed analysis of the transcripts of students in five colleges and universities indicated that more than half of the students who took a literature course had taken only two years—and frequently only one—of prior training in that language. The consequent limitation on the classroom use of the language is apparent. In fact, many courses on foreign literatures are given entirely in English. And given the low level of language competence of the typical student, the serious introduction of foreign-language materials into international studies courses other than literature is even more unlikely. Moreover, while data on the extent of monolingualism among the faculty in international studies are unavailable, the incidence of that malady is known to be quite high.

The Earlham College Model

In some places, there have been deliberate attempts to foster foreign-language use in substantive international courses. Earlham College has had such a program for at least a decade. It involves both faculty development, that is, raising the language competence of international studies faculty, and the deliberate introduction of foreign-language textual materials and realia into courses in anthropology, political science, and history. At Earlham it was discovered that the low level of students' language competence when they enrolled in the courses required the creation of elaborate special glossaries and translation crutches to make the courses accessible for most students.

Language Faculty Roles

Much more needs to be done in this area not on just one campus but on many, and not in just three disciplines but in a wider range of specialties. Indeed, if the students encountered both an expectation and an encouragement that they would actually use their foreign-language competence in the rest of their education, it might motivate the acquisition of the competence level necessary for its use. Moreover, the construction of substantive courses with a foreign-language component can bring the language faculty and the rest of the international studies faculty closer together. The language faculty clearly have an interest in raising the level of foreign-language competence among faculty members in key social science and humanities departments, both by affecting the initial hiring process to encourage the employment of those that have foreign-language skills and by becoming advocates for overseas faculty development programs that include the acquisition of language competencies. Language departments might also consider setting up language training facilities for faculty members in other departments who need to rejuvenate, reinforce, or upgrade foreign-language skills formerly acquired.

MAJORS, MINORS, AND CONCENTRATIONS

The penetration of individual international studies courses with foreign-language materials and raising the language competence of faculty members are important steps in the linguification—to coin an awkward neologism—of international studies. A more concentrated leverage point in the curriculum is in the specialized internationally focused majors, minors, and concentrations. One or more of these is found on most campuses. For instance, 84 percent of universities and 46 percent of baccalaureate institutions have both an international specialty major and a minor (Lambert 1989a: 130). They come in three basic varieties, each representing a different opportunity for articulation with foreign-language instruction: international studies, international relations, and area studies.

International Studies

The first, international studies, tends to group together all internationally oriented courses. It is an increasingly popular undergraduate concentration. On a number of campuses it is becoming one of the five most popular student majors. In structure, it may specify one of two overarching courses as a requirement for the major and, if the program has been in place for a while and has a large student enrollment, it may have a language requirement. If it is a new major on a campus or has low enrollments, however, the tendency is to skimp on requirements of any kind, recruiting as many students as possible by allowing the maximum of flexibility in courses to be counted toward the major. Precisely because of its flexibility, however, and the fact that it tends to involve many of the internationally oriented faculty on the campus, the international studies concentration is a fertile ground for collaborative experiments between language and nonlanguage faculty.

International Relations

The second major, minor, or concentration is in international relations. These are usually anchored in political science departments and deal mainly with political relations among nation-states or topically defined aspects of the international politico-economic system. International relations programs are usually not hospitable to foreign-language requirements, and, if they were, it is difficult to know which language students could be urged to learn, since they typically deal with political and economic relations among a number of world regions. Nevertheless, because of their traditional roots in European studies and their concentration on international organizations with headquarters in Europe, French, German, and sometimes Russian are often specified as language requirements for these students. As the study of international relations broadens to include the Third World in comparative studies, a wider variety of languages is accepted for the language requirement, where there is one. Unfortunately, neither those languages nor the Western European languages show up very often in the reading materials or classroom discussion of the substantive courses. Our students tend to read about the world system exclusively in English through American eyes.

Area Studies

The third model for international majors, minors, and concentrations is area studies. Their breadth depends on the size of the institution and how far along it is in developing international studies more generally on the campus. Where international studies is a mature industry, a single country may be the focus of an area program, particularly such large ones as the Soviet Union, India, China, or Japan. More often at the undergraduate level they cover broad world regions. The least developed programs will put the entire Third World or developing countries under the same rubric. More typically, there will be a regional grouping of countries as in Asian Studies or Latin American Studies. As these examples illustrate, most of the area studies concentrations are outside of Western Europe, on whose languages most of the foreign-language courses are focused. Western European languages represent more than 90 percent of the college enrollments in languages. There are a few Western European area studies concentrations, but they tend to be at the graduate level. Hence, for most of the foreign-language faculty, ties with area studies concentrations is problematic, whereas it is a natural association for those in the less commonly taught languages. Nevertheless, with their tendency to focus on one or a few languages, and with their emphasis on a diversified instructional package for the student, area studies majors, minors, and concentrations are the most natural points of contact between foreign-language education and the rest of international studies.

Study Abroad

A vital part of international studies for students is study abroad. Indeed, in Europe international studies means study abroad. European governments, under a European Community program called ERASMUS, are attempting to ensure that 10 percent of the student body in each EC member country studies in some other EC country. The American system of study abroad is much less centrally orchestrated, being typically managed by the colleges and universities themselves. Most institutions—91 percent of universities, 63 percent of all four-year institutions (Lambert 1989a: 14)—maintain their own programs, and, in addition, there are numerous consortia, broker institutions, and foreign institutions involved in our national system for promoting overseas study.

In the aggregate, in the United States study abroad is a major enterprise: some 50,000 students study in other countries for credit every year. Nonetheless, on any one campus, while there may be many separate programs—an average of 8 for all four-year institutions—the percentage of the undergraduate student body that studies abroad varies by class of institution. About 4 percent of undergraduates in the average research university study abroad, while in baccalaureate institutions the average is 22 percent. Some liberal arts colleges, such as Kalamazoo, try to have all, or almost all, their students go abroad for study.

Foreign Language Faculty and Study Abroad

Even though on most campuses only a minority of students go abroad for study, such programs are important to foreign-language teachers in a number of ways. First, most foreign-language departments urge their majors to study abroad, even though, for a variety of reasons, only about 33 percent of undergraduate majors do so (Lambert 1989a: 21). Second, study abroad is a favorite student device for fulfilling part of the language requirement. Treating a summer of study abroad as equivalent to a full second year of language study at home is a tempting bargain for many American undergraduates. Third, the study of language and literature is a major purpose of those going abroad for study: 65.3 percent of the some 307 programs reviewed in the ACE survey said their primary purpose was the study of a foreign language and 59.6 percent focused on the study of a foreign literature (Lambert 1989a: 22). Looked at another way, it would appear that a substantial portion of the language courses taken by American undergraduates are taken abroad. Fourth, language faculty are often called on to manage study-abroad programs from the home institutional base as well as abroad. And finally, and most important, study abroad can provide an important opportunity for students to use their language competence both in their studies and in real-life situations.

Current Inadequacies

It is surprising, therefore, that there is so little collective planning in the foreign-language community for this vital part of their enterprise, and that so few evaluations have been made of what actually happens during language study abroad. A major agenda for the foreign-language community is the rationalization of this period of overseas language study. It is now, like the rest of study abroad, a demand-driven process. Those students go abroad who can afford it, who choose to invest their or their institution's resources, and who want to and can take time off from study at their home institutions. As a result, the participants in study abroad are a skewed subset of all students—for instance, more women, more students from four-year colleges, more humanities and social science majors go abroad—and where they go and why is the result of idiosyncratic personal choice. The largest percentage go to Great Britain, where no foreign-language exposure takes place, and go to a foreign-language area for a summer only. Consequently, the amount of time spent is far too short to make a real improvement in language competence. What is most troubling of all is that, in general, very few American students reach a high enough level of competence in a foreign language, particularly a non-European language, to have genuine access to instruction given in that language in a foreign educational institution. Even though they may have every intention of making full contact with their host culture, they are automatically enslaved by their limited knowledge of the local language. European students assume that they will have to have a substantial competence in the language of the host institution before they study there. Our students do not.

Another major agenda challenge for college language teachers with respect to study abroad is to assure students returning home with an advanced language competence that they will have an opportunity to use that competence in their further studies. It is the students returning from abroad with advanced language competence who are the natural clientele for substantive courses actually using foreign languages in the classroom.

APPLIED AND PROFESSIONAL STUDENTS

In the main, foreign-language instruction in our formal educational system is not aimed at occupational use (Lambert 1989b). Indeed, when foreign-language skills are needed by adults for their work, it tends to be government or commercial language training organizations that serve that need. This situation has obtained in part because there was little demand for, indeed a resistance to, foreign-language instruction on the part of the many students on campus who were seeking degrees in applied fields. In only 9 percent of American universities are the language requirements extended beyond the arts and science students. This lack of participation in foreign-language education has been mirrored in a lack of exposure to international studies more generally on the part of students in applied or professional disciplines. Most telling of all, the lowest participation is among education students, an ominous portent for the future of our educational system.

Within the past few years, however, as the global scope of many of the professions has become increasingly clear, a number of the applied and professional schools and departments have become caught up in the international studies movement. Leading universities and national professional associations in business studies, engineering, nursing, and other fields have begun to stress the introduction of an international dimension to their education. This has led many of them to recognize the need for foreign-language competence among their students. This need has been particularly strongly felt by a few universities who, as a consequence, have sought to develop substantial study-abroad and foreign-internship opportunities for their professionally oriented students. For instance, ten leading engineering schools in the United States have formed a consortium to provide both foreign-language training and overseas internships to their students.

Moves of this type present a major opportunity for the foreign-language community, one that is in danger of being lost as some of these institutions seek to provide their own training in the face of what they perceive as the inflexibility of the traditional language departments on their campuses. There are obvious hurdles. Many in such programs think there is a quick fix for language learning. If only we had a pill or a shot that would provide instant language competence! Every language teacher knows how long and how difficult the second-language acquisition process can be, even with motivated students. Furthermore, to add to their problems, such programs often choose languages like Japanese, where the difficulty level and length of study to reach competence are both very high.

The nation desperately needs more businesspeople, engineers, scientists, physicians, nurses, and other professionals who have a global competence, including command of one or more foreign languages. Other parts of the international studies community are seeking to assist in the education of such people. The foreign-language community needs to address this issue directly. In particular, it must help create the mechanisms for providing language instruction in a context suited to the special needs of these students. I am not referring just to courses that introduce a specialized vocabulary as happens in too many courses in business French or Spanish. Professional students often cannot or will not fit into the usual rhythm, instructional style, and time demands of regular campus-based language courses. A rethinking of the nature of the organization of language instruction is in order if these growing needs are to be met.

RECOMMENDATIONS

International studies is a major movement on American campuses. In one sense foreign-language study is an integral part of international studies. In many other ways it stands apart. The foreign-language community must take steps to integrate foreign-language education more fully into other aspects of international studies. Faculty members in international studies must both increase their own foreign-language competence and work together with the language faculty to make a more internationally literate student body. The language faculty should play a more direct role in the internationally oriented general education requirements over and above the language requirement itself. Ways should be found to utilize foreign languages in substantive courses in other disciplines dealing with international matters, and language faculty should participate strongly in international majors, minors, and concentrations. Language educators should take stock of and plan more fully the role of study abroad in foreign-language learning and work to raise the level of language competence of students before they go abroad, so that they can use their language skills in the substantive courses they take in other countries. They should help create substantive courses using the returnees' advanced level skills after they return home. They should also join with applied and professional schools to find new ways to meet the needs of students in those areas for international studies more generally and for foreign-language education in particular.

If foreign-language faculty are to expand their linkages with the rest of international studies, it will be necessary to think afresh about the ways in which foreign-language instruction can participate more fully in the drive to internationalize the campus more generally. Just pressing for an extension of the language requirement will not do this. It will be up to the faculty on both sides to create a new format, one in which language learning and disciplinary learning are both taking place. The language faculty must become fully aware of the wider body of disciplinary knowledge about the countries with which they deal and incorporate it in their language courses and in preparation for students studying abroad. Other international studies faculty must both raise their own language competencies and work in tandem with the foreign-language faculty to make possible the inclusion of relevant foreign materials in the instructional process. There is much to be done on the part of both groups, who to date have been barely aware of their natural affinity and their need for each other in the achievement of their goals.

NOTES

1. For a recent national survey of college-level language instruction as part of international studies, see Lambert 1989a.

2. At Harvard University there are several courses in the Foreign Cultures section of the Core Curriculum that combine foreign-language instruction and use with foreign culture content.

3. A national survey of college freshmen and seniors did not show a correlation between foreign-language competence gained in college and greater transnational knowledge and empathy (Barrows 1981).

REFERENCES

Andersen, Charles J. 1988. *International Studies for Undergraduates, 1987: Operations and Opinions.* Higher Education Panel No. 76. Washington, DC: American Council on Education.

Astin, Alexander, et al. 1987. *The American Freshman: National Norms for Fall 1987.* Los Angeles: Higher Education Research Institute, University of California.

Barrows, Thomas A., et al. 1981. *College Students' Knowledge and Beliefs.* New Rochelle, NY: Change Magazine Press.

Fetters, William B., and Jeffrey A. Owings. 1984. *High School and Beyond: Foreign Language Course Taking by 1980 High School Sophomores Who Graduated in 1982.* Washington, DC: National Center for Educational Statistics.

Kramsch, Claire J. 1989. *New Directions in the Teaching of Language and Culture.* Occasional Papers of the National Foreign Language Center, no. 4. Washington, DC: NFLC.

Lambert, Richard D. 1981. "Language Learning and Language Utilization." *ADFL Bulletin* 13,1: 8–13.

_____. 1989a. *International Studies and the Undergraduate.* Washington, DC: American Council on Education.

_____. 1989b. *The National Foreign Language System.* Occasional Papers of the National Foreign Language Center, no. 6. Washington, DC: NFLC.

15

The Program Director or Coordinator, the LTCS, and the Training of College Language Instructors

Wilga M. Rivers
Harvard University

*A*s MODERN LIFE BECOMES MORE COMPLICATED AND CAREER PREPARATION must continually be revised and updated, tertiary colleges are being called upon to provide higher education for a broader and broader swathe of the population. No longer can the university and college professoriate relax with the academically gifted and motivated. In the future, even more nontraditional students will be in our classes—as more and more students are admitted to higher education in institutions practicing open admissions, and as adult students return to acquire higher qualifications for new career demands. Languages will be playing a major role in a world that is drawing closer in collaborative unions.

Colleges and universities must now adapt teaching to a diversity of student learners. Even those preparing for a career in literature will spend a number of years teaching language and culture. It follows then that our college teachers must know much more than they have in the past about how students learn, and learn languages, and how to design courses so that students can learn language more efficiently and usably for the purposes they themselves envisage. The two go together. The other essential element for the future success of the language and culture teaching enterprise at this level is an increase in the respect of college departments for activities associated with language learning, so that promotion and academic rewards are available equally to literature professors, linguistics professors, and experts in language learning and the teaching of languages and cultures. For this to be achieved, it is not sufficient for language and culture professors to be good, even excellent, teachers; they must also be good researchers and as proficient at communicating their ideas and findings in professional books and journals as their colleagues in literature and linguistics. The MLA Commission on Foreign Languages, Literatures, and Cultures concluded that "oppositions between scholarship and pedagogy are essentially untenable" (1986: 1).

To ensure a future of good language teaching and course design, we need a four-pronged effort:

1. Training our future professors in language and literature departments in understanding the processes of language learning and teaching

2. Giving them knowledge of the fundamentals of course design and evaluation to provide for a diversity of student objectives, with experience in applying this knowledge appropriately in an array of varied courses

3. Opening up to them areas of research that will provide them with a continuing intellectual interest, inform and refresh their teaching, and enable them to contribute worthwhile research of their own to the development of their chosen fields

4. Fighting administratively for realistic recognition of the value of the work of language teaching and culture specialists (LTCS's) in terms of access to the rewards of promotion, tenure, and appropriate financial remuneration

We must also instill in those who train others to teach the need to demonstrate themselves the kind of teaching they are advocating. Why, we may ask, do so many teacher trainers lecture to their trainees about interactive activities, small-group work, and the like, without ever using these techniques in their own classes? If they expect their students to understand processes of learning, they should demonstrate this understanding in their own teaching. Young teachers tend to teach as they were taught, reflecting the attitudes and implicit assumptions they absorbed from their college and university professors: "Of course you must innovate and put the student first," we say, "but I myself am far too busy to change my course; the department (or university) structure is too rigid to allow much change anyway; my colleagues are such fuddy-duddies; in my experience the computer can't cope with variation from established formats. That's a wonderful idea! I'd just love to come one day and evaluate the way you apply it." With such well-meaning neglect, not only classroom practice but also the structure and content of undergraduate and graduate programs, as well as attitudes toward courses with specific aims related to emerging needs of society, all become set in concrete. Not surprisingly, the system becomes self-perpetuating in a new generation.

TRAINING THE PROFESSORIATE

It is appropriate first of all to pose the question: What kind of professional training for teaching is most appropriate for college professors of language, literature, and culture studies, always remembering that all will be involved in language teaching at some level? In our departments, we already provide subject matter training, but is this sufficiently broad? All selection of subject matter involves a choice that reflects certain attitudes and values. If future needs are to be met in developing programs for all types of students (see chapters 1 and 2) future professors, whether of literature, linguistics, or language and culture will need a background that includes the following components:

1. *Knowledge about the language:* linguistic structure, phonology, history and evolution of the language to be taught (with some attention to variants and dialects), discourse structure, sociolinguistic factors, and evolving lexicon. Even future literature professors should have this foundational understanding of the language of which they are to teach one of the interlocking manifestations. Without such basic knowledge, how can literature professors discuss meaningfully how authors use language,[1] or linguists analyze its formal features? Along with this theoretical preparation should come a solid control of the language in oral and graphic form, wherever possible through a period of immersion in the language and culture in an area where they are indigenous (see chapter 11). Every departmental program should have a built-in evaluation of the ability of the student who will be a future professor and teacher *to use the language at a high level,* both in speech and writing, whether that future lies in language and culture teaching, literature, or linguistics. This should be a *sine qua non* of graduation, not just for high school teachers, but also for future college teachers, who will need to teach in the language as well as write and conduct research in it.

2. *Training in studying other cultures:* their underlying patterns of beliefs, values, and expectations and the semantics, pragmatics, and discourse features that distinguish them from each other. This understanding, if it is to be more than superficial, requires some training in the principles and methods of cultural anthropology and ethnomethodology, so that

future teachers of language, literature, or culture can continue to study the evolving culture in a scientifically sophisticated way, regularly updating their knowledge as they visit, read about, or watch films of target-language areas. The period of immersion in a culture where the language is spoken (proposed above) should include a research project that applies the knowledge and methodology they have acquired.

3. A thorough study of *approaches to the teaching of language, literature, and culture* with attention to the nature of the skills involved and the psychological aspects of their acquisition, including individual learning strategies. The place of foreign languages, literatures, and cultures in the liberal arts curriculum will be discussed, as well as the accountability of teachers for ensuring the best possible educational experience for each student. Participants will consider course design for a diversity of course objectives; the thorny question of the place of grammar in language learning and how it can be integrated into active performance; the way culture is embedded in language and literature, and how coping in another culture can be inculcated without developing stereotypes; strategies of listening and reading as personal skills, and how to design materials and tests in these areas so as to evaluate student comprehension in an authentic way; recent theories of memory in relation to vocabulary acquisition; and, that most difficult task of all, how to stimulate genuine communication via language in culturally acceptable ways. They should understand principles of assessment and evaluation of learning and be able to apply these in quizzes and examinations at all levels (see chapter 10). Beginning teachers also need opportunities to discuss classroom management and different instructional formats: large-group, small-group, pair work, peer-to-peer assistance, and team teaching. Nor should the teaching of literature be neglected, since this will be a lifelong commitment of many of the students (see chapter 12). More mundane but equally important matters must receive attention: materials development and adaptation; textbook selection; grading policies and practices; the use of media; the preparation of materials for new media as they become accessible; and specifically how to incorporate available materials effectively into the ongoing language learning experience.

A course of this type should have as its aim the preparing of future college teachers for continuing growth in a professional career, not just for what will take place in class on Monday. It should broaden their views of areas of language-related research and be as intellectually challenging and demanding as any other credit course in the student's graduate studies; it should provide ample opportunity for exploration of areas of personal interest to the student, be they in language, linguistics, literature, or culture.[2]

The course should be accompanied, as part of the graduate degree, by supervised teaching experience and guidance in self-evaluation. Coaching in classroom teaching techniques as such should take place in a separate practicum, which will be closely related to the actual supervised teaching experience and materials used in courses. Here students will practice teaching techniques in microteaching format and prepare exercises, tests, and activities that will be shared with and critiqued by their fellow teachers. The practicum will provide opportunities for students to see and discuss videotapes of their own performance in the classroom and that of exemplars.[3] Audiotapes of their own teaching for self-evaluation are also useful. The practicum instructor should visit the classes of these students, as does the course head (and ultimately the Program Director or Coordinator). After this initial training, young teachers will continue to be assisted by their course heads as mentors, who will meet regularly with all the section instructors in their course for preparation of materials and tests in common, sharing of ideas, and discussing of problems and policies.

Every person connected with a language and literature department needs this kind of preparation for work that is a mutual responsibility. The emphasis in training the future professoriate should be on developing the initiative and personal teaching style of each instructor. There should be no stifling imposition of someone else's convictions on young instructors, beyond an initiation into well-tried techniques that give neophytes a sense of confidence and control while they are mastering classroom management. We are training future leaders in whom we should applaud and encourage initiative and innovation; this we can further by involving them in a well-developed program of courses, within which they will have experience in teaching at different levels with different contents and approaches and be encouraged, as their training proceeds, to develop courses or segments of courses that reflect their own experimental interests.

TRAINING THE LANGUAGE TEACHING AND CULTURE SPECIALIST (LTCS)

Beyond this common core of studies, those who have chosen careers as foreign-language acquisition specialists and teachers of language and culture should receive in-depth preparation in the following additional areas:

4. The *psycholinguistic and cognitive factors* that enter into language learning and adaptation to another culture, so that approaches to teaching and

techniques may be readily adapted to the needs of different types of students of all ages and to courses with varied objectives

5. Recent theoretical research and experimental methodology in *second- and foreign-language acquisition,* as well as first-language acquisition, bilingualism, and multiculturalism

6. An intimate acquaintance with the *literature* associated with the language, particularly that of the nineteenth and twentieth centuries, not only for its intrinsic interest and its value in developing a feel for the culture of speakers of the language, but also so that suitable literature, in language reasonably close to the contemporary, may be selected as content for language development programs. This is the element most frequently provided for future members of the professoriate. The canon should be broadened, however, so that literature from all areas where the language is spoken are included, as well as the contributions of sections of the population whose work has been underrepresented in the more exclusionary past. In this way the future LTCS will gain a deeper and richer understanding of evolving national and international values and attitudes, and be prepared to choose materials that represent whole peoples, not just literary elites.

7. An in-depth study of some aspect of *the culture of a target-language area,* preferably as an independent study on a self-selected subject, employing the methodology and techniques of cultural and sociological research; this study should result in production, not just of a written exposition of what has been discovered, but also in gathering and combining material in teaching units for different levels.

8. Specialized *preparation in a specific area of research* through which the LTCS will make his or her personal contribution to the advancement of knowledge in the field. The area chosen for research may be in linguistics, psycholinguistics, pragmatics, cultural studies, foreign-language acquisition, learning theory, cognitive psychology, the teaching of literature, psychometrics, or theoretical aspects of materials preparation, including the use of new technologies. Departments must be willing to recognize these interdisciplinary areas as legitimate subjects for research and writing for LTCS's, acceptable for promotion and tenure. What is expected in the way of research and production for a favorable decision on promotion and tenure must be made clear to the LTCS early in his or her period of employment in the department. Serious involvement in some such personally selected area of productive endeavor will ensure that the specialist keeps mentally alert, exercises leadership, and continues to progress in new knowledge of significance to the field. Such a continuing interest is the best antidote against staleness and burnout.

LTCS's, of course, are not different as a genus. The need for training in teaching and presentation of material is equally important for professors of history, science, law, or medicine. Many universities and professors themselves are now realizing the need for all who teach at the college level to be so trained. Consequently centers for faculty development are opening their doors to all who seek their help, beginners and senior professors alike. In many institutions, professors are experimenting with ways of teaching, not only in the humanities but in the professional schools, to ensure that they prepare graduate students to go out and exercise their professions in all kinds of unforeseen circumstances. LTCS's can learn a great deal from participating in these faculty development efforts and, through them, getting to know a network of faculty with similar interests.

THE ROLE OF THE LTCS

To return to our own bailiwick, what should be the responsibilities of the language/culture teaching and foreign-language acquisition specialist in a language and literature department? For what are we preparing them? I am not thinking merely of the responsible task of preparing teachers of language for elementary and secondary school level, where no one disputes the fact that teachers should know how to teach. Nor am I thinking only of young instructors and doctoral students who teach undergraduates—an onerous task for many in American colleges and increasingly elsewhere. The LTCS will provide this clientele with courses like 1, 2, and 3 on pages 297–98, as well as carefully guided and critiqued early teaching, on videotape or in the classroom, and through self-evaluation audiotapes.

Beyond these tasks, the LTCS should be deeply involved in the development of a series of courses for diversified objectives at different levels. These will exemplify the different approaches and course objectives discussed in the training course, and be continually updated as undergraduate language students' preoccupations and needs evolve. For experimental interest, to keep the profession moving forward and demonstrate to young instructors what can be done at other levels than the ones they themselves teach, these courses will incorporate, among other things,

The use of video and computer-assisted learning materials

Learning language through drama

Purposeful task-oriented activities

The use of simulations in which students act out the evolution of complicated situations requiring on-the-spot decision making (these may be based on sociological or cultural dilemmas or situations arising within the plot of literary works)

Content teaching in association with other disciplines

Language learning through culturally authentic experiences in the surrounding community or experienced vicariously on interactive videodisc

Combined projects with students in other disciplines via computer in which progress in a joint endeavor (e.g., business or investment decisions) depends on the expertise of the language students

Direct collaborative projects via computer and videophone with students in classes in a country where the language is spoken

Development and videotaping of students' own episodes based on televised human-interest serials taken from satellite telecasts in a country where the language is spoken, or based on the life stories of notable persons in the other culture

The potential for cross-disciplinary courses in international studies should be explored—courses in which current political and economic problems in specific areas of the world are discussed by experts in those fields, while instructors from the language departments conduct discussion sections in the foreign language, using documentation and contemporary comment in the language from newspapers, magazines, and reports in books and archives; in this way, as students learn, they refine their linguistic skills. Many other possibilities for lively opportunities to use the language interactively in diversified courses have been discussed in other chapters in this book. LTCS's will come up with many more of their own.

LTCS's need also to be aware of the rapid changes taking place in what students already know, before coming to class, of a language and culture and in what contexts they are learning it. Students are becoming less and less dependent on what teachers provide. They learn from radio, television, advertisements, internationally distributed newspapers and magazines (where they follow the activities of the latest rock and punk stars or international sporting or cinema heroes and heroines), from music, song, rock videos, contact with native speakers, whom, with the rapid movement of populations, they now meet in shops, streets, and clubs, and even in their own homes. LTCS's need to study how these environmental factors affect what we do in the classroom and the way we encourage our students to pursue acquisition of the language; they need to experiment with ways in which these new elements can be incorporated into language study and exploited to enhance language learning.

What has all this to do with training graduate teacher assistants?[4] Much. If language programs in colleges and universities are to keep up with rapidly evolving societal needs for usable language control in a diversity of circumstances, our training must be extremely flexible, encouraging individuality, original thinking, and a capacity for autonomous action; our LTCS's will have a vital role to play in this endeavor.

To establish a coherent program of language and culture courses to an advanced level of near-native proficiency to meet a diversity of expectations, LTCS's must develop some expertise in ferreting out the current needs of constantly changing student populations. They need experience in administering carefully constructed questionnaires, opportunities to develop effective interview techniques, and time for wide reading. They must also keep the teaching group in their courses alert and interested in innovation and adaptation to changing climates, while undertaking new approaches only when the existing staff are ready for and capable of such change and development. Helping and encouraging the teaching group to grow and mature professionally is an essential part of the leadership role. LTCS's must also cultivate their own garden, keeping abreast in developments in the field and ahead in their own area of research. All this is very demanding and time-consuming; consequently, their own teaching loads should be reasonably adjusted to allow for the time and energy demands of leadership.

The Future of LTCS's

What about the fourth prong of our original analysis—the rewards of the profession? The status of specialists who are developing language teaching and culture programs must be taken seriously in the decisions of the academy. No longer should these hardworking individuals face a revolving door or permanent relegation to the lower ranks of the hierarchy, to carry an unreasonable share of the department load in obscurity and less-than-benign neglect. They should be able to expect through the development of successful programs and fruitful research to receive the same rewards of promotion, tenure, and financial recompense that their colleagues in other areas of the department enjoy.

Here we are perhaps caught in a vicious circle. Because so many of the present faculty in charge of language teaching programs are graduates in literature who have been allotted this role as untenured junior faculty with little say in their departmental assignments, most have never received any particular preparation in linguistics, psycholinguistics, or the study of cultures, let alone innovative teaching and course design. Consequently, they have no specialized area of research in which to develop. They do well, even brilliantly, in the classroom, they may even be excellent organizers and teaching coaches and have useful ideas for new courses; they are, however, unfamiliar with the areas on which they should be opening wide vistas for those working or training with them. In the area in which they labor they have no specific expertise for which academic rewards may be expected, and they rapidly lose touch with developments in the area of literature in which they wrote their theses.

Unfortunately, these pinch-hitters are often considered prototypes for all LTCS's, trained or untrained. Here is where the vicious circle turns back on itself: until proper training and specialization are developed within our departments and respected in appointments, we will not see specialists emerging; yet, until they emerge and are recognized, they will not be there to be rewarded nor there to prepare other specialists for the future. Consequently, the few specialists in our departments (some trained, some self-developed) come up as a surprise in the rewards process, and neither the departments nor the administration knows what to do with them. (In many institutions other cross-disciplinary and interdisciplinary specialties are similarly regarded as suspect by many in leadership positions who advanced in a simpler, more compartmentalized era.) Decisions to promote these new leaders are, therefore, shelved, sending a negative signal to younger scholars who may be attracted to this work.

This is a veritable Catch-22 situation. To break the vicious circle, a clear decision must be reached in institutions to which other schools look for a lead to break with the past by appointing fully trained and experienced LTCS's at a senior level and charging them with the responsibility of training the new leaders our institutions so badly need.

It is essential that LTCS's be given time to develop professionally and acquire experience in their many responsibilities. For these reasons, LTCS's should not be appointed program directors or coordinators as soon as they step in the door. They should be given course head responsibilities where they work closely with section instructors in developing course content and assist with the practicum, supervision, and some segments of the teacher training course, while teaching a moderate number of language and culture sections themselves. One of these courses will often be a demonstration class, which new instructors will attend daily until they have acquired confidence and skill in their own teaching. In this way, LTCS's are acquiring administrative and supervisory skills and taking an active role in program development and course design, while having enough time and freedom from responsibility to keep up with their field, initiate or continue research and experimentation, and begin establishing a record of publication. They should also be initiated into their professional leadership role by being encouraged to make presentations and give workshops at language-related conferences. Without this opportunity for professional growth, many burn out from overwork or are thrown out by nontenure decisions, just as they had begun to show what they could offer the institution and the profession.

The pinch-hitters with literary backgrounds who have decided that they wish to continue as LTCS's should be encouraged early to recycle into this area by undertaking such essential theoretical studies as 4, 5, 7, and 8 on pp. 299–300. They should not be so burdened with work that they have no time for retraining in an area that is new to them, and they should be clearly informed of the tenure and promotion criteria that will determine their future.

What kind of publication record may we expect from an LTCS under consideration for promotion and tenure? There are many theoretical areas in which fully trained LTCS's have been prepared:

- Theoretical linguistics (particularly synchronic studies of contemporary target-language features)

- Psycholinguistics, particularly related to language acquisition and use

- Sociolinguistics of target-language communities

- The pragmatics of discourse in the target language and in different settings and relationships

- Phenomena of contemporary culture in a target-language country (including popular culture)

- Second- and foreign-language acquisition

- Problems of language learning in formal settings, including testing

- Cognitive strategies for different age groups

- Historical studies of leading figures and movements in foreign-language teaching

- Development of the theoretical bases of new methodologies

- Empirical research in any of these areas and in the dynamics of the classroom

- In-depth studies of the acquisition of specific language skills

This nonexhaustive list is sufficient to indicate that there is plenty of scope for research and leadership in language-related areas that will lead to valuable practical applications.[5]

One unresolved problem is what value to place on the publication of textbooks for classroom use and the production of teaching materials (tapes, videotapes, films, and, increasingly, computer software, authoring languages, and videodiscs); all these materials are very time-consuming to produce, indispensable to the language-teaching enterprise, and underestimated in the rewards process. Here a distinction must be made, as in other areas of study, between imitative hack work and materials that reflect a great deal of research and an extensive knowledge of the field and theoretical developments within it. Questions that should be asked in individual cases are the following:

- Are the materials under consideration innovative?

- Do they reflect a knowledge of current language learning and teaching theory and a rational application of it?

- Do they demonstrate that the writer has kept up with the present state of the language in its varieties and levels of use, and with linguistic findings in this regard?

- Do they reflect intimate knowledge of the evolving culture in target-language areas?

- Do these materials contribute to an advance in the effectiveness of language teaching and learning?

If textbooks and programs are not written by the most well-informed of teaching specialists, classroom teachers who depend so much on these aids will continue to teach in conventional, outmoded ways that research has demonstrated to be ineffectual. Teachers who trained years ago also need recycling, and teachers' manuals written by well-qualified LTCS's help those who are unable or unwilling to take refresher courses in methodology, revitalize their teaching through extensive reading, or study contemporary language and culture *in situ*. The publications of LTCS's bring such knowledge in applied form to many who do not have the time to keep up with basic research nor the scholarly preparation to work out its applications for themselves. College and university faculty are obligated, because of their specialized training, to give a responsible lead in this task. A change of attitude toward such scholarly contributions is long overdue.

THE PROGRAM DIRECTOR OR COORDINATOR

Rank

It is important for the efficient functioning of the language program that the person at the head of the program be a tenured member of the faculty at full professor level. (A tenured associate professor with potential and assured prospects of promotion in the near future might be considered.) This tenure and rank ensure the autonomy of the program, reflecting the degree to which the department values its contributions, and tenure and rank assign to the

Director the authority to develop it in new directions without undue interference. It also permits the Director to concentrate on program development and professional leadership without the insecurity of trying to please all with an eye to the future, and consequently hesitating to make unpopular but necessary decisions. To merit this high rank, the Director or Coordinator should be a fully trained LTCS who has had experience in program development and teaching-assistant training and supervision, and who has demonstrated leadership in research, publications, and professional activity. Persons preparing for the role must be able to foresee, as they survey the profession nationwide, the same academic rewards for their work as those accorded their colleagues in literature or linguistics.

Coordinators or Directors of this rank should have under their control the language program at all levels (elementary, intermediate, and advanced), even those courses taught by colleagues, not so that they can dictate, change, and harass unnecessarily, but so that cooperatively, and after group deliberation, a cohesive and coherent program can be built. Such a program will offer a reasonable degree of articulation across levels to obviate unnecessary repetition and duplication. Students will be presented, then, with an interesting and varied sequence into which they can integrate or through which they can leap, according to their talents, interests, and the time at their disposal.

Responsibilities   With an appointment at the proper level of authority and autonomy, the Director or Coordinator now has an important role to play, not only in the development of the program but also in the nurturing of the teaching staff and the professional preparation of the graduate students.

Professional development in the program   The Program Director/Coordinator as a leader is responsible for the professional development of all who teach in the program, whether junior faculty, lecturers, adjunct instructors, or graduate teaching assistants. The future of the program in this institution, and in other institutions later on, lies with these important participants, each of whom should either be fully trained or should audit the training being provided for graduate teaching assistants and incoming nonstudent instructors (exchange students or adjunct personnel). In this way, everyone in the program will share a common background in theory and practice of language learning and teaching, which will enable them to think flexibly and innovatively about the program. The Director/Coordinator will help the instructional staff in course design and in incorporation of new techniques and technologies, keep them informed of new developments, encourage their participation in professional activities, help them develop funding proposals and writing for publication, and advise and collaborate with them on experimentation and research.

In this way, a dynamic, active, and innovative team is established that can be relied upon to keep the program moving forward smoothly and effectively.

The Director/Coordinator should be alert to new possibilities for enriching curriculum and content and encourage the course heads in the team to experiment and innovate, according to findings of student needs analyses and new directions in professional thinking. The Director/Coordinator does not impose, but works through the members of the team—informing, proposing, encouraging, helping with developments, discovering resources perhaps not known to the members of the team, seeking additional funds, materials, and equipment where needed, and always praising and attributing credit where it is due.

Public relations   The Director/Coordinator is the public relations agent for the teaching team, making sure that the department and the wider university community are aware of successful innovations, increasing enrollments, favorable student evaluations, or special recognition from outside the institution.

Supervision of instructors   The Director/Coordinator takes the time to visit the class of each trainee or new instructor, and others on request, and then discusses the class personally with the instructor. This should be done in an indirect way, drawing as much as possible first of all from the instructor about the class session, its successes and failures, and then encouraging, praising, giving guidance and advice, and making recommendations for future development and improvement. Each class session should be evaluated as an organic whole; the evaluator should judge what is going on in relation to the goals of the instructor and the cooperative contributions of the students, rather than following some sterile taxonomy of features drawn up by someone outside of this particular class and based on someone else's idea of what constitutes a model class.[6] Through these visits, the Director/Coordinator gets to know each member of the team well, giving them coaching, when and as often as needed, and is thus able to incorporate them into future scheduling in a very individualized way that utilizes their greatest strengths. This close knowledge of each instructor's pedagogical style and classroom performance provides fresh and telling material for detailed and informative recommendations when these are needed for future advancement or appointment in other institutions.

Administration   Administrative duties are, of course, part of the Director/Coordinator's role. Budgeting should be adventurous, keeping in mind the future development of the program. ("The money goes where the students are!") Scheduling of assignments should respect not only the needs of the program and its students, but the particular gifts of the instructors, the breadth of experience at different levels that they have a right to anticipate, and their preferences and those of the course heads with regard to working relationships. In this way, a happy, harmonious team ensures a happy, harmonious program.

Communication   Communication is not only a keyword in language teaching; it is the essence of any administrative success. The program administrator must keep everyone clearly informed of every detail that affects them, and also of the overall operation of activities, so that they can see where their segment fits into the whole. For graduate teaching assistants and new instructors, a detailed handbook should be available, informing them of departmental and college regulations and policies, what is expected of them administratively and what they can expect from the administration (salary rates and increments, funds available for materials, departmental and college services, term dates and deadlines, opportunities for supplementary work and regulations regarding such work, how student problems are to be handled administratively— waivers of requirements, absences, ethical misconduct, late assignments, deferred grades, and so on). There can never be too much concisely expressed and focused information available.

Orientation program   To ensure the effective launching of the year's program, a well-planned and comprehensive orientation session is essential. Running preferably for a week, it should be a shared exposition and training session that is shared equally by course heads (LTCS's) and the Director/ Coordinator. Obligatory for all new instructors in the program, it should incorporate discussion on the approach taken to the program and to classroom teaching; coaching in some rapidly acquirable techniques for the first few weeks of class, with videotaping of microteaching, which will be critiqued individually with participants; information on administrative details of immediate concern (e.g., the form of the requirement, if there is one, and the nature of the waiver system; how technological assistance for teaching operates)— anything that will smooth the path for novice instructors in their initial period of teaching.

Trainees always listen eagerly, too, to young instructors in their second year as they describe their own initial experiences in classroom management and student relations; these young peers have much useful and practical advice to give. Time should be allotted for trainees to discuss materials and activities with the heads of the different courses to which they have been assigned, with particular attention to ways of presenting material in the early weeks, to ensure a smooth and confident beginning. (These instructors will be meeting each week with their course heads and other more experienced members of the course team to work out collaboratively the development of the course, but they need special support for their initial experiences.)

Nor should native speakers from outside the country be forgotten (exchange students or new adjunct instructors); it is essential to explain to them how American colleges operate, how instructors relate to students in this country (in and out of class and in office hours); how learning is assessed and evaluated, and particularly the kind of instruction that is expected.[7]

Problem-solving   The Director/Coordinator is a trouble-shooter. Most student problems will be handled directly by instructors and course heads, but the thorniest will always come through the program director's door, as will certain problems of individual instructors in their relations with students and with course heads. The Director/Coordinator, then, must be a good listener and develop skills of mediation, persuasion, and negotiation—soothing and calming, while proposing judicious and acceptable solutions. Frequently this will require unraveling bureaucratic knots, so the Director/Coordinator must be well-informed about regulations and contact persons across the university.

Advocacy   The Director/Coordinator is an advocate, representing the cause of foreign languages (all languages) to bodies within the university and without, fighting for decisions that affect the program, as well as for the rights and advancement of those teaching in it; drawing together LTCS's from all languages on campus in collaborative projects; helping colleagues in high schools and elementary schools in their struggles with school boards and administrators, and entering into frequent discussions with them on problems that concern foreign-language teaching in all settings, sharing information and expertise, and ensuring smooth articulation from one level to the next.

Director/Coordinators are not deities, but it seems at times that for success and effectiveness they need some of the compassionate and all-knowing attributes of the superhuman.

Tout se tient within the web of interrelated work and interrelated roles. We are all engaged in an interlocking enterprise. If the work of LTCS's and Director/Coordinators is to be respected and rewarded, we must push ahead together in different institutions to bring about change. We must keep up with our students' needs and those of our institutions in developing worthwhile and efficient programs. As one junior faculty member in the United States remarked in a survey on the level of preparation for college language instruction:

> Our discipline is wide-ranging, full of possibilities, if only we would
> see it that way and take the initiative to redefine it; and if we agreed on its
> importance in intellectual life generally we would treat questions of
> methodology in teaching language and literature with the seriousness they

deserve. Potential college professors should have a sense of the large inclusive scope of the foreign language field. . . . Unless we develop a sense of our common base as students of language and culture (including literature), the regressive horizons and fragmentation of our profession will continue. Language teaching at the college level differs greatly from the teaching in other subjects. It is a special opportunity, for both instructor and student, to engage actively in a process instead of reporting on some process from the outside. Learning to communicate is a magical phenomenon and one that can be for the college student a deeply satisfying, even stabilizing psychological and emotional force. (Rivers 1983: 340)

If we are to provide this kind of college language instruction, we must take it more seriously than we have in the past and see that it is in the hands of persons who not only love what they are doing, but have the background of training and scholarship to make it a highly respected and respectable area of the department's work.

Notes

1. For the importance of linguistics in the language and literature department, see chapter 13, and S. Fleischman (1986).

2. R. Waldinger (1990) describes in detail her experience in planning and executing such a course at the City University of New York Graduate School.

3. M. Mueller (1990) has prepared a computer program with video for teacher training. This program provides students with segments of classroom teaching that they can analyze and evaluate through leading questions, with opportunities for personal commentary. A program of this type should lead to educated self-assessment—an important factor as the young teacher develops and experiments.

4. In this chapter, graduate students teaching undergraduate courses are referred to as "teaching assistants"; in some universities they are called "teaching fellows."

5. Areas for publication and research for LTCS's are discussed in detail in Sadow (1989).

6. For a detailed discussion of supervision of graduate teaching assistants, see Walz, ed. (forthcoming).

7. For advice to non-American teaching assistants/teaching fellows and exchange students on teaching American undergraduates in an American academic setting, see Sarkisian (1990).

REFERENCES

Fleischman, S. 1986. "Getting Calliope through Graduate School? Can Chomsky Help? Or the Role of Linguistics in Graduate Education in Foreign Languages." *ADFL Bulletin* 17,3: 9–13.

MLA Commission on Foreign Languages, Literatures, and Linguistics. 1986. "Resolutions and Recommendations of the National Conference on Graduate Education in the Foreign Language Fields." *ADFL Bulletin* 17,3: 1–4. [See Appendix 15A.]

Mueller, M. 1990. *A Training Videodisk for Teachers of Elementary French.* Cambridge, MA: Harvard-Danforth Center for Teaching and Learning (now Derek Bok Center).

Rivers, Wilga M. 1983. "Preparing College and University Instructors for a Lifetime of Teaching: a Luxury or a Necessity?" pp. 327–41 in J. Alatis, H. H. Stern, and P. Strevens, eds., *Applied Linguistics and the Preparation of Second Language Teachers: Toward a Rationale.* Georgetown University Round Table on Languages and Linguistics. Washington, DC: Georgetown Univ. Press.

Sadow, S. A. 1989. "Methodologists: A Brief Guide for Their Colleagues." *ADFL Bulletin* 21,1: 27–28.

Sarkisian, E. 1990. *Teaching American Students: A Guide for International Faculty and Teaching Fellows.* Cambridge, MA: Harvard-Danforth Center for Teaching and Learning (now Derek Bok Center).

Waldinger, R. 1990. "Training PhD Students to Teach in College." *ADFL Bulletin* 22,1: 20–23.

Walz, J., ed. Forthcoming. *Issues in Teaching Assistant Supervision.* Madison: AAUSCDFLP/Univ. of Wisconsin Press.

APPENDIX 15A:
RESOLUTIONS AND RECOMMENDATIONS OF THE NATIONAL CONFERENCE ON GRADUATE EDUCATION IN THE FOREIGN LANGUAGE FIELDS
MLA Commission on Foreign Languages, Literatures, and Linguistics

On 15–17 November 1985 the MLA's Commission on Foreign Languages, Literatures, and Linguistics convened at the University of Virginia in Charlottesville a national conference on graduate education in the foreign language fields. The conference was supported by a grant from the National Endowment for the Humanities, with additional funding from the University of Virginia, the National Council on Foreign Language and International Studies, and Educational Testing Service. Sixty-two participants, including chairpersons and other representatives from forty-five institutions, met in plenary sessions and in three simultaneous discussion groups during the three-day period. Group I, which dealt with recruitment and selection of graduate students, was cochaired by Raymond Gay-Crosier (Univ. of Florida) and E. Michael Gerli (Georgetown Univ.). Group II, asked to focus on graduate curriculum, was chaired jointly by Charles Babcock (Ohio State Univ.) and Phyllis Zatlin (Rutgers Univ.). Group III was concerned with preparation for teaching and was cochaired by Gerard Ervin (Ohio State Univ.) and Ralph Hester (Stanford Univ.).

At the closing plenary session on 17 November, the participants accepted by consensus the following statement, which originated in group II, as a preface to the full set of recommendations from the three groups:

The MLA believes that departments of foreign languages and literatures form an integral part of the humanities, that is, those disciplines concerned with the reading and interpretation of literary texts and cultural artifacts. Graduate programs in foreign languages and literatures need to maintain an ideal of original scholarship and teaching so that outstanding students will be attracted to the profession and will continue to provide vitality in the understanding and transmission of culture. This ideal implies a constant exploration of what literature and cultures are, what purposes they serve, what perceptions of humanity they provide. The study of foreign languages offers an indispensable means of access to the study of culture and must be vigorously and professionally pursued in order to enable students to make original contributions to cultural understanding.

Oppositions between the study of language and literature, between scholarship and pedagogy, are essentially untenable. We believe in a continuum in the study of reading and interpretation, from the elementary to the most advanced levels. The significant texts of any culture represent language in its most challenging uses, and understanding these uses is a form of intellectual empowerment. We urge departments of foreign languages and literatures to provide training in textual analysis, in poetics, in rhetoric, in theories of interpretation, in literary history, and in linguistics. The study of literature should be placed in broad and significant contexts, so that students may understand that what is at stake in the study of language and literature is an ever-renewed understanding of the ways in which human beings create meaning in the world.

The recommendations from the three discussion groups are listed below, arranged by topic. They are followed by numbers in parentheses identifying the groups that presented them to the final plenary session of the conference. *It must be noted that the recommendations in their present form represent the views of the participants in the Virginia conference and do not constitute a statement of policy by the Modern Language Association or the MLA Commission on Foreign Languages, Literatures, and Linguistics.*

Recruitment

1. Given the renewed interest in the United States in the study of foreign languages and literatures, the improving conditions of the profession, and the growing need for foreign language teachers, the MLA should encourage the most promising students in foreign languages and literatures to pursue graduate work and careers in the field (I).

2. The issue of quality should be central to all graduate education and paramount in budgeting decisions. Recruitment of graduate students solely to meet the staffing needs of lower-division language programs is deplorable; universities must reaffirm the primary identity of graduate students as students (I).

3. The MLA should publish a brochure aimed at graduating seniors, addressing the following concerns:

   a. Preparation for graduate work and generally expected standards for admission and successful completion of a graduate program

   b. Sources of information about programs for graduate studies in each language

   c. Materials generally needed for admission and financial aid

   d. Guidelines and criteria for evaluation of programs (I)

Programs

Program Objectives

1. Foreign language departments should develop programs that offer students a range of meaningful academic and career goals. Given the need for foreign language proficiency among professionals in a variety of fields, appropriate departments should be encouraged to develop cooperative programs with professional schools (e.g., management, law, health professions, social work) (I, II).

2. Universities should find supplementary funding resources (e.g., a revived NDEA, special state funds, private endowments) for graduate programs and should coordinate program goals with the identification of possible funding sources (I).

3. Without losing sight of the intrinsic humanistic value of the study of literatures and languages, the profession should redefine graduate studies and the role of the departments in terms of international and interdisciplinary studies (I).

4. Students should be encouraged to pursue studies in languages and literatures as a means to careers in teaching as well as for pure research. (I).

Curriculum

5. Curricular modification or augmentation to meet anticipated teaching needs at primary, secondary, and college levels must be made with full attention to the central role of subject content in graduate education and with the guarantee of increased staff and support for such program development. The response to the new state mandates must not be allowed to deflect from the present and continuing mission of foreign language departments.

   Additional funding is also essential to facilitate the retraining of present faculty so that they may introduce into their curricula new components suggested by the state mandates or by recent scholarly developments in the field. Such retraining may be particularly important for smaller departments. In the training of graduate students, however, cooperative efforts among departments or institutions should be considered. Electives outside the home department may be the most effective vehicle for providing graduate students with the necessary diversification in their course of study (II).

6. The MLA should approach the Linguistic Society of America with the intent of establishing a joint commission to make recommendations to graduate programs that will invite complementary and appropriate emphasis on literature and linguistics in the respective programs of each set of disciplines (I).

7. Foreign language and literature faculty should develop and maintain good working relations with schools of education and with programs in linguistics, using certain of the offerings and faculties of these fields and incorporating them into teacher-training programs (III).

8. Language and literature departments should strive to achieve good working relations with interdisciplinary programs and with certain programs in the social sciences and professional schools, in order both to train graduates and to offer expanded models of the truly wide scope of the foreign language and literature field (III).

Less Commonly Taught Languages

9. The MLA recognizes the importance of concentrated foreign language study in a graduate curriculum in the humanities. In the case of the less commonly taught languages, however, we are concerned that the present practice at some universities of awarding less credit to graduate than to undergraduate students in beginning- and advanced-level courses in effect constitutes for graduate students a disincentive to the acquisition of these languages (II)

10. The MLA should convene a working group to examine ways and means of shifting, in appropriate fields and areas, the present Eurocentric orientation of the field. Issues to be addressed include not only policies relating to second-language acquisition but also the expansion of the literary canon to include non-European texts. To this end, the MLA should seek greater contact and cooperation with professional associations representing specialists in non-European languages, literatures, and area studies (II).

Preparation for Teaching

Statement by Participants in Discussion Group III

The MLA Commission on Foreign Languages, Literatures, and Linguistics should be no less concerned with preparation for teaching in 1985 than were the contributors to the MLA's 1981 report *The Teaching Apprentice Program in Language and Literature* (ed. Gibaldi and Mirollo). The consensus of group III suggests that more attention than ever should be given to the role of training in pedagogy in those institutions from which come future teachers in our discipline. Unlike the 1981 report, the findings of the present commission must respond to the phenomena of rapidly increasing enrollments in language study accompanied by a declining availability of competent instructors, already manifest at the precollege level. Emergency certification of teachers without adequate language preparation is becoming frequent at a time when there is a national feeling not only that foreign language training is necessary but also that it should produce functionally able users of bilingual ability. Federal agencies, private foundations, and specialists in related disciplines (e.g., international studies) have demonstrated their interest in, and support for, programs aiming to improve the teaching of foreign languages and literatures.

Group III has concluded that the MLA must encourage graduate programs to respond, through their trainees, to the needs, expectations, and aspirations of the profession and of the nation as a whole. Both practitioners and researchers in foreign languages and literatures should applaud the broad-based concern expressed by sectors hitherto only marginally interested in our discipline. We must continue to nourish the humanities with our fundamental contribution of teaching, research, and scholarship in letters and language, while at the same time we take into account the needs of the schools and the requirements of the profession. We believe our enterprise should remain under the banner of the humanities as we seek ways, in the training of our graduates, to enable them to collaborate with researchers in certain of the behavioral sciences and learn how to participate in and conduct classroom experiments. Such collaborative work in language teaching parallels interdisciplinary activities in other areas (e.g., humanities, international relations, law, medicine, science) and deserves respect and support.

Group III recommends that departments of foreign languages and literatures establish serious and systematic programs of training for teaching using the following specific points as guidelines:

Elementary and Secondary School Training

1. The profession in general, whether through individual institutions or in the MLA or ADFL, should take cognizance of the opportunity presented by the mandating of foreign language instruction by many or most of the states. This matter is of concern to all institutions, including those that give the BA degree only and those that offer work toward the PhD. Each institution should examine its degree structure to see which of its programs might be adapted to meet the new mandate or whether a new program needs to be established. In devising curricula for any programs under consideration, departments should emphasize language competence and insist on an appropriate level of intellectual attractiveness through courses in literature, linguistics, and culture. Since the terms of the mandate will differ from state to state,

departments should be urged to make contact with the agencies in their states that have responsibility for carrying out their mandate. Close cooperation between the language and literature faculty and the faculty of the school of education is essential (II).

2. The MLA should encourage interaction between secondary school and college level faculty and give high priority in its publications to reports and discussions of such interaction (I).

College and University Teaching

3. Recognizing the central role of teaching in PhD programs in language and literature, departments should take steps to develop training programs for graduate students both in second language learning and in the teaching of literature. Where appropriate, graduate departments should consider the appointment of faculty qualified to introduce such training in the teaching of language (II).

4. Departments should develop programs to provide their graduate teaching assistants with all required competencies in language, literature, and linguistics. They should also seek ways to maintain these abilities and to reinvigorate the competencies of teachers already in the field (III).

5. Preparation for teaching should include training in the approaches or methodologies for teaching language-skill courses at all levels, as well as courses in other areas (literature, culture, civilization). Trainees must also be introduced to new technologies. Preparatory experiences should precede or occur simultaneously with the trainees' first teaching experience and may take a variety of forms. The teaching done by trainees should be evaluated regularly (III).

6. At least one tenured or tenure-track faculty member in a department should be charged with responsibility for training graduate students. Ideally, the task should be shared among several colleagues whose esteem for the activity will ensure it the prestige it deserves. Whether shared or assigned to only one person, the work of the methodologist and the supervisor-coordinator of language instruction is labor-intensive, bears heavy administrative responsibility, and deserves recognition in the form of salary, tenurability, and released time (III).

7. A department of foreign language and literature should require, and recognize the legitimacy of, faculty members' research and publications in language teaching methodology and second-language acquisition (III).

Professional Standards

Hiring and Staffing

1. The MLA should exert pressure on universities to increase full-time faculty positions and reduce their dependency on part-time personnel and graduate teaching assistants (I).

2. To assist in meeting the staffing needs created by the state mandates, funding agencies at state and national levels should support postdoctoral teaching fellowships and other special initiatives designed to retrain PhDs who were forced to leave academe during the years when the job market for foreign language faculty was in decline (II).

Standards for the Profession

3. In the light of the preeminent need for criteria of quality in the pursuit of graduate education and the responsibility of each department to the total profession, some departments may need to reassess their graduate programs and suspend those that cannot maintain high standards (I).

4. Believing that the monitoring and maintenance of high standards is an ongoing process, we urge the MLA to formulate a list of evaluative criteria for graduate programs, and we urge departments to seek opportunities for outside review of their programs (I).

5. Since the expectations and needs of the different language and literature programs vary widely among fields and institutions, the issue of language proficiency standards is one that must be approached separately by faculty in each program (I).

Maintenance and Continuity

6. Finding great value in the dialogue established at the Virginia conference, we urge the MLA to collaborate with a set of universities to organize yearly meetings on various campuses (I).

16
The Four-Year College: Prospects for the Future

Truett Cates and Bernice Melvin
Austin College

*W*HAT CHANGES ARE IN STORE FOR FOREIGN-LANGUAGE DEPARTMENTS IN the smaller institutions in the 1990s? Which responses to these changes are likely to be successful in the coming decade? Which responses should we avoid? Before making these projections, we must come to grips with powerful societal trends.

THE DYNAMICS OF CHANGE

By the 1980s sweeping changes in postsecondary education in the United States had effectively challenged the traditional positions not only of foreign-language study, but of the humanities in general. In the mid 1980s a number of official studies and commissions, not to mention best-selling books, decried the decline of the humanities, including foreign-language study, in American higher education. For example, William Bennett asserted in 1984 that "the humanities have lost their central place in the undergraduate curriculum" (Bennett 1984: 2). To these analysts it seemed that the deterioration was an aberration of recent origin, something that rededication to enduring principles, or curricular reform, or pedagogical innovation, or clever administrative

321

management, or greater government involvement could overcome. Each commission or report had its own, often political, perspective on the problem and its own suggestions for remediation. The decline has been real, and perhaps more severe in recent decades than previously. The process of decline of clientele for the humanities is, however, not actually of recent origin. As Sachs (1985) has pointed out,

> the charge [that the humanities are losing their central place in the undergraduate curriculum] was not less true fifty years ago, during the Depression, when both the University of Chicago and tiny St. John's College attempted to institute a "Great Books" program, with the express purpose of putting the humanities back into the center of the undergraduate curriculum from whence they had long since been displaced. (p. 1)

He further argues that one really must look even further back in time, to the first half of the nineteenth century, to find humanities truly at the core of undergraduate curricula.

In those days colleges served the sons of the elite families of the nation by lending depth to already established cultural grounding acquired in similarly elite secondary schools. Foreign-language study was centrally placed in the curriculum. This meant, of course, study of Classical and Western European languages, the languages of High Culture, culminating in the reading of the literary monuments of those languages. To the question, "Why should I study a foreign language?" if an intrepid student of fifty years ago should even dare to ask such a question, the answer would have been easy, because it would have derived from the generally accepted conception of what it meant to be an educated person. "It is good for you; every educated person must have studied French (or German or Italian)"; or "You'll have a greater understanding of Culture"; "No one can call himself educated who has not read Molière (or Goethe, or Dante)"; and so on. The legitimacy of language study was seldom questioned, especially in the elite liberal arts colleges. Students were well grounded in classical languages in grammar school. On application for admission to college, they typically presented one modern foreign language as well, the study of which they continued in college.

DECLINE OF ENROLLMENTS
IN THE HUMANITIES

The general decline in the numbers of students in the humanities in general, and foreign languages in particular, has been documented in several empirical studies. Since the late seventies, demographic studies have warned of the decline in college-age students in the 1990s. College and university administrators are planning for the possibility of institutional reduction in the coming decade because of fewer entering freshmen. Educational analysts have speculated that at least 10 percent of America's 3100 colleges and universities will close their doors or merge with other institutions by 1995 (Keller 1983). Many of these will be small liberal arts colleges, whose endowments are not big enough to carry them through a decade of low enrollments.

As postsecondary institutions plan for a decade with fewer 18–20 year-olds, they will also be faced with a decline in the popularity of the traditional liberal arts disciplines. Data collected by the Cooperative Institutional Research Program (CIRP) in surveys of college freshmen between 1966 and 1986 revealed dramatic declines in the humanities, the fine and performing arts, and the social sciences (Astin et al. 1987). According to the CIRP analyses of trends, freshman interest in English declined by almost 80 percent during this period, and similar statistics emerged for foreign languages, philosophy, and theology. The authors concluded that "the data point to sharp and continuing declines in student interest in virtually every field that has traditionally been associated with a liberal arts education" (p. 15). For the humanities, the implications of such trends are grim: "the aggregate freshman data," Astin et al. continue, "are very good predictors of aggregate final choices and behaviors. In other words, the trends in freshman aspirations have been followed by similar trends in bachelor's degrees" (p. 16). These and other studies completed in the early and mid 1980s provided data that haunt the humanities faculties at many postsecondary institutions.

Effects in Foreign-Language Departments

Foreign-language departments have already felt the effects of these changes in attitudes. Enrollments, observed nationally, have been declining in advanced courses. By 1984 Bennett reported that there had been a 50 percent drop in foreign-language majors since 1970 (Bennett 1984, cited in Carney 1986). As colleges and universities dropped or reduced their language requirements in the seventies, registrations in modern foreign languages dropped from 16.1 percent of total college enrollment in 1960 to 7.8 percent in 1986 (Brod 1988). The total college enrollment, however, grew from 3.78 million to 12.24 million during this same time, so the overall number of students studying languages increased from 608,749 students to 960,588 (Brod 1988). This meager gain is no cause for rejoicing. The drop in the total number of freshmen in the 1990s may lead to a loss in foreign-language enrollments that reflects the decrease in interest revealed in the CIRP study.

Enrollment patterns, however, indicate that declines will not have the same impact on all languages. Between 1983 and 1986 Arabic lost 0.5 percent of total enrollments nationally; German lost 5.6 percent, Ancient Greek 9.0 percent, and Hebrew 14.1 percent. Meanwhile French gained 1.9 percent, Latin 3.3 percent, Russian 11.8 percent, Portuguese 14 percent, and Spanish 6.5 percent. Nationally the greatest increases were recorded by Chinese (28.2 percent) and Japanese (45.4 percent) (Brod 1988). Should these trends continue, some languages could experience a net gain in students, even during a period of diminished overall student commitment to language study.

Profile of Current Incoming Students

The student clientele has in this same period been diversifying its interest to match the increasing complexity of society. For some time now, the clientele of colleges has not been made up of a culturally homogeneous social elite (Girash 1987; Astin et al. 1987). Students now have an altogether different preparation for college, with more extensive backgrounds in the natural and social sciences and less background knowledge of Western European culture than fifty years ago. Furthermore, they come to college with much less preparation in language learning. On graduation they enter into an altogether different and decidedly more complicated world. These factors, combined with the smorgasbord served up as a response to student demands for variety and diversity in the academic cafeteria, have combined to deflate interest in literary and linguistic study.

The growing indifference to humanistic study among college students may correlate with the shift in values, clearly observable even over the last twenty years. In 1967 the most important value for entering freshmen was "developing a meaningful philosophy of life." By 1985 "being well-off financially" had replaced this as a major goal, and values dealing with matters of social concern and altruism had declined significantly (Astin et al. 1987). These shifts in values (it is possibly too early to designate them as permanent changes in the social landscape) have brought about an accelerating diversification of the curriculum. These changes coincide with the growth in many institutions of majors in business, engineering, and computer science, and the decline of student interest in education, the humanities, and the arts. Since at present there are no indications that these trends are about to be reversed, it is likely that students will increase pressure on colleges to change requirements and diversify offerings to accommodate their interests.

Meanwhile the structure of the foreign-language major at most liberal arts colleges has retained into the nineties the basic features of the past. Professors are trained predominantly as literary scholars, still poised, as they were before the First World War, to mediate the transmission of High Culture to the scions of the great families. Yet, for better or for worse, historical change has swept away, for the majority of the society that colleges serve, the humanities-rich conception of the educated person. In the wake of this loss, institutions are adjusting their priorities. Departments, including foreign-language departments, must choose their responses.

POTENTIAL RESPONSES

Trends like those discussed above already led many colleges in the seventies and eighties to revoke, reduce, or revise their foreign-language graduation requirements. Four-year liberal arts colleges, including their departments of foreign languages and literatures, will find it especially difficult to survive these trends in the nineties without retrenchment. Because larger institutions seem better equipped to attend to students' career orientations, smaller colleges may find themselves attracting a smaller fraction of the undergraduate population. As the competition for the smaller number of students increases, scholarship programs and financial aid packages will also become a more significant factor in student decisions about which schools to attend. Institutions with the largest endowments will be able to offer more attractive financial packages, and thus entice the elite students, the students most likely by cultural upbringing to be interested in what traditionally structured departments of foreign languages and literatures have to offer. It is within this context that the language faculties of liberal arts colleges may do well to reconsider their philosophy, goals, and responses to the challenges of the nineties.

Generally speaking, three types of responses to the situation are possible, which we will call the defensive, the tactical, and the strategic responses.

The Defensive Response

For a number of professors, the clear preference would seem to be to reaffirm the traditional curriculum of departments of foreign languages and literatures (Williamson 1987). A decision to maintain and strengthen literary studies as the goal of foreign-language study capitalizes on the professional training of the faculty and can be justified by the traditional arguments that are used to support a liberal arts education. Such a posture may be particularly appealing to small liberal arts colleges, since it is precisely these institutions that have carried down into the second half of the twentieth century a commitment to the central role of the humanities. This may, however, mean heavy enrollment losses in courses not protected by graduation requirements.

Such an approach may succeed for elite schools whose reputation for excellence and a strong liberal arts tradition will attract dedicated students eager to become literary scholars. These same schools have the financial resources to maintain departments at full strength, despite low enrollments, provided that such maintenance is an institutional priority. In most liberal arts colleges, a foreign-language department that continues to offer the traditional curriculum culminating in literary analysis may seriously fail to meet the needs and interests of the majority of its undergraduates who are interested in engaging in language study.

The Tactical Response

In the context of prospective retrenchment, foreign-language instructors have come up with a truly impressive list of remedies that modify some aspect of the program, without, however, radically modifying the departmental curriculum. Such tinkering offers the possibility of adding something new to a department without calling into question cherished assumptions about the role of the department in the college and in the profession. A survey of the literature reveals that foreign-language departments have

- Introduced commercial and professional courses for students majoring in business (Tcachuk 1982)

- Collaborated in curriculum planning with other departments such as English or History (Klein 1987; Reichardt 1985)

- Initiated a campuswide collaboration that entailed encouraging colleagues in all departments to incorporate foreign-language content into their curriculum (Jurasek 1982)

- Experimented with incorporating content from other disciplines into intermediate and advanced offerings in the language department (Lindstrom 1982)

- Offered self-instructional courses in critical languages for which there was student demand but no qualified instructor (Morehouse and Boyd-Bowman 1973)

- Intensified efforts to provide language-relevant extracurricular activities and heighten interest in study abroad (Shepard 1982)

Most of these innovations have involved beginning and intermediate language instruction, perhaps in part because this is where the majority of enrollments are and where the attrition takes place. The search for something that works has introduced foreign-language teachers to new technologies.

Computers, videodiscs, videotapes, and satellite dishes have been adopted and adapted in the hope that they would enhance learning and increase motivation. Other tactical responses have included experimenting with new textbooks, approaches, and methodologies, again in the hope that better language instruction at lower levels would pay off in greater enrollments at the upper levels of the curriculum.

A particularly promising avenue of approach for enriching existing courses and initiating new ones involves taking advantage of the surrounding community of the college. Where feasible, instructors can take the language out of the classroom to speakers of that language and bring native speakers into the classroom. This possibility is not so restricted as one might think. Most communities in the United States possess a wealth of untapped language resources. Spanish speakers, along with radio and television, are perhaps the most obvious, but native speakers of French and German can be found virtually everywhere. Many corporations, for example, have international operations that bring foreign nationals to installations all over the United States for short periods of time. Native speakers of our target languages whom fate has brought to remote areas will often respond to newspaper invitations for a French film series, for example, or for a German Christmas celebration. Once located, the cooperation and assistance of these native speakers is usually easy to obtain, and they can serve as resource persons for cultural topics and as interview candidates for linguistic and conversational study.

At some colleges language house programs exist. These provide further vehicles for innovations that will have positive impact on the departmental curriculum. In addition to usual language house activities, departments might consider the feasibility of using foreign students, who frequently choose small colleges, for buddy pairs with American foreign-language students. Such enrichment would not only help integrate the foreign student into the college community, but would also give practice and cultural experience to the foreign-language student.

Depending on geography, collaboration with other small colleges may often provide a chance to expand the curricula, for developing study-abroad programs, and for pooling technological resources. A tactical response will be more likely to succeed in the long run if it entails institutional commitment. Cooperation with neighboring institutions must involve the administrators of the colleges concerned, and usually entails making the institutional commitments matters of record. Administrators may be predisposed to favor a program that will be seen to improve the institution's offerings at a low cost. In such negotiations it must be up to the foreign-language departments to ensure that the benefits are real and programatic and not simply token improvements on paper. If properly thought out and executed, such commitments will benefit the departments of foreign language.

The success, or failure, of any tactical response in curricular innovation often depends heavily on one or two faculty members who propose, lobby for, and implement the changes. The energy and enthusiasm that accompany the inauguration of something new and different are often crucial factors in its success. The tactical innovators and their programs reap the rewards of their good efforts for a time. A department may be well served by committing itself to a series of innovations, as the conditions call for them and as the personnel and energy become available. But when the innovators move on, their interests evolve, or local conditions change once again, then another tactical response is called for. Tactical solutions, however positive, do not generally provide long-term solutions.

Strategic Responses

Finally, a department may opt for fundamental change. Such responses entail displacing literary study from the top of the curricular pyramid. Rivers noted in the early seventies that the curricula of language departments were no longer meeting the needs of a significant number of college students and that rekindling student interest in foreign-language study would involve major curricular changes (Rivers 1972). Few language faculties have been able to make these changes. Strategic responses are difficult, for they require a pragmatic attitude toward the traditional curriculum.

One must take a dispassionate look at the past and future and reconceptualize the department of foreign languages and literatures. For many colleagues this may seem a potentially humiliating defeat, for others an exciting new challenge. Not many colleges to date have chosen this route. Any successful reform would have to address the societal changes we have been discussing in this chapter, while still capitalizing on the actual competencies of foreign-language professors in language, linguistics, cultural history, and contemporary societal analysis, as well as literary study.

Any significant change cannot be effected by a department unilaterally. Broad-based consultation, and perhaps collaboration, with colleagues in other departments will be required. Furthermore, small colleges will be most likely to succeed in their reforms if they capitalize on their institution's own strengths in neighboring disciplines. When a department sees a real strength in history, then a curricular reform capitalizing on expertise of colleagues in that department, even co-opting already existing courses, is likely to be a more efficient approach. In fact, reforming departments should consider building on strengths wherever they find them, whether in history, business, communications, international relations, or wherever (Rivers 1983: 166–82; and chapter 2 in this volume).

Four basic outlines for reform, then, present themselves.

- Departments can focus on advanced language study, with emphasis on oral and written proficiency, stylistics, linguistics, and critical reading in a variety of fields. In such a plan, literary texts would perhaps maintain a prominent, though probably not dominant, role.

- Departments can establish programs in cultural history and cultural trends. The German Studies model adopted by several universities serves as an example (see chapter 2). Many larger universities already have in place a "culture track," which could in some instances be adapted for smaller colleges choosing this approach. In this case, collaboration with colleagues in the humanities and social sciences would be essential to ensure the intellectual rigor of the reformed curriculum. This model might also be coordinated with campuswide efforts to internationalize the curriculum.

- Colleges can move literary study into a department of its own, say, a department of comparative literature or European literature, and maintain a basically service oriented department for beginning and intermediate language courses. The economics of this line of attack seem inherently problematical for smaller colleges; furthermore it ignores the interest of many students who need or want experience with the language at an advanced level.

- Colleges can assess the career orientations of a majority of their students in relation to local professional opportunities and provide a carefully developed sequence of career-oriented language courses, where possible linked with an interinstitutional study-abroad program, whether for business, health professions, engineering, or international service (see chapter 6). Internships, both abroad and with domestic firms or institutions, might be a productive accompaniment to such an endeavor.

In addition to the defensive, the tactical, and the strategic response, we might also name a fourth approach: no response at all. The posture of the ostrich seems to us bound to fail, given the quite serious realities that face the four-year colleges in the nineties. Inaction, however, may well be the response in those small colleges where rewards for faculty have little relationship with teaching performance and curricular stewardship. Curricular stagnation might, for instance, be an unexpected consequence of a college administration's decision to seek institutional prestige by assigning highest priority to research and publication. Faculty would then have little incentive to put time and effort into their curricular responsibilities.

Against the backdrop of threatened decline, there is much room for hope. Small colleges are not without their strengths, and, if departments of foreign language can capitalize on these, they can survive and thrive into the next decade and century. The liberal arts college, despite its inability to offer everything under the sun, provides a total experience of learning of a special kind that many students and parents evidently still prefer. The relative intimacy of contact for faculty with colleagues in other disciplines makes collaboration more likely to succeed. The less cumbersome bureaucracy and greater access to administrators makes it easier to initiate tactical curricular responses: new courses can be instituted almost instantly and all courses can be modified in midstream, without fear of losing coordination with instructors in other sections (because there are almost no multisection courses at small liberal arts colleges). These same features make strategic adjustments easier to develop and implement.

Deep societal changes are acting to make our long-cherished notions of foreign-language study untenable. A language department in a small liberal arts college can thrive in the coming decade, but only if it is willing to exploit its fundamental advantage of flexibility in order to accommodate to these changes in a way consonant with its educational mission, its own constellation of faculty and students, and its vision of the future.

REFERENCES

Astin, W., K. Green, and W. Korn. 1987. *The American Freshman: Twenty Year Trends.* Los Angeles: American Council on Education.

Bennett, William J. 1984. *To Reclaim a Legacy: A Report on the Humanities in Higher Education.* Washington, DC: National Endowment for the Humanities.

Brod, Richard I. 1988. "Foreign Language Enrollments in U.S. Institutions of Higher Education—Fall 1986." *ADFL Bulletin* 19,2: 39–44.

Carney, W. J. 1986. "Integrating Commercial French into the Traditional Foreign Language Curriculum: A Marriage of Convenience That Works." *ADFL Bulletin* 17,2: 43–49.

Girash, D. 1987. "And Guess Who's in the Bull's Eye—You, Ladies and Gentlemen: A Report on SCUP-22." *Planning for Higher Education* 16,2: 43–59.

Jurasek, R. 1982. "Practical Applications of Foreign Languages in the College Curriculum." *Modern Language Journal* 66,4: 368–72.

Keller, G. 1983. *Academic Strategy—The Management Revolution in American Education.* Baltimore: Johns Hopkins Univ. Press.

Klein, Richard. 1987. "Advanced Literary Study in the Smaller Department: Leaving the Past and Moving toward an Uncertain Future." *ADFL Bulletin* 18,2: 9–12.

Lindstrom, N. 1982. "Foreign Languages and Social Sciences: Shifting Ground." *Improving College and University Teaching* 30,4: 179–82.

Morehouse, W., and P. Boyd-Bowman. 1973. "Independent Study of Critical Languages in Undergraduate Colleges." Washington, DC: Institute of International Studies (DHEW/OE).

Reichardt, Paul. 1985. "English and Foreign Languages: Patterns of Collaboration." *ADFL Bulletin* 17,1: 14–17.

Rivers, Wilga M. 1972. "From the Pyramid to the Commune: The Evolution of the Foreign-Language Department." *ADFL Bulletin* 3,3: 13–17. [Revised version in Rivers 1983, pp. 154–65.]

————. 1983. *Speaking in Many Tongues: Essays in Foreign-Language Teaching.* 3d ed. Cambridge, Eng., and New York: Cambridge Univ. Press.

Sachs, Murray. 1985. "Upon the Shoulders of Giants: Some Present Imperatives for Humanities Education." *ADFL Bulletin* 17,1: 1–4.

Shepard, Joe W. 1982. "Beyond the Language Requirement: The Role of Foreign Languages in the Upper-Level Curriculum." *ADFL Bulletin* 14,2: 14–16.

Tcachuk, A. 1982. "Teaching Professional Spanish: The Experience of a Small, Liberal Arts College." Paper presented at the Eastern Michigan University Conference on Spanish for Bilingual Careers in Business, March 18–20, Ypsilanti, MI.

Williamson, R. 1987. "Moving a Graveyard: Or Revising the Major in the Small Liberal Arts College." *ADFL Bulletin* 18,3: 21–24.

17

Foreign-Language Learning in Adult Education: Program and Practice

Raymond Comeau
Harvard University

MANY FOREIGN-LANGUAGE INSTRUCTORS ACCUSTOMED TO TEACHING traditional full-time undergraduates have already had the experience of teaching part-time adult learners, and many others will share that experience in the future. The purpose of this article is to provide these instructors with practical guidance derived from research on adult development and learning. The first half of the article presents some key sociological, physiological, psychological, and pedagogical characteristics of adult learners; the second half offers ten precepts for teaching adults.

For the past twenty years adult learners have been quietly changing the student landscape of higher education. Between 1970 and 1989 part-time enrollments increased by 109 percent, while full-time enrollments increased by only 32 percent. Today one-third of all undergraduate enrollments are part-time, as are two-thirds of all master's degree enrollments, and nearly half of the students enrolled at all levels in higher education attend on a part-time basis. This increase in the number of part-time students has helped to maintain enrollment growth in higher education despite the decline in the traditional college-age population since 1981 (NUCEA 1990: 3).

Adult students at present are generally white, middle-class, and well-educated, and they earn at least a moderate income (Long 1983: 87). They are likely to be women in their 20s and 30s. Most are pragmatic learners who enroll in noncredit courses or pursue a certificate in order to obtain a new job, advance in their present job, or obtain a better job. Adult learners who pursue traditional liberal arts courses are in the minority. Adults display a preference for evening courses offered on on-campus sites, although off-campus sites are also fairly popular (Cross 1981). Some developing forms of distance learning, including courses using radio, television, and telephone, are gaining in popularity (Stringer 1982; Twarog and Pereszlenyi-Pinter 1981; Whiting 1988). No doubt computer-assisted learning will join the list shortly (Garrison 1987).

Since foreign languages possess both a practical and academic dimension, they have proved to be popular among adult learners. At the Harvard Extension School, for example, about 10 percent of the student body of 14,000 were enrolled in one of 16 foreign-language programs in the academic year 1989–90. In a 1989 survey of the graduates of the Harvard College classes of 1978, 1980, and 1983, 28 percent reported they had studied at least one foreign language since graduation, 10 percent said they had studied two, and 5 percent reported they had studied three. When asked why they studied these languages, 29 percent claimed professional reasons, 17 percent named travel, and 11 percent pointed to personal or family reasons (Hokanson 1989).

THE ADULT LEARNER

The "Older Is Better" Hypothesis

There is a strongly held belief, which Snow (1983) calls the "folk psychology of language learning," that children are better language learners than adults (p. 147). This belief was strengthened by the widely accepted "critical period hypothesis," which claimed that the critical period for learning foreign language ends at puberty (Lenneberg 1967).

In an article summarizing more recent research findings by other investigators, Krashen, Long, and Scarcella (1982) concluded that "adults and older children in general acquire the second language faster than young children (older is better for rate of acquisition), but child second-language acquirers will usually be superior in terms of ultimate attainment (younger is better in the long run)" (p. 161). While this finding may appear on the surface to be encouraging for adult educators, it must be pointed out that researchers often classify traditional college-age students as adults, and in the Krashen summary only 3 of the 9 studies cited compared children with adults over 26.

One study of older learners was the Snow and Hoefnagel-Höhle (1978) investigation of 42 English-speaking subjects learning Dutch, conducted in 1974. The subjects ranged in age from 3 to 55 years and included 11 adults, most in their 20s and 30s, 6 teenagers, and 25 children 10 years old or younger. The results of the test, which included pronunciation, auditory discrimination, morphology, sentence repetition, translation, and the Peabody Picture Vocabulary Test, showed that older learners generally seemed to have an advantage over younger learners in acquiring rule-governed aspects of a second language—morphology and syntax. This advantage of age was, however, limited, as the teenagers did better than the adults. Age differences on these tests diminished and disappeared with longer residence in Holland. In addition, there were very small age differences for tests reflecting control of the phonetic system, and a native level of performance was not achieved by any of the groups of nonnative speakers on these tests.

Snow (1983) maintains that "older is better" (p. 143) despite the fact that the teenagers performed better than the adults. To support this conclusion, she points to the fact that all the nonadults in the study learned primarily in Dutch schools, from teachers and from classmates, and they needed to acquire the language to get along in school. The adult subjects, on the other hand, had relatively little contact with Dutch speakers and were able to communicate in most situations using English. She also stresses that the one subject who scored best on almost all the tests was a young adult attending a Dutch university and therefore experiencing the same kind of sociolinguistic environment as the nonadults. Snow concludes, "It does not surprise me that adults turn out to be better second-language learners than children—after all, adults are better than children at almost every other learning task" (p. 149).

Despite this and other encouraging findings, such as Neufeld's study (1978) demonstrating that adults can achieve a nativelike proficiency in pronunciation within a limited amount of time, there is clearly a need to corroborate these findings with more research focusing on older foreign-language learners.

Andragogy or Pedagogy?

Although many foreign-language instructors are and have been successful teachers of adults without the benefit of formal training in the theory and practice of adult education, there can be little doubt that a deeper understanding of adult learning and development would benefit both present and future instructors. The most popular model of adult learning is called *andragogy,* first proposed in this country by Malcolm Knowles (1968). Knowles has consistently offered his model in contrast to pedagogy, which he first defined as a model of childhood learning. He now considers andragogy and pedagogy, however, as "two parallel sets of assumptions about learners and learning that need to be checked out in each situation" (1989: 80). Since andragogy is perhaps the most popular adult learning model, it is useful to consider its most recent formulation by Knowles (1989: 82–85):

Regarding the need to know   *Pedagogical:* Learners need to know what the teacher teaches if they want to pass and get promoted. *Andragogical:* Adults need to know why they need to learn something before undertaking to learn it.

Regarding the learner's self-concept   *Pedagogical:* The teacher's concept of the learner is that of a dependent personality; therefore, the learner's self-concept becomes that of a dependent personality. *Andragogical:* Adults have a self-concept of being responsible for their own lives. They develop a deep psychological need to be seen and treated by others as being capable of self-direction.

Regarding the role of experience   *Pedagogical:* The learner's experience is of little worth as a resource for learning. *Andragogical:* For many kinds of learning, the richest resources are within the learners themselves.

Regarding readiness to learn   *Pedagogical:* Learners become ready to learn what the school requires them to learn if they want to pass and get promoted. *Andragogical:* Adults become ready to learn those things they need to know or to be able to do in order to cope effectively with their real-life situations.

Regarding orientation to learning.   *Pedagogical:* Learners have a subject-centered orientation to learning. *Andragogical:* Adults are life-centered (or task-centered or problem-centered) in their orientation to learning.

Regarding motivation to learn   *Pedagogical:* Learners are motivated by extrinsic motivators—grades, the teacher's approval or disapproval, parental pressures. *Andragogical:* While adults are responsive to some extrinsic motivators (better jobs, promotions, salary increases, and the like), the more potent motivators are intrinsic motivators (the desire for increased self-esteem, quality of life, responsibility, job satisfaction, and the like).

While the andragogical assumptions proposed by Knowles are consistent with principles of adult development and have been used successfully by many adult educators, it is unfortunate they are made in contrast to assumptions referred to as *pedagogical.* The term *pedagogy* is universally understood to mean, in Webster's words, "the art and science of teaching," whether it be teaching children, adolescents, or adults. Even when it is used in reference to the teaching of children, it does not imply the divorce from life that Knowles assigns to it. John Dewey, whose philosophy has had perhaps the greatest influence on childhood education in this century, stated that "education must be conceived as a continuing reconstruction of experience" (Dworkin 1959: 27), a statement that could serve as a cornerstone of Knowles's own model of andragogy.

The andragogical concept of the adult as a self-directed, responsible, intrinsically motivated learner must be qualified further when it is applied to foreign-language students, especially beginning students. Foreign-language students are asked to display an unusual vulnerability by temporarily replacing their comfortable cultural and linguistic habits with new ones. They invest a great deal of trust in the instructor, who becomes an immediate model of cultural and linguistic behavior. This complex relationship between the instructor and the student admits of both the independent relationship of adult to adult and the nurturing relationship of parent to child (see Rivers 1964: 90–98). In other words, this "adult-child" (that is, this adult who becomes like a child in the classroom) displays both andragogical and pedagogical tendencies, as Knowles has defined them.

Some Physiological Characteristics

As the body grows older, it experiences certain physiological changes that have an effect upon learning. For example, there is a slowing down in reaction time, which peaks at around 18 and gradually decreases during middle and old age. Vision and hearing are also affected. Vision is at its best at about age 18, declines gradually until about age 40, declines more sharply between 40 and 55, then begins to deteriorate more moderately. Hearing decreases gradually until the fifties and then decreases more rapidly (Knox 1978: 275–87).

Intelligence also changes with age. Cattell (1963) makes an interesting distinction between two kinds of intelligence, fluid and crystallized. Fluid intelligence, which peaks during adolescence and declines gradually through adulthood, is the ability to perceive complex relations, use short-term memory, form concepts, and engage in abstract reasoning. It is innate and unlearned, and "flows into" various intellectual activities easily and naturally. Independent of experience and education, it comes into play in tests of rote memory, common word analogies, verbal reasoning, and adaptation to novel situations. Crystallized intelligence, on the other hand, which continues to increase gradually throughout adulthood, is much more dependent on education, experience, and acculturation, and it draws on this knowledge and experience to perceive relations and engage in abstract reasoning. It comes into play in tests of general information, vocabulary, reading comprehension, and arithmetic reasoning. As one grows older, the growth of crystallized intelligence tends to compensate for the decrease in fluid intelligence (Knox 1978: 419–21; Cross 1981: 161–63). A good deal of research has been conducted on the effects of age on memory. It is thought that short-term memory and the ability to retain information for immediate access remain relatively stable throughout adulthood, if the material is meaningful and not too complex. Although there is a general decline in the ability to recall, the decline can be minimized if adults organize the information in clusters, a technique that most adults, unfortunately, do not employ (Knox 1978: 434–36). Summarizing some of the findings on memory, Cross (1981) concludes that "the greatest problems with memory for older people occur with meaningless learning, complex learning, and the learning of new things that require assessment of old learning" (p. 163). Some recent studies suggest, however, that the poorer performance of older learners on some memory tests may be simply a factor of speed of response; it is an accepted fact, after all, that older learners require more time to do just about everything. One study provides the interesting hypothesis that older people actually retrieve information more efficiently than younger people if the size of the data base is taken into account (Ogle 1986: 9–10).

While some memory functions are adversely affected by age, creativity, an important mental ingredient in many foreign-language classes, does not seem to be. According to Knox, "there is some evidence regarding creativity during adulthood which indicates that it is both feasible and desirable and that educational activity can facilitate it" (p. 446).

Some Personality Characteristics

What is the effect of age on personality? According to Cross (1981), "perhaps the major conclusion that can be drawn from all the research on personality is that people show a remarkable consistency throughout life" (p. 165). She points to studies that show that personality differences between 50-year-olds and 20-year-olds have more to do with life experiences than with age. Other studies she cites show that personality characteristics such as wide-ranging interests, aesthetic reaction, intellectual level, and verbal fluency, which psychologists refer to as "style of cognitive development," remain stable throughout life (p. 165).

For adult educators, certain aspects of personality development are especially important. One factor is the concept of individual differences. As people grow older, they accumulate more life experiences, hence their individual differences become more pronounced. A group of 50-year-olds, for example, will display more variability in learning aptitude than a group of 20-year-olds. A second important variable in adult personality development is the tendency to put accuracy before speed. To compensate for their slower reaction time, adults tend to rely more on accuracy, deliberation, and efficiency. They are more likely to rely on previously learned solutions than to take the risk of trying out novel solutions. Finally, although young and middle-aged adults generally display a growth in self-confidence and goal-directedness, there is some evidence that adults in their middle years gradually experience an increase in anxiety and the fear of failure, which can result in response inhibition. If the pace is slowed down, however, this response inhibition can be reduced (Cross 1981: 167; Joiner 1981: 17–18; Long 1983: 226–27).

Some Developmental Characteristics: Life Phases

Popularized by Gail Sheehy's 1976 best-seller, *Passages,* research on the phases of the life cycle describes the changes that people undergo as they pass through important age and social periods. Cross distilled phase research into the following seven phases: leaving home (18–22), moving into the adult world (23–28), search for stability (29–34), becoming one's person (37–42), settling down (45–55), mellowing (57–64), and life review (65+) (Cross 1981: 174–75). All phase researchers warn against taking these distinctions too literally and recommend a flexible approach when seeking implications.

While it is not necessary for adult educators to become experts in phase research, an awareness of the various life-cycle phases can provide them with a better understanding of their students. Consider, for example, Cross's distilled version of the marker events in the "search for stability" life-cycle phase (1981: 174–75): establish children in school; progress in career or consider a change; possible separation, divorce, remarriage; possible return to school.

Keeping these marker events in mind, the foreign-language instructor can encourage students in this phase to carry out activities that deal with the issues of children, career, marriage, or school. Compositions, role-play activities, and simulation exercises that respond to these preoccupations will in all probability interest these students. An appreciation of these issues may also help the instructor understand certain student behaviors and attitudes in and out of class. A student working overtime, for example, or one who is having personal difficulties, will perhaps need special consideration from time to time.

Ten Precepts for
Teaching the Adult Learner

The following ten teaching precepts are intended as points of departure for implementation and discussion. Some instructors will find them compatible with their teaching style; others will want to modify them to meet their needs. Although they are derived from research on adult development and from experience in teaching adults, many may be applied with equal efficacy to the teaching of traditional college-age undergraduates (who, after all, are in the beginning stages of adulthood), and even, with adaptation, to younger students.

Assess Student Level and Interests

An accepted practice in most teaching environments, the assessment of student level and interests becomes more imperative with adult learners because their individual differences and motivations are more pronounced (Thorndike 1935: 139). In addition to asking for the names, addresses (work and home), and telephone numbers (day and night) of students, language instructors should also ask how much previous exposure students have had to the language, for what reasons they are studying it, and what experiences they have had that are pertinent to their study of the new language. (e.g., Have they been successful or unsuccessful learners of other languages? Have they had the personal experience of living in other cultures? Do they hear this new language around them at work or in the family?)

An understanding of the student's previous exposure will help to determine proper level placement. Some adults, for example, have traveled extensively in a country where the target language is spoken but have not studied the language formally; others may have studied the language formally, even for long periods of time, but many years earlier; yet others have heard the language spoken in the family, but can neither speak nor read it. Consideration of previous experience, along with the results of a short placement test given on the first day, should yield enough information to determine who should stay in a particular course and who should be encouraged to take a more elementary or more advanced course. Since adults can be independent and persuasive, instructors should be prepared to negotiate their position; they may even want to encourage a trial period to allow students to convince themselves of the most comfortable level that will ensure progress.

It is often useful—and always interesting—to learn the reasons students have for studying the language. Typically, the reasons will vary considerably, ranging from institutional reasons such as satisfying a language requirement or preparing for a graduate reading exam to more adult-related reasons such as traveling and working abroad, communicating with a friend or family member, usefulness for career or leisure purposes, or simply being attracted to the language. Instructors can keep these reasons in mind when making up assignments and even design assignments that respond to certain interests. A student taking the language to carry out a journalistic assignment in the country where the language is spoken might be encouraged to write an article as a composition assignment; another who is planning a vacation to a country where the language is spoken might want to prepare an oral presentation on an imaginary journey to that country (disastrous?, adventure-packed?, bizarre?, amusing?), which would involve consulting authentic materials such as maps, schedules, or brochures.

Devise Assignments That Respond to Individual Differences

Instructors have two major options for dealing with a class of diverse adult students: (1) to focus on the individual by creating an individualized learning plan for each student based on his or her interests and learning style; or (2) to focus on the class as a whole by devising many varied activities and allowing individuals to choose among them. Since most adult education programs have neither the staff nor the resources to allow for the first kind of individualization, they rely on the second option, which works very well and is more consistent with the usual classroom teaching environment. In keeping with the view that adult learners are independent and know what they want to study, the most effective activities are those that allow for the greatest freedom of choice and expression. As Even (1987) says, "the key to working with adults with a variety of differences is the use of a variety of examples, techniques, and approaches to accommodate the various alternatives of choice" (p. 25). For a composition on the theme of cuisine, for example, the following subjects could be assigned: an interview with a waiter, a letter of complaint to the owner of a restaurant, a dialog with a mouse that resides in the kitchen, a dialog between a gourmet and a gourmand, an essay comparing a restaurant in the country and a Mcdonald's, an original poem about food, a presentation and brief commentary on favorite recipes, and a free choice. Instructors should not shy away from creative activities, as research shows that creativity is not adversely affected by age.

Another exercise that puts the individual differences and experiences of adults to good use is the writing of student autobiographies. This activity, properly devised (in three or four segments, each corresponding to a different life period such as childhood, grammar school, high school, working life) and conveniently spaced (one every month or so, leaving enough time for rewriting) allows for the use of a rich variety of personalized vocabulary and grammar.

Once the versions have been corrected, they can be read to the class as a whole and discussed, thereby serving as pronunciation, intonation, listening comprehension, and speaking exercises as well. This kind of activity takes full advantage of some of the strengths of crystallized intelligence, namely experience, breadth of vocabulary, and general information, and it also serves as a memory aid by organizing meaningful vocabulary in clusters.

Adopt a Deliberate, Unhurried Approach to Teaching

There are many reasons for instructors to adopt a deliberate, unhurried approach when teaching adults. First, adults have a tendency to slow down both physically and mentally as they grow older. They have a slower reaction time than younger people, and their hearing and vision are not as acute; mentally, they neither recall information as readily nor process it as quickly or easily. They compensate for this speed deficiency by being accurate, efficient, and deliberate, and by calling on their experience and general knowledge.

Other factors, more situational in nature, also call for this approach. For example, since most adults work full time, they may be somewhat tired when they arrive for their evening class. In addition, they sometimes have less classroom contact than traditional daytime students, with many seeing the instructor only once a week. Fortunately, their interest in the subject matter and their motivation to learn make up for low energy level or infrequent classroom contact.

A deliberate, unhurried approach to teaching maximizes the strengths and minimizes the weaknesses of adult learners. Careful, planned, and economical, it stresses the essentials at the expense of the superfluous. Adapting one's approach does not imply that adults are somehow inadequate learners, but it does recognize that each is a unique learner.

Experienced instructors of adults allow extra time for students to respond to questions, stress the essentials when presenting new material, and, while varying classroom activities because this is a universal pedagogical principle, move from one activity to the next in an orderly, careful, and logical fashion. They assign homework that corresponds clearly with classroom activities, reinforce oral work with written board work, and stay with an activity until students feel comfortable with it. They write clearly on the board and speak loudly and distinctly enough to be easily heard. While they occasionally quicken the pace of drills to interest and challenge their students, they never rush through activities or cover too much material, preferring to extract the essential elements and teach them thoroughly. In order to avoid ambiguity and misunderstanding, they are clear and precise when explaining course objectives, requirements, and grading standards.

Provide Frequent Reinforcement and Feedback

An important aspect of deliberate, unhurried teaching is frequent reinforcement and feedback. The following chart is an example of how a discrete grammar point (e.g., the present tense of one category of verbs, object pronouns, or basic interrogative adverbs) might be sequenced over a number of class meetings for maximum reinforcement. In most cases below, the reinforcement occurs immediately in class; in cases where quizzes are graded by the instructor, the feedback is delayed until the next class meeting. To aid recall and maintain a serious attitude toward the learning process, every effort should be made to hand back all graded work at the next class meeting.

Class	*Student Activity*
First	• Listens to and repeats grammar point in meaningful contexts in class
	• Prepares oral and written assignments on that point at home
Second	• Selected students put assigned written homework exercises on board for group correction
	• Does assigned oral exercises in groups
	• Takes written practice quiz on point covered this day
Third	• Takes written quiz on grammar point for a grade
Fourth	• Selected students write corrected quiz on board while other students or instructor explain troublesome questions
Fifth, sixth, etc.	• Takes quizzes that review grammar point, which is included in different contexts with grammar points learned later

In the above sequence there is a progression in level of difficulty: from meaningful repetition to oral interaction, and from taking a practice quiz to taking a quiz for a grade. There are also frequent opportunities for reinforcement, including cumulative quizzes and written exercises that reinforce oral responses.

Providing a fixed sequence of activities that can be used for every class, leaving room for some variation to avoid monotony, also provides for effective reinforcement, especially for adults who have limited classroom contact and are pressed for learning time. One possible set class sequence for teaching grammar might be the following: (1) make the initial presentation of the next day's material; (2) return corrected quizzes that were taken the previous day and have answers written on the board; (3) give a quiz on the material covered during the previous class; (4) have written exercises for the day's assignment written on the board and correct them together (to save time and allow more time for activity 5, this activity might take the form of pair correction with a fair copy); (5) do various oral activities; (6) assign work for the next day.

In this class sequence, the initial presentation of the next day's material is made at the beginning of class. This is done in order to avoid having to present it at the end of class, when there is often less time, and also to allow the instructor to return to it periodically during the class, thus actually reinforcing the next day's new material before the student has even opened the book to study it. By having the written exercises put on the board before practicing them orally, the instructor reinforces the material visually before the oral practice.

Create a Playful Learning Atmosphere

There are many reasons why the language classroom can be a threatening place for adults. Self-directed, independent, and responsible for shaping their own lives outside of class, they may feel out of place in an environment where they do not exercise the same level of control. For those who have been away from study for some time or who have never before set foot in a college classroom, the typical classroom may appear cold and unwelcoming. Although most students will be taking the course voluntarily and will be motivated and eager to learn, others, perhaps because they have had a bad learning experience in a previous language course or need to satisfy a language requirement, will take the course with some reluctance or trepidation. Even the instructor, if inexperienced or unwilling to teach adults, can contribute to their sense of uneasiness (David 1979).

Deliberate, unhurried teaching, with its emphasis on structured and reinforced learning, can help to reduce anxiety. An equally powerful tool for breaking down emotional barriers, however, is playfulness, which serves as a light counterbalance to the deliberate, unhurried approach. A playful give-and-take between the instructor and the class, and between individual students, alleviates tension and lays the foundation for meaningful interaction. It allows adults to shed their inhibitions and dare to experiment freely and naturally without the fear of making mistakes.

Playfulness includes kidding with students, individually and as a class. It may consist of the instructor's pseudo-menacing remark, such as "la guillotine!," at appropriate moments, or clapping together as a class after a student has made an oral presentation in front of the class, or hissing together when a student has willingly and daringly told a "bad" joke. It may also include humorous written comments on an especially good quiz or a supportive comment on an unusually bad quiz ("oops!"), or inserting unexpected humorous examples in an otherwise serious grammar exercise. It also includes spontaneous retorts and unexpected improvisations.

Playfulness, as a technique, presumes equal rights for students to tease the instructor and other students (sympathetically, of course). This reciprocity is particularly important with adults, who are frequently as old as, or older than, the instructor. Wherever this playful give-and-take is present, it brings people together and, as Highet has expressed it, "togetherness is the essence of teaching" (1950: 64).

On a questionnaire, adult students of elementary French in a Harvard Extension School class were asked to rate the activities they liked best from 1 to 10. The twenty-two-item questionnaire covered virtually every activity they performed in and out of class, including such items as "preparing oral exercises at home," "writing written exercises on the board," and "working with a partner in class." The activity that received the highest average score was "kidding around in French in class."

Maintain High Academic Standards

While adults appreciate a playful attitude in class, they expect a serious attitude toward learning in general. Since they often pay for their own education and take classes at some personal sacrifice, they are determined to get the most out of their educational experience. They expect to work every bit as hard as full-time students and to be graded according to the same rigorous standards.

High academic standards also help to compensate for being out of the academic mainstream. As part-time students on campus, adult learners are sometimes denied the status and rights that full-time students are afforded. They sometimes suffer from the feeling of being "different," of having a "different" classroom, a "different" faculty, and "different" requirements. Instructors should see to it that there is no difference in the quality of instruction they receive.

Maintain a Flexible Classroom Management Style

Unlike traditional college students whose primary responsibility is to attend class on a full-time basis, adults are forced to fit their part-time education into a crowded personal and professional schedule. Circumstances such as caring for a sick family member, being required to work overtime, or having to take a business trip can sometimes conflict with their academic schedules.

Instructors should be flexible in accepting situations of this kind and be prepared to provide direction in ways of dealing with them. For example, if students take a certain number of quizzes per semester, they may be allowed to miss a certain number without jeopardizing their grades. In the name of fairness, those who take all the quizzes should be allowed to drop the same number of their lowest grades. Instructors should also be considerate about accepting late work without penalty in special circumstances, reviewing written homework assignments out of sequence, and arranging make-ups on important tests for students who are unexpectedly forced to miss a class. Harvard Extension School has adopted a policy of duplicating laboratory materials on cassettes and lending them to students so they can listen to them at a convenient place and time.

Adapt Teaching Materials to Adult Interests

Most teaching materials are written with the traditional college student in mind. The learning styles, needs, and abilities of 22-year-olds will often differ markedly, however, from those of 30-year-olds or 50-year-olds. Exercises and readings dealing with parental authority, school dances, or college rap sessions may appear curiously out of place in the adult classroom.

Since it is sound pedagogy to adapt materials to students' interests and needs, it is often useful to make adaptations in readings, activities, vocabulary, and exercises for adult learners. The degree of adaptation will depend, however, on a number of factors, including the kind of course, the expertise of the instructor for adapting material, and the perceived need for adaptation by the instructor and the students. Some instructors using the four-skills approach to teach adults in a university continuing education class may make only a few adaptations, while an instructor teaching a specialized group, such as fire fighters, police, or nurses, may be forced to make many more.

Some published texts are more suited to adult interests and abilities than others. Instructors considering texts should look for the following features: grammar explanations in English, particularly at the beginning level, to avoid confusion and save time in individual study; a strong emphasis on reentry of vocabulary and grammar to reinforce material and aid recall; vocabulary organized in meaningful clusters to aid retention and recall; and a wide range of activities and exercises to respond to individual differences by allowing for maximum freedom of choice. Joiner (1981) recommends materials that present grammar deductively, deal with real-world issues, avoid memorized dialogs, provide intensive practice and review, and display an awareness of the notional-functional syllabus, which gives practice in using language purposefully (p. 44–47).

While it is advisable to choose materials that present subjects of interest to adults (e.g., office intrigues, buying a house, moving) in order to enhance interest and motivation, it is important to point out that adults have passed through various phases of life and are often willing to appreciate them in retrospect. Many also have children who are in different phases from their own. Adults enjoy doing an occasional role-play between a child and a mother or between two college roommates. They are also very much interested in topics of general interest, such as art, sports, films, current affairs, and cuisine.

Is one teaching method more suited to the interests and abilities of adults than others? The answer depends on the kind of student one is teaching and the goals of the course. Here, it is best to keep in mind Rivers's (1987) advice: "Teachers should not be looking for the one best method for teaching languages (or helping students learn languages), but rather the most appropriate approach, design of materials, or set of procedures in a particular case" (p. 6).

Listen and Respond to Student Feedback

Generally speaking, adults take courses for specific reasons and understand quite clearly what they want to get out of them. They also demand high standards and possess the social adroitness to inform the instructor if their expectations are not being met. It is not unusual for adults to complain if class is dismissed too early, if the syllabus is not followed closely, or if a test or composition is handed back late. On the other hand, they will often demonstrate their appreciation if they like a particular activity or assignment. They may ask for additional work or information relating to specific points of personal interest, and even request a change in class format or assignment.

If instructors take the point of view that adult learners are responsible and serious, they will listen carefully to all student feedback and, if appropriate and feasible, accommodate the schedule to address it. Instructors may even want to elicit feedback in the middle of the semester in order to sample student satisfaction with the course and get ideas for improving the course in the second half. This may be done anonymously in writing.

Be as Supportive as Possible

Foreign-language courses require precisely what adults most often lack—time. Even when motivation is high, it is sometimes difficult for adults to find adequate time in their busy schedules to do all the required study and assignments as completely as they would like (although, surprisingly, most do).

At times they do not do as well as they would like; some even fall behind and are then tempted to drop out.

Instructors should talk with students at the first sign of difficulty. If possible, the conversation should take place in a quiet office setting rather than during five or ten hurried minutes before or after class. If, after evaluating the seriousness of the student's problem, the instructor thinks that additional help is required, extra tutoring should be recommended. Since language learning is a cumulative process, tutors should be engaged at the earliest moment and given assistance in integrating their work with that of the class. Support is especially critical in courses offered at a distance because of the limited personal contact involved (Finkel 1982).

Even students who are doing well need support occasionally. Praise given orally and in writing can help, as can the instructor's demonstrated understanding if a hardworking student receives an occasional low grade on a quiz (the "oops" referred to earlier). The instructor's playful attitude will also lighten the spirits of a student who may be having an off day.

In conclusion, I would like to share the results of an unpublished survey conducted in 1984 among all 30 of the Romance Language faculty members of the Harvard University Extension School. Asked to compare their experience in teaching traditional undergraduates and adult students, 21 responded that their adult students were more motivated, and 24 that they were more appreciative, than the undergraduates they had taught. Significantly, they reported no major differences in student achievement and, by the highest margin of agreement in the survey (25 of 30), they even found the age range of their students to be an advantage. Not surprisingly, they considered their Extension School teaching to be more rewarding (22 of 30). These results are consistent with other findings comparing these two groups (Cross 1981: 70). With this in mind, an eleventh precept for teaching adult learners might be: "Enjoy the experience!"

REFERENCES

Cattell, R. B. 1963. "Theory of Fluid and Crystallized Intelligence." *Journal of Educational Psychology* 54: 1–22.

Cross, K. P. 1981. *Adults as Learners.* San Francisco: Jossey-Bass.

David, R. L. 1979. "Full-Time Faculty Resistance to Adult Higher Education." *Lifelong Learning* 2: 14–16, 29, 38–39.

Dworkin, M. S., ed. 1959. *Dewey on Education.* New York: Teachers College Press.

Even, M. J. 1987. "Why Adults Learn in a Different Way." *Lifelong Learning* 10: 22–25, 28.

Finkel, A. 1982. "Designing Interesting Courses," pp. 94–96 in J. S. Daniel, et al., eds., *Learning at a Distance: A World Perspective*. Edmonton, Alta.: Athabasca University, International Council for Correspondence Education.

Garrison, D. R. 1987. "The Role of Technology in Continuing Education," pp. 41–53 in R. G. Brockett, ed., *Continuing Education in the Year 2000*. San Francisco: Jossey-Bass.

Highet, G. 1950. *The Art of Teaching*. New York: Knopf.

Hokanson, K. 1989. *Harvard Alumni Survey*. Unpublished survey, Harvard University Assessment Seminar, Cambridge, MA.

Joiner, E. G. 1981. *The Older Foreign Language Learner: A Challenge for Colleges and Universities*. Washington, DC: Center for Applied Linguistics. [EDRS ED 208 672]

Knowles, Malcolm S. 1968. "Andragogy, Not Pedagogy." *Adult Leadership* 16: 350–53.

————. 1989. *The Making of an Adult Educator*. San Francisco: Jossey-Bass.

Knox, A. B. 1978. *Adult Development and Learning*. San Francisco: Jossey-Bass.

Krashen, Stephen D., Michael H. Long, and R. C. Scarcella. 1982. "Age, Rate, and Eventual Attainment in Second Language Acquisition," pp. 161–72 in S. D. Krashen, M. H. Long, and R. C. Scarcella, eds., *Child–Adult Differences in Second Language Acquisition*. Rowley, MA: Newbury House.

Lenneberg, E. H. 1967. *Biological Foundations in Language*. New York: Wiley.

Long, H. B. 1983. *Adult Learning*. Cambridge, Eng., and New York: Cambridge Univ. Press.

National University Continuing Education Association. 1990. *Lifelong Learning Trends*. Washington, DC: NUCEA.

Neufeld, G. G. 1978. "On the Acquisition of Prosodic and Articulatory Features in Adult Second Language Learning." *Canadian Modern Language Review* 34: 163–73.

Ogle, S. E. 1986. "Memory and Aging: A Review and Application of Current Theories." *Lifelong Learning* 9: 8–10, 27.

Rivers, Wilga M. 1964. *The Psychologist and the Foreign-Language Teacher*. Chicago: Univ. of Chicago Press.

————. 1987. "Interaction as the Key to Teaching Language for Communication," pp. 3–16 in Wilga M. Rivers, ed., *Interactive Language Teaching*. Cambridge, Eng., and New York: Cambridge Univ. Press.

Snow, C. E. 1983. "Age Differences in Second Language Acquisition: Research Findings and Folk Psychology," pp. 141–50 in K. M. Bailey, M. H. Long, and S. Peck, eds., *Second Language Acquisition*. Rowley, MA: Newbury House.

————, and M. Hoefnagel-Höhle. 1978. "Age Differences in Second Language Acquisition," pp. 333–44 in E. M. Hatch, ed., *Second Language Acquisition. A Book of Readings*. Rowley, MA: Newbury House.

Stringer, M. H. L. 1982. "Learning French at a Distance: The Student's Perspective," pp. 236–39 in J. S. Daniel, et al., eds., *Learning at a Distance: A World Perspective*. Edmonton, Alta.: Athabasca University, International Council for Correspondence Education.

Thorndike, E. L. 1935. *Adult Interests*. New York: Macmillan.

Twarog, L. I., and M. Pereszlenyi-Pinter. 1988. "Telephone-Assisted Language Study at Ohio State University: A Report." *Modern Language Journal* 72: 426–34.

Whiting, L. R. 1988. "The Television Renaissance in Extension Education." *Lifelong Learning* 11: 19–22.

18
Language Centers: Models and Caveats

June K. Phillips
Tennessee Foreign Language Institute

CENTERING IN ON CENTERS

The mid eighties have witnessed the growth on many campuses of "centers" with a variety of disciplinary and interdisciplinary focuses. Formerly, centers that maintained connections with language departments were associated primarily with Title VI Area Studies Programs. The new generation of foreign-language centers appears to have no standard definition; in fact, the actual use of the designation *center* has been studiously avoided on some campuses and terms such as *program, project,* or *institute* have been substituted. The center concept has also expanded beyond the single institution, with concomitant labels such as *consortium, collaborative,* or *alliance.*

Regardless of the label, the fact that a variety of institutions has given birth to foreign-language centers suggests that an impetus or motivation is at work that envisions a mission beyond that of the traditional department. Existing centers feature rather specific structures so that no two seem exactly alike. If models are being built, they remain at the stage of infancy; nevertheless, centers now exist in sufficient numbers that one can review their potential for departments at other institutions.

Given the newness of most centers on which this chapter focuses, it must be stated that the literature on centers is virtually nonexistent. Information gathered has been through personal contact with directors and through printed mission statements, brochures, descriptions in newsletters, and the like. Many centers are in a formative stage and are taking shape according to successful funding efforts and grants. A listing of identified centers, their directors, and their addresses is appended to this chapter; readers are encouraged to contact these individuals for additional and updated information. The list is not exhaustive, and new centers are in various stages of planning and implementation.

MOTIVATIONS FOR A "FOREIGN-LANGUAGE CENTER"

The reasons for which centers have been established differ greatly from institution to institution. Yet a common thread running through all models relates to the desire for greater visibility for the language teaching component of departments, greater opportunities for research, and greater chances for faculty interested in language teaching (as contrasted with literary pursuits) to obtain funding. The Center for Language Studies at Brown University states explicitly in its charge that it serves as "the intellectual center for language related research and knowledge by providing an academic 'home' for those faculty with scholarly interest in the teaching of language *quod* language and in interdisciplinary research that is pertinent to language studies" (Charge for the Center for Language Studies, 1987).

In the case of the Language Research and Development Project at the University of Michigan (Coffin 1990), the impetus came from the Applied Linguistics Committee of the College, which requested that the Dean of Literatures, Science, and Arts "construct a community" of those interested in language teaching. The mission of the project is to address all language needs, especially at advanced levels, and to carry out this mandate within a strong research base. The LRD Project studiously avoided the label *center* in order to differentiate its structure from the numerous centers on the campus.

In some cases the original motivation for a center arose from administrative concerns at universities where languages were dispersed among multiple departments. At The Ohio State University, with six separate language departments, the original chief tasks of the Foreign Language Center were (1) organizing and conducting placement testing for the large number of entering students; and (2) assuming responsibility for coordinating the growing teaching-assistant training program ("Foreign Language Center" 1988). The

University of Pennsylvania's Penn Language Center also works with some seven language departments to serve instructional needs not covered by regular offerings; much of the work of the Center involves research, instruction, and materials development in the less commonly taught languages *(Penn Language News* 1990).

The Center for French and Francophone Studies at Louisiana State University differs from the preceding in that the cultural roots the state nurtures with the French-speaking world provided the climate for outreach and awareness. The Center receives a portion of its funding from an endowment and uses its resources to sponsor speakers, symposia, and publications that foster the study of literature, culture, and pedagogy. The French Education Project is the pedagogical branch of the Center, and it has become nationally known for its activities in promoting and improving the teaching of French (Lafayette 1990).

The rationale for interdisciplinary centers and consortia resembles that established for single-institution centers. The desire to bring together those interested in language teaching as an area of scholarship and research, as distinct from the dominant and dominating role of literature as departmental focus, drives the consortia. Thus, the Consortium for Language Teaching and Learning, with its office at Yale University, seeks to "reaffirm the central importance of the study of foreign languages" among its eleven private research institutions (Patrikis 1988).

The driving issue in the Five College Foreign Language Resource Center was that of literally building centers where new technologies could be developed and materials collected. By pooling the resources of the five collaborating institutions, Amherst, Hampshire, Mount Holyoke, and Smith Colleges and the University of Massachusetts, a strong research and development effort was possible (Lyman-Hager 1990).

A consortium that predates most of the centers already mentioned is the Computer Assisted Language Learning and Instruction Consortium (CALICO). Founded in 1983, CALICO serves as an international clearinghouse for computer-assisted language instruction. Its goal is to unite those interested in specialized areas of technology and language through a membership structure open to individuals, institutions, and corporations (*Welcome to CALICO* nd).

THE MISSIONS OF THE CENTERS

A review of the mission statements of language centers confirms that they affirm strongly the language teaching/learning agenda from which they are derived. In some cases, the mission is research oriented, in others it promotes languages for special purposes or for special audiences. Service across language departments is a fairly consistent mission of centers. The Foreign Language Center at the Ohio State University describes its present mission as fivefold: research, instruction, testing, outreach, and publication. In all of these, it is both a coordinating body and a body that can focus on issues common to all the language groups, such as the use of technology, sponsorship of a conference, or materials development in less commonly taught languages ("Foreign Language Center" 1988).

Likewise, at the University of Hawaii at Manoa, The Second Language Teaching and Curriculum Center's mission includes that of providing curriculum development services, supporting faculty in second-language research and teaching, sharing information on faculty's activities, and disseminating current news on research on language teaching (Second Language Teaching and Curriculum *Newsletter* 1990).

At the University of Michigan, the Language Research and Development Project was mandated to serve not only the language departments but also the professional schools (Coffin 1990). Similarly, at UCLA the Language Resource Program maintains strong links with the university's International Studies and Overseas Program (ISOP). The Language Resource Program sponsors many special-purpose language courses (e.g., Spanish for Social Welfare Workers) and facilitates collaborative programs between the Applied Linguistics Department and language departments, area studies centers, professional schools, and institutions overseas (Campbell 1988).

The French Education Project at LSU (a center within a center) states its mission in terms of improvement of the teaching of French in schools. No other center indicates this degree of outreach to precollegiate education, although a number list outreach among their objectives. The FEP seeks to carry out these goals by addressing five major areas: initial certification of teachers, in-service education, maintenance of a resource center, research, and graduate programs (Lafayette 1990).

Another mission, whether stated or implied, of any center is its participation in grant writing for externally and internally funded projects. There is strength in numbers, especially where dollars are at issue; the center can become an attractive administrative hub for seeking and receiving grant monies. As we know, success breeds success, and expertise gained through fund-raising experience becomes self-perpetuating. The very existence of a center gives the grant writer an advantage in demonstrating institutional commitment, and the center or consortium is a viable vehicle already in place for carrying out a proposed project. University administration has an outlet for funneling to language teaching personnel matching funds, clerical support, or faculty release time when doing so through a department might pose problems of priority or "turf." Faculty members of one department can join forces with colleagues in others and become part of a larger grant submission or a more competitive one than could be sustained through an individual request. In a way, this is the humanist learning from the scientists who have effectively used research centers to attract specialized funding for a long time.

GOVERNANCE AND STAFFING

While the structures of the centers differ in specific details, there are a few commonalities. Most centers have a faculty director who tends not to be a current departmental chairperson. Most directors report to an administrator above the level of department chair, usually to a dean. The majority of the centers have advisory councils that formulate policy, give direction, or provide oversight; these councils or boards also represent departments, colleges, administration (including the development office), and often the business and government community. Most important, this representation, by reaching into disciplines other than foreign languages, maintains a broader mission than the departments would if the center were not a factor.

The Center for Language Studies at Brown University exemplifies the more flexibly structured side of the organizational spectrum. The CLS exerts no control over faculty, who retain appointment in their departments and who affiliate voluntarily with the Center according to their interests or projects. Administrative responsibility for the Center lies with a Director, appointed by the Provost upon recommendation of the Dean of the Faculty. The Director carries a full-time appointment to a department at the same time. There is a Coordinator, primarily charged with grant writing, plus one and one-half clerical positions assigned to the Center (Wrenn 1990). The Language Research and Development Project at the University of Michigan also depends primarily upon faculty who associate with the Project for special activities. The Director works part-time for the Project; permanent appointment is in a department. The request for a center was made to and accepted by the Dean for a three-year term, already renewed as a result of successful program funding by IBM (Coffin 1990).

The Foreign Language Center at The Ohio State University has a full-time Director, Assistant Director, and secretary all supported by hard money, that is, budgeted university funds. The Director and Assistant Director hold faculty appointments to a department, but all their time is devoted to the Center. Joint or visiting appointments are made for special projects and faculty may come from any of the language departments or programs represented on the Center's advisory committee. Governance is through the Dean of the College of Humanities, who provides principal funding (Ervin 1988).

The University of Hawaii at Manoa is unusual in that there is a College of Languages, Literatures, and Linguistics, which includes departments of English as a Second Language (ESL), European Languages and Literatures, and East Asian Languages and Literatures. Thus the Second Language Teaching and Curriculum Center is constituted as an academic support unit within this college and reports to its dean. The Center's Director is a faculty member appointed by the Dean with the agreement of an advisory committee composed of faculty interested in language teaching (Second Language Teaching and Curriculum *Newsletter* 1990).

The UCLA Language Resource Program receives its administrative support from the International Studies and Overseas Program, but its academic home lies in the Department of Applied Linguistics. Both a faculty-level Director and an administrative assistant serve half-time in the LRP; the Director's time is supported by a discretionary fund of the Chancellor; and the administrative assistant, research assistants, and students on work-study are supported through grants and contracts (Campbell 1988).

The Center for French and Francophone Studies at LSU has as its Director a Distinguished University Professor. His appointment is to the Center, which is housed in the Department of French and Italian. Within the Center is the French Education Project, which is administered through a Coordinator (who receives release time for work in the project) and through a full-time Attaché Linguistique supported by the Services Culturels Français. Both the Center and the Project have graduate student assistants and clerical help. The FEP's Coordinator holds a joint appointment to the departments of Curriculum and Instruction and French and Italian. Funding for the Project comes from the Center itself and from the Association pour la Promotion de l'Éducation et de la Formation à l'Étranger (Belgique), the Bureau de Québec en Louisiane, and the Services Culturels Français (Lafayette 1990).

The Consortium for Language Teaching and Learning has a very different structure, since it crosses institutional lines. Policy setting is achieved through a large Governing Board, which meets annually and is composed of three representatives from each of the eleven universities within the consortium: an academic dean, a language professional, and a staff member from the office of corporate and foundation relations. The seven-member Executive Council (three deans, three language professionals, and one staff member from development) acts for the Governing Board and also meets annually. The offices for the consortium are donated by Yale University; staff consists of an Executive Director and Coordinator and an assistant to the Director. Funding comes from major foundations (Patrikis 1988).

CALICO, a consortium with a topical mission concerning computer-assisted instruction, is housed at Brigham Young University. The Executive Director is a full professor in the Department of Linguistics and support staff and space are provided by the university and augmented by grant funding and membership fees. CALICO draws upon the expertise of faculty from across the nation through a system of advisors. There are eight SIGs (Special Interest Groups) and three committees (Journal, Symposium, Summer Institute) whose chairpersons assume responsibility for their topics in publications and at professional meetings of the consortium (*Welcome to CALICO* nd).

In sum, the trend for staffing and governance is for faculty to retain their appointment, rank, and tenure in their departments, although exceptions exist. This is true for those with administrative responsibilities in the center as well as for those who serve mainly by participation in center-related activity. Reporting structure for the centers usually bypasses the departmental chair and occurs at least at the dean's level; this is a natural outcome, since no center exists strictly within a single department. Staffing tends to be minimal, with one or two professional-level appointments and one or more clerical staff on hard money; expansion occurs as grant or project money, that is soft money, permits.

Activity:
The Contributions of the Centers

The major question for existing centers and for ones in a conceptualization stage is: What can the center do that a department does not or could not do? Answers to this question often reflect "willingness" rather than "possibility." Activities seem to coalesce around topics ranging from the concrete to the more affective.

On the concrete side, centers frequently take responsibility for institutional tasks that cross language department boundaries such as placement testing or teaching-assistant training. Externally, centers and consortia often assume the organizing role for conferences, publish newsletters, and conduct outreach programs to schools. While one area of activity purports to deal with research, focusing the research mission to give the center an identity has not occurred in most cases. Rather, we see centers supporting individual research interests for faculty through funds or in-kind resources. This activity, however, does not necessarily define a "research area" for the center itself or for its supporting institutions. A last point: although activities of centers become more abstract when one attempts to assess their ability to foster a better climate for faculty interested in language teaching/learning, this is an area clearly stated in missions and identified by advocates as a major benefit of the centers.

Coordination, Dissemination, and Outreach

In institutions that have a number of separate language departments, the center can certainly fulfill a coordinating function that avoids duplication of effort and facilitates reasonable program compatibility. With the center's assuming that role, it relieves an individual department from either the burden of serving all at its own expense or the benefit of doing so to the exclusion of colleagues. The likelihood of a better organized and a more efficient program results from a center's having both resources and responsibility for the "generic" duties associated with issues such as placement testing, teaching-assistant orientation, preparation and publication of brochures promoting languages, or even presenting the case for foreign-language study to the university community. It can also serve as a resource center for books and teaching materials useful to a number of departments and to teachers in the region. Information for students concerning options for language study, such as overseas programs and career opportunities, can be housed there as well.

Coordination   In this vein, examples of coordinating activities can be identified in current centers:

- Proficiency testing in the required sequence at the Language Research Center at the University of Pennsylvania

- Placement testing, TA training for approximately 100 students per year, and a brochure describing opportunities for foreign-language study at OSU at the Foreign Language Center of The Ohio State University

If the centers did not exist, these functions would revert to individual departments, probably with a great deal of duplication, which is particularly cumbersome for smaller departments. Furthermore, students tend to react positively to knowing that similar procedures for assessment are in place for the various languages or that information on language study and related matters is available at a central location.

Conferences and newsletters   Many centers use their resources to organize conferences either in the form of seminars for faculty or as meetings open to a wider audience. They also use newsletters as a means of communicating with colleagues and keeping them informed; the audience for these activities may be internal or external. Examples include the following:

- The Second Language Teaching and Curriculum Center at the University of Hawaii at Manoa publishes a newsletter that contains conventional announcements as well as summaries of books or conference sessions written by faculty for their colleagues. Annotated lists of resource materials available for loan from the SLTCC, a directory of grant opportunities, and information on Center activities are featured.

- *ISOP Intercom* is the UCLA newsletter produced by the International Studies and Overseas Program, and the Language Resource Program contributes to it. The newsletter highlights campus events and speakers from various disciplines with an international focus and includes lists of fellowship and grant opportunities for students and faculty.

- *Penn Language News,* a publication of the Penn Language Center, addresses students and faculty by highlighting Center activities in teaching and in research. The first issue alerted readers to the various resources in the computing office at the University of Pennsylvania, such as optical scanning, interactive video, and text archive searches.

- CALICO publishes a journal and a monograph series; it has also ventured into software production, including videodiscs.

- The Consortium for Language Teaching and Learning at Yale has no regular publication, but it provides data about language programs to constituents and disseminates results of funded projects. It has funded the development of an intermediate Chinese text at Princeton and held workshops on needed materials, especially for less commonly taught languages in the United States. The CLTL has sponsored conferences and published their proceedings; recent topics included governance of language teaching and learning programs, the role of language learning in an undergraduate liberal education, foreign-language acquisition research, and cross-disciplinary and cross-cultural perspectives on language study.

- The French Education Project at Louisiana State University has produced a survival kit for teachers of elementary school French through its Center for French and Francophone Studies. The Project also conducts colloquia and summer workshops and produces a newsletter, *La Plume du Tigre.*

- The University of Michigan's Language Research and Development Project has sponsored a number of technology fairs, speakers, and conferences on testing and topics that utilize its excellent language laboratory facilities.

- The Foreign Language Center at The Ohio State University hosts an annual conference, Research Perspectives in Adult Language Learning and Acquisition, with the cooperation of the *Modern Language Journal,* which considers the papers for publication.

This listing of activities of existing centers is strictly representational, not comprehensive, but it does point out that the centers promote significant activity in the domains of news dissemination and conferences. Could departments do this without centers? Probably, but the interdepartmental strengths outweigh the potential of a single department. The means for maintaining the momentum from conference to conference, or from issue to issue of newsletters, are available because personnel are assigned to that task as part of center responsibilities. In many cases the crossing of college boundaries, such as those between education and liberal arts at LSU, or the combining of programs and academic departments, as at UCLA, occurs because the center has a structure and mission that rises above the department level.

Course Development in the Center

Another key area of activity is the development of courses and course materials that meet special program needs. As interests expand beyond the commonly taught languages and beyond commonly taught topics at advanced levels (in the past, mostly literature), colleges and departments are faced with the question of whether to incorporate these into departmental offerings or to allow them to become the prerogative of other university entities. Critical questions arise in many institutions, particularly smaller schools: Does the faculty of French, German, or Spanish find a faculty line for Chinese, Korean, or Bahasa Indonesia? Are they willing to see advanced level coursework expand to teaching in the foreign-language content courses such as economics, political issues, or history, or do they prefer to remain with a literary organization of century, genre, and writer? How do language departments or sections with a small number of faculty, which is often the case with the less commonly taught languages (LCTs), retain credibility and visibility and compete for resources with the established language departments and their larger student enrollments? A center can often meet these needs in innovative ways without draining resources from departments.

Centers that have provided leadership in course development include the following:

- The University of Pennsylvania's Penn Language Center provides instruction in languages not covered by departments in the School of Arts and Sciences. It seeks to bring students to a level of intermediate competence. Languages administered by the Penn Language Center include: Classical Greek, Modern Greek, Latin, Swahili, Yiddish, Portuguese, Arabic, Biblical Hebrew, Korean, Persian, Turkish, Ukrainian, Gujarati, and Nepali. Expansion is planned for Czech, Lithuanian,

Malayalam, Panjabi, Sindhi, Tibetan, and Yoruba *(Penn Language News* 1990).

- The French Education Project at LSU offers a summer program of minicourses for school teachers, which may be taken for graduate, extension, or continuing education credits in French or in Education.

- The Language Resource Program at UCLA established a number of courses and programs through joint efforts of the Department of Applied Linguistics and the applicable language departments. As examples: Applied Linguistics and the Department of Spanish and Portuguese created a course in Spanish for Spanish speakers; Applied Linguistics and the Department of East Asian Languages developed a televideo class in intermediate Japanese and a course in Korean for Korean-Americans; Applied Linguistics and the School of Social Welfare offer a class in Spanish for professional social welfare workers.

Research Agendas

Certainly one way in which most centers hope to advance research is through the grant-seeking process. A secondary means is by providing a place to which faculty can be assigned for research projects, where they can tap into data and where they can collaborate in areas of expertise. In most cases, the interests of faculty drive the research agenda, although several centers plan to focus energies on research topics that fit in with institutional or funding priorities. Whereas much of the current research activity in centers must be characterized as formative at best, many are making progress in assigning value to language acquisition and language pedagogy as viable scholarly domains in literature-dominated departments and colleges.

Research activity at some of the centers includes the following:

- The Consortium for Language Teaching and Learning has a regranting authority wherein it funds directly proposals submitted by faculty from participating universities, preferably those that involve a benefit to several institutions within the consortium. Among projects with research elements are a cooperative effort at Harvard and Stanford on collaborative writing in French via modem, research on the informal acquisition of Japanese, and the design of a computer workstation for the humanities.

- The Foreign Language Center at The Ohio State University seeks to promote interdisciplinary research between the College of Humanities and the College of Education. One avenue suggested is that of having doctoral candidates in Foreign Language Education use the Center as an entity through which to coordinate empirical research on language teaching and acquisition. No specific evidence of joint research has been cited, and the Center has primarily dealt with institutionally driven research, for example, by evaluating the Computer-Adaptive Placement Test from Brigham Young University and the individualized language instruction program operational in several languages at OSU.

- The Language Research and Development Project at the University of Michigan builds upon the strong reputation of its language laboratory and a three-year IBM grant to develop and assess multimedia instruction in world languages.

- The UCLA Language Resource Program targets content-based language instruction as a central research area, because part of its mission concerns instruction within the university's cooperative programs for overseas and home-based students. It is also looking at issues such as the effect of telecommunications on instruction (Japan), computer-aided instruction (Mexico), and conservation of language (Korea).

- The Second Language Teaching and Curriculum Center at the University of Hawaii at Manoa has initiated "inquiry groups" that bring together faculty to explore research topics. This informal setting has identified areas in which faculty would like to collaborate; the dialog generated has also suggested potential areas for grant development. Currently, reading and listening comprehension have come to the fore as areas of shared faculty interest.

- The Penn Language Center supports research programs under its aegis and as a member of the Consortium for Language Teaching and Learning. The Center regularly sponsors Oral Proficiency Interview Testers' Workshops, applies a proficiency perspective to materials development (e.g., a new syllabus for Modern Standard Arabic), works with the Language Analysis Center at the University of Pennsylvania to integrate technology and linguistics, and encourages faculty members in a variety of independent research projects (*Penn Language News* 1990).

- CALICO's research is market-driven, because many of its projects are supported by soft money. An area of significant research and development for CALICO is that of technology-utilizing tests, interactive software, and courseware authoring systems.

At a meeting convened by the National Foreign Language Center in fall 1988 for directors of centers, a number of research questions were raised. Most attenders saw their centers as becoming more active in research after becoming more solidly established. Among future research interests discussed were: (1) content-based education; (2) second languages for special clientele (e.g., nontraditional, special needs, ethnic populations); (3) high technology and language learning; (4) advanced skills; (5) overseas focus; (6) testing; (7) language retention; (8) learning styles; and (9) factors that make language-learning centers effective. Clearly this is a continuing agenda that will require time for implementation.

Improving the Climate for Language Teaching/Learning Pursuits

In any discussion of the reasons for which centers were founded, their missions, goals, or outcomes, the ever-present dissonance experienced in so many colleges and universities between the belle-lettrists and the language teaching faculty sounds loud and clear. In spite of the fact that in many places faculty teach courses in both literature and language, the dichotomy continues to divide departments. The effect is felt most keenly on issues of promotion and tenure. Departments, and often deans, caught up in the throes of these divisive forces, look to the new "center" concept as a means of providing opportunity for teaching faculty to produce scholarship that might be recognized by their senior colleagues.

The ultimate success of centers in achieving parity for faculty will depend upon the quantity and quality of scholarly activity these groups can generate in the next few years. In the meantime, the centers can be credited with having created a positive environment for faculty with language teaching interests through the conferences, workshops, symposia, projects on materials development, and newsletters they have organized and produced.

NATIONAL, STATE, AND OTHER GOVERNMENTAL CENTERS

The main thrust of this article concerns the relationship of foreign-language centers and departments, but it might be useful to take a brief look at centers that are not institutionally connected.

The National Foreign Language Center was established in 1986 with headquarters in Washington, D.C., but administratively it is part of The Johns Hopkins University. The NFLC is funded primarily through four private sources: The Exxon Education Foundation, the Ford Foundation, the Andrew

W. Mellon Foundation, and the Pew Memorial Trusts. It sees its principal mission as the formulation of public policy. Staffing of the NFLC includes a Director, several Deputy Directors, some scholars on short-term appointments, and other researchers on fellowships as soft money permits. There is a National Advisory Council, which consists of individuals from business, government, philanthropic organizations, education, and the universities.

Several initiatives of the National Foreign Language Center hold relevance for language departments at higher education institutions. The Mellon Fellowship program supports faculty undertaking empirical research in second-language pedagogy for a year, a semester, or for shorter projects during the summer. Both individual and collaborative research proposals are considered. The NFLC has convened a number of meetings to discuss issues of concern to the language teaching community; these have included forums on campus-based foreign-language centers, on foreign-language instruction at liberal arts colleges, and on developing less commonly taught languages. The NFLC sponsors publication of a newsletter and of invited submissions to its Occasional Papers, and it has received funding for several surveys, results of which will influence departments directly and indirectly in their potential for policy setting. Through its resident research faculty and Mellon Fellows, it has been having an impact on commonly taught and less commonly taught languages alike.

In 1990, after a competitive proposal process, the United States Department of Education designated three centers as National Foreign Language Resource Centers (NFLRC): the University of Hawaii at Manoa, San Diego State University, and Georgetown University/Center for Applied Linguistics. Each NFLRC has proposed specific missions within the general charge of improving the teaching and learning of foreign languages.

The University of Hawaii at Manoa is building upon the activity of its existing Second Language Teaching and Curriculum Center, and its NFLRC will support a fellowship program to bring internationally known professors to the University of Hawaii and an intern program for teachers of Indo-Pacific languages.

The Language Acquisition Research Center (LARC) at San Diego State University was established in 1987 with a major financial commitment from the university. The designation as an NFLRC will enable it to expand its program significantly. Current and proposed projects include investigating video stimuli in oral proficiency testing; evaluating and developing interactive courseware; and training instructors in improved methods of teaching languages (Robinson 1990).

It must be noted that at both San Diego State University and the University of Hawaii at Manoa the prior establishment of a foreign-language center within a college was a key ingredient in their successful competition for major federal funding and for a greatly expanded regional and national presence.

The third NFLRC results from a joint proposal by Georgetown University and the Center for Applied Linguistics. Under this arrangement, CAL will be a subcontractor to Georgetown. The GU / CAL Center will conduct basic research on second-language acquisition and language-learner strategies, develop proficiency-based tests for commonly and less commonly taught languages, provide workshops to train teachers in proficiency testing and the use of technology, expand the database of the Survey of Materials for the Study of the Less Commonly Taught Languages, and widely disseminate information through the Georgetown Roundtable on Languages and Linguistics (GURT) and CAL's Educational Research Information Clearinghouse (ERIC). This Center's cooperative agreement provides two already strong entities with the potential to make even greater impact in the future (Stansfield 1990; Thompson 1990).

The Tennessee Foreign Language Institute was created by the 1986 Tennessee state legislature with a mission to education as well as to business and government. Foreign-language departments at universities in the state supported the initiative and have cooperated in numerous ways with the Institute. The Institute has an Executive Director and a staff assistant, with additional staffing based on soft money. A Board governs the TFLI, and the agency's report structure is to the Board, the state legislature, and the governor. In terms of relationships with existing departments, the Institute seeks to conduct projects that are collaborative in nature and permit involvement of faculty with appropriate interests or credentials. Thus, a federally funded summer project for elementary teachers was held on one campus with faculty coming from three institutions. Another federal project involved collaboration among the TFLI, an urban public school, and departments in two colleges at a state university. A grant-writing workshop was sponsored by the Institute for all language departments in the state, both public and private.

A number of states are looking at these models and other ways of promoting international education. Departments should be vigilant to ensure that a foreign-language component is included in these programs, for, in the past, government has been known to attempt internationalizing without including world languages. Furthermore, foreign-language professionals must make the case for the academic side of language learning to balance the false, but widely held, belief of the community that economic competitiveness can be achieved by spending "30 minutes a day" on foreign-language learning. When foreign languages are highlighted in these broader centers, the ensuing opportunities for faculty to engage in research, teaching, materials development, and outreach result in greater visibility for the profession. Examples of other state initiatives include: The California International Studies Project, the

Corporation for Indiana's International Future (Becker 1989/90), and Florida's House of Representative's Advisory Council on International Education.

Guidelines and Caveats

As universities see an increase in foreign-language centers, many departments will be faced with addressing the rationale for establishing one on their campus or of joining a consortium. Factors that operated to found those described in this chapter continue to influence administrators and to attract a number of faculty. The following guidelines may be useful in the conceptualization stage.

Motivations

It would be useful for departments to consider existing conditions on the campus. If a number of those listed below play a role, a foreign-language center might be a way of dealing with them:

- The university has multiple language departments that would benefit from a center's playing a coordinating role for common language-based issues.

- Strong divisions exist between faculty with primary responsibility or interest in language teaching and those in literature. A center might play a supportive role for scholarship and research with a pedagogical focus.

- Course development at the advanced level for students with interests other than literary or linguistic (international education, history, architecture, engineering), expansion into less commonly taught languages, or courses for in-service teachers are not presently provided in the departments' programs. A center might be a vehicle for creating and offering such courses.

- Pressure emanates from higher administration for more interdisciplinary service or for research and innovation that broadens the departments' mission from traditional skills and literature. A center could provide the impetus for piloting courses and serve as a temporary home until attitudes in the departments become more accommodating.

- Current efforts at obtaining funds for foreign-language projects would be enhanced through a center or through a consortium with like-minded faculty on sister campuses within a system or in colleges with some commonality of interests.

- High interest by some faculty on a given topic such as technology, study abroad, or nontraditional learners could be encouraged by opportunities for research and practice in a center or through a consortium.

Mission and Expectations

It is important that a realistic mission be established for the center or consortium at the outset and that procedures for assessing the success of the endeavor be thought out in advance:

- The mere existence of the center does not automatically ensure that outside funding will accrue, that collegiality will improve, that research will take root and grow, or that the broader student community will flock to courses.

- The mission should also have enough flexibility to adjust to priorities established in competitive grants and program shifts at the institution.

Organizing Procedures, Governance, Staffing

Should the decision to establish a center be taken, a number of procedural questions must be addressed:

- The level of support from the institution and the expected level from outside sources must be established. This includes assigning of academic personnel such as directors, assistant directors, or graduate students; and the portion of their time dedicated to service in the center must be precisely defined. Clerical support sufficient to maintain ongoing activity must be balanced with soft-money support for special projects. The term of the center must be established along with preconditions for continuance; that is, does the center become dependent upon outside money after a given period, or will an institutional budget line be continued?

- Governance structure must delineate lines of report and evaluation, role and make-up of an advisory council, and responsibilities of center staff.

- Budget outlines and projections must address issues of space, equipment, resources, and salaries. Provisions for handling grant monies and indirect costs should be established in advance. Authority for spending and contracting by the center must be specified.

Cautions and Concerns

Even with a fairly short history to date and a relatively small number of operating centers, one can urge that departments move cautiously and thoughtfully when considering such an undertaking. Establishing a center to resolve issues of collegiality seems a drastic step and, even worse, one that can probably not solve problems of promotion or tenure by itself. A center does have the capacity for enhancing the academic environment so that faculty with the ability and desire to conduct research or improve teaching of languages receive more support for their efforts.

Centers lend themselves to the enthusiasm of advocates, who may be administrators, philanthropists, businesspeople, or government leaders with a wish to improve language teaching and the availability and range of programs. Frequently, their dreams stretch beyond the resources they provide, and the result is understaffing or underbudgeting. Then the "center" will have been deemed a failure when, in reality, the necessary support was never solidly in place.

Finally, as the profession cries out for more research of an empirical nature, most centers remain at a stage where research is more contemplated than completed. The research agendas delineated by centers are lengthy; their research results are sparse. This occurs for a variety of reasons, not least among them the fact that the majority of the faculty in the language teaching profession have minimal background in second or foreign-language acquisition research, and it is really improvement of instruction and materials development and use that many of them are pursuing.

CONCLUSION

For further, more specific information on centers, readers are encouraged to make direct contact with individuals involved with those that have been discussed. No model fits itself exactly to any institution other than the one that generated it; at the same time, elements of these models should be applicable to others, and over time some centers may well serve as prototypes as they take final form. The decision to establish a center should not be taken in haste in response to a transitory problem. The center has the potential for accruing greater financial benefits to departments and for generating research and outreach, but some initial investment will also be required. If it is to succeed, it must evolve from careful consideration of existing conditions and aspirations, and the missions of the departments.

REFERENCES

"Foreign Language Center Established at Ohio State." 1988. *AATF National Bulletin* 13,4: 15.

Becker, J. 1989/90. "International Education." *Educational Leadership* (December–January): 89–90.

Blumenthal, A. L. 1970. *Language and Psychology.* New York: Wiley.

Campbell, R. N. 1988. Discussion at meeting at NFLC.

Charge for the Center for Language Studies. 1987. Brown University. [Mimeo.]

Coffin, E. A. 1990. Telephone communication.

Ervin, Gerard. 1988. Discussion at meeting at NFLC.

Foreign Language Study at The Ohio State University. Brochure.

Lafayette, R. C. 1990. Telephone communication.

Lyman-Hager, M. A. 1990. "Development of the Five College Foreign Language Resource Center." *CALICO Journal* (June): 39–47.

Patrikis, P. C. 1988. Discussion at meeting at NFLC.

Penn Language News 1. 1990.

Robinson, G. 1990. Letter.

Second Language Teaching and Curriculum *Newsletter* 1,1–2 (1990).

Stansfield, C. W. 1990. Fax, October 24.

Thompson, R. 1990. Letter.

Welcome to CALICO. n.d. Brochure.

Wrenn, J. 1990. Telephone communication.

APPENDIX 18A:
FOREIGN LANGUAGE CENTERS

CALICO
Brigham Young University
3078 JKHB
Provo, UT 84602
(801) 378-7079
Frank Otto, Executive Director

Center for Language Studies
Brown University
Box E
Providence, RI 02912
(401) 863-2895
James J. Wrenn, Director

**The Consortium for Language
Teaching and Learning**
111 Grove Street
P.O. Box 2497 Yale Station
New Haven, CT 06520-2497
(203) 432-0590
Peter C. Patrikis, Executive Director

Foreign Language Center
The Ohio State University
155 Cunz Hall
Millikin Road
Columbus, OH 43210-1229
(614) 292-4361
Ivan Dihoff, Acting Director

**Foreign Language Education
and Testing**
Center for Applied Linguistics
1118 22nd Street NW
Washington, DC 20037
(202) 429-9292
Charles W. Stansfield, Director

French Education Project
Louisiana State University
202 Peabody Hall
Baton Rouge, LA 70803
(504) 388-6662
Robert C. Lafayette, Coordinator

**Georgetown University/
Center for Applied Linguistics**
School of Languages and Linguistics
ICC 303
Georgetown University
Washington, DC 20057
(202)687-6045
Richard Thompson, Director

**Language Acquisition
Resource Center**
College of Arts and Letters
San Diego State University
San Diego, CA 92182-0230
(619) 594-6588
Gail Robinson, Director of Research
and Development

**Language Research and
Development Project**
University of Michigan
3083 Frieze Building
Ann Arbor, MI 48109
(313) 764-0314
Edna Amir Coffin, Director

Language Resource Program
University of California, Los Angeles
405 Hilgard, 11250 Bunche Hall
Los Angeles, CA 90024
(213) 825-2510
Russell N. Campbell, Director

The National Foreign Language Center at The Johns Hopkins University
1619 Massachusetts Avenue NW
Washington, DC 20036
(202) 667-8100
Richard D. Lambert, Director

Penn Language Center
University of Pennsylvania
651 Williams Hall
Philadelphia, Pennsylvania 19104
(215)898-6039
Michael Lenker, Director

Second Language Teaching & Curriculum Center
University of Hawaii at Manoa
Webster Hall; 2528 The Mall
Honolulu, HI 96822
(808) 956-2795
Robert Bley-Vroman, Director

Tennessee Foreign Language Institute
1620 Parkway Towers
State of Tennessee
Nashville, TN 37243-0840
(615) 741-7579
June K. Phillips, Executive Director

19
Ten Principles of Interactive Language Learning and Teaching[1]

Wilga M. Rivers
Harvard University

We set out from the assumption that languages are difficult to learn and no less difficult to teach. —H. H. STERN (1983)

There is much stale air in language classrooms. Typically, when our class is assembled, we close the door, even lock it against latecomers. There is a big, wide world out there for whose inhabitants language is a living, pulsating thing—ever-changing, ever-adapting, and indispensable for human activity. Language is the expression of communal life. Bees have language; cats, dogs, and birds have language. Human language has enabled us to build societies, keep our heritage, and plan for the future. As language teachers we must make our classrooms microcosms of life, with real relationships and purposeful use of language. All our techniques should be directed toward achieving this goal.

As I reflected on these facts about language and language use, I began to think about what to me, and to many other teachers of language, are basic beliefs about effective learning and teaching in formal situations. This process led to the elaboration of *ten principles of interactive language learning and teaching,* which we must keep in mind if our classes are to become really communicative.

It has been said that we cannot teach a language—students learn a language. This is very true and is basic to an understanding of the Ten Principles. It is time, however, to rehabilitate the term *teaching* so that its definition no longer reflects all that is most authoritarian, imperious, and manipulative in the teacher–student relationship. Teaching is an art and a craft of great antiquity and high honor throughout the world. One may throw fresh light on the mysteries of its influence and success through such paraphrases of *teacher* as "facilitator of learning," but these terms merely describe the process of helping people draw from a deep well of knowledge and understanding to which the teacher already has some access. Language learning and language teaching may be seen as one interactive process: the teacher's work is to foster an environment in which effective language learning may develop. In so doing, the teacher also learns many things. Seneca observed that "while we teach we learn."[2] The teacher is a learner and the learner is a teacher. In the words of an old proverb, "who is too old to learn is too old to teach." It is this interaction of teaching and learning that successful teachers have always understood. It is vividly represented by the use in the French language of one verb, *apprendre,* for both teaching and learning. This reciprocal use of the terms *teaching* and *learning* is basic to the discussion of the Ten Principles.

PRINCIPLE ONE:
The student is the language learner

As early as 1836, W. von Humboldt had concluded that no one can really teach a language; one can only present the conditions under which it will develop spontaneously in the mind in its own way.[3] Bronson Alcott maintained that we should "teach nothing that pupils cannot teach themselves."[4] This radical paradox, so applicable to language teaching, is echoed by Gattegno (1972), who observes that in teaching we are nurturing inner criteria in learners that enable them to advance in their learning. "Only self-education," he says, "will lead any learner to the mastery of a skill" (pp. 31–32).

In learning a language, each learner must acquire and consolidate mental representations that are basic to both understanding a language and expressing oneself through it (whether in speech or writing). We know that people possess even their native language to differing degrees and levels of control and operate differently in the way they use language to serve their purposes. In teaching a language, we are facilitating the individual's acquisition and increasingly fluent use of the language in the best ways we know. (Our ways of proceeding are often intuitive, since our ignorance at this point is great.) We can present clearly and provide opportunities for observing the language in use and for using the language, but only the learners themselves can assimilate the language and make it theirs. This they do in very individualistic ways, or do not do because they lack motivation to do so. For this reason, in an interactive approach, self and peer-to-peer consideration of errors is promoted. The students must realize that they are responsible for their own progress; they will take responsibility more seriously if they themselves discover and work at their own weaknesses.

Corollary 1: Motivation springs from within; it can be sparked, but not imposed from without

There is a misconception among some teachers that their task is to "motivate" their students. "My students are completely unmotivated," they complain. Corpses and mummies are "completely unmotivated," but every living being is motivated. One student may be motivated to get through each language class hour with the least personal hassle while acquiring the barest minimum of the language being studied; another may be motivated to get high grades by supplying what the teacher seems to be seeking on tests; yet another may be motivated to learn as much as possible of the language to achieve personal goals, which are not always those of the course or the teacher. The teacher's task is to discover the springs of motivation in individual students and channel this motivation, through course content and classroom activities, in the direction of language acquisition. (This approach is discussed further under Principle 2.) Frequently, the intrinsic attraction of the subject matter and the interest aroused by classroom activities will spark motivation to persist with language learning, until some degree of language control satisfying to the learner has been attained.[5]

PRINCIPLE TWO:
Language learning and teaching are shaped by student needs and objectives in particular circumstances

Student needs and objectives are not just personal. They are shaped to a considerable degree by societal pressures and political exigencies. These outside forces exert a largely subconscious influence on what are perceived as individual choices. One such subtle influence is that of career opportunities for the language learner, which are derived from social and political currents.

Another is the growing importance in public perception of certain speech communities at a particular point in time: Should our students be learning Japanese, Chinese, or Russian, for instance, instead of German? Or Spanish or Italian instead of French? Is it pointless and time-wasting for English speakers to learn any other language at this particular period in history? Factors such as these influence students' decisions and attitudes.

Language teachers must study the language learners in their classes— their ages, their background, their aspirations, their interest, their goals in language learning, their aptitude for language acquisition in a formal setting— and then design language courses that meet the needs of specific groups. Decisions on course content and orientation will affect the way the language will be presented and the types of materials that will be used.

Corollary 2: Language teaching and course design
will be very diverse

The days of a monolithic approach to a language course, imposed on all learners, are well past (or should be). As students and their perceived needs and objectives change, so will the content and techniques of language courses. In some countries, languages are still studied by an elite group of academically oriented students who are preparing for university or college entrance examinations written by academics whose main concern is the students' preparedness to enter their literature courses. There is much more to a language program than this.

In 1951 in Turkey, Buck cited the accusation against active, direct methods of language teaching that students were being taught to speak "comme des perroquets, en négligeant le côté intellectuel de l'enseignement" (1951: 30). This accusation has been repeated elsewhere in relation to other methodologies. Language courses, however, need not lack intellectual content. Language teachers are fortunate in that any kind of content (philosophical, literary, scientific, commercial, aesthetic) is appropriate for a language course, as long as it provides opportunities for contact with and use of the language.

Wherever there are enough students for diversification, several parallel courses or sections should be offered, allowing for student selection of content and approach. Should such diversity not be possible at each level for practical reasons, different contents and approaches should be available as the student advances through the language sequence (see chapters 1 and 2).

Let us be imaginative in devising course content and classroom activities to meet the needs of all comers.

PRINCIPLE THREE:
Language learning and teaching are based on normal uses of language, with communication of meanings (in oral or written form) basic to all strategies and techniques

Learning to use a language naturally requires much practice in using that language for the normal purposes language serves in everyday life. This is in contradistinction to the artificial exercises and drills on which so many language learners spend their time. A glance at some of the textbooks in common use will reveal that the situation today is not so different from that described by our Danish predecessor, Jespersen, in 1904. "By reading schoolbooks," he says, "one often gets the impression that Frenchmen [substitute Germans, Russians, Greeks] must be strictly systematical beings, who one day speak merely in futures, another day in passés définis, and who say the most disconnected things only for the sake of being able to use all the persons in the tense which for the time being happens to be the subject for conversation, while they carefully postpone the use of the subjunctive until next year" (1961: 17–18).

In normal interaction, people use language to give and get information; to explain, discuss, and describe; to persuade, dissuade, promise, or refuse; to entertain or to calm the troubled waters of social contact; to reveal or hide feelings and attitudes; to direct others in their undertakings; to learn, teach, solve problems, or create with words. There are many more such uses for language, in speech and writing. Suffice it to say that facility in conveying meanings in purposeful acts is the true end of language instruction. The most direct route to this end is to provide many opportunities to use language in communication within and outside the classroom from the earliest stages. Students learn to communicate in the form that natural interaction takes for speakers of the target language, which includes acquaintance with the structure of natural discourse within the culture—ways of opening and closing conversational interludes, ways of negotiating meaning and of asserting conversational control, of filling pauses, of interrupting or not interrupting, or of navigating so that the conversation is channeled in a direction of interest to the interlocutor (Allwright 1984: 156–71). Many of these features of natural interaction are related to the wider expectations within the culture, as discussed under Principle 10.

In our language classes, we prepare students to interact in normal ways by creating or simulating culturally authentic situations that stimulate them to communicate real meanings, thus preparing them to choose confidently and rapidly from the many possibilities within the language for expressing their intentions comprehensibly and acceptably in natural interaction.

Principle Four:
Classroom relations reflect mutual liking and respect, allowing for both teacher personality and student personality in a nonthreatening atmosphere of cooperative learning

Language teaching and language learning are distinctly different from other school disciplines. Speaking and writing what one really thinks and feels means revealing one's inner self: one's feelings, prejudices, values, and aspirations. Those new to a language can do this only in a roughly approximate, unnuanced way, that is, in a simplified form of language that is perhaps incorrectly formulated, so that they readily give a false impression of who they are (or would like people to think they are). This experience can be very inhibiting and ego-threatening, if not traumatic; students frequently seek to avoid it. They may also approach other people with lack of subtlety because of their ignorance of either certain nuances of the linguistic system or the associated pragmatics and cultural expectations.

In a highly structured methodology, like the grammar-translation method or the teacher-directed audiolingual approach, in which students perform according to instructions in a well-planned, emotionally neutral, and predictable sequence, students are protected from such wounds to self-esteem. Once a teacher tries, however, to stimulate interactive activities where more than the student's intellect and memory are involved, then the whole personality of the student comes into play. The language learning becomes, in Curran's terminology, a "unified personality encounter" (1976: 41). The student must now "establish," as Leontiev (1981) has put it, "an independent *communication activity*, . . . the aim of which is not the immediate satisfaction of concrete practical objectives, but the setting up of contact and mutual understanding, the establishment of interaction with the other members of his [or her] social group, . . . [impacting] on the knowledge, skills, system of social values (convictions), or emotions of another individual or group" (p. 23). There is now place for emotional hurt and embarrassment, even the hostilities that arise from frustration. The teacher must be aware of the many emotional factors in the encounter, which can either depress or exhilarate the student, depending on how they are handled.

An interactive language-learning environment requires that students and teachers, and students among themselves, reach a stage of being comfortable with each other, interested in each other, and respectful of each other's personal temperament-imposed limits. To achieve this equilibrium, teachers must feel comfortable with what they are doing, just as students must be comfortable with what they are expected to do. For students, the emotional threat comes as much from fear of the reaction of peers as the reaction of the teacher, so time should be allowed for peer-with-peer bonding and the development of mutual trust and confidence as students share enjoyable and successful experiences. Teachers need to develop a realistic understanding of their own strengths and weaknesses in interpersonal relations and allow themselves time to get to know their students. Both teachers and students have to be willing to take risks and laugh together when things go wrong. Together they must exorcise the fear of failure (as real for teachers as for students).

To stimulate the interaction that leads to communication via language, both teachers and students must work toward a nonthreatening atmosphere of cooperative learning. Cortese calls this "a sense of place . . . where people feel that they belong, that they are accepted" (1987: 37). This does not mean that teachers and students must be effervescently cheerful and amusing at all times. Some teachers, as well as some students, are reserved and take time to unbend with strangers. We like and respect people of widely varying personalities, and each has a contribution to make in a cooperative atmosphere. Not all students, nor all teachers, wish to interact with each other at a very deep level, and this attitude must be respected. If this is the case, we involve our students in surface activities—games, simulations, dramatizations, informative activities through which they communicate. For interaction at a deep personal level, students will find their own partners and arrange their own activities. Respect for the privacy of the individual to interact as he or she feels the need or desire is another aspect of cooperative learning. "In cooperative learning, all can succeed because each has something unique to contribute to the enterprise" (Rivers 1983: 78).

PRINCIPLE FIVE:
Basic to use of language are language knowledge and language control

Basic to language use is a mental representation of how language works.

All languages are organized at several levels (the phonological, syntactic, semantic, and pragmatic). Once we have learned the outlines of this organization (linguists are still seeking to systematize the details), we have a basis for the expression of an infinity of meanings. Grammatical structure and vocabulary, which are interrelated in their functioning, provide the tools for expressing semantic and pragmatic meaning. As Halliday expresses it: "Reality consists of 'goings-on': of doing, happening, feeling, being. These goings-on are sorted out in the semantic system of the language, and expressed through the grammar of the clause" (1985: 101).

A ballet dancer learns basic steps and then can fly. Scientists learn basic principles and can then build new knowledge: experimenting, applying, and thinking creatively. Scientists may not fully understand the principles (research is continuing), and their findings may even cast doubt on some of these or even cause them to restructure the basic framework, but the basic framework is there to be reinterpreted. Linguistic scientists continue to research linguistic structure. They may propose a distinctly new model to explain what is there, but they cannot restructure it; they can only reinterpret the operation of the basic framework or bone structure of the language.

Is the problem for language learning an inadequate or incomplete description of the linguistic structure of the language? People have learned languages for millennia while awaiting discovery and description of the ultimate adequate model, just as people have grown wheat and lit fires without a complete understanding of the processes underlying these phenomena. Language learners need a functional mental model of linguistic structure that works for producing, at a basic level, speech that communicates meaning, while they await final decisions on the structural model that will describe the actual inner workings of the basic framework.

We cannot use language without a mental representation, no matter how personal and idiosyncratic, of the basic framework or mechanism. (I shall call this *knowledge of language*.) Teachers can help students acquire an understanding of this basic mechanism that will enable them to use it to comprehend language and produce comprehensible speech. Teachers can also help their students refine this understanding as they progress. Without expert help, students will acquire some form of mental representation; with help, they will acquire more rapidly one that works for them more satisfactorily. Years of experience with learners of many languages in the Federal Institutes of the Interagency Language Roundtable have shown that, when language learners try to express their meanings freely without a firm structural framework, "*incorrect* communication strategies . . . fossilize prematurely," and "their subsequent modification or ultimate correction is rendered difficult to the point of impossibility, irrespective of the native talent or high motivation that the individual may originally have brought to the task" (Higgs and Clifford 1981: 74). Precise construction is important, however, for fluent expression of meanings that native speakers will understand.

Students acquire this precision of expression through performing rules, not through memorizing or discussing them. They acquire knowledge of the structure of the language actively through use. In this way it becomes part of the learner's mental equipment and can be called upon readily, if more and more without conscious focus, to express personal meaning or to comprehend and re-create the meanings others are trying to convey. It can also be reexamined consciously, should there be a need to reinterpret its potential. As

William James observed: "Experience is never yours merely as it comes to you, facts are never mere data, they are data to which you *respond,* your experience is constantly transformed by your deeds" (quoted in Rugg 1947, p. 91).

Sharwood-Smith (1981) expresses the necessity for performance practice succinctly when he says: "Whatever the view of the underlying processes in second language learning . . . it is quite clear and uncontroversial to say that most spontaneous performance is attained by dint of practice. In the course of actually performing in the target language, the learner gains the necessary control over its structures such that he or she can use them quickly without reflection" (p. 166). Recent experimentation in Sweden has demonstrated that this performance practice should be through student-initiated utterances (Ericsson 1986), which constitute student response to the data in James's sense and which gradually transform the student's mental representation.

Performing rules, then, provides the natural bridge to using these rules in creating personal messages. (I shall call this *control of language.*) Control of language necessarily includes the ability to understand messages and their full implications in the context, interpreting tone of voice, stress, intonation, and kinesics, as well as actual words and structures. Once students attain some degree of language control, they can use the language "as a medium which will engage [their] thought, perception, and imagination" (Leontiev 1981: 65).

The development of control of language is further discussed under Principle 6.

PRINCIPLE SIX:
Development of language control proceeds through creativity, which is nurtured by interactive, participatory activities

The ultimate goal for our students is to be able to use the language they are learning for their own purposes, to express their own meanings, that is, to create their own formulations to express their intentions. That use of language is creative, not imitative, has been emphasized by language-teaching theorists, linguists, and psycholinguists for years, yet many language teachers continue to teach as though imitation, repetition, and reconstruction or transformation of models were the be-all and end-all of language learning. In 1966 Chomsky drew our attention to the fact that "ordinary linguistic behavior characteristically involves innovation, formation of new sentences and new patterns" (p. 44). He succinctly alluded to this feature as "the creative aspect of normal language use" (p. 44). Belyayev (1963) maintained that "when using language, one is always dealing with new verbal formulations, irrespective of whether they are created by others or by oneself" (p. 29). And Blumenthal cites Wundt as stating in 1912 that "the mind of the hearer is just as active in transforming and creating as the mind of the speaker" (Blumenthal 1970: 37).

Creating new utterances in a language that one only partially controls is not easy. It frequently leads to cognitive overload: learners pause and hesitate (both phenomena of natural native speech); they misuse elements of the new language when they are well aware of the accepted forms; they self-correct or let it be, depending on the situation and the amount of time available (conversations veer off in different directions, depending on the comprehension of the interlocutor); they frequently feel embarrassed or humiliated by their poor showing and may give up their attempts because the effort is too great.

Yet one cannot acquire facility in expressing meanings in a foreign language without much experience in doing just that. Experience in expressing meanings requires interactive situations within which the students' motivation to communicate personal messages is stimulated.[6] The motivation is strengthened and maintained in situations where there is a low level of ego-threat and frustration. (See the discussion under Principle 4.) Through interactive activities, students experience the use of the new language as an important social skill, and success in conveying meanings and evoking a response encourages them to seek more success.

How does a teacher promote interaction? The teacher encourages participatory interactive activities that engage the students' attention so that they become involved, and frequently exhilarated, by activities that make them use the language. I use the word *encourage* because many of these activities may be student-initiated. When they are teacher-initiated, they should be student-sustained and student-developed. Purposeful and task-oriented, such activities are frequently conducted through peer-with-peer or small-group discussion and elaboration. Some object that mistakes are made in such activities, and this is true, but the experience in creating utterances that carry personal meanings and the confidence it engenders are vital to future autonomous language use. Students are encouraged to learn from their peers, with unobtrusive teacher assistance as they feel the need for it.

Activities may be amusing or serious. Games, competitions, skits, simulations, and dramatizations enliven the interaction; problem-solving and information-getting activities encourage persistence and probing and involve the intellectual skills of the students. Interactive activities may be related to content being studied in the language, whether literary, historical, philosophical, scientific, commercial, or sociological: For example, students may

- Work in groups to gather information

- Set up experiments

- Develop alternative dénouements for literary works to understand further the author's intent

- Use the case-study method for investigating legal or economic aspects of the society that uses the language

- Prepare meals according to the cuisine of a country where the language is spoken

- Engage in appropriate social activities of the culture

- Develop plays, radio or television programs, soap operas, or videos

- Write poems that they then discuss with each other

- Prepare entertainments for other students, parents, or the community

In these ways students learn by doing.[7]

PRINCIPLE SEVEN:
Every possible medium and modality are used to aid learning

Carroll (1966) made the point that "the more numerous kinds of association that are made to an item, the better are learning and retention" (p. 105). In communicative interaction, language learners need to draw on all kinds of unpredictable items to express their meaning—items they learned the previous day, even items they learned on the first day they had contact with the language. What they have learned of the language must then be firmly established in memory with many associative triggers so that it becomes readily available, in some cases for recognition in speech or writing and in others for retrieval for active use.

Context is an important factor in recall as well as a guide to possible and appropriate meanings. Context, it must be remembered, may be linguistic or nonlinguistic; aural, visual, kinesic, olfactory, or tactile; situational; and even emotional. Language teaching or learning that restricts itself to presentation and practice in one modality (for example, the visual in a traditional grammar-translation approach or the aural-oral in a conservative audiolingual approach) does not prepare the learner for the full array of contexts in which items may recur. For these reasons, interactive learning needs to draw on every possible type of experience to reinforce what is being learned. Among these experiences are physical response, aural input, reading materials, written expression, the act of drawing what is meant, the manipulation of objects (in the Pestalozzian tradition), interpretation of pictures, the acting out of scenes, music, song, dance, purposeful tasks (such as making things or preparing and eating them), gestures, facial expressions, and so on. Gattegno (1972) emphasizes the importance of breathing and kinesics; Lozanov, the suggestive impact of paintings and music,[8] and Curran (1976) calls for the involvement of the "whole person."

At the present time, it is much more possible for the learner to have a well-rounded experience of the language: to see, hear, and live it in all kinds of ways. Teachers are no longer limited to the book, the chalkboard, their own vocal apparatus, an occasional picture or chart, and a few objects to be handled to bring a sense of reality and a broader context to the elements of the language and how they combine to create meanings. First came the disc, then radio, film, the telephone, television, magnetic tape, videocassettes, ready availability of foreign-language newspapers and magazines, and now audio and visual material beamed by satellite and computer software that may be integrated with videodisc—each new medium has presented additional opportunities for teachers to provide multiple associations with language as used by native speakers and insights into their ways of thinking and reacting, as well as opportunities for students to view and hear themselves as they attempt to use the language in authentic ways.

In 1921 Palmer, that most enduring of methodologists, advocated that "we select judiciously and without prejudice all that is likely to help us in our work." He called this "the multiple line of approach" (p. 141). Now is the time for teachers to investigate, experiment, and use judiciously the many possibilities for increasing language impact for the learner and for enabling their students to interact with speakers of the language (in actuality or vicariously) in order to increase their motivation to communicate. Now even autodidacts and students far from their teachers (distance learners) can have access to many of the same advantages for language contact as those in more formal situations.

All is not sunshine and light in language-learning land, however. Much that is available ostensibly to "help us in our work" does not promote or encourage the interaction that leads to communication through language. A great deal of attention, time, and energy need to be devoted to what passes over the airwaves or is stored on disc, film, or cassette. "Garbage in, garbage out" is still as true as it ever was. Teachers need to reflect very carefully on how to use this almost mesmerizing quantity of materials so as to ensure that it increases opportunities for learning and improves quality of learning.

Before acquiring new materials, teachers need to consider three questions.

• Will these materials fit in with the aims and approach of my course?

- Will they enhance language learning in ways that less expensive materials cannot?

- Am I prepared to devote the time and energy necessary to incorporate them effectively into my course?

PRINCIPLE EIGHT:
Testing is an aid to learning

Testing has so often been punitive. Students become very nervous about tests, which as often as not seek to uncover what students do not know or cannot immediately recall, rather than providing them with an opportunity to demonstrate to the examiners and themselves what they can do with the language. *"Chercher la petite bête"* is a very illuminating expression in French that can well be applied to the attitude of test writers who concentrate on the minutiae of the language rather than the broader aspects of comprehensible and acceptable language use. (Why otherwise do teachers need answer keys to help them correct tests?)

First of all, then, tests should concentrate on enabling students to demonstrate what they can do with whatever level of language they possess. In this way, the test is a guide to the student, as well as the teacher, as to what has really been assimilated so that it is available for some form of realistic use. The test becomes an aid to learning, not an intentionally tricky hurdle.

Next, the test itself should be a learning experience that is part of the ongoing course. If the test acts as a guide to the student (and the teacher), then it cannot be final. The student goes on to relearn and consolidate what has been found to be lacking or misunderstood, and then retests (not "is retested") to see how the learning is progressing. Opportunities should be provided for students to relearn and then retake tests to inform themselves, as well as the teacher, about how well they now understand or can use the language.[9] In brief, the test stimulates further learning.

That the test should reflect the objectives of the course (which, as discussed in Principle 2, already reflect the objectives of the student) cannot be overemphasized. For too long we have taught and students have learned one thing while the test has concentrated on another, because we preferred a kind of test that was easy to prepare and correct, thus putting large groups through the same wringer for our own convenience. Even in cases where the teaching seems to be congruent with the testing, this may be because the form of the test is already familiar to the teacher and the students and has been allowed to dominate the design of the course. Consequently, the teaching and learning are directed first and foremost toward preparing students to perform well on the test, with scant attention paid to their linguistic needs or to creative use of language. Expedience is thus put before educational objectives.

Finally, the test should be interesting. Students should enjoy taking the test. If thought is given to creating a test that involves students in working out interesting problems, comprehending and reacting to stimulating ideas, expressing their own ideas (or at least producing original utterances), and in taking the initiative in some way related to the interactional nature of the preceding learning, then the test will be motivational and a means of growth for the students. This approach to testing will reduce the emotional and stressful element that discriminates against students of certain temperaments when faced with the once-for-all, future-determining character of much present-day testing.

Can student-centered testing be conducted for large groups (across sections in large institutions, across a number of schools in a local area, or for all students of a certain level in national examinations)? A more appropriate question would be: Is there genuine educational value in wide-scale impersonal testing?

PRINCIPLE NINE:
Language learning is penetrating another culture; students learn to operate harmoniously within it or in contact with it

Language and the cultural values, reactions, and expectations of speakers of that language are subtly melded. Gattegno (1972) brings this out when he says that "only when one is really imbued with the literature or soaked in the environment of the people using the language can one express oneself in speech or writing as a native would. It is the spirit of a language that has to get hold of one's mind" (p. 20). Not even consciously realized by the culture-bearers themselves, these values, expectations, and presuppositions frequently pass unperceived by the learners of the language, who bumble and fumble their way through relations and contacts with native speakers quite unaware of their cultural faux pas and unintentional offensiveness. Plunged into the culture, they suffer from depressing shock and stress and confidence-destroying frustrations that affect their ability to interact harmoniously with those with whom they come in contact. Frequently they end up loving the language but hating its users. As Cortese (1987: 32) expresses it,

> If the social compact requires the observation of pretty, polite tech-
> niques for the avoidance of conflict [these are frequently taught to the

learner] it is also, at a deeper level, built on negotiation of and respect for individual values and traits. It is to this level that a formative language learning process must reach, both in the sense of helping the individual to shape his [or her] own values and in the sense of comprehending different value orientations.

This type of learning, she says, distinguishes "production performance" from the mere "imitation of politeness norms" (p. 32).

While seeking to understand from her own experiences what brought about ease of interaction in new social and cultural situations, Robinson (1985) developed four principles:

1. On a one-to-one basis, the differences between people divided them, the commonalities brought them together.

2. Understanding, in the sense of smooth interaction, was probably least affected by awareness of how people were going to act, or the ability to anticipate culturally different events. Understanding happened through all modes of perception [physiological, emotional, kinesthetic, tactile, as well as cognitive].

3. . . . The new cultural experiences were not "add-ons." They seemed to be interpreted through and integrated with the learner's previous experience.

4. Understanding—getting over the barriers to communication—. . . took time. (pp. 3–5)

To help students operate harmoniously within another language and culture requires more than talk about cultural differences. Bringing out cultural similarities combats stereotypes more effectively than focusing on differences (Robinson 1985: 71). We develop the students' ability to interact initially with those who are linguistically and culturally different by teaching social amenities that oil wheels and open doors of acceptance (Cortese's pretty politenesses), but these merely provide opportunities to advance further in understanding. As we proceed, we need to understand culturally diverse interaction styles (Robinson 1987: 141–54), and, in many cases, adopt them ourselves, if our progress is not to be arrested. We need to learn different pragmatic routines, ways of opening and closing conversations, taking turns, and so on.

As we come into closer contact with the other culture through these outer doors, we begin to understand patterns of beliefs and behavior and recognize that what may appear to be exotic, discrete acts or ways of expressing oneself are in fact manifestations of societal features (such as recognition of a hierarchy of respect; rejection of discriminatory distinctions; dislike of vanity, bombast, or servility; deep-seated needs for individualistic expression or, contrariwise, a tendency to take refuge in group conformity). These reactions, even in the form of verbal formulas, cannot be learned piecemeal; they need to be acquired in culturally probable situations. They may be observed in films, plays, novels, soap operas, or radio talk shows, as well as in newspapers or magazines, when actually living and working with native speakers is not possible. Interactive practice is supplied through the acting out of problem situations within the culture. Students work out possible, culturally appropriate solutions as they are interacting, facing up to the unpredictable as native speakers might do. Later discussion brings out areas of cultural understanding and misunderstanding that surfaced during the interaction.[10]

Through attempting to understand the cultural-linguistic behavior of others, we come to understand our own value systems and culture-laden language use. As a result, we emerge enriched as we broaden our experience of human ways of thinking and behaving; we develop a tolerance for difference, even within apparent similarity; and we learn to interact harmoniously and comfortably with others from different backgrounds, within our own and other societies, without confusion of our own sense of identity.

Such a result does not come of itself. It requires hard work, hard thinking, and persistence on the part of both teacher and learner.

Principle Ten:
The real world extends beyond the classroom walls; language learning takes place in and out of the classroom

"Language is a natural function of human association," according to Dewey (1925: 179). Consequently, the more opportunities for human association with speakers of the language, presumably the more potential for growth in control of language for normal uses and spontaneous expression. Second-language teachers and bilingual teachers with interactive aims have already been creating opportunities to strengthen language learning through arranging contacts between second-language learners and the native-speaker community surrounding them. They arrange for host families to invite foreign students for holidays and family festivities. They set up interview assignments that help their students overcome their diffidence and nervousness so that they can talk with native speakers in a purposeful way. They send students out to discuss prices and the quality of goods in shops or to use the telephone to inquire about a local sports club or the availability of videocassettes for rental. They take them to local restaurants, the bank, or the post office. They request reports on films, television shows, or radio broadcasts (ranging from commercials or news hours to sitcoms or soap operas). They encourage their students from overseas to give talks to local service clubs or in schools.

This kind of immersion in the "real world" has generally been considered impossible for foreign-language learners, who have remained inside their classrooms behind closed doors—taking an occasional peek at the passing crowd if the windows are not placed too high. Need this continue to be the situation? As the world opens up through travel, technology, and shared interests, the advantages second-language learners can enjoy are being taken more and more seriously as options for all language learners.

In most communities, a little searching will lead to the discovery of some native speakers (expatriates, spouses, exchange students, business executives and their families, or newly arrived immigrants) in the environs. Where there has been immigration, another source is the retirement community or old people's home. Sometimes these older speakers of the language are isolated and lonely and are reverting gradually to monolingualism. The "Adopt a Grannie" idea, which has proved so successful in social work, might be adopted here, as well as the fostering of phone friendships with elderly speakers of the language or shut-ins. Sometimes students can help monolingual speakers of the language with filling out forms or getting information.

In Clyne's book on second-language classes in Victorian schools, Kipp (1986) reports that motivation to speak the language being learned was dampened among students by the lack of a "sizeable native [second-language] speaking peer group either inside or outside the school environment." Where there was a local community of speakers of the language, second-language learners enjoyed contacts that were readily available to them but did not actively search for further language speech partners (pp. 104–5). These facts emphasize the need for the teacher's leadership in assigning projects that will be integrated into classwork, so that students enjoy a sense of achievement after all their effort. Students whose motivation is stimulated by a language-related assignment or group project will ferret out opportunities to use the language that the teacher did not dream were available. But there must be some incentive such as a project to research some subject (an elderly person's early education, a migrant's memories of "old country" customs) that will be presented to the class, be reported in the school or local newspaper, or form part of a group writing project on unusual features of the local community for eventual dissemination within and beyond the school. Where there are no such resources, the community is contacted from a distance—through pen pals; tape pals; twinned classrooms; sister city projects; a commercial campaign ("France" or "Italy in Our Town" at the department store); or language camps where teachers from different schools become the "native speakers" for the weekend.

Opportunities now extend to videos and satellite broadcasts. We must seize every imaginable opportunity for taking the language (and its learners) out of the classroom, vicariously or in reality.

Once students see the advantages and experience the satisfactions of undertaking these kinds of projects, they will think of others on their own. Like barbecues, students need a little "starter."

Each of these principles expresses a philosophical or psychological position or attitude. We each teach according to firmly held attitudes of this kind. Ours may not be explicit, even to ourselves; we may not have stopped to think what they are; but, if challenged or confronted with other views, we respond in a way that reveals "where we are coming from," to use a contemporary expression. I hope that this exposition and explication of my deeply held and cherished positions may bestir other teachers to a deeper consideration of their own, and perhaps to a reexamination of some of them in the light of the needs of our language learners, who must remain our preeminent preoccupation.

NOTES

1. Revised version of keynote address to the Sixteenth World Congress on Language Learning of the Fédération Internationale des Professeurs de Langues Vivantes, Canberra, Australia, January 4, 1988.

2. Seneca, *Ad Lucilium,* V, vii.

3. W. von Humboldt, "Über die Verschiedenheit des Menschlichen Sprachbaues" (Berlin, 1836), as cited by N. Chomsky in *Aspects of the Theory of Syntax* (Cambridge, MA: MIT Press, 1965), p. 51.

4. A. Bronson Alcott, *General Maxims,* in the *Alcott Journals,* 1826–27, Maxim XXXIV. This was also the approach of Maria Montessori.

5. This subject is considered in greater detail in "Motivating through Classroom Techniques," in W. M. Rivers, *Speaking in Many Tongues: Essays in Foreign-Language Teaching,* 3d ed. (Cambridge, Eng., and New York: Cambridge Univ. Press, 1983), pp. 108–19.

6. For further discussion of interaction as an essential prerequisite for communication through language, see W. M. Rivers, "Interaction: The Key to Communication," in M. A. K. Halliday, J. Gibbons, and H. Nicholas, eds., *Learning, Keeping and Using Language: Selected Papers from the Eighth World Congress of Applied Linguistics.* Vol. 1. (Amsterdam/Philadelphia: John Benjamins, 1990), pp. 7–17.

7. Many suggestions for participatory interactive activities may be found in W. M. Rivers, ed., *Interactive Language Teaching* (Cambridge, Eng., and New York: Cambridge Univ. Press, 1987).

8. G. Lozanov's *Suggestopaedia,* as discussed in S. Ostrander and L. Schroeder, *Psychic Discoveries behind the Iron Curtain* (Englewood Cliffs, NJ: Prentice-Hall, 1970).

9. For suggestions on how to arrange the retaking of tests, see Rivers et al. (1988–89), chapter 10.

10. Proposals of this type are made by R. C. Scarcella, "Socio-Drama for Social Interaction," *TESOL Quarterly* 12 (1978): 41–46; and R. J. Di Pietro, *Strategic Interaction: Learning Languages through Scenarios* (Cambridge, Eng., and New York: Cambridge Univ. Press, 1987). Further ideas for bringing students to awareness of another culture are found in W. M. Rivers, *Teaching Foreign-Language Skills,* 2d ed. (Chicago: Univ. of Chicago Press, 1981), chapter 11.

REFERENCES

Allwright, R. L. 1984. "The Importance of Interaction in Classroom Language Learning." *Applied Linguistics* 5 (1984): 156–71.

Belyayev, B. V. 1963. *The Psychology of Teaching Foreign Languages.* Tr. R. F. Hingley. Oxford, Eng.: Pergamon, 1963. [Originally published in Russian in 1959.]

Blumenthal, A. L. 1970. *Language and Psychology.* New York: Wiley.

Buck, E. 1951. *L'Enseignement du français: une méthodologie.* Istanbul, Turk.: "La Turquie Moderne" Basimevi.

Carroll, John B. 1966. "The Contributions of Psychological Theory and Educational Research to the Teaching of Foreign Languages," pp. 93–106 in A. Valdman, ed., *Trends in Language Teaching.* New York: McGraw-Hill.

Chomsky, Noam. 1966. "Linguistic Theory," pp. 43–49 in R. G. Mead Jr., ed., *Language Teaching: Broader Contexts.* Report of the Northeast Conference on the Teaching of Foreign Languages. Middlebury, VT: The Northeast Conference.

Clyne, M., ed. 1986. *An Early Start: Second Language at Primary School.* Melbourne, Australia: River Seine Publications.

Cortese, G. 1987. "Interaction in the FL Classroom: From Reactive to Proactive Experience of Language." *System* 15: 27–41.

Curran, Charles A. 1976. *Counseling-Learning in Second Languages.* Apple River, IL: Apple River Press.

Dewey, J. 1925. *Experiences in Nature.* Chicago: Open Court.

Ericsson, E. 1986. *Foreign Language Teaching from the Point of View of Certain Student Activities.* Göteborg Studies in Educational Sciences 59. Göteborg, Sweden: Acta Universitatis Gothoburgensis.

Gattegno, Caleb. 1972. *Teaching Foreign Languages in Schools: The Silent Way.* 2d. ed. New York: Educational Solutions.

Halliday, M. A. K. 1985. *An Introduction to Functional Grammar.* London, Eng.: Edward Arnold.

Higgs, Theodore V., and Ray Clifford. 1981. "The Push toward Communication," pp. 54–79 in T. V. Higgs, ed., *Curriculum, Competence, and the Foreign Language Teacher*. The ACTFL Foreign Language Education Series, vol. 13. Lincolnwood, IL: National Textbook Company.

Jespersen, Otto. 1961. *How to Teach a Foreign Language*. London, Eng.: George Allen and Unwin. [First published in 1904.]

Kipp, S. 1986. "Student Reaction," pp. 99–111 in M. Clyne, ed., *An Early Start: Second Language at Primary School*. Melbourne, Australia: River Seine Publications.

Leontiev, A. A. 1981. *Psychology and the Language Learning Process*. Oxford, Eng.: Pergamon.

Palmer, Harold E. 1921. *The Principles of Language-Study*. London, Eng.: Harrap. [Reprinted London, Eng.: Oxford Univ. Press, 1964.]

Rivers, Wilga M. 1983. "Individualized Instruction and Cooperative Learning: Some Theoretical Considerations," pp. 65–79 in Wilga M. Rivers, ed., *Communicating Naturally in a Second Language: Theory and Practice in Language Teaching*. Cambridge, Eng., and New York: Cambridge Univ. Press.

————, et al. 1988–89. *Teaching French / Spanish / German / Hebrew: A Practical Guide*. Lincolnwood, IL: National Textbook Company; Tel Aviv, Israel: University Publishing Projects.

Robinson, G. L. N. 1985. *Crosscultural Understanding: Processes and Approaches for Foreign Language, English as a Second Language and Bilingual Educators*. New York: Pergamon.

————. 1987. "Culturally Diverse Speech Styles," pp. 141–54 in Wilga M. Rivers, ed., *Interactive Language Teaching*. Cambridge, Eng., and New York: Cambridge Univ. Press.

Rugg, H. 1947. *Foundations for American Education*. Yonkers-on-Hudson, NY: World Book.

Sharwood-Smith, M. 1981. "Consciousness-Raising and the Second Language Learner." *Applied Linguistics* 2: 159–69.

Stern, H. H. 1983. *Fundamental Concepts of Language Teaching*. Oxford, Eng.: Oxford Univ. Press.

Appendix A:
ILR Correspondence
with ACTFL Proficiency Levels

The following correspondence was established with the Interagency Language Roundtable (ILR) scales for speaking proficiency (formerly the Foreign Service Institute, or FSI, scales).

ILR Scale	*ACTFL/ETS* Scale*
0	Novice–low
No practical proficiency	Novice–mid
0+	Novice–high
1	Intermediate–low
Elementary proficiency	Intermediate–mid
1+	Intermediate–high
2 Limited working proficiency	Advanced
2+	Advanced plus
3 Professional proficiency	
3+	
4 Distinguished proficiency	Superior
4+	
5 Native or bilingual proficiency	

SOURCE: *Educational Testing Services (Princeton, New Jersey)*

Appendix B: Expected Levels of Absolute Speaking Proficiency in Languages Taught at the Foreign Service Institute (Revised April 1973)

THE FOLLOWING CHART WAS DRAWN UP BY THE SCHOOL OF LANGUAGE Studies of the Foreign Service Institute. It summarizes our experience with students as taught in our own classes rather than our judgments about the relative difficulty of these languages for speakers of English, though there is undoubtedly some correlation. The expected speaking proficiency for a student with a given background and a given aptitude, in a given language, after a given number of weeks, will depend not only on the difficulty of the spoken language itself, but also on the amount of time and effort that the student has had to spend in concurrent study of the writing system.

GROUP I:
Afrikaans, Danish, Dutch, French, German, Haitian Creole, Italian, Norwegian, Portuguese, Romanian, Spanish, Swahili, Swedish

Length of Training*	Aptitude for Language Learning		
	Minimum	Average	Superior
8 weeks (240 hours)	1	1/1+	1+
16 weeks (480 hours)	1+	2	2+
24 weeks (720 hours)	2	2+	3

*The number of hours is the theoretical maximum at 30 hours a week.

GROUP II:
Bulgarian, Dari, Farsi, Greek, Hindi, Indonesian, Malay, Urdu

Length of Training	Aptitude for Language Learning		
	Minimum	Average	Superior
16 weeks (480 hours)	1	1/1+	1+/2
24 weeks (720 hours)	1+	2	2+/3
44 weeks (1320 hours)	2/2+	2+/3	3/3+

GROUP III:
Amharic, Bengali, Burmese, Czech, Finnish, Hebrew, Hungarian, Khmer (Cambodian), Lao, Nepali, Pilipino, Polish, Russian, Serbo-Croatian, Sinhala, Thai, Tamil, Turkish, Vietnamese

Length of Training	Aptitude for Language Learning		
	Minimum	Average	Superior
16 weeks (480 hours)	0+	1	1/1+
24 weeks (720 hours)	1+	2	2/2+
44 weeks (1320 hours)	2	2+	3

GROUP IV:
Arabic, Chinese, Japanese, Korean

Length of Training	Aptitude for Language Learning		
	Minimum	Average	Superior
16 weeks (480 hours)	0+	1	1
24 weeks (720 hours)	1	1+	1+
44 weeks (1320 hours)	1+	2	2+
80–92 weeks (2400–2760 hours)	2+	3	3+

SOURCE: *School of Language Studies, Foreign Service Institute*

Index of Topics

Index of Authors Cited

Pica, T., 53, 55
Polsky, Marion, 162, 189

Q, R

Quinn, Gerald M., 168, 186
Randall, John G., 168, 189
Rassias, John A., 229, 233, 243
Rehorick, Sally, 69, 71
Reichardt, Paul, 326, 331
Reinhold, Meyer, 157, 189
Rheingold, Howard, 40
Richlin, Amy, 171, 190
Richterich, R., 113
Rieber, L. P., 134, 139
Rivers, Wilga M., 4, 5, 6, 7, 9, 11, 15, 18, 19, 22, 23, 29, 39, 40, 47, 55, 79, 86, 89, 93, 99, 106–7, 115, 208, 253, 258, 311, 312, 328, 331, 337, 347, 349, 379, 390, 391, 392
Robinson, F. P., 89
Robinson, G., 364, 369
Robinson, G. L. N., 387, 392
Robinson, Gail L., 136, 139
Rocher, R. 219, 222
Rodman, R., 270, 278
Roessler, H. R., 219, 221
Rosenbluth, P., 211, 221
Rosmarin, A., 254, 259
Rosovsky, Henry, 245, 252, 256, 259
Rowland, Robert J., 171, 188
Rubin, Joan, 133, 140
Rugg, H., 381, 392
Rumelhart, David E., 75, 89
Ryan, Joseph T., Jr., 111, 113, 114

S

Sachs, Murray, 322, 331

Sadow, Stephen, 113, 311, 312
Sako, S., 200, 221
Salerno, Dorsey P., 167, 190
Santirocco, Matthew S., 160, 190
Sapir, Edward, 271, 279
Sapon, S. M., 203, 221
Sarig, Gissi, 77, 80, 90
Sarkisian, 311, 312
Sartre, Jean-Paul, 59
Scanlan, Richard, 170, 190
Scarcella, R. C., 334, 349, 390 n. 10
Scebold, 157
Schade, R., 39
Schaeffer, John N., 168, 185
Schroeder, L., 390 n. 8
Schutte, L. E., 219, 221
Scott, Nathan A., 249, 259
Segerstråle, U., 246, 252, 259
Seligson, Gerda, 168, 190
Sharwood-Smith, M., 381, 392
Sheehy, Gail, 339
Shepard, Joe W., 326, 331
Sheppard, M., 130, 140
Shohamy, E., 217, 222
Sidwell, Keith C., 168, 186
Skinner, Marilyn B., 172, 190
Slater, S., 226, 242
Smuckler, R., 239, 242
Snow, Catherine E., 268, 279, 334, 335, 349
Snow, M. A., 97, 114
Sola, D. F., 128
Sosa, Julie Ann, 181, 184
Stansfield, C. W., 203, 205, 219, 222, 223, 365, 369
Steele, R., 53, 55
Stern, H. H., 261, 279, 373, 392
Sternfeld, S., 231, 243
Stevenson, D. K., 203, 223

Strasheim, Lorraine A., 162, 167, 190
Stringer, M. H. L., 334, 350
Styker, S. B., 97, 115
Sullivan, L., 94, 115, 160
Sussman, Lewis A., 162, 170, 190
Swaffar, Janet K., 74, 77, 82, 84, 90
Sweet, Waldo, 172

T–Z

Taylor, Martha C., 168, 190
Tcachuk, A., 326, 331
Tebben, Joseph, 172, 190
Terrell, Tracy D., 7, 19
Terry, R. M., 212, 223
Thompson, R., 365, 369
Thorndike, E. L., 340, 350
Trim, J. L. M., 113
Troy, J. F. de, 61
Twarog, L. I., 334, 350
Ullman, B. L., 167, 170, 190
Underhill, 200
Underwood, J. H., 136, 140
Valette, Rebecca M., 200, 220, 223
Vaughn, John, 172, 190
Vendler, H., 249, 252, 259
Vergil, 162
Via, Richard, 16, 20, 32, 40
Voght, G. M., 96, 109, 111, 115
Waite, Stephen V. F., 169, 191
Wakefield, R., 48, 54, 55
Waldinger, Renée, 167, 191, 311, 312
Walker, Galal, 85, 90, 155
Walton, A. Ronald, 154, 155
Walz, 311, 312
Wang, L. S., 219, 223
Wesche, M. B., 97, 114
West, Andrew F., 157, 191
Whalen, Paul, 169, 184

NTC PROFESSIONAL MATERIALS

ACTFL Review

Published annually in conjunction with the American Council on the Teaching of Foreign Languages

NEW PERSPECTIVES, NEW DIRECTIONS IN FOREIGN LANGUAGE EDUCATION, ed. Birckbichler, Vol. 20 (1990)

MODERN TECHNOLOGY IN FOREIGN LANGUAGE EDUCATION: APPLICATIONS AND PROJECTS, ed. Smith, Vol. 19 (1989)

MODERN MEDIA IN FOREIGN LANGUAGE EDUCATION: THEORY AND IMPLEMENTATION, ed. Smith, Vol. 18 (1987)

DEFINING AND DEVELOPING PROFICIENCY: GUIDELINES, IMPLEMENTATIONS, AND CONCEPTS, ed. Byrnes, Vol. 17 (1986)

FOREIGN LANGUAGE PROFICIENCY IN THE CLASSROOM AND BEYOND, ed. James, Vol. 16 (1984)

TEACHING FOR PROFICIENCY, THE ORGANIZING PRINCIPLE, ed. Higgs, Vol. 15 (1983)

PRACTICAL APPLICATIONS OF RESEARCH IN FOREIGN LANGUAGE TEACHING, ed. James, Vol. 14 (1982)

CURRICULUM, COMPETENCE, AND THE FOREIGN LANGUAGE TEACHER, ed. Higgs, Vol. 13 (1981)

Professional Resources

CENTRAL STATES CONFERENCE TITLES (annuals)

A TESOL PROFESSIONAL ANTHOLOGY: CULTURE

A TESOL PROFESSIONAL ANTHOLOGY: GRAMMAR AND COMPOSITION

A TESOL PROFESSIONAL ANTHOLOGY: LISTENING, SPEAKING, AND READING

THE COMPLETE ESL/EFL RESOURCE BOOK, Scheraga

ABC'S OF LANGUAGES AND LINGUISTICS, Hayes, et al.

AWARD-WINNING FOREIGN LANGUAGE PROGRAMS: PRESCRIPTIONS FOR SUCCESS, Sims and Hammond

PUZZLES AND GAMES IN LANGUAGE TEACHING, Danesi

GUIDE TO SUCCESSFUL AFTER-SCHOOL ELEMENTARY FOREIGN LANGUAGE PROGRAMS, Lozano

COMPLETE GUIDE TO EXPLORATORY FOREIGN LANGUAGE PROGRAMS, Kennedy and DeLorenzo

INDIVIDUALIZED FOREIGN LANGUAGE INSTRUCTION, Grittner and LaLeike

LIVING IN LATIN AMERICA: A CASE STUDY IN CROSS-CULTURAL COMMUNICATION, Gorden

ORAL COMMUNICATION TESTING, Linder

ELEMENTARY FOREIGN LANGUAGE PROGRAMS: AN ADMINISTRATOR'S HANDBOOK, Lipton

PRACTICAL HANDBOOK TO ELEMENTARY FOREIGN LANGUAGE PROGRAMS, Second edition, Lipton

SPEAK WITH A PURPOSE! Urzua, et al.

TEACHING LANGUAGES IN COLLEGE, Rivers

TEACHING CULTURE: STRATEGIES FOR INTERCULTURAL COMMUNICATION, Seelye

TEACHING FRENCH: A PRACTICE GUIDE, Rivers

TEACHING GERMAN: A PRACTICAL GUIDE, Rivers, et al.

TEACHING SPANISH: A PRACTICAL GUIDE, Rivers, et al.

TRANSCRIPTION AND TRANSLITERATION, Wellisch

YES! YOU CAN LEARN A FOREIGN LANGUAGE, Goldin, et al.

LANGUAGES AT WORK (VIDEO), Mueller

CULTURAL LITERACY AND INTERACTIVE LANGUAGE INSTRUCTION (VIDEO), Mueller

For further information or a current catalog, write:
National Textbook Company
a division of *NTC Publishing Group*
4255 West Touhy Avenue
Lincolnwood, Illinois 60646-1975 U.S.A.